We the **Poor** *People*

WITHDRAWN

We the Poor People

Work, Poverty, and Welfare

Joel F. Handler and Yeheskel Hasenfeld

A TWENTIETH CENTURY FUND BOOK

YALE UNIVERSITY PRESS   New Haven and London

BKL 3403-4/3

Designed by Richard Hendel
Set in Minion type by Keystone Typesetting, Inc.
Printed in the United States of America.

Library of Congress Cataloging-in-Publication Data
Handler, Joel F.
    We the poor people : work, poverty, and welfare / Joel F. Handler, Yeheskel Hasenfeld.
        p.   cm.
    "A Twentieth Century Fund book."
    Includes bibliographical references and index.
    ISBN 0-300-07248-1 (alk. paper). — ISBN 0-300-07250-3 (pbk. : alk. paper)
        1. Public welfare—United States.   2. Welfare recipients—Employment—United States.
    3. Poverty—United States.   I. Hasenfeld, Yeheskel.   II. Title.
    HV95.H264   1997
    362.5'0973—dc21   97-17475
                    CIP

A catalogue record for this book is available from the British Library.

The paper in this book meets the guidelines for permanence and durability of the Committee on
Production Guidelines for Book Longevity of the Council on Library Resources.

10   9   8   7   6   5   4   3   2   1

In memory of my beloved
colleague and friend Julian N. Eule

JOEL F. HANDLER

In memory of my father, Zvi, who
taught me the importance of caring

YEHESKEL HASENFELD

Contents

Foreword

As of this writing, America is in the midst of an enviable period of sustained economic growth. The value of financial assets, especially stocks, has increased enormously. Some salaries are going through the roof, but overall inflation is modest. There is even a strong political movement contending that the consumer price index is substantially overestimated. All these developments add to the many continuing economic advantages the nation enjoys when compared to most of the rest of the world.

Americans, as a group, are enormously rich. We spend less of our income on food, water, clothing, fuel, and shelter than almost anyone else in the world. Looking at necessities, we spend exceptionally only on health care. We not only have the smallest current public deficit, we also pay the smallest share of income in taxes of any industrialized nation.

But we are neither happy nor satisfied.

In spite of these favorable developments, many, probably most, Americans are disappointed with their economic circumstances. This reaction is understandable. Over 85 percent, for example, of the rapidly growing financial assets are in the hands of only 10 percent of Americans. In fact, half of families have less than a thousand dollars in net financial assets. For the majority, real wage growth has either been limited or even negative. Many feel burdened by debts and insecure about the future.

The median American family, in any case, does not compare its living standard to the British, for example, and feel rich. We are a people accustomed to constant and rapid improvement; we experience sharp disappointment when progress is slow. Our personal economic disappointment feeds antipathy to government, stunting our sense of national mission. We think small, undertaking little, underestimating our strength, and exaggerating the harmful consequences of public debt.

Tax revolts, the ideology of selfishness, and other elements of the backlash against the bipartisan liberal activism of the post–World War II era have spread rapidly through the voting public. People feel hurt and defeated by their personal failures to make economic progress. The generous impulses of the public sector in the 1960s and 1970s, in this pessimistic view, have been rewarded in the 1980s and 1990s by steady deterioration in the economic condition of the average family. Even as the average level of education rose, even as an ever larger proportion of the population joined the workforce, families—even two-income families—saw the American dream of rising income, upward mobility, a home of their own move further away.

As a result, although our economy easily could afford better health care and education for the young, we despair of finding the necessary resources. Even though we easily could save and invest more in public as well as private projects, we do not. In truth, no constraint of national poverty or solvency forestalls the possibility of calling on government for constructive change. But individually, many of us feel that *we* cannot afford to bear our share of the "burden" of building a better society.

In this context the persistence of poverty, while seen as unfortunate, increasingly is viewed as simply a problem for those who are affected by it. For the great bulk of workers, charity, whether personal or through taxes, is just too much to ask.

At least this is one interpretation of the astonishing fact that the federal budget for the nation's basic welfare program, which amounts to only 1 percent of total spending, has consistently been at the center of national political campaigns. In 1996, all this attention culminated in a Democratic President and Republican Congress agreeing on a welfare reform plan that drastically alters the federal role in helping the nation's poorest. The restructured system reflects pessimism about those on welfare (they could be working, but they're not). But it also reflects optimism about the job market (if you look, you'll find work). The authors of this volume are quite sure that this new experiment will not succeed.

Joel F. Handler, professor of law at the School of Law, University of California, Los Angeles, and Yeheskel Hasenfeld, professor of social welfare at the School of Social Welfare, also at the University of California, Los Angeles, have studied welfare and poverty for many years. They understand both its intransigence and the difficulty of finding workable programmatic solutions. In this volume, they go well beyond finding fault with past efforts, proposing ideas that would break the pattern of previous policies and even current reform efforts. Setting aside the many attacks on the current system that depend on emotion and prejudice, serious students of what to do about welfare agree that the focus needs to be on two major questions: first, do we need a new conception of what welfare programs are meant to accomplish; and second, is it possible to realize improvement in the system by restructuring it?

Handler and Hasenfeld offer provocative answers to both questions. Regardless of one's view about poverty in America, it would be a leap of faith indeed to conclude that the welfare reform program enacted in 1996 is the end of the story. The ideas set forth in this book are therefore likely to receive the attention they deserve as the nation struggles, in the years to come, with the inevitable process of "reforming the reforms."

On behalf of the Trustees of the Twentieth Century Fund/Century Foundation, I thank the authors for their thorough and most interesting treatment of this important aspect of American public life.

Richard C. Leone, President
The Twentieth Century Fund
June 1997

Acknowledgments

We survived and thrived—a University of Michigan–trained sociologist and a mushy lawyer type. Ten years, two books, several papers, many conferences and talks about poverty, welfare, social policy, foreign policy, whatever. On vacations, while our wives browsed, we plotted. It's a great friendship, a great collaboration, and we are still going strong.

Along the way we have had lots of great support. For this particular project, we wish to express our thanks to Sandy Danziger, Sheldon Danziger, Mark Greenberg, Rena Hasenfeld, Julia Hastings, Julia Henly, Katherine Hill, Frank Munger, and Lucie White. Margaret Kiever is a wonderful secretary, and it is hard to exaggerate the excellence of the research staff of the UCLA Law Library.

The project was funded by the Twentieth Century Fund. We particularly want to thank Greg Anrig, Jr., William Grinker, and Beverly Goldberg. We are grateful to John Covell, senior editor, and Harry Haskell, manuscript editor, at Yale University Press, and to the press's readers, Lucy A. Williams and Gary D. Sandefur. Part of the writing was done at the Rockefeller Foundation Bellagio Study and Conference Center. We thank the foundation for that opportunity.

Part One

The Fixation on Work versus Welfare

It is not bread the poor need, it is soul;

it is not soup, it is spirit.

Chapter 1

The Choices We Make

In *The Structures of Everyday Life,* Fernand Braudel describes medieval European welfare policy:

> The peasants lived in a state of dependence on merchants, towns and nobles, and had scarcely any reserves to their own. They had no solution in case of famine except to turn to the town where they crowded together, begging in the streets and often dying in public squares. . . .
>
> The towns soon had to protect themselves against these regular invasions. . . . Beggars from distant provinces appeared in the fields and streets of the town of Troyes in 1573, starving, clothed in rags and covered with fleas and vermin. They were authorized to stay there for only 24 hours. But the rich citizens . . . soon began to fear that "sedition" might be spread among the poor inside the town or in the surrounding countryside, and in order to make them leave, the rich men and the governors . . . were assembled to find the expedient to remedy it. The resolution of this council was that they must be put outside the town. . . .
>
> The attitude of the bourgeois hardened considerably towards the end of the sixteenth century, and even more in the seventeenth. The problem was to place the poor in a position where they could do no harm. In Paris the sick and invalid had always been directed to the hospitals, and the fit, chained together in pairs, were employed at the hard, exacting and interminable task of cleaning the drains of the town. In England the Poor Laws, which were in fact laws *against* the poor, appeared at the end of Elizabeth's reign. Houses for the poor and undesirable gradually appeared throughout the West, condemning their occupants to forced labour in workhouses. . . . In Dijon the municipal authorities went so far as to forbid the town's citizens to take in the poor or to exercise private charity. "In the sixteenth century, the beggar or vagrant would be fed and cared for before he was sent away. In the early seventeenth century, he had his head shaved. Later on, he was whipped; and the end of the century saw the last word in repression— he was turned into a convict." This was Europe.[1]

ertain themes leap from Braudel's description—danger, containment, ~~natization~~, deterrence. That was Europe.

What is welfare policy today? We often think about the poor—or at least the welfare poor—in much the same way, as threats to dominant values and the social order. The failure to support oneself and one's family has always been considered more than just being poor. Violating the work ethic is a moral fault; as such, it contaminates other areas of personal and family life. In Braudel's Troyes, Paris, Dijon, and London, as well as in the contemporary United States, those considered able to work but fail to work—the "unworthy" poor—are associated with sin, vice, disease, and crime.

Today's welfare mothers, it is said, do not work or marry. They have children out of wedlock and engage in other forms of antisocial behavior, including drugs and crime. As a consequence, it is widely believed that welfare children grow up in poverty; they suffer from bad environments, do poorly in school, and, for the most part, follow the paths of their parents in dependency or worse. The stereotypical image of the "welfare recipient" is the young, unmarried woman, more likely an addict, who has children in order to get on and stay on welfare. Her children, in turn, will at best become welfare-dependent, but more likely substance abusers and criminals. The subtext is the African American "underclass" or the inhabitants of the Latino barrios. Race, ethnicity, and religion reinforce the moral condemnation of welfare. Whereas the unworthy poor used to be called the "dangerous classes," now the polite euphemism is "counterculture poverty" or the more pejorative "underclass." In prior periods of welfare crises, threats to the social order were often riots or the fear of riots; today, it is the fear of the spreading underclass.

Accordingly, welfare policy is deeply involved in preserving the moral order—the work ethic and family, gender, race, and ethnic relations. Welfare policy is fundamentally a set of symbols that conveys what behaviors are virtuous and what are deviant. It is continually identifying and categorizing the deserving and undeserving poor. Thus, welfare symbols are addressed not only to the welfare poor but equally to the nonpoor. As in most symbolic systems, especially those engaged in primal moral struggles, the "myths and ceremonies" of welfare are ambiguous and at times contradictory. The debate over welfare policy is both moralistic and ritualized, less concerned with the experience and needs of the poor than with validating dominant norms about who the poor are, why they are poor, and how social control is justified.

Welfare policy both contributes to and is shaped by the larger moral debates in society. In the United States, race, ethnicity, and gender have always had a significant impact on welfare policy. As we shall see in Chapter 2, patriarchy decisively influenced early state aid to dependent children's programs; race and gender had a similar impact on the twin pillars of the New Deal—Social Security and Unemployment Insurance. Today, welfare policy is part of the larger debates over immigration, changing family structure, sexual behavior, cultural pluralism, and growing inequality.

Welfare policy is also part of the debate over the role of government. The control of the deviant, the "dangerous classes," has always been seen as primarily a *local* issue; it is in the community that the worthy can be separated from the unworthy. When "government" (national or state) tries to interfere, it becomes the problem rather than the solution to controlling the unworthy poor. At the same time, delegating the "welfare problem" serves the interests of upper-level politicians; it pushes the moral conflicts to the local level and buffers them from contending interest groups.

As symbolic politics, as an exercise in myth making serving majoritarian values, welfare policy diverts attention from the fundamental issues of growing inequality, poverty, and the deterioration of the low-wage labor market. Instead, welfare becomes the *cause* of societal ills; therefore, the remedy for the disease is to exorcise welfare rather than confront the more fundamental problems and search for workable solutions. Welfare policy ignores the lives and the actual experiences of the poor. In short, welfare programs are more interested in blaming the victim than in disturbing labor markets or redistributing income.

The latest welfare reform is part of this long history of misconception, mythology, and diversion.

The Current Welfare Reform

Predictably labeled a "crisis," welfare became an issue in the 1992 presidential campaign when candidate Bill Clinton promised to "end welfare as we know it." Welfare dependency, he said, had become a "way of life." Clinton was referring to Aid to Families with Dependent Children (AFDC), the welfare program primarily for single mothers and their children. Candidate Clinton proposed a two-year time limit on welfare during which the recipient would be required to participate in training. At the end of two years, if the recipient had not been able to secure a job, she would be offered a public job for a limited period of time; but, in any event, welfare would end.

Over the next four years, welfare reform was the subject of partisan politics. The Republicans and Democrats in Congress and the state governors all submitted proposals. Twice the President vetoed Republican-sponsored bills. While welfare reform was stalled in Washington, the states were reforming welfare on their own under waivers granted by the U.S. Department of Health and Human Services. Then, on the eve of the 1996 election, Clinton signed the Personal Responsibility and Work Opportunity Reconciliation Act of 1996—a comprehensive bill that formally abolishes AFDC, JOBS (the work and training program for welfare recipients), and Emergency Assistance to Families with Children, and replaces them with a block grant of federal funds given to the states, known as Temporary Assistance for Needy Families (TANF).[2]

The new legislation is complex and comprehensive—it covers several programs in addition to AFDC[3]—and it is ambiguous. Consequently, it will be years before the major provisions of the legislation, let alone the details, will be sorted out, and undoubtedly changes will continue to be made. Despite the claims of "ending welfare as we know it," TANF is not the last word on welfare. Throughout this book we discuss specific provisions of the act, and in the concluding chapter we give our overall assessment of the reforms and our predictions as to the future. Here, we briefly summarize the major welfare provisions.

The new legislation can be summarized in terms of four major themes. The first is that the legislation ends the "entitlement status" of welfare by folding that program, along with several others, into block grants to the states.[4] In general, a state will receive the TANF grant, based on a formula, when the Department of Health and Human Services approves the state plan. In return, the states are required to meet a basic maintenance of effort, which is no less than 80 percent of a "historic spending level."[5] There are several purposes in the block grant provision. Ending "entitlement status" sends the message that recipients can no longer count on welfare. The block grant provision would allow states more easily to reduce the amount of money they spend on welfare or shift funds to other programs. Even though there are federal restrictions, the block grants will allow the states to manage welfare free from federal interference. As will be discussed in the next chapter, contrary to political rhetoric, the states have always had a great deal of control over AFDC, including the all-important benefit levels, but the block grants would significantly increase state authority over all aspects of AFDC. For example, under TANF individuals and families have no entitlement to assistance. Presumably, states are free to determine which families receive assistance, how much, and under what circumstances; if a state runs out of funds, applicants can be placed on waiting lists or rejected. In other words, there no longer is a guarantee of aid.

The second major theme combines time limits for welfare with work requirements. Under TANF, there are two sets of time limits. The first is the two-year time limit. Starting in fiscal year (FY) 1997, a quarter of each state's recipients must participate in "work activities"; the percentage of the caseload increases annually to 50 percent by FY 2002. Up to 20 percent of the state's caseload can be exempted from this requirement. The requirements are considerably higher for two-parent families. A state risks a penalty for failure to meet the annual rate.[6] Second, recognizing that many welfare recipients cycle on and off welfare, there is a cumulative lifetime five-year limit on welfare.[7]

Time-limited welfare addresses the perceived lack of work ethic on the part of welfare recipients. Other aspects of welfare reform speak to different issues. A cluster of provisions deals with so-called family values. Unless states specifically opt out, they cannot provide aid to children who were conceived while the mother was on welfare (called the "family cap") or to minor parents unless they are attending school (called "learnfare") and living at home. Nor can they provide aid to reduce or eliminate assistance if the family does not cooperate in the establishment of paternity and obtaining child support. States would also have the option to deny aid to mothers under eighteen.

Further provisions deny aid to immigrants, both legal and illegal. For example, future legal immigrants who have not become citizens would be ineligible for most federal welfare benefits during their first five years in the United States. Supplemental security income (ssi) and food stamps would end for noncitizens now receiving benefits. Other provisions would also affect poor families. For example, thousands of children would lose ssi disability benefits under stricter standards. Unless a state opts out, people convicted of drug felonies cannot receive assistance.

Almost forty states have either received or are applying for waivers from the Department of Health and Human Services. Under TANF, states may continue to operate welfare according to the waivers. Waiver provisions vary—and not all of them are punitive—but the most popular deal with time limits (usually two years, although some states are opting for shorter periods), increased work requirements, and family values. Several states, for example, along with strict time limits, are mandating quick entry into the low-wage labor market, or requiring recipients to work off the welfare grant at community service jobs. The state time limits are cumulative; nonexempt families who cannot find a job or otherwise participate in state-approved work activities (for example, a community service job) will lose their cash assistance at the end of one or two years rather than the five-year federal limit. Other states mandate family caps and the establishment of paternity, in addition to requiring that teenage mothers live with their parents and attend school. Counting the number and variety of state waivers, either already granted or in the works, even before TANF, it is clear that the country was already in a full-blown welfare reform.

Although it is hazardous to predict how TANF and the state programs will eventually sort out, the Urban Institute, based on "optimistic" assumptions (that is, that the states will maintain current benefit levels and exempt 20 percent of the caseload), estimates that when fully implemented, government spending on the major welfare programs will be reduced by nearly $16 billion annually; AFDC by $5.3 billion, with almost a million families losing all benefits; SSI by nearly $5 billion, with 900,000 individuals losing benefits; food stamps by $5.5 billion, eliminating 850,000 families. The number of people in poverty will increase by 2.6 million; most of this increase will occur in families with children. About 1.1 million more children will be poor. The poverty gap will increase by about $6 billion for all families.[8]

The Assumptions Behind the Current Welfare Reform

Why has welfare reform become such a prominent political issue? And why such harsh provisions? It's not as if welfare has suddenly become a "problem." For more than thirty years, repeated attempts have been made to change welfare, always with the promise of "major reforms." As recently as 1988, the Family Support Act was enacted, also hailed as a major reform. And why the particular reforms? It's certainly not because reducing welfare will affect taxes and government spending. Welfare is quite small compared to other social welfare programs. In 1993 the total amount spent on AFDC—by both the federal government and the states—was $22.3 billion. The big-budget items are: Social Security Retirement and Disability ($419 billion), Medicare ($143 billion), and Medicaid ($132 billion). The federal share of AFDC costs was $12.2 billion, or 1.5 percent of all federal spending.[9]

Furthermore, if costs are the major consideration, politicians and policymakers know that welfare is the *cheapest* alternative. It is certainly cheaper than doing anything constructive for welfare recipients, such as providing meaningful education, training and work, day care, and health benefits. And it is cheaper than drastically reducing welfare, since higher shelter and foster care costs are likely to occur. After all, most welfare recipients are children. When one compares welfare with health, crime, substance abuse, AIDS, low wages, education, child protection, and many other problems, the fixation on welfare is puzzling.

Even though welfare is a relatively small part of government budgets, when welfare rolls and costs rise—or when the electorate *thinks* they are rising—welfare comes under attack. It's not the amount of money that is being spent, it's what the money is being spent for. It's the specter of the welfare recipient. Welfare, it is believed, is no longer a temporary measure to help single mothers and their children over a bad patch. Instead, it encourages and perpetuates dependency; it has become "a way of life." The resentment may also be fueled by the large numbers of middle- and working-class mothers who are now in the paid labor force, working hard, and paying for their own child care and health care. They not only do not receive any support from government, but they pay taxes. The middle class is hurting; real wages are stagnating or declining and families need two, if not three, jobs to stay even. It may be that the political focus on welfare draws attention away from the plight of the middle class.

Conservatives became increasingly concerned over the perceived connection between welfare and the lack of work ethic in the Reagan years. It was during that period that Charles Murray popularized the idea that welfare induced people to quit work and to break up homes.[10] As part of the general campaign against liberalism and the Great Society, the idea of entitlement to welfare was attacked. The very idea of an entitlement was seen as a corrupting influence on recipients. Besides, why should welfare recipients have "entitlements" when no one else had? Citizens have *responsibilities*, not entitlements, some conservatives said. This is the social contract; it was a matter of fairness, of equity. The "truly needy" deserved to be helped, but they must also contribute to society by supporting themselves and their families if they can.[11] The theme of responsibility became very popular, and is now endorsed by liberals as well. In fact, time-limited welfare was first proposed by the liberal left.[12] Dependent mothers will be helped—by income and by education and training—but after a reasonable period of time, they must help themselves.

It used to be thought that mothers should stay at home and take care of their children. Welfare was designed so that poor mothers could do the same. But times have changed. The argument today is that because the majority of women are now in the paid labor force, including mothers of young children, welfare mothers can no longer expect to stay at home and take care of their children. However, there is more to the argument than mere symmetry. The failure of the able-bodied to support themselves and their families is a moral fault that compromises other areas of personal and family life.

Several long-standing assumptions are behind today's apparent political consensus on what is wrong with welfare and what to do about it:

First, "dependency," as used in the welfare context, is not simply being poor. It is not simply being out of work. Rather, welfare dependency is a problem of attitude, a moral failure to have the proper work ethic. It is a way of life.

Second, the assignment of moral fault is rarely unidimensional. When those with whom we are familiar, who are "like us," fall on hard times, it is because of "bad luck" or "misfortune." Moral condemnation is reserved for those who are not only poor but different—in terms of race, ethnicity, country of origin, or religion—or who violate patriarchal norms. The poverty of our neighborly, aged, white widow is different from the dependency of the inner-city young black mother or single male, and, increasingly, immigrants. Race and ethnicity have always been fault lines in American history. In the last century, immigrant Catholic families, especially from Ireland or the Mediterranean, suffered the multiple burdens of harsh discrimination. Today, it is primarily people of color. Throughout welfare history, poor women have had to work but were condemned for doing so. "Proper" wives and mothers stayed home and took care of their husbands and children. Working mothers raised the specter of vice, promiscuity, illegitimacy, and unsupervised, delinquent children—in short, the destruction of traditional family values. Although this book will emphasize work, it is essential to keep in mind the multiple dimensions of moral condemnation in trying to understand the nature and continuities of American welfare policies. Race, gender, and threats, whether real or imagined, to the socialization of children are never absent in American politics.

The third assumption is that providing aid destroys not only the work ethic but other family values as well. Because of the multiple aspects of moral fault, welfare is not simply a matter of "economics," that is, providing income support. Welfare policy is concerned with "reformation" rather than redistribution.

Fourth, welfare reforms (that is, reformation) are directed at changing *individual* behavior rather than the environment. Self-sufficiency through work is to be achieved by changing the mothers rather than labor markets or other institutional arrangements that contribute to successful, independent lives. Since "decent" people can find work, it is assumed that people who want to work can find work. Focusing on the individual relieves policymakers from confronting the more difficult issues of labor markets, redistribution, or other institutional change. It allows policymakers to isolate the recipient, to blame the victim. It is the politics of exclusion.

Fifth, the reforms are directed at adult welfare recipients, who are almost exclusively women. Despite the obvious importance of men to family support and the socialization of children, men are virtually ignored, except for child support. Despite the origins of AFDC—concern for poor children—and its popular name, the "children's program," and despite the seemingly strong concern to prevent the transmission of deviant values, with relatively few exceptions (such as requiring school attendance), welfare children are also largely ignored, except when teens become pregnant. From its earliest days, AFDC (then ADC, for Aid to Dependent Children) has been concerned with regulating the mothers. It is easier, of course, to ascribe moral fault and justify punishment for adults and teenagers than for infants and toddlers.

The current welfare reforms, both enacted and proposed, are being hailed as "new," the first time welfare will really have been changed. This sort of political rhetoric, of course, accompanies most legislative changes. In fact, both the underlying assumptions about welfare reform and the remedies seem to be timeless. In Chapter 2 we will provide a brief historical overview of welfare. Our purpose is to show the continuity of the basic assumptions, myths, and ceremonies of welfare policies. As the new round of welfare reforms take hold, we are just a couple of years shy of the 650th anniversary of the Statute of Laborers (1349). This statute, enacted in the reign of Edward III, is usually considered to be the first legislative attempt to deal with welfare—the origin of "social security" in England and the United States.[13] The continuous similarities between welfare reform at the close of the twentieth century and in the previous half millennium are striking. Both the "menace" of welfare and its "cures" have not changed that much. Welfare policy is still in the shadow of the sturdy beggar. It's time for a new approach.

An Honest Approach to Welfare Policy

Our approach can be summarized as follows:

- The problem we are facing is poverty, not welfare.
- Poverty is caused primarily—not exclusively—by the deterioration of the low-wage labor market.
- Most welfare recipients are part of the working poor; therefore, the surest way to help most welfare recipients is to help the working poor.

Poverty is extensive and it is much larger and more serious than welfare. Although causality is not well understood, there seems little doubt that poverty is the single most important predictor of poor outcomes for families—the issues we usually ascribed to welfare families: single parenthood, out-of-wedlock births, poor physical and mental health, substance abuse, school failure, crime, delinquency, unemployment, and generational dependency. Single-parent families are not supported in this country as they are in most industrialized countries; consequently, they have much higher rates of poverty. Unless we confront poverty—not just welfare—serious efforts to do something about the problems of families in poverty and the well-being of children will be ineffective.

Poverty is caused primarily—not exclusively, to be sure—by changes in family composition and transformations in the low-wage labor market. To put the matter most bluntly: Because of the deterioration in the low-wage labor markets, working families are finding it increasingly difficult to escape poverty. Although the issue of poverty is most acute for single-parent households, it is also a serious issue for increasing numbers of intact families. Therefore, unless the issues of the low-wage labor market are addressed, our country will make little headway against the harmful effects of poverty, let alone welfare.

The economy in the United States, especially as compared with industrialized Europe, is creating millions of jobs. The problem is that they are lousy jobs. Wages have declined for the low-skilled worker and increasing numbers of jobs are part-time or temporary, often with no benefits. Finally, even though poverty policy always *assumes* that jobs are there if recipients are willing to look for them, the best evidence indicates that there are many more job seekers than job vacancies. The result is that poverty is increasing for millions of people, despite the fact that they are working, and working harder. The problems are more acute for women, minorities, and the less educated.

We would prefer an economy that provided enough *good* jobs for the those seeking work or working in poorly paid jobs. By good jobs, we mean stable jobs that pay a decent wage and that carry decent health and child care benefits. We recognize that this type of economy is not likely in the near future. Therefore, what is called for in the immediate future is reforming the low-wage labor market. There has to be job creation for those who are able and willing to work. Earnings from low-wage work have to be supplemented by income and benefits—the Earned Income Tax Credit (or other forms of wage supplementation), raising the minimum wage, child support, health care, subsidized child care, improved unemployment benefits, as well as other mechanisms to reduce income instability. Many have advocated these proposals, and we build on their work.

How would reforming the low-wage labor market affect welfare recipients? Contrary to the myth, most welfare recipients are part of the working poor. Although welfare recipients vary, a large majority of recipients are either in the workforce or have recently left a job and had to return to welfare. Then they try again and often succeed in leaving welfare. Belying the myth of welfare as a way of life, many are relatively short-termers; another significant portion cycle back and forth between welfare and work, but eventually leave after about four years; only a small fraction are long-term dependents. The long-term dependent is usually the young, poorly educated mother of color: in addition to suffering discrimination, she has more child care needs and fewer employment skills. But even in such cases long-term dependency is the exception.

The problem for most welfare recipients is not a lack of work ethic; it is a lack of jobs that will enable them to become independent. Many low-skilled women move in and out of jobs that disappear, or have to leave work because of child care or health or other family problems. There is no support for these wage earners. Because of the labor market and the lack of social support, recipients cannot make it on either welfare or work alone. The dismal employment prospects of AFDC recipients demonstrates that welfare reform is not simply a matter of dependency versus work. *Welfare reform has to be part of labor-market reform.*

Attacking poverty by reforming the low-wage labor market will be a major, costly undertaking—we are talking about the politics of redistribution. We are dealing with an unprecedented—and ominous—development in the American economy. Despite an impressive overall growth rate (4.1 percent in 1994), an outstanding increase in jobs, record corporate profits, and a revival of growth in productivity, progress toward equality has been reversed and inequality is rising. While income and wealth increased for the top 1 percent of the population, for the rest of the country family income stagnated during the 1980s—declines were prevented only by the continued rise in two-earner families—and they actually began to decline in the 1990s.[14] At the present time, the gap between the rich and the poor in the United States is the widest since the end of World War II.[15] The United States has the most unequal distribution of income of any Western industrialized country.[16] And there is no reason to expect that these trends will not continue, at least in the immediate future. At the lower end of the labor market, there is an increasing lack of mobility and increasing pressure from low-skilled immigration. Despite the growth in jobs, there are high levels of permanently un- and underemployed people, particularly young people who lack education and work experience. *These people are in danger of never making a permanent connection to the labor force.* It is because of the concentration of poverty and the very high levels of joblessness that we witness the rise of the "new urban poverty" in so many of our major cities. The loss of steady work has meant the loss of society's primary mechanism for the organization and socialization of life.[17]

It is not surprising that, on the rare occasions that the issues of the low-wage labor market are seriously addressed, reform proposals are both fundamental and expensive: changing our views as to what is the "natural" rate of unemployment; insuring rather than assuming that jobs are available; making serious public investments in skills and technology; changing corporate strategies from short-term profits to long-term investments in skilled workers; changing trade policies that reward the lowest-paid labor; and reempowering workers.[18]

Establishment economists believe that in time wages will rise; but this has not happened so far, despite the growth in productivity. In the meantime, wages are stagnant and inequality continues to grow. The choice, then, is between an increasingly unequal society—more poverty with its attendant ills (crime, suffering, urban decay, an impoverished urban underclass)—and policies that improve the returns from labor. The stakes for our country are very high.

Reforming the Labor Market

Our approach focuses primarily, but not exclusively, on work in the paid labor force. We believe that this is the surest, most sensible, most pragmatic, and most humane way to reduce family poverty and deal with many of the other ills that plague poor families today. Further, reforming the low-wage labor market is the *only* way to reduce the number of single mothers who have to rely on welfare either because of a temporary setback or to facilitate more stable exits from welfare via work. Therefore, to help most welfare recipients, as well as to reduce poverty, reform has to begin with the low-wage labor market. How we free ourselves from the so-called iron law of international economics, which says that all wages have to be as low as those of Chinese prison laborers, is beyond the scope of this book.[19] What we can address, however, is a more attainable near-term program—how to increase jobs and earnings income and benefits in an economy still characterized by relatively high levels of low-wage jobs.

Reforming the labor market by both creating jobs and supplementing low-wage work will accomplish the following:

- Poverty will be reduced, but primarily through attachment to the labor force; and because these benefits only apply through participation in the labor market, they reinforce the work ethic.
- Welfare rolls will be reduced by lessening the need for welfare in the first place, hastening welfare exits via work, and reducing the recycling between welfare and work.
- These are "targeted universal" programs—they apply to all the working poor. Thus, welfare mothers are incorporated into the working poor, where, in truth, they belong. Thus, it is hoped, they will no longer be stigmatized.
- This approach applies to men. We believe that the economic viability of men has to be part of the solution to poverty and welfare reduction, as well as family formation and the raising of children.
- If income supplementation and job creation are made available to all the working poor, those unable to make a satisfactory connection with the labor market will be a relatively small proportion of the previous welfare population. The reduced size, plus the fact that the majority of previous recipients will be absorbed into the working poor, should reduce the "crisis" politics of welfare and stigma surrounding this group and allow for more individualized services.

A number of objections can be raised to our approach. Some argue that even under the best of circumstances, the economy cannot provide enough jobs, and therefore what is called for is a basic citizens' income regardless of work effort; others object to proposals because they are universal rather than targeted on those most in need; and others argue that the low-wage labor market is inherently degrading and discriminatory. There is merit in these positions, and we address them in the concluding chapter. We believe, however, that the best route, at least in the near term, is to try to reduce poverty and welfare through reform of the low-wage labor market. Policy should concentrate on preventing single mothers who are already in the labor market from falling into welfare and facilitating those who are trying to leave welfare via work. The majority of welfare recipients and potential recipients will be incorporated into these more universalized programs. They will become part of the growing numbers of mothers in the paid labor force, some of whom work full-time, but most of whom combine work with family responsibilities and work part-time. Work and work-related supports and other kinds of social supports will be combined. These recipients will lose their identity as a separate, stigmatized class. They will be part of the working poor, as in fact they are already.

Most important from our point of view is that our approach will reduce *poverty*. This is a crucial issue that should not be lost sight of. The traditional approach—concentrating on the long-term recipient—does nothing about the conditions of poverty for the great bulk of welfare recipients, let alone the working poor. The current approaches to welfare reform—both Democratic and Republican—define "self-sufficiency" as the absence of welfare, *not the reduction of poverty*. Sooner or later, our country must address the problems of growing inequality and the spread of poverty among the working poor.

The specific policy options we favor are not new. In fact, one of the most important—the Earned Income Tax Credit—has been in place for two decades, and others, such as health care, child support, and child care, have been on the policy agenda for some time. In Europe, various provisions are designed to mitigate both job and income instability, as well as providing a better social safety net, apparently without adverse effects on flexibility of employment.[20] Universal approaches to welfare have also been proposed. What we are trying to do is combine the potential of the universal policies with a demonstration of the futility, indeed the cruelty, of the traditional approach.

The package that we present is the way to attack welfare dependency. Welfare recipients are incorporated into the more broadly based programs for the working poor; thus, rather than separating welfare from work, we combine work with redistribution. Whatever the disguise, the Earned Income Tax Credit, subsidized health care, and child care are redistribution.

The welfare system that we envisage is one in which the bulk of recipients move on their own into the labor market—one hopes permanently—with a variety of other supports. The job of welfare is to provide a safety net for those who return and for those who find that they cannot leave. Although we argue that the resulting welfare rolls will be substantially reduced, this depends ultimately on the state of the labor market and the levels of supports.

The Long-Term Dependent

The next question is what, if anything, should be done about those who find they have difficulty leaving welfare—the potentially longer-term dependents. There is great variation in this group. Some lack information about the job market or basic job-finding skills, such as preparing a resume or handling an interview. Others need more help; they may have more than the normal share of difficulties—child care, health problems, personal problems, work-related problems, whatever. This group needs more ongoing support. Then there are recipients who have more long-term problems. They are usually young, lack education and work experience, and have very young children. They may also be less motivated to increase their human capital. More intensive efforts are needed, but in truth we know very little about what "works" with the more difficult cases.[21]

We propose creating a separate employment services agency to work with all of these recipients, rather than trying to deal with them in regular welfare departments. Welfare agencies are not equipped to provide the kind of services that these recipients need—prompt, supporting, cooperative relationships that may have to extend over a considerable period of time. The employment services agencies, we believe, should be locally based and open to all. They would offer employment-related services along with whatever else is appropriate for their particular community. For the recipient, becoming part of a general clientele would lessen the stigma of welfare. The agencies would be encouraged to experiment, which is important, since we know so little about how to work with the harder cases.

The Issue of Mandatoriness

The welfare departments would refer clients to the general social service agency, but the relationship would be voluntary. There would be no sanction if the client refused. We believe that if the agencies have something of value to offer, there will no shortage of volunteers. We also believe that if clients still refuse to take advantage of what is being offered, sanctions will only make them poorer. Finally, we believe that sanctions would be inconsistent with the mission of the general social service agencies. The argument is made that even if sanctions are not necessary for welfare mothers who are already working, or trying to work, they are necessary for those who are not motivated. We will present evidence that agencies have a hard time doing both—they cannot successfully run programs that rely on cooperation, trust, and support, and at the same time rely on sanctions. Agencies that use sanctions become regulatory and distant from clients, and have higher sanction rates than agencies that minimize sanctions (they are presently required by law) and emphasize cooperation. We recognize the specter of the welfare abuser; we argue that this relatively small group should not distort welfare reform.

Why, then, the persistence of sanctions? They are clearly not needed for the bulk of recipients. The answer, again, lies in symbolic politics—the age-old practice of validating dominant ideologies by condemning the unworthy poor. Majoritarian society feels in control when it can punish, even if the punishment is futile.

We take the same approach with at-risk youth. We would make no distinction between teen parents or teen males and females. The current welfare reforms that focus on mandatory family values—the family cap, learnfare, requiring teens to live with their parents, and so forth—are singularly unsuccessful. We have evidence of better approaches.

Are These Proposals Feasible?

Reforming welfare by reforming labor markets will reduce welfare *rolls* but not necessarily welfare *costs*. Although long-term dependents are a minority of recipients, they absorb a disproportionate share of welfare costs. It is difficult to judge how much welfare would cost with a reformed labor market. This depends on the size of the long-term dependent population, the kinds of services offered, and, most crucial, the state of the labor market. Assuming a relatively full-employment economy, with adequate income supplementation and benefits, welfare rolls ought to decline by at least two-thirds (the present proportion of those in and out of the labor force), and should be even greater with more effective services. However, the costs of welfare are not the real issue fueling the welfare "crisis."

On the other hand, making work pay will cost *much more* than welfare. This is because the programs apply to all the working poor, including the men, not just the welfare recipients. And the proposed programs are much more expensive than welfare. The Earned Income Tax Credit alone will shortly cost more than AFDC. Job creation and adequate health and child care benefits are very costly. (We present estimates in Chapter 5.) We are talking about billions of dollars.

We must face reality: There is no cheap way to reduce poverty and welfare through work. We have noted the deep, serious problems of wage inequality in the U.S. economy, which is unique among the Western industrialized countries. The magnitude of the gap between the rich and the poor in this country has reached the dubious characterization of "astonishing."[22] We have noted the serious, harmful consequences of poverty on families and children. In the most recent Gallup study, physical abuse among families earning less than twenty thousand dollars was three times higher than in upper-income families, and sexual abuse is seven times more common among low-income families.[23]

Millions—yes, millions—of children are at risk because of mediocre child care and lack of adequate health care. The costs of poverty are real, they are tragic, and they are large. In short, we are talking about the politics of major redistributions. The Republicans proposed tax cuts for the middle- and upper-income brackets on the order of $270 billion over five years. We are urging that this kind of money be redirected. Under our proposals, the public money will go toward reinforcing the values of work and, we believe, strengthen the bonds of social life that have been so weakened by poverty.

By redefining the bulk of the welfare population as part of the working poor, we change the terms of the debate. The issue of welfare reform now becomes the issue of the low-wage labor market. In answer to the question, Can we afford to reform welfare? we must ask:

- Can our country afford not to seriously address the problem of low-wage work?
- Can our country afford not to seriously address the growing inequality throughout society?
- Can our country afford not to face the social costs of millions of children living in poverty?

When we look around the world, we ask: What kind of society do we want our children to live in? Do we want a society which strives to provide opportunities for all, which tries to assure decent standards for health and growth, and which fosters social cohesion? Or do we want a society which increases economic and social division and polarization? The choice is ours.

Chapter 2

Welfare Programs History and Structure

Two claims are made by the current welfare reformers: first, *these* reforms, as distinguished from earlier ones, are really new; they will change welfare; second, the new feature is that now welfare recipients will have to work rather than remain on the dole; welfare will no longer be a "way of life." In the following brief review of welfare history, our purpose is to show that both claims have repeatedly been made for more than six hundred years, but that none of the reforms accompanying them have, by themselves, resulted in significant change.

This raises a puzzling question. If welfare is such a persistent social problem, why do policymakers keep trying the same failed remedies? In this chapter we will examine, through both historical and contemporary examples, the *myth* and *ceremony* of welfare policy. The myth of welfare, as described in Chapter 1, is that the primary problem of the poor is individual moral fault—the lack of work ethic. The remedy, therefore, is to force the poor to accept work rather than welfare.

Yet because welfare policy fails to address the labor market, this creates a dilemma for officials who are supposed to implement welfare policy: What are they to do if there are no jobs or the poor are unable to work? Are the poor still to be punished? It is here that charity conflicts with ideology and difficult decisions have to be made. The tension is resolved through the use of ceremony— some of the hapless poor are punished to deter the able-bodied; at the same time, a few "succeed" by finding work and leaving welfare. The examples—the ceremonies—are sufficient to lend credence to the ideology. Victims can be blamed by pointing to the few, visible "successes." But the reality is that for the vast majority of the poor not much will change—at least through the administration of welfare policy. Local officials cannot control labor markets and, for the most part, are not willing to risk the costs of imposing widespread, visible, dramatic suffering.

The term *local officials* calls attention to the third point of this chapter. The current reforms, responding to the current crisis over welfare, are making a big point about returning AFDC to the states. "The states know best" is the current mantra of reform. This too is a puzzle since, in fact, AFDC has always been run primarily at the state and local levels, with comparatively slight federal influence. Furthermore, within the states AFDC is most often a county-run program, with a great deal of discretion exercised at the individual field offices. We will show through historical examples that when welfare boils up politically, the typical response at upper levels of government is largely symbolic: delegation to lower levels. In other words, delegation is used to manage political conflict. Why delegation to the lowest levels of government? Because it is there that the conflicts between charity and ideology are most keenly felt. Local officials believe that they know best how to resolve the moral dilemmas, how to distinguish the deserving poor from the undeserving. At the same time, delegation serves the interests of upper-level politicians. They can claim to be taking the moral high ground, to be "solving" the welfare mess, while leaving the moral conflicts to be sorted out at the local level, out of sight (they hope). It is uncanny how the current welfare reforms follow the historical script.

In many major aspects, the local offices are the crucial determinants of welfare policy administration. It is there that the ambiguities, conflicts, and discretionary judgments get sorted out. Starting in the 1960s, the local AFDC offices became extensively bureaucratized, staffed by overworked, underpaid, undertrained eligibility clerks and technicians driven by the demands of administering a huge, complex income-maintenance program, obsessed with work quotas, errors, and sanctions. There are hundreds of rules and requirements covering family relationships, residence, income, assets, expenses, health, schooling, employment, and so forth. Yet, the local offices, despite their oppressive income-maintenance burdens, have been called upon to become not only employment agencies but employment agencies dealing with a very hard-to-employ clientele. In this chapter, we will describe the transformation of the local AFDC offices. This transformation helps explain the generally dismal results of the welfare-to-work programs, discussed in the next chapter.

The history and structure of the U.S. welfare state illustrate how these social welfare programs have reinforced dependence on the private labor market rather than providing alternatives to paid labor.[1] Contributory retirement based on earnings, restrictive unemployment insurance and disability, and miserly poor relief provide strong incentives for families to achieve self-sufficiency primarily in the private labor market. But the labor market upon which the American welfare state was constructed—full-time jobs paying a family wage to the male breadwinner—no longer exists for millions of families. We increasingly have a labor market of low-paying jobs, with the majority of women in the paid labor force and families requiring two and sometimes three wage earners. Thus, the task is to reform not only the low-wage labor market but also related social welfare programs.

In the Shadow of the Sturdy Beggar

The key section of England's Statute of Laborers (1349) deserves to be quoted: "Because that many valiant beggars, as long as they may live of begging, do refuse to labor, giving themselves to idleness and vice, and sometimes to theft and other abominations; none upon said pain of imprisonment, shall under the color of pity or alms, give anything to such, which may labor, or presume to favor them towards their desires, so that thereby they may be compelled to labor for their necessary living."[2] At the time of the statute, begging was a widespread and accepted form of behavior. The purpose of the statute was to force beggars to seek work by preventing the giving of alms—in other words, by cutting off welfare.

By the middle of the fourteenth century, begging had become a social problem. Feudalism was giving way to capitalism, the woolen industry had been introduced into England, land was being foreclosed, and employed labor was replacing serfdom. During periods of economic dislocation, the unemployed roamed the countryside and migrated to the towns looking for work. These migratory workers, it was claimed, were responsible for mendacity and crime. Landlords were not only losing control over their labor but also feared threats to their safety and property. The more immediate precipitating cause of the Statute of Laborers was the acute labor shortage caused first by a period of famine, and then by the Black Death (1348–49). As a consequence, wages rose. In addition to prohibiting the giving of alms, the statute sought to restrict movement, require work, and fix wages. Thus—and this is the key point—the first statute dealing with "social security" was not about poverty and destitution. It was about forcing individuals to seek work rather than welfare.[3]

Capitalism, wage labor, and poverty continued to grow. Subsequent statutes filled out the basic contours of English welfare policy. It was recognized that certain categories of the poor were outside the labor market—the aged, impotent, sick, feeble, and lame. For this class, the work ethic, or moral behavior, was not at issue. At first, the "worthy poor" were given licenses to beg in designated locations; then publicly gathered alms were provided so that they would not have to beg.[4] Children caught begging were apprenticed. On the other hand, the able-bodied were required to work. The various provisions were codified in the Elizabethan Poor Law of 1601. Work was provided to the needy able-bodied. Administration was local. Strangers were removed. Those who violated the statutory requirements were imprisoned.[5]

The basic English poor law principles—direct aid for the unemployable, work (or imprisonment) for the able-bodied, and local administration—influenced welfare in colonial and early eighteenth-century America.[6] During this period, significant poverty was caused by rapid economic changes, depressions, fluctuating wages, low wages, even lower wages for women, seasonal labor, immigration, lack of public transportation, sickness and disease, and old people without families. According to Michael Katz, there were no clear lines between the destitute and the ordinary working family. With no safety net, there were increasing numbers of beggars, tramps, and criminals in the growing cities.[7]

By the mid-seventeenth century, several colonies had enacted poor laws patterned after the English legislation. In general, there were four basic responses to poverty: auctioning off the poor, contracting (placing the poor in private homes at public expense), outdoor relief, and the poorhouse. Administration was at the smallest unit of government. Communities responded to the needs of friends and neighbors. On the other hand, they were decidedly less generous to strangers, and, as transiency increased, attempts were made to restrict movement and immigration. Strangers were asked to post bond as a condition of settling. Those who were thought likely to become dependent were told to leave ("warned away"). If they returned, they were severely punished.[8]

A sharp distinction was made between those who were unable to care for themselves and the able-bodied. Religion, the need to hold down taxes, and the need for labor meant, in no uncertain terms, that those who could work should work. As Cotton Mather put it, "For those who indulge themselves in idleness, the express command of God unto us is, that we should let them starve."[9] As in England, there was a clear difference between being poor and being a pauper. The latter was a moral issue. The idle able-bodied were viewed as criminals, as threats to themselves as well as the community. They were either bound out as indentured servants, whipped and expelled, or jailed. By the beginning of the eighteenth century, they were confined to workhouses and their children were apprenticed. Putting the pauper to work was considered beneficial to both the pauper and the community.

Throughout the nineteenth century, the major welfare concern developed over outdoor relief; that is, aid given in the community rather than within an institution. Outdoor relief, it was believed, released the poor from the obligation to work. By the 1820s and 1830s, in both England and the United States, reformers began advocating poorhouses as the principal form of relief of the poor. Poorhouses, workhouses, or almshouses already existed in several of the major American cities, but the new emphasis was to make the poorhouse either the exclusive (in England) or the primary method of relief.[10] The famous Royal Poor Law Commission Report, published in 1834, reiterated the basic moral distinction between being poor and pauperism. Although there were several causes of poverty—urbanization, immigration, and intemperance—the primary cause of pauperism was assumed to be the indiscriminate giving of aid, which destroyed the desire to work.[11] From this premise followed the doctrine of "less eligible"—that is, "that the condition of welfare recipients, regardless of need or cause, should be worse than that of the lowest paid self-supporting laborer. While relief should not be denied the poor, life should be made so miserable for them that they would rather work than accept public aid."[12]

But why did the Elizabethan poor laws have to be reformed? After all, poor relief was only to be given to those who could not work; the able-bodied were required to work as a condition of aid. The reason was that it came to be held that the distinction between the malingerer and the disabled was too hard to administer in practice: "Character and circumstance were too intimately related, misery and vice too much a part of each other, to lend themselves to such distinctions. Besides, even if they could be distinguished, what magistrate would let a poor man die because it was his own fault he was dying?"[13] Other problems with the Elizabethan poor law resonate in today's debates. When relief became a "right" and the poor could count on it as "income," all "stimulus to industry and economy" was "annihilated or weakened. . . . The just pride of independence, so honorable to a man, in every condition," was "corrupted by the certainty of public provision"[14] (read "welfare as an entitlement" today).

The poorhouse would maintain the principle of "less eligible" and, at the same time, avoid the pitfalls of line-drawing between the worthy and unworthy poor—as long as the conditions of the poorhouse were sufficiently miserable; that is, "less eligible than any other mode of life, only the most severe destitution would induce a man to enter it." In this way, the poorhouse would serve as a "self-acting test of the claim of the applicant. . . . If the claimant does not comply with the terms on which relief is given to the destitute, he gets nothing; and if he does comply, the compliance proves the truth of the claim, namely his destitution." "Thus the instrument of relief was itself the test for relief."[15]

But what about the worthy poor, those who could not work? Since all outdoor relief had to be abolished to avoid line-drawing, the worthy poor also had to go to the poorhouse. And since the conditions of the poorhouse were to be sufficiently miserable to deter the able-bodied, the worthy poor—who had no other alternative—had to endure misery in order to deter the able-bodied. In Katz's telling phrase, the worthy poor were held "hostage" to deter the able-bodied.

In America, too, outdoor relief was blamed as a prime cause of pauperism.

Although the reforms were far less draconian, and in fact were also designed to eliminate some of the harsher practices, such as auctioning off the poor, the emphasis was on the increased use of the poorhouse. Within a few years after the reforms took hold in the mid-nineteenth century, the reports on the poorhouses documented a disaster. There was graft, corruption, and brutality; alcohol was smuggled in; inmates came and went; there was a general climate of filth and disorder; criminals, alcoholics, prostitutes, mothers, children, and infants were all mixed together. Mortality rates were high. Poorhouses were described as "living tombs" or "social cemeteries."[16] The able-bodied inmates were supposed to work, but in many houses it was cheaper to support them in idleness, especially in the winter. In many instances, work was used for deterrence only.[17]

In both England and America, poorhouse reform was regarded as a failure. In England, there was strong opposition to what quickly became a detested institution. Neighbors protected friends and relatives; there were local riots; and rural landlords wanted a ready supply of cheap labor. Local relief administrators found loopholes in the law and other ways to avoid institutionalization. One of the most powerful objections to the new Poor Law was the stigma that flowed from the very attempt to so sharply distinguish the pauper from the poor. Poverty had indeed become a crime.[18] In the United States, there was no rehabilitation; there was great and needless suffering, certainly for those who were not in the labor market but nevertheless confined; and, in the end, institutionalization turned out to be more expensive than outdoor relief.

The reasons for the failure transcend the particular experience of the poorhouse reform. First, the poorhouses tried to do two things that proved to be inconsistent. They sought to be compassionate to those who were truly needy, but at the same time they had to deter the able-bodied from applying. In the end, deterrence won and the poorhouses were universally feared and despised.[19] Second, the reforms focused on the individual poor person; fault was the cause of poverty; and the cure was moral reformation. No attention was paid to the supply of jobs; it was assumed that work was available for those who had the right attitude.

In the meantime, outdoor relief continued to grow. In the latter part of the nineteenth century, despite severe economic depressions, attempts were again made to restrict outdoor relief. This time it was to be replaced by "scientific charity." Although clothed in new theory, the assumptions as to the causes and cures of poverty were the same. Once again, the distinction between the two classes of poor was cast in moral terms, but in practice all who needed welfare were condemned as moral failures.[20] Economic causes of poverty were not mentioned; instead, vice and misery, laziness and immorality were held responsible. The emphasis on moral defect was strengthened by the rise in immigration. The alien newcomers, often confined to ghettoes, were blamed as one of the largest sources of pauperism.[21] Private charity was the preferred substitute for public assistance, for several reasons: because assistance would not be a right, there would be more uncertainty, and thus it would not weaken the work ethic; charities would be more resistant to political pressure to liberalize benefits, and charities would be more effective in exerting "those moral and religious influences that would prevent relief from degenerating into a mechanical pauperizing dole."[22]

Katz points out that—then, as now—the reformers' view was sharply at odds with that of those who actually received outdoor relief. Most recipients were in fact widows, children, the aged, and the sick. Very few, he says, could work. The reformers, however, considered outdoor relief a threat, not necessarily because of whom it helped, but because of those who *might* be helped. The "respectable working class just might learn the possibility of life without labor."[23] Many charity officials strongly opposed the "excess" of relief. "Next to alcohol, and perhaps alongside it, the most pernicious fluid is indiscriminate soup."[24]

In many communities, outdoor relief was either abolished or drastically reduced. The result was that by the end of the century, the number of children placed with agencies or in orphanages soared. Mothers sought jobs as live-in maids. Husbands went on the road looking for work, and local officials began to complain about the increase in tramps, who were mostly younger men in search of work. As with the new Poor Law in England, the opposition to abolishing outdoor relief was at the local level. There, the superintendents of the poor had to face local resistance to sending friends and neighbors to the poorhouse. Local merchants wanted the vouchers for food and coal. Local officials made the distinction between the truly needy and the unworthy. They knew the residents. However, "for strangers, nothing would certify worthiness as well as the willingness to break stone."[25]

These, then, were the attitudes toward the poor as America entered the twentieth century and began to build the current welfare state. For more than five hundred years, relief had focused on the individual rather than on labor markets or other social conditions. People were viewed as naturally slothful and would work only if required to. The goal of relief, therefore, was not primarily to relieve misery but rather to preserve the work ethic. Although preservation of the work ethic was the central theme, dependency was complex and multicausal. There was vice, filth, criminality, and above all, intemperance. Always present was hostility to strangers and immigrants—people who were different not only in habits but in race, ethnicity, and religion. Self-sufficiency, therefore, not only was morally valuable in itself but also served other goals of family, socialization, conformity, and citizenship. Those who were clearly not in the labor force would be helped, but drawing the line between the truly needy and malingerers was difficult. Therefore, the conditions of relief had to be sufficiently miserable and stigmatic to deter the working poor.

The Development of the American Welfare State

The characteristic feature of the American welfare state is its categorical nature. There are separate, distinct programs for specific categories of the poor—for example, Social Security pensions for retired workers and their survivors; disability for those who are permanently disabled; AFDC for single mothers and their children;[26] unemployment insurance; workers' compensation; Medicare for Social Security pensioners; Medicaid for the poor; and general assistance for the residuals—those who do not fit the categories, who are mainly childless adults under sixty-five years old.

The American welfare state is usually dated from the Social Security Act of 1935. Although that act established a national retirement system, it also continued and hardened the categorical programs that had been enacted by the states between 1910 and the 1920s, but that in fact had their roots in the early nineteenth century. Initially, the general mass of the poor were handled at the local level. Categorization began with the institutional movement. In the 1830s, the states began to separate out those categories of the poor who were morally blameless—that is, for whom the work ethic was not at issue—and provided separate institutions for the blind, the deaf and mute, and the insane. Subsequently, children were removed from the poorhouses and placed in orphanages. The institutional movement was not a matter of custodial efficiency; rather, it was a clear recognition that those who were dependent by misfortune did not deserve the stigma of the unworthy poor.

The Civil War resulted in a further categorization. The states created separate institutions for Civil War orphans and separate relief programs for indigent veterans and their families. The major program of that era was the Civil War pension program, which by the end of the century grew into a massive national income-maintenance system. Indigent veterans were morally excused from work—needy soldiers are not a "class of professional paupers, but are poor by misfortune."[27] In 1910, the program was terminated amid charges of extravagance, corruption, and partisan politics.[28]

At the close of the nineteenth century, single mothers and their children were in a very difficult position. In practice, they were not differentiated from the general mass of poor. They were not considered outside of the labor market. They were part of the "unworthy poor." From time to time, they, along with the rest of the poor, were helped, but mostly under severe conditions. They had to work, and when they could not support their families, the children were placed in orphanages.[29]

Poor single mothers not only carried the pauper stigma, but because they had to work, they threatened patriarchal conceptions of "proper" women and mothers.[30] Under the patriarchal "domestic code," proper women stayed home and took care of their husbands and children. The myth of the availability of work went hand in hand with the myth of the "family wage"—that the hardworking husband could earn an amount sufficient to support the family.[31] Husbands alone were supposed to provide for the material well-being of their families. Proper wives and mothers were not suited to the rough, vulgar world of commerce and paid labor; rather, they were to nurture husbands and children. Thus, poor mothers and their children were in a double bind. They were considered to be in the labor market. They were part of the undeserving poor, which meant that they had to work in the paid labor force. Mothers took in laundry, had boarders, were domestics, and, if lucky, worked in factories. The children also worked. But the families were also condemned for working. Poor working mothers were suspected of vice, immorality, and intemperance. This was a deviant class.[32] Immigrants and women of color bore the additional burdens of discrimination. Immigrants, especially Catholics and southern Europeans, were considered to be a different race, threatening the United States unless they became "educated, self-controlled, disciplined." Blacks were barely in the social conscience.[33] In Linda Gordon's terms, they were all but outcasts.[34]

In the later part of the nineteenth century, poor children began to be distinguished as a separate category that deserved attention. It was the children of these women—poor, immigrant, minority, working, often alone—that the Progressive Era Child Savers were concerned about.[35] The Child Savers, fearful of threats posed to middle-class Protestant America by the urban slum children growing up in these baleful circumstances, asserted public social control over these families by expanding the concept of abuse and neglect. Through child protection laws and the newly created juvenile courts, poor children were removed from their mothers and sent to institutions or farms in the Midwest. The Child Savers claimed that children were never removed for poverty alone, but poverty was never alone. There were always other factors.[36]

Around the turn of the century, the idea began to develop among some of the Child Savers that if the problem with children was in fact only poverty—if the mother was otherwise fit and proper—then perhaps a solution was to support the mother rather than to break up the home. This idea was endorsed in a White House conference in 1909, and the first aid to dependent children (ADC) statute was enacted in 1911—the Illinois Fund to Parents Act. The idea spread rapidly; by 1925, similar statutes were enacted in almost all the states.[37] At the time of enactment, ADC was popularly known as "mothers' pensions," although most statutes simply used "aid to dependent children."[38]

In order to understand the significance of the initial ADC programs—what they purported to do and what they did not do—it is essential to keep in mind the moral context of that time. This was the full flowering the patriarchal domestic code. The Progressive social reformers—for the most part, upper-class women—were fully committed to the domestic code and the family wage.[39] Those who opposed ADC, including many prominent social reformers, feared that aid to single mothers would weaken the responsibility of fathers and encourage single parenthood. Accordingly, aid should be given only to "children of worthy character, suffering from temporary misfortune, and children of reasonably efficient and deserving mothers."[40]

The apparent popularity of ADC has led some observers to regard the mothers' pension movement as a turning point in American social welfare history; now, poor mothers of young children could stay at home. They were morally excused from work; they were the "deserving poor."[41] However, when one looks more closely at what these statutes said and what the practice was in fact, aiding single mothers was still morally problematic. The indiscriminate giving of aid continued to raise great concern. The Charitable Organization Society (COS), the most influential organization at that time, vigorously opposed all forms of outdoor relief, including ADC. The statutes only included single mothers—intact families were excluded. This made no sense if poverty alone was the deciding factor. The reason for excluding husbands and fathers was that public relief would encourage idleness, lack of responsibility to the family, and compromise the moral socialization role of the working male.[42]

There were other restrictions. Aid would only be given if the mother was "fit and proper." Single mothers were suspicious; aid, it was thought, would encourage separation, further weaken the role of husbands and fathers, and increase the vulnerability of the mothers and children to temptation. The statutes did not define "fit and proper"—that was left to local administrators. In most jurisdictions, it was not the welfare departments but the juvenile and county courts that administered the program. These were the same courts that could, in addition to giving aid, adjudicate children delinquent, dependent, or neglected, break up the homes, and incarcerate the children either in reformatories or in state schools. Assisting the courts in many jurisdictions were the local COS chapters; they would make sure that aid would not contribute to vice. Programs were means-tested and "morals-tested" and supervised to make sure that the mothers learned proper work habits and morals that the reformers thought they lacked. By locating the programs in the courts, and having organizations such as the local COS supervise the recipients, ADC was, in effect, an alternative form of probation.

From the earliest days, ADC was an exercise in myth and ceremony. The myth was that poor mothers would be allowed to stay at home and take care of their children—hence the popular name "mother's pensions." The ceremony was that a small number of "deserving" white widows were helped; this served to validate the myth. The reality was that for most poor single mothers and their children, at best, nothing had changed; at worst, they were further stigmatized by being excluded from the mother's pension program.[43]

In practice, ADC programs remained small. Relatively few families were enrolled; they were almost exclusively white widows; and grants were small. Excluded were most poor single mothers—those who were divorced, deserted, never married, of color, or who engaged in questionable behavior. In short, the myth was that poor mothers and children were now the deserving poor. The reality was that the vast majority of poor mothers and their children were still morally problematic; they were still considered part of the paid labor force; they were denied aid. They were the undeserving poor.

Programs to aid the blind were enacted contemporaneously with ADC, but the contrast between the two was striking. Blindness was a "sufficiently well-defined cause of poverty"; therefore, the blind were the deserving poor. Eligibility was clear-cut—in addition to blindness, the determinants were age, residence, and need. In some states, the only moral condition was that the applicant not be a beggar. In contrast to ADC legislation, aid to the blind statutes were administered by welfare departments, not juvenile or county courts.[44]

Old-age assistance (OAA) was introduced in the 1920s, but it resembled ADC more closely than aid to the blind. Before the Depression, a standard retirement age had not been agreed upon, and the aged poor were viewed with as much suspicion as the rest of the poor. Aid to the aged poor, it was thought, would threaten the values of hard work and saving and family responsibility. Not only was it harder to enact OAA programs, but, like ADC, they were small, uneven in coverage, and contained many provisions designed to weed out the unworthy—for example, in many states aid would be denied persons who had deserted their spouses or failed to support them, or had been convicted of crimes, or were "habitual tramps, vagrants, or beggars."[45]

This, then, was the pattern on the eve of the New Deal: when consensus formed as to the nature of a social problem and its solutions, program design was transparent and ideologically consistent. This was true whether programs were benign—such as separate state institutions, veterans' pensions, and aid to the blind—or repressive—such as workers' compensation. Conversely, when moral responsibility was at issue, there was ambiguity and conflict. Here, programs were delegated to the local level and decided on a case-by-case basis. Aid to single mothers and their children, old-age assistance, as well as general relief to the undifferentiated able-bodied, raised issues of work, responsibility, race, gender roles, moral behavior, and child protection.

The immediate problems that the Roosevelt administration faced were massive numbers of unemployed, unprecedented poverty, and threats to the social order.[46] The administration quickly launched the Federal Emergency Relief Administration (FERA), which provided both work relief and direct relief. This, and its successor, the Works Progress Administration, was the largest work-for-relief experiment in our history. Between 1.4 and 2.4 million people per month worked at wages higher than direct relief, and at times higher than prevailing market wages as well. Two other work programs were also established at this time: the Civilian Conservation Corps and the Public Works Administration.[47] Despite their apparent success, however, the federal programs were vehemently attacked by the business community on the grounds that they compromised local labor markets, wasted public funds, and abandoned traditional welfare work requirements—that is, failed to preserve the historic distinction between work relief and "regular" employment. Despite the pressure, the administration launched the Civil Works Administration (CWA) to supplement the FERA. The accomplishments of CWA, too, were "heroic": it employed 4.26 million people in public jobs, with no means test and at relatively high wages.[48] Yet it too provoked a storm of protest. Congress imposed a means test. Roosevelt himself considered both programs temporary, and they were shortly replaced by the smaller Works Progress Administration (WPA), but it too was mired in political, economic, and administrative difficulties. It was short-lived and produced meager results.[49]

The Roosevelt administration turned its attention from job creation and welfare to its real concern: Social Security retirement and unemployment insurance. The centerpiece of the Social Security Act was the establishment of a contributory national pension program for the retired worker—old-age insurance (OAI), ("Social Security"). Consensus settled on a retirement age; those over sixty-five were now excused from work. Contributory insurance meant protection for clearly defined "risks." There would be no means test, so that beneficiaries would not have the stigma of the dependent poor. The Roosevelt administration fought vigorously and successfully to include only workers who contributed and to exclude the poor aged, lest the program be considered "welfare." The South also insisted that agricultural workers not be included; hence, most African Americans were not covered. In short, Social Security was for the deserving white worker and remained relatively small until the after World

War II, when most of the poor aged were finally blanketed in. OAI was a national, uniform program administered by the Social Security Administration.

The biggest fight the administration had was over unemployment insurance (UI), or more particularly, the jurisdictional location of UI. One would have thought that unemployment, especially on the massive scale of the Depression, would be considered a national problem requiring national solutions. But the unemployed were different from the aged. Not only was the work ethic involved, but also race. In the end, race relations and control over local labor markets prevailed. UI was handled at the state and local levels; at the local level, programs failed to reach those most in need—employees of small firms, agricultural workers, women, African Americans, and migrants. State benefits were low and short-term, more in the nature of temporary, emergency relief. A variety of eligibility provisions in state laws were designed to make sure that benefits were paid only to deserving workers, that is, workers who had been steady and reliable in covered employment. Workers who quit or were fired or discharged because of a labor dispute or who failed to register at a public employment agency and be available for suitable work were not eligible.

ADC, along with OAA and aid to the blind, became one of the grants-in-aid. There were a few federal requirements; basically, the states and local governments continued to administer the program as they saw fit. ADC began to expand in numbers, in racial composition, and in eligibility requirements (in addition to widows, it embraced children of mothers who were divorced, deserted, or never married).[50] But until the late 1950s and early 1960s, it remained relatively small. Since there were no other welfare programs (except the very uneven and miserly local general relief), poor mothers, those who were divorced, separated, or never married, and those of color, and their children had to work or otherwise obtain money as best they could. That is, despite ADC, the vast majority of poor single mothers and their children were treated no differently than the other categories of undeserving poor; relief was denied and they were subject to the paid labor market.[51]

Dramatic changes came in the AFDC program in the late 1950s and 1960s. The previous system of exclusion collapsed and the rolls and costs exploded. In 1950, two million people were on the AFDC rolls; in 1960, three million; by 1970, nine million; and the numbers increased, more or less steadily, to twelve to thirteen million today. The demographic characteristics of the rolls changed from mostly white widows to divorced or never married, with increasing proportions of nonwhites. Expenditures also rose dramatically, from about $500 million in 1950 to $4.8 billion in 1970, $9.2 billion in 1975, and then gradually to today's level of about $23 billion.[52]

There are various reasons for the changes—the massive migrations of African Americans to the northern cities; the entry of women into the paid labor force; the severe unemployment in the inner cities, with the accompanying increase in poverty, rising social unrest, disorder, crime, and riots; the pressure exerted on local governments by the War on Poverty, the welfare rights movement, and the legal rights movement; the courting of inner-city voters by the Democratic Party; and the rise of mother-only families.[53] This was a period of growing liberalism—witness the Civil Rights Act (1964) and the Voting Rights Act (1965)—and political elites were becoming more responsive to the demands of inner-city African Americans, including antipoverty measures. This was the era of the Great Society. A variety of federally sponsored local initiatives and activist groups attacked local institutions and practices, including welfare. The federal courts, War on Poverty lawyers, and welfare rights activists, such as the National Welfare Rights Organization (NWRO), forced open the state ADC gates; welfare became a "right"; social movement groups actively recruited potential eligibles, reaching more than 90 percent in the early 1970s.[54]

In streamed the previously excluded—African Americans, the divorced, separated, deserted, and increasingly the never-married.[55] Were these previously excluded morally problematic recipients now to be treated as the deserving poor and excused from work? Not so. Welfare was now in "crisis." From the very beginning, the liberalization of AFDC was strongly contested. Congress and the states tried to increase support from absent fathers; eligibility was tightened; benefits were cut.[56] Nevertheless, costs and numbers rose steadily and the program appeared out of control. Political and popular concern focused on the large of number of African Americans, out-of-wedlock births, single parenthood, and generational dependency.[57]

The federal and state governments offered three major responses to the welfare crisis. The first was short-lived. Reflecting the liberal moment, the Kennedy administration thought that the rolls and costs would be reduced by using social services to strengthen families and helping them toward self-support. The 1962 "social service amendments" renamed the program Aid to Families with Dependent Children (AFDC). In fact, very few social services were delivered; agencies, in general, simply took the additional federal money and continued to do business as usual. AFDC continued to grow, and the social service approach was abandoned in 1967.[58]

The second approach returned to first principles—requiring work by the reduction of grant levels by the state governments and the introduction of required work programs. (In Chapter 4, we will discuss in detail the administration of the various work programs.) Beginning in 1967, and continuing through the Family Support Act of 1988, the current array of state waivers, and now the Personal Responsibility and Work Opportunity Reconciliation Act of

1996, federal and state work requirements were to be applied to able-bodied welfare mothers. Prior to the recent consensus, liberals vigorously fought the work requirements; they argued that if nonwelfare mothers were not required to work, it was unfair and punitive to impose work requirements on single poor mothers. Conservatives thought otherwise. Single poor mothers did not shed their historical undeserving status simply because misguided liberals let them into AFDC. They were morally different from mothers who were either man-dependent or self-sufficient. Thus, they should be required to work.

Over the next twenty years, there was a standoff. As we will discuss in Chapter 4, the work requirements never succeeded in the sense of either reducing rolls through employment, or setting the poor to work, or imposing sanctions for failure to comply. The vast majority of welfare recipients were either declared ineligible for the programs or otherwise excused from the requirements. Just as with the earliest ADC "mothers' pensions," the country collectively engaged in myth and ceremony. The myth was that we were going to reduce welfare by imposing the moral values of work; the ceremony was the small number of recipients who did leave welfare through employment (whether they did so as a result of the work programs is another matter). In the meantime, the vast majority of welfare recipients were condemned for their continued dependency. They were still the undeserving poor.

Both sides remained unhappy. Conservatives continued to attack the "entitlement state" on the grounds that there are *responsibilities* as well as rights in the social contract. Then, in the late 1980s, the liberals changed tack. Instead of arguing that it was unfair to require AFDC mothers to work, they now argued that AFDC mothers should be *expected* to work. Two reasons were given. First, social norms concerning female labor have changed. Since the majority of nonwelfare mothers, including mothers of young children, are in the paid labor force, it is reasonable to expect welfare mothers to work. Second, the families are better off, both materially and socially, when the adults are gainfully employed. It is bad (morally) when families are continually dependent.[59] Many liberals supported the state work demonstration projects and the JOBS program created by the Family Support Act of 1988, and the recent legislation which combines work requirements with time-limited welfare.[60]

As is customary in American politics, the current reforms designed to enforce work by limiting welfare are being hailed as "new" when in fact they are old, painfully old. As we have seen, they perpetuate beliefs as to the causes of poverty and the remedies that date back almost 650 years. The reason for poverty among the unworthy poor is the lack of the work ethic, which is an individual moral responsibility. This brief review of the history of welfare shows two things: (1) poor mothers, including those on welfare, *always* were required to work; it is a myth to think that *new* "responsibilities" are now to be asked; and (2) although contemporary welfare policies are often described in so-called objective terms—labor markets, wage rates, incentives, demographics—they are heavily ladened with moral judgments. Who the poor are, whether they should be helped, and under what circumstances are social issues that affirm moral norms of work, family, gender roles, and attitudes toward race and ethnicity. Accordingly, whether and how to help those who cannot support themselves necessitates making a moral judgment.

The first two responses—social services and work requirements—were largely myth and ceremony. As we show in Chapter 4, nothing really happened very much to the great bulk of welfare recipients, at least as a result of the work requirements. This is not true with the third response, however. As a result of the dramatic changes in the welfare rolls—the size, the demographic composition, and the costs—AFDC administration at the state and local levels underwent profound changes. In a word, the system became highly bureaucratized. And it is these changes that seriously compromise the administrative capacity of the local AFDC offices to respond to the various welfare-to-work programs that have been imposed upon them over the past thirty years.

Administrative Changes

Prior to the 1960s, the AFDC program could be characterized as highly discretionary as to both eligibility and aid. For example, caseworkers could determine, among other things, whether the home was "fit and proper," the suitability of child rearing, and whether there was a man in the house. The AFDC budget was individualized. Caseworkers would calculate each family's resources and expenses, then compare the total with a need standard to determine the amount of aid that the family would receive. Many states also had special programs to meet individual needs (emergencies, health, household, and so on). The budget calculations were not a one-time process, since family resources and needs would change over time. Individualized treatment served a number of purposes. Since different families have different needs—for example, requiring a special diet for a sick child—recognizing those differences would treat dissimilar families according to a common standard. Although the principle was horizontal equity, individualized budgets served the moral or social control functions of welfare. Budgets for clothing, food, rent, and other household expenses reflected judgments about the character and behavior of individual families.[61]

Starting in the 1960s, several of the more restrictive eligibility rules were declared illegal by the courts or by the federal government.[62] Pressures to standardize the budget also began to mount. There were many reasons—legal rights lawyers, for example, pressed for uniformity in place of administrative discretion—but the two principal reasons were the sheer volume of cases and issues of program integrity. The two reasons are related. All systems of administration must adopt routine to handle volume, and welfare is no exception. As the rolls expanded, in the large offices it became impossible to verify information, process cases, review cases, make required home visits, and adjust budgets as individuals' circumstances changed. Working conditions deteriorated and administrative costs and error rates rose to what seemed to be alarming proportions. As a result, whatever benefits individualized budgets had provided turned into vices. It was widely believed that error, fraud, mismanagement, informal administrative practices, the failure to respond to individual needs, and the lack of information on the part of both clients and staff led to gross inequities in the actual administration of aid.[63] AFDC began to be described in terms of "administrative chaos."

A consensus developed that AFDC had to be simplified to reduce these problems. Standardized budgets replaced individualization; special needs were largely eliminated. Most significant, the federal government and the states reasserted quality control. Ostensibly designed to address the accuracy of eligibility and budget determinations, quality control quickly concentrated on erroneous overpayments. Programs became computerized; social workers were replaced by clerical and intake workers, now supervised under strict rules. Cases were monitored by both federal and state governments for errors. States were to be penalized if the AFDC program exceeded a certain error rate; individual workers and supervisors were held to strict quotas and error rates, under threat of sanction.[64]

The vigorous pursuit of overpayments through the quality control system transformed AFDC into a bureaucratic, rule-bound system. In a relatively short time, there was a dramatic tightening of administrative practices.[65] Meanwhile, quality control, along with monthly reporting, produced great distortions in the program. There was a sharp increase in procedural denials. Under great pressure to get the work out, and get it out correctly, the staff would no longer offer assistance to clients or give them full information. Instead, the staff would cut corners to manage the work load and to avoid tasks that would create delays. Client requests for changes—for example, adding a baby, or deductions for work expenses—were placed at the bottom of the pile. Staff would close cases for paper errors (for instance, missing Social Security numbers, birth certificates, and other required documentation) rather than try to contact the client and risk having an auditor finding a case error. Clients were placed under greater burdens to produce documentation and to correct errors on their own. The result was what Michael Lipsky called "bureaucratic disentitle-ment"—the controlling of welfare costs through the hidden, obscure decisions of the bureaucracy.[66] Error rates (defined as overpayments) did go down. Many of the errors were on paper only, and although some proportion of the clients were restored to the rolls when the missing documents were supplied, there are no reliable figures on those who never made it back.[67]

The importance of this change—the bureaucratization of AFDC—cannot be exaggerated. To a large extent—though never completely—management was able to assert control over the line staff by routinizing large parts of the pro-gram, instituting strict monitoring controls, and replacing the staff with eligi-bility clerks and technicians. The emphasis was, and still is, on strict adherence to eligibility and income-maintenance requirements. At the same time, local welfare offices have been hard hit. The staff are undertrained, underpaid, and overworked. In testimony before the General Accounting Office, welfare ad-ministrators from Cleveland described their offices in the following terms: "Many human services departments cannot manage to answer the telephone, let alone conduct a civilized interview. They have been stripped of staff; the staff they have has been downgraded—some have only an eighth- or ninth-grade education; and they have been buffeted, blamed, and drowned in impos-sible regulations and requirements."[68]

This is the context of the local welfare office. It is the culture of eligibility and compliance. There are widespread accounts of negative attitudes on the part of workers toward recipients. Many workers see themselves as but a short step away from welfare themselves; yet they work hard, "play by the rules," and no one is giving them benefits and favors. Workers trained, socialized, and supervised in this manner will apply rules strictly, impose sanctions, avoid errors, and get through the day as quickly and painlessly as possible. This is why clients with problems become problems. Requests for change or required change consume scarce administrative time and run the risk of error. Yet it is rare for policymakers to take these organizational constraints seriously; most of the time, they are content to make the political, symbolic gestures of reform and not worry about administration. As we shall see in Chapter 4, this is especially true with the welfare-to-work programs.

The path that welfare has taken is thus contradictory. It has kept its long-standing moralistic, social control ethos. Applicants and recipients are viewed with suspicion. The emphasis is on moral reformation and the control of waste, fraud, and abuse. The former has resulted in the reinstitution of in-creasingly strict work requirements, which, as we shall see, requires intensive, close caseworker management. But the latter has resulted in bureaucratization, computerized rule enforcement, and the proletarianization of the workforce—

in short, an organization that is administratively incapable of carrying out work programs. The basic incompatibility between welfare agencies and the demands of work programs will be amply demonstrated in Chapter 4, after we look more closely at who welfare recipients are and how they respond to both welfare and the low-wage labor market.

Chapter 3

Work, Recipients, and Poverty

The American welfare state is designed to provide strong incentives for private labor market employment. For the last thirty years, the dominating characteristics of AFDC reform have been to try to move recipients into the workforce through low benefits and work requirements. The current welfare-to-work reforms, through a combination of expanded work requirements and time limits, intend to move many more recipients as quickly as possible into low-wage, entry-level employment—to "end welfare as we know it." The assumptions behind this approach are that jobs are available in the regular economy for people who want them; that recipients are choosing welfare rather than work; and that welfare dependency not only costs taxpayers but is harmful to the recipients and their families. It is assumed that with the proper incentives and sanctions, recipients will get jobs, and that even though these will be low-wage, entry-level jobs, if people stick with these jobs, they will obtain better-paying jobs, thereby transcending the harmful consequences of dependency and poverty.

In this chapter, we question these assumptions. The first section deals with the low-wage labor market—the kinds of jobs that are available for the less-skilled worker, the low pay, the lack of benefits, and the lack of mobility. Increasingly, the labor market is no longer a route out of poverty. Second, we examine the welfare population. Contrary to the popular stereotype, most welfare recipients are either working or trying to work, but have great difficulty in securing jobs that will allow them to leave welfare permanently. Third, we examine the poverty consequences of both the low-wage labor market and AFDC. The harmful consequences usually attributed to welfare families—the decline in "family values"—are more accurately consequences of poverty.

The Low-Wage Labor Market

There are a great many people who are working but still in poverty. Of the nearly 40 million people in poverty in 1993, 8.2 million were employed at least some time during the year, and 4.7 million usually worked full-time.[1] Among the 28 million near-poor (those with incomes 150 percent of the poverty line), there were 6 million full-time and 5.5 million part-time workers.[2] If so many working people are struggling, then what is happening with the low-wage labor market?

Our particular concern is with the low-wage worker—basically, the less skilled man or woman who has only a high school diploma or less. We look at (1) trends in wage rates for low-wage jobs, for both men and women, and for single- and two-parent households, including the important issue of mobility; (2) employment; (3) the rise of contingent or part-time employment; and (4) the future of the low-wage worker.

Declining Wages; Rising Inequality; Consequences for Families

There have been several studies of the growing inequality of earnings, all reaching pretty much the same conclusion: that the real earnings of less skilled, less educated workers have declined substantially since 1973.[3] Moreover, this decline occurred during a period of economic expansion and aggregate growth in employment. In 1973, for men with one to three years of high school, the median income was $24,079 (in 1989 dollars); in 1989, it was $14,439. For men with a high school diploma, income dropped from $30,252 to $21,650. For women with one to three years of high school, the median earnings were $7,920 in 1973; by 1989, they dropped to $6,752. For women with a high school diploma, the figures were $11,087 (1973) and $10,439 (1989).[4] Furthermore, the decline in income was not because of the shift in jobs from manufacturing to service; real wages declined in both sectors. Between 1973 and 1990, the median income declined almost a third for families headed by parents under age thirty. Real wages of the less skilled worker have deteriorated significantly—so far that low-wage earners in America have lower earnings than workers in all advanced countries.[5]

Overall, less-skilled women's wages have not experienced the same declines as men's wages. The primary reason is that less skilled women are in occupations and industries that have not suffered such severe wage declines. Although men's and women's wages are closer, however, women still earn substantially less. For example, as late as 1987, "more than 80% of women still earned less than the median male worker and over one-quarter remained in the bottom decile of the men's distribution. . . . The gains that women did make over the 20 years from 1967 to 1987 largely consisted of movement out of very low earnings, not into high earnings levels."[6] Moreover, women's relative progress vis-à-vis men will probably slow in the future, primarily because of increasing labor-market segmentation along race and gender lines. Women are concentrated in the lower end of the service jobs; and (as we will discuss shortly) the growing use of involuntary part-time labor will increasingly block entry-level workers from traditional career-ladder jobs.[7]

Although the expansion of low-wage (below poverty-level) jobs affected all workers, its greatest impact was on minorities. Between 1979 and 1987, the proportion of African Americans in these jobs increased from 33.9 to 40.6 percent, for Latinos from 31.7 to 42.1 percent, and for whites from 24.3 to 29.3 percent.[8]

Earnings opportunities are seriously affected by household composition. In 1960, about a quarter of female-headed families were poor; now, the proportion is nearly half (47 percent).[9] These families are poor because there is typically only one earner, they usually have child care expenses, and women earn less than men, even when they work the same number of hours.[10]

Although the problem is most acute for single-parent families, most two-parent families have been able to maintain their relative position only by having both parents working. As a result, within marriage, the role of women is changing. In fact, the most dramatic changes in women's labor force participation has occurred among married women with young children. Increasingly the "breadwinner-husband" family is being replaced not only by the wife-contributor—since 1980, most wives have provided some earned income to the family—but by the "coprovider" wife, who brings in a significant percentage of the family's income.[11] There are positive sides to this development—marriage no longer has to be viewed as subordination for women; on the other hand, research on trends in delayed marriage, increasing nonmarriage, marital instability, and marital formation suggests that "marriage is more likely to occur when *both* men's and women's economic prospects are good."[12]

Economic viability for working people may not require only two earners; there is an increasing trend toward three jobs per couple. Seven million Americans, or 6 percent of the workforce, hold 15 million jobs. Most multiple-job holders are married, and, increasingly, as many women as men. No other country approaches these numbers of multiple-job holders.[13]

Today, the majority (61 percent) of children have mothers who are in the paid labor force; moreover, these mothers are working longer hours—more than 30 percent longer than a decade ago.[14] Married mothers, who still have the great bulk of child care responsibilities, are working longer hours in a poorly paid, gender-discriminatory labor market. It is estimated that the amount of time that children spend with their parents has fallen by half since 1964.[15] Not surprisingly, these developments have important consequences for family life and child care, which will be discussed in Chapter 6.

With the decline in real wages, it is not surprising that the poverty rate of full-time workers is increasing. According to the latest figures, in 1992, 18 percent of full-time workers earned less than the poverty line, which is a 50 percent increase over the last thirteen years. The poverty rate of full-time workers increased for both men and women but was particularly steep for those without a high school diploma. For these men, the rate rose from 15 percent in 1979 to 32 percent in 1992—and this is for full-time workers.[16] As a result, over the last two decades, there has been a steady decline in work among men in families in the bottom fifth of the income distribution.[17]

The argument is made, however, that wage inequality is less worrisome if there is sufficient mobility. In a recent paper, Moshe Buchinsky and Jennifer Hunt, using data from the National Longitudinal Survey of Youth, examined both hourly wages and annual earnings, for both men and women, and also took into account unemployment. They found that mobility has fallen significantly over time, especially "at the bottom part of the distribution" as compared with more educated and more skilled workers.[18] This research is also consistent with the findings of Roger Waldinger, who examined low-wage employment in Los Angeles. There was little mobility out of the ethnic labor niches. Low-wage ethnic workers increasingly are stuck in their jobs.[19]

Although the low-income employment rates of married women increased over the the past two decades, higher proportions of single women, even with children, work more than married women, with or without children. Almost half (48.3 percent) of poor single mothers work, as compared to 29.8 percent of married women without children, and 39.9 percent with children. But the most important point is the decline in real wages for all of these groups.[20]

Employment and Unemployment

Not only did earnings decline, but so did employment for both high school graduates and dropouts. Although the unemployment rate for all workers was roughly the same in 1974 and in 1988, it doubled for these two groups. Continued levels of unemployment exacerbate the problems of the less educated worker. Of the workers who lost their jobs in 1988, by 1990 78 percent were reemployed. Sixty percent, however, had been jobless for five or more weeks, almost 10 percent were still unemployed, and just over 12 percent were no longer in the workforce. Many of the displaced workers experienced earnings losses when rehired. The likelihood of being reemployed depended on the length of time with the previous employer, number of years in school, age, gender, and the local unemployment rate. High school dropouts, older workers, women, and minorities were less likely to be reemployed.[21] It is this combination—declining real earnings and rising unemployment—that has resulted in increasing poverty among these young families. They simply cannot work their way out of poverty.

Contingent, Part-Time Work

The nature of employment is shifting from full-time work for a single employer to various forms of part-time, contingent work or other types of flexible work arrangements that lack job security. It is estimated that as of 1988, there were 32 million contingent workers, accounting for almost a quarter of the workforce. The contingent workforce grew rapidly in the 1980s and will probably continue to increase, since new jobs are expected to be almost entirely in the service sector, where contingent employment is most likely to occur.[22] According to the Bureau of Labor Statistics (BLS), almost two-thirds of the new entrants into the labor force by the year 2000 will be women, and they are more likely than men to hold part-time and temporary jobs. Although most part-time workers are women, men now account for a significant fraction.[23] It is estimated that by the turn of the century 40 percent of jobs could be part-time.[24]

There are two views of part-time work. At its worst, it is a disguised form of unemployment. But it is good for some workers. It provides additional income, flexible hours, and continued attachment to the labor force for those workers who pursue other activities. With the rapid growth of nontraditional families, many workers are interested in part-time work. This would be true for both single parents and two-earner families with children. More than three-quarters of part-time workers say they voluntarily choose this status. It is not clear what "voluntary" means as measured by the BLS. The data do not reveal why part-time workers look only for part-time work—for example, child care, transportation, and health costs may operate as constraints. Further, if female heads of households are more constrained than male heads to working part-time, income inequality (and poverty) will increase as the sex distribution of family heads continues to change.[25] More than a quarter of women work part-time, making them 1.5 times more likely to be so employed than the average worker. "While women are more likely to *choose* part-time work, they are also more likely to be *stuck* in part-time jobs against their will. The female rate of involuntary part-time work is 44 percent greater than that for men."[26] In any event, the real growth in part-time employment was with involuntary part-time jobs, indicating that employer, not employee, preferences are predominating.[27]

Part-time jobs are more likely to be dead-end. Part-time workers keep their jobs for shorter periods than full-time workers. The average job tenure for a part-time worker is 3.4 years, as compared to 5.7 for full-time working women and 8.1 years for full-time working men. Part-time workers often lack health and pension benefits. Controlling for education, gender, and age, part-time workers receive about 40 percent less per hour than full-time workers in the

same jobs. Part-time workers are disproportionately in the low-wage distribution. Part-time workers constitute 65 percent of all people working at or below
minimum wage.[28] As a result, families headed by part-time workers are four
times more likely to be below the poverty line than families headed by full-time
workers. A fifth of families headed by part-time workers are in poverty, and 12
percent also receive welfare, as compared to 2 percent of families headed by
full-time workers. Again, single-parent families were worse off—40 percent
were poor and 26 percent were on welfare.[29]

The significant portion of employees in part-time work, and the expected
proportional growth of this form of employment, indicate that underemployment is going to be a continuing concern.

The Future for the Less Skilled Worker

The future does not look good for the less skilled worker. First, sectoral
shifts in employment have resulted in declining manufacturing opportunities
for this group. Wages in the service sector are lower but skill levels are higher.
Second, although unemployment rates in general have stabilized, younger, less
educated workers, especially African Americans, are the last to be hired and the
first to be fired. For both men and women, unemployment rates are considerably higher for people of color than for whites. Third, although the impact of
immigration varies, there has been a large increase in less educated immigrants
and this has contributed to the decline in labor market for high school dropouts.[30] Fourth, imports of manufacturing goods from third world countries
continue to have an uncertain effect on the labor market.[31]

The decline in union membership has meant a loss of higher-wage jobs.
(Until recently, the minimum wage has declined significantly in real terms.[32]
When it is raised to $5.15 per hour [on September 1, 1997] for a full-time worker
in a family of four, earnings still will be only two-thirds of the poverty line.) Almost 5 million workers are stuck in minimum-wage jobs. Other factors contributing to the bleak picture for the less skilled worker include what is called
the "spatial mismatch"—jobs continue to leave the inner city for the suburbs.
There continues to be discrimination against nonwhite men and women,
especially African Americans, who are associated with inner-city culture.[33]

On the supply side, it is often argued that the decline in basic reading and
math skills accounts for the decreased earnings of the less educated. However,
earnings for African Americans fell while test scores and academic achievement
rose, and earnings of less educated cohorts fell as they aged. The more likely
explanation is that academic skills have not kept pace with job requirements.[34]

Crime, of course, affects employment. It provides not only an attractive alternative for the less educated but also a disqualification for legitimate employ-

ment. The number of young, less educated males, especially African Americans, who are involved in the criminal justice system is staggering.[35]

This is the labor market confronting the majority of welfare recipients—low wages, spells of unemployment, jobs that do not last, jobs without health or child care benefits, jobs where there is gender and race discrimination. We now turn to the recipients. Who are welfare recipients? And how do they fare in this world?

The Welfare Population

The stereotypical welfare recipient is a young black woman, without education or skills, who bears lots of children to get more welfare, who is a long-term dependent and whose dependency is passed on from generation to generation. In fact, we find that most of the recipients are not African American; very few are teenagers, especially young teenagers; welfare families have about the same number of children as nonwelfare families; most are on welfare for relatively short periods of time; but most remain quite poor, and this probably accounts for their children being more likely to have welfare spells when they are older as compared to children whose parents did not experience welfare. We also find that a great many are working. They may be working off the books, but they are working. And, in time, despite significant odds, most work their way off welfare.

In 1994, the average monthly family enrollment in AFDC was 5 million families. This is an all-time high; recently, AFDC rolls have been declining. The 5 million families translates into 14.2 million recipients, of which 4.6 million are adults (virtually all mothers) and 9.6 million are children.[36] This represents about 63 percent of the children in poverty.[37] "Welfare" is often used interchangeably with poverty, but in fact the AFDC welfare population is only about a third of the poverty population.[38]

In 1994, the total AFDC bill for assistance payments was $22.8 billion; the federal share was $12.5 billion.[39] Although this is not a trivial amount, it is well to keep in mind that AFDC is a small program, in terms of both recipients and budget dollars. The food stamp program, for example, is twice as big— 26.6 million people costing $27.4 billion in federal funds. The really big programs are the Social Security Retirement and Disability program ($339 billion), Medicare ($180 billion), and Medicaid ($185 billion).[40]

How does welfare support these families? Adjusting for inflation, in 1970, the average grant per three-person family was $713 (1995 dollars). In 1995, it was $377—a 47 percent reduction.[41] Nor has this decline been made up by the cost-of-living increase in food stamps. Between 1972 and 1992, the combined value of AFDC and food stamps declined from $874 (1992 dollars) to $649—a 26 percent reduction. And since 1991 several states have cut benefits.[42]

The largest, most recent increases in the AFDC population occurred between 1988 and 1992—from 10.9 million to 13.6 million. The most recent research found that the pattern of AFDC receipt closely follows the unemployment rate, especially the unemployment rate of female heads of households.[43] Still, at its highest levels, AFDC recipient rates for the total population actually declined by 4.8 percent between 1975 and 1992.[44] And recently rates have continued to decline.

Whites account for 37.4 percent of the AFDC population, African Americans 36.4 percent, and Latinos 19.9 percent. Most (55.7 percent) mothers are never married; about a quarter (26.5 percent) are divorced or separated.[45]

Between 1970 and 1995, the average AFDC family size *decreased* from 4.0 persons to 2.8. Most AFDC families are two-member families. In 72.7 percent of the families, there are two or fewer children. In another 15.5 percent, there are three children. There are four or more children in 10.1 percent of the families. The average AFDC family is about the same size as the average non-AFDC family. About half of the children are less than six years old, with a quarter being under three.[46]

Very few AFDC mothers are teenagers (see table 1).

TABLE 1

Age of AFDC Mothers

Under 20	6.3%
20–24	24.6%
25–29	22.6%
30–39	34.9%
40 and over	11.5%

Source: *1996 Green Book,* 473.

Teen mothers, of course, are of special concern. Of the 6.3 percent teens, more than half were nineteen, more than 80 percent were over eighteen, more than 90 percent were over seventeen, and fewer than 2 percent are fifteen or younger. In fact, the rate of teen births was much higher in the Eisenhower years than it is today. What has changed is that the teens are not getting married. Teen pregnancy became a social problem in the 1970s, when attention began to be paid to the harmful effects of teen mothers and their children.[47] We will discuss teen parents in Chapter 8.

At this point, we have established that AFDC parents are mixed racially, are for the most part in their twenties or thirties, and have one or two children, about half of which are pre-school age. We turn now to education and welfare spells.

About half of the mothers have not graduated high school. Only about 10 percent have attended post-secondary school. Only about 1 percent have graduated from college. And most score in the bottom quarter on standardized tests of general aptitude and ability.[48]

How long do they remain on welfare? The stereotype behind the current debates on welfare reform is that although some recipients are on welfare for a relatively short period, welfare becomes a way of life for most. In fact, the welfare population is very dynamic. Not only do people go on and off welfare, a significant fraction (about one-third) have more than one spell. It is estimated that during the first year of welfare, half the recipients exit AFDC within one year and about three-quarters within two years.[49] However, many women who leave welfare very rapidly also return within the first year. The longer a woman can stay off, the more the probability of return declines. Counting multiple spells, 30 percent are still on welfare less than two years and 50 percent less than four years; only about 15 percent stay on welfare continuously for five years. The overall picture is that one group uses welfare for relatively short periods and never returns. A middle group cycles on and off, some for short periods and others for longer periods, but again not for five *continuous* years. And a third, quite small, group stays on for long periods.[50]

The most powerful predictor of long-term welfare receipt is the young, never-married mother. She is usually disadvantaged at least threefold, having no high school diploma, no significant employment experience, and a very young child. She probably also is a minority. But even among this group, no more than a third will be on welfare for as long as ten years. "Long-term welfare is still very much the exception."[51]

Several studies have now documented that the most common route out of AFDC is through work.[52] Many attempt to exit via work, but for a variety of reasons—lack of health care, a breakdown in child care, low wages, and jobs that do not last—return to welfare; we will address this issue shortly. Still, by the end of six years, more than 40 percent will have left to enter the labor force.[53] Of those who leave welfare through earned income, about 40 percent remained poor after their exit. The picture that emerges from the studies of welfare spells and exits is that for most recipients, welfare is a safety net rather than a way of life.

Generational welfare is also a myth. In Frank Furstenberg's longitudinal study of African American welfare families in the inner city of Baltimore, a significant majority (80 percent) of daughters who grew up in highly dependent homes (defined as receiving at least 25 percent of average family income as welfare payments) do *not* become dependent themselves. Only 20 percent were themselves highly dependent on AFDC in their early twenties; and 64 percent of daughters with welfare backgrounds received no AFDC.[54] There is, however, a higher likelihood of welfare receipt among women with welfare backgrounds. The fraction of daughters from highly dependent homes who themselves become highly dependent (20 percent) is much greater than the fraction of daughters from nonwelfare families who become highly dependent (only 3 percent). And although more than three out of five of the daughters who grew up in AFDC-dependent homes received no AFDC themselves, more than nine-tenths of those who grew up in nonrecipient families received no AFDC in their early adult years.[55]

Although there is a relationship between intergenerational welfare, there is no solid evidence that welfare *causes* welfare dependency in the next generation. What is probably happening is that the powerful effects of poverty and single parenthood are making it more likely that daughters growing up in these conditions will be poor themselves. As Peter Gottschalk, Sara McLanahan, and Gary Sandefur state:

> Because families receiving welfare are poor—indeed, poverty is a condition of welfare receipt—we would expect children from welfare families to have higher rates of poverty and welfare use as adults than children from non-poor, nonwelfare families. Intergenerational correlation, therefore, does not necessarily indicate a causal relationship. Daughters and their mothers may simply share characteristics that increase the probability of their both receiving assistance. For example, if both mother and daughter grow up in neighborhoods with poor-quality schools, both will be more likely to have lower earnings and, hence, a greater need for income assistance . . . . Changing the quality of the school the daughter attends . . . will raise her income and, in turn, lower the probability that she receives public assistance.[56]

We have seen that most welfare recipients are neither teenagers, nor long-term dependents, nor having lots of children. What about dependency or, more specifically, their work ethic? Is it true that welfare saps the work ethic?

We have both qualitative and quantitative data that address the work ethic of welfare recipients. A recent study by Kathryn Edin and Christopher Jencks examined empirically the economic position of AFDC recipients in Chicago.[57] They found an extensive amount of work for the simple reason that single mothers on welfare cannot pay their bills on welfare alone; they have to obtain additional income, often without telling the welfare department. The authors' conclusions are based on a study of the Illinois welfare system between 1988 and 1990. At that time, a single mother with one child, counting both the welfare grant and food stamps, received $399 per month, or $4,800 per year. Benefits rose per additional child, to $9300 if she had four, but were still only

60 to 75 percent of the poverty line. Edin interviewed fifty welfare families in Chicago and the suburbs to see how they got along.[58]

Virtually all of the recipients obtained additional income, both legal and illegal, to cover their expenses, either by working, or by taking money from friends and relatives, or by relying on someone else to pay their expenses. Recipients had to obtain this income because unless they lived in subsidized housing, the AFDC check would not even cover rent and utilities. For those in unsubsidized housing, rent and utilities came to $37 more per month than the welfare check; those in subsidized housing would have $197 extra—still not enough to get through the month. Food stamps help, but again, very few were able to feed their family for the entire month on the stamps alone. Taking the sample as a whole, $314 was spent for food, rent, and utilities. This left only $10 for everything else—clothing, laundry, cleaning supplies, school supplies, transportation, and so forth. Edin calculated that her sample spent about a third of what the average mother in the Midwest spends on these items. Still, it amounted to $351 more than the welfare grant, and almost all of this came from unreported income.

Almost half of the extra money needed to live was earned but not reported. Jobs varied. Some held regular jobs under another name and earned $5 per hour. Others worked off the books (bartending, catering, babysitting, sewing), earning an average of $3 per hour. A small number sold drugs, but earned very little ($3–5 per hour). The only high earners ($40 per hour) were occasional prostitutes (in the sample, five).

The families' expenses were about $1,000 per month, or $12,000 per year. The federal poverty line in 1994 was a $11,852 for a family of three.[59] As will be discussed shortly, the poverty line is low and most Americans think it should be considerably higher. Edin estimates that the public would put the figure for her sample at about $16,000, or $4,000 higher than the recipients were presently consuming. Almost all of the sample (88 percent), in varying degrees, lacked basic necessities and material comforts. Edin reports that they lived in bad neighborhoods in run-down apartments, often without heat and hot water. Roofs and windows leaked. The sample had no telephones or money for entertainment. They could not afford fresh fruits or vegetables. There were some small "extravagances" such as a video, fast food, cigarettes, and alcohol, but these amounts were only 6 percent of the sample's expenditures.

The Chicago results have been replicated in Cambridge, Massachusetts, Charleston, South Carlina, and San Antonio, Texas.[60] Urban welfare mothers need about $1,100 per month to live on, which they get from work, family, male friends, and absent fathers. Working mothers need even more money to pay for transportation, clothing, and child care. These mothers typically spent between $12,000 and $15,000 per year.

The authors argue that circumstantial evidence suggests that their findings can be generalized. There seems to be little variation in terms of both rent and living necessities across major metropolitan areas.[61] If these estimates are only reasonably accurate, then in no major American city can welfare recipients get by on their grants. Furthermore, in several states grants are less than $200 per month for a family of three, and no family can get by on that amount of money.

The authors compared their results with the Consumer Expenditure Survey (CES) for 1984–85. Despite the problems with that survey, more than 80 percent of the single adult welfare families report outside income. The average is about 40 percent in excess of AFDC and food stamps, which is consistent with Edin's findings.

If these mothers are so willing to work, why, then, are they also on welfare? The argument of the authors is that "single mothers do not turn to welfare because they are pathologically dependent on handouts or unusually reluctant to work—they do so because they cannot get jobs that pay better than welfare."[62]

This conclusion is supported by quantitative research that examined the dynamics of work and welfare.[63] Greg Duncan and his colleagues examined welfare patterns from 1969 through 1978. He reports: "Families rarely rely exclusively on welfare income; instead, welfare appears to be used to supplement income from labor market earnings and other sources or as an alternative source of income when other sources dry up."[64] Roberta Spalter-Roth, Heidi Hartmann, and Linda Andrews, on the basis of 1986–87 data from the U.S. Census Bureau, reached similar conclusions. The majority of welfare recipients combine paid work and welfare in various kinds of income packaging, either simultaneously or cycling between work and welfare.[65] The employment experience of welfare recipients, as described by Spalter-Roth, was as follows: at least 40 percent of the recipients averaged 1,800 hours over the two years— *which is about the average number of hours of all working mothers*—either by combining work with welfare or by cycling between work and welfare. They held an average of 1.7 jobs over that period, and 44 percent held two or more jobs, for about 54 weeks. The average hours per week was 34, which suggests that these recipients held "sporadic full-time jobs rather than steady part-time jobs." They averaged about four months either laid off or looking for work.[66]

These women worked as cashiers, nursing aids, food service personnel, janitors, maids, and machine operators; the average pay was $4.40 per hour (1990 dollars). Most held food service jobs, which were of the shortest duration (thirty weeks) and paid the lowest wages ($3.73 per hour); sales and cleaning services paid $3.94 and $4.08, respectively. The jobs in these categories were more likely to be part-time. The blue-collar jobs paid between $4.38 and

$4.65; the white-collar jobs paid between $5.24 and $6.40. Spalter-Roth found no evidence that changing jobs improved wages, overall length of employment, or duration of individual jobs. The picture is one of intermittent, low-wage jobs.[67]

Spalter-Roth and her associates draw attention to the cycling phenomenon: most recipients leave welfare for work; moreover, a great many (more than half) leave during the first year; the problem is that many also return, and then try again and again. There is significant movement between welfare and work. At least one-half work at least some of the time they are on welfare. Although there is some variation depending on the survey, significant numbers—as many as two-thirds—of welfare exits occur when the mother finds a job or continuously works until she leaves welfare.[68] The failure to make a successful exit from welfare is not due to a failure of the work ethic—these women say they prefer to work *and they validate their attitudes by their behavior*. They simply cannot make it in the labor market. Not surprisingly, those who are the most disadvantaged in terms of employability are the least successful. As Gary Burtless puts it, "Even if welfare recipients had no young children to care for— and almost half have children under six—most face severe problems finding and holding good jobs. Limited schooling and poor academic achievement doom most AFDC mothers to low-wage, dead-end jobs."[69]

When we look at the characteristics of AFDC recipients, we readily see how disadvantaged they are in competing even for these low-wage, entry-level jobs. They have very low levels of education (half have not completed high school); they have major child care responsibilities and uneven or sparse work experience; and more than 60 percent are of color. And even if they do manage to find and keep jobs, "the upper-bound estimate of their earnings should they work *full time-year round* . . . is no more than $12,000–$14,000; given their family sizes, this level of earnings will not remove them from poverty." And this assumes full-time work. In fact, most recipients only find temporary jobs paying less than average wages. "Indeed, the typical former recipient earns about one-half of this 'outer limit' earnings level."[70] Nevertheless, in the words of Kathleen Harris, "work is much more common in poor single mothers' lives than previously thought, in spite of their very low wages, risk of losing medical care provisions, and child-care constraints."[71]

The same evidence of work ethic holds true for those considered most at risk of long-term dependency—inner-city, teenage black mothers. It is believed that the large majority of these single mothers "have no interest or desire to work their way off welfare and support themselves and their families with an earned paycheck."[72] Harris examined work behavior of a sample of black teenage mothers living in the inner-city of Baltimore that has been followed for seventeen years.[73] The sample consisted of 288 women who had their first child at age eighteen or younger. All were pregnant for the first time, most were unmarried, nearly all were black and grew up in very poor families, many of which were on welfare at the time of the pregnancy.

More than 80 percent of the mothers started out on AFDC. Work increased as the young mothers finished school and raised their children. At the end of the study, although a quarter of the women were still on welfare, more than half were also working. In fact, the more extensive the welfare experience, the more likely the recipients were to be supplementing welfare with work.[74] Practically all of the women who had been on welfare for nine or more years were supplementing their income through jobs.

Consistent with other research, Harris found that most welfare spells for the teenagers ended through work—either they found a job that enabled them to leave welfare, or they combined welfare and work until eventually they left welfare. Spells ended rather quickly—almost half within two years. Beyond that period exit rates declined, and a quarter of the teenage mothers remained on welfare for ten years or more. In other words, "one group of women finds work, and it moves them off welfare, whereas another group finds work, but it does not provide sufficient wages or hours to move them off welfare. The latter group continues working on welfare until they either increase their hours or wages by gaining a promotion or finding a better paying job."[75]

Not surprisingly, "women who have a more advantaged family background [two parents, better-educated, nonwelfare], who were older at first pregnancy, who have smaller families, and who finished high school were more likely to leave welfare when they entered the labor market than were younger women with fewer family resources, more children, and less human capital."[76] Harris found that education (graduating from high school) was particularly important in exiting welfare through work. These mothers could find the higher-quality jobs. Family size, of course, was important, since more children would entail both more child care and fewer hours of work. A surprising result was the negative effects of previous work experience. This suggests, according to Harris, that women who *substitute* work for education—that is, who drop out of school and prematurely enter the labor market—will experience longer periods of welfare than women who combine welfare with education. The differences between these two groups, in Harris's words, are "dramatic."[77]

The important conclusion is that work was "surprisingly widespread" among this group of recipients who started as teenage mothers. Most left welfare through employment. Those mothers who stayed in school and graduated exited via work more rapidly than the others. This was especially true if they no longer had preschoolers to care for. "For high-risk teenage mothers, graduating from high school is their ticket out of dependency through a high-paying job or a promotion and increase in earnings. Without a high school degree, mothers can find only unstable, low-wage jobs that provide little chance for advancement or further job training, requiring them to remain dependent on welfare income."[78]

What happens when women leave welfare? Why do some return and not others? In a recent paper, Harris looked more closely at exits from welfare.[79] "Repeat dependency is quite prevalent. Women are especially vulnerable in the first 12 to 18 months following welfare exit such that 42 percent of women return to welfare within 2 years of leaving welfare. However, the return transition is only one point in a highly dynamic pattern of welfare recycling as most of the women who return to welfare, exit again quite rapidly. Overall more than three-quarters of those who return exit again, and nearly half do so within 12 months of the return. The most important factors influencing repeat dependency are those factors that determine a woman's economic security and earnings potential—age, education, which operates indirectly through wages, marriage to a working husband, and labor market conditions. Clearly, the economic factors override the importance of the social context."[80]

The most successful permanent route off welfare is employment. What Harris found is that the women who were most successful in remaining off welfare via work where those who had the most investments in human capital, primarily age (a proxy for work experience) and education, especially if beyond high school. Education, in particular, had strong effects in increasing the likelihood of economic independence. Women who have these investments in human capital are able to maintain their wage rates, continue to work, gain additional education and experience, reduce their poverty (although a third still remained poor after three years), and also increase their chances of marriage or cohabitation. Those with less human capital investment are less likely to obtain additional education, more likely to suffer a decline in their wage rates, less likely to marry or cohabit, more likely to return to welfare, and more likely to remain poor.[81]

Summing up both the qualitative and quantitative research, most welfare mothers are adults, they have few children, and they are not long-term welfare recipients. Furthermore, there is no problem about their work ethic. Contrary to myth, most either work or try to work while on welfare, and most leave welfare via work. The "problem" of welfare dependency is not the recipients. Rather, it is the job market and the conditions of work. In addition to poorly paying, unsteady, increasingly part-time work, the problem has to do with the lack of benefits, especially critical health insurance, and the difficulties of child care. There is no support for these wage earners. Because of the labor market and the lack of social support, recipients cannot subsist on either welfare or work alone. Even if they work full-time, their families remain in poverty.

The Nature and Consequences of Poverty

Poverty is extensive, and it is growing. In 1995, the official poverty line for a family of four was $15,150. Using this threshold, more than 38 million people—about 14.5 percent of the population—were in poverty.[82] That number included 15.2 million children, or more than a fifth of all American children. Moreover, in 1995, 15 million Americans (almost 40 percent of the poor) reported incomes of less than *one-half* of the poverty line. Most Americans, according to a 1993 Gallup poll, thought that a family of three had to have about $16,000 a year to get by—considerably more than the poverty line at that time, which was $11,522.[83] An additional 30 million Americans live on 150 percent of the poverty line, which is approximately $21,000 for a family of four. At this income level, there is barely enough to get by—and certainly nothing at all for what most of us take for granted, such as meals out, vacations, lessons or allowances for children, haircuts, and so forth.[84]

Even at these low levels, how accurately the official poverty line reflects reality is questionable. The official poverty line, adopted in the 1960s, was arrived at by multiplying the cost of a minimum adequate diet (the Economy Food Plan, the least expensive food plan adopted by the U.S. Department of Agriculture in 1961) by three. Cash income, before taxes, determined a family's poverty status.[85] The thresholds were updated annually for price inflation.

The Committee on National Statistics of the National Research Council has recently proposed a new measure.[86] The committee recommended that the poverty threshold be based on basic needs—food, clothing, and shelter, with a small amount added for other needs—and that nondiscretionary expenses should be deducted from income, including out-of-pocket medical expenditures and insurance premiums, income and payroll taxes, actual child care expenses up to a cap for working parents, an allowance for other work-related expenses, and child support payments to another family. At the same time, in-kind resources such as food stamps, subsidized housing, school lunches, and home energy assistance would be included. Rather than a specific poverty line, the panel recommended a range. For a family of four (two adults, two children) the range would be from $13,700 to $15,900 (1992 dollars).[87]

Under the committee's recommendations, the number of people in poverty would remain about the same. However, the composition of the poverty population would change. About 20 percent—7.4 million—would be "new," and roughly the same number would be above the poverty line.[88] The most important change, for our purposes, is the higher proportions of poverty rates for families with one or more workers. The new definition includes *3.6 million more people living in families where the primary worker was a full-time worker.* Although the number of poor children would remain the same, more poor children would be living in two-parent families. The poverty rate of children in single-parent families would remain disproportionately high. The number of poor families that do not have health insurance would increase; in fact, the largest marginal increase in the number of poor (5.3 million) comes from deducting out-of-pocket medical expenses. Conversely, when the 1996 expansion of the Earned Income Tax Credit takes effect (as discussed in Chapter 5), 2.4 million people will cross the poverty line.[89] Whether or not the official poverty line is revised, there is little doubt that poverty is growing, both in numbers and in severity. In fact, "the severity of poverty is greater today than at any point since the late 1950s."[90]

Two principal reasons are given for the dramatic rise in poverty—the deterioration of the low-wage labor market, which we have discussed, and the dramatic changes in family structure during the last two decades. Although most children still live in two-parent families, there has been a significant growth in single-parent households, mostly female-headed, accounting for about 25 percent of all children. Single-parent households are much more likely to be poor than two-parent households. Although female-headed households represent about 10 percent of the population, they account for more than a third of the poverty population, and more than half of the increase in poverty since 1990.[91] Almost three-quarters of all children in single-parent households will experience at least some poverty while they are growing up. For African American children, the poverty spell will be extended. Since almost all of these single parents are women, gender discrimination limits their ability to earn a living. Despite participation in the labor market, the economic circumstances of the family decline after divorce primarily because of the lack of child support. It is thus no surprise that "single parents are twice as likely as married couples to be worried about 'making ends meet' and concerned that their children will 'get beat up,' 'get pregnant,' 'not get a job,' or 'drop out of school.' "[92]

Two-parent households will not necessarily escape poverty. In most of the poor households, there is only partial employment or unemployment, but even among families with two wage earners, a fifth remain poor. In these poor households, less than half of the unemployed workers receive unemployment compensation, and jobs found after unemployment usually pay, on average, about a third less than the previous jobs. David Ellwood thinks that because many of the working full-time poor families fail to qualify for benefits such as Medicaid, they may actually be the poorest of the poor.[93]

Although low income is not the exclusive cause of family problems, the fact remains that poverty is the most powerful predictor of the harmful behavioral consequences that are most commonly ascribed to welfare families.[94] McLanahan and Sandefur state: "Low income or income loss is the single most important factor in accounting for the lower achievement of children in single-parent families. It accounts for half of the difference in educational achievement, weak labor force attachment, and early childbearing."[95] Not surprisingly, parents in these families suffer more emotionally and are more anxious about their children's future than parents who are better off. Poor families are more likely to disintegrate and become single-parent households, and single parents, in turn, are less likely to engage in "good" parenting practices. Even allowing for the problems of official reporting, the highest incidence of child neglect and abuse and the most severe injuries to children occur in the poorest families. Economic instability and hardship and social stress among adults are related to marital conflict and harsh and inconsistent punishment, rejection, and noninvolvement. Brain dysfunctions, caused either by exposure to lead, injuries from abuse, or mothers' substance abuse—all highly correlated with poverty—interfere with language and cognition development, resulting in learning and social problems at school. Early school failure, in turn, is one of the strongest predictors of adolescent problems, including violent behavior. It is not surprising that children growing up in poor families are more likely to suffer from poor physical and mental health problems, do poorly at school, and compromise successful development by early sex, pregnancy, substance abuse, delinquency, and crime.[96] One of the important factors increasing the risk of adolescent deviant behavior is leaving kids alone. Understandably, overloaded single parents are more likely to give their children more autonomy.[97] It is estimated that the average parent spends 11 fewer hours per week with their children than in 1960; fewer than 5 percent of families have another adult living in the house, such as a grandparent, to relieve the burden, and as a result children are increasingly on their own. The National Commission on Children estimated that 1.3 million children aged five to fourteen are on their own after school.[98]

Education is a crucial determinant of future employment, and low income (less than 150 percent of the poverty line) seriously affects educational achievement. Poor children attend schools of inferior quality; they cannot afford after-school enrichment activities; their parents are less likely to be involved with their schooling; and they have lower expectations and are less likely to invest in themselves.[99] Not surprisingly, low income is the strongest predictor of school dropout, regardless of race.[100] People without a high school degree or its equivalent are severely disadvantaged in an already difficult job market.

Because there is such a high correlation between poverty and single-parent households, it is hard to separate out the effects. It's a case of double jeopardy, for both the parents and the children. As Uri Bronfenbrenner says,

> Because many single-parent families are also poor, parents and their children are in double jeopardy. But even when two parents are present, . . . households living under stressful economic and social conditions, processes of parent-child interaction and environmentally oriented child activity are more difficult to initiate and sustain.
>
> To be sure, . . . when the mother, or some other adult committed to the child's well-being, does manage to establish and maintain a pattern of progressive reciprocal interaction, the disruptive impact of poverty on development is significantly reduced. But, among the poor, the proportion of parents who, despite their stressful life circumstances, are able to provide quality care is, under present circumstances, not very large. And even for this minority, the parents' buffering power begins to decline sharply by the time children are five or six years old and exposed to impoverished and disruptive settings outside the home.[101]

The risks of poor outcomes are increased when the parent is a teenager. The children of these parents are even more likely to do poorly in school and engage in compromising behaviors. Again, it is hard to separate out the effects of teen parenting from low income. There are some differences between white and black teenage mothers. While the former are more likely to marry, the latter are more likely to live in an extended household. While black teenage mothers stay longer on welfare, they are also more likely to graduate from high school.[102]

The effects of both poverty and low wage labor reinforce each other. Children growing up in poverty approach adulthood already overburdened. They face a labor market that offers little rewards. Most of these young adults will work, but a great many will remain in poverty. Many, especially women and their children, will have to rely on welfare. They, too, will struggle in the low-wage labor market, but most are also likely to remain in poverty. Neither welfare nor work will greatly improve their lives or the lives of the next generation. Self-sufficiency has been defined by policymakters as not being on welfare. It does not mean a decent life.

Hugh Heclo sums up the effect of low wages and poverty as follows:

> In 1990, of the 2 million married couples with children living below the official poverty line, 63 percent of the adults were working at least some of the year, and over a third had work levels approaching the equivalent of full-time work all year. Likewise, half of the 3.7 million poor single mothers with children worked some of the year, and almost a fifth were in, or close to,

full-time, full-year employment. . . . If anything, the adults in such poor families with children were working more in 1990 than in 1975. To define the poverty problem as simply a matter of unmotivated, unfunctional people who need government's tough love to make them seize the opportunities surrounding them is absurd.[103]

Chapter 4
Work Programs Myth and Reality

We have described the state of the low-wage labor market and employment disadvantages of welfare recipients. It is small wonder, then, that the history of work programs for the poor in general, and for welfare recipients in particular, at best points to rather dismal results. The programs never set more than a very small number of the poor to work; they tend to be used to benefit local interest groups other than the poor; they are beset by serious administrative problems; and their services are overwhelmed by client-control problems. Their persistence, in the face of limited success, suggests that they serve mostly symbolic purposes, affirming dominant beliefs about the importance of the work ethic—that jobs are available to all who want to work, and that by failing to work the able-bodied poor are morally deficient.

As noted in Chapter 2, there is remarkable continuity in our efforts to set welfare recipients to work. Despite the periodic reinvention and modification of the work programs, the assumptions behind them, and the difficulties and failures they produce, are amazingly similar. In this chapter, we examine contemporary work programs. Most are not particularly successful. A few, however, are being acclaimed for getting recipients into the paid labor force and saving welfare costs. It is these programs that have provided the justification for the work requirement in Temporary Assistance for Needy Families (TANF) and influenced state initiatives in welfare reform. We will show that these claims are vastly exaggerated; in fact, the so-called positive results are extremely modest. Furthermore, in view of the more general failure of most contemporary work programs as well as the general characteristics of welfare agencies, it is highly doubtful that the acclaimed ones can be replicated.

At the conclusion of Chapter 2, we discussed the transformation of local welfare offices into highly bureaucratized, rule-bound, overworked staffs, burdened with excessive details, straining to reduce eligibility and income-maintenance errors. Welfare-to-work reforms require these offices to administer the work programs and to become, in effect, employment offices. One of the more important conclusions to be drawn from the transformation of the welfare office is that income eligibility determination is fundamentally inconsistent with the work of an employment office, especially one that has to deal with generally hard-to-employ recipients in the low-wage labor market. We will show that the notion of changing the welfare department into an employment agency is untenable and largely unrealistic.

The Work Incentive Programs

Contemporary policies to set welfare recipients to work were launched in earnest in 1967 with the Work Incentive program (WIN).[1] This is the period when welfare rolls and costs exploded, and when AFDC became increasingly associated with African Americans and those who had never married.[2] Two strategies can be used to increase the work effort of welfare recipients—regulatory requirements and incentives (the stick and the carrot)—and Congress has regularly employed both. The older strategy is the regulatory one. It controls behavior (that is, requires work) by either denying aid altogether and forcing the poor into the low-wage labor market or requiring work as a condition of receiving aid. Symbolically, a regulatory strategy separates the working poor from the welfare poor by stigmatizing the latter. In an earlier age, it was confinement in the poorhouse and required work or "pauper labor," such as chopping wood or breaking rocks. The work ethic is affirmed by deterrence and stigma. The dependent poor are outcasts.[3]

In contrast, the incentive strategy attempts to encourage recipients to work by reducing the effective marginal tax rate on their earnings. By combining work with welfare, recipients will always be better off financially. Symbolically, the incentive strategy blurs the distinction between welfare recipients and the working poor; therefore, it is strongly resisted by those who believe that labor discipline must be enforced through segregation and stigmatization. It should be emphasized, however, that the two ideologies have a lot in common. They both view welfare dependency as a personal deficit rather than a structural, societal problem.

The WIN program combined both strategies—recipients were able to keep more of their earnings—but it was the regulatory strategy that predominated. Its core policy was coercive. Welfare was contingent on participation. By all accounts, the WIN program was a dismal failure.[4] Only 2–3 percent of the eligible recipients were successful in obtaining jobs through the program. Moreover, only 20 percent held their jobs for at least three months. At the same time, very few recipients were sanctioned. The vast majority of AFDC recipients were excused from participation by local level officials.[5] The program served mostly a symbolic function. It was myth and ceremony. The myth was that now recipients were going to be required to reduce their dependency through training and work. This affirmed the symbols of the work ethic, which was being threatened by rising welfare rolls. The ceremony was requiring able-bodied recipients to register for training and employment.

With these kinds of results, the welfare crisis continued to boil. President Nixon's Family Assistance Plan (FAP), which would have greatly expanded the incentive approach, was defeated by both the right and the left due to fears that it would further erode the work ethic, increase poverty, and be perceived as blatantly racist, and in 1971 Congress enacted WIN II.[6] The effect of WIN II was to toughen the program. Mothers with children aged six or older were now required to participate, direct job placement was emphasized over education and training, and sanctions were strengthened. The able-bodied welfare poor were to be forced into low-status work. Mandatory job search became the primary focus. The program was simple to administer, at minimal cost, and the responsibility was placed on the recipient to find a job.[7]

WIN II failed for the same reason as WIN I.[8] The funding formula created incentives to cream—that is, put resources in those recipients who were most employable to begin with. Local offices were faced with the triple problem of uncontrollable local labor markets, multiple employment barriers facing AFDC recipients, and a demand for services that far outstripped resources. It's no wonder they resorted to creaming and paper registration. Finally, because of lack of resources and the desire on the part of local offices to have good evaluations, sanctions were minimal. In other words, at the field level workers, in exercising their discretion, were able to modify the program to fit their organizational needs.[9]

WIN was followed by a series of WIN demonstration projects initiated by several states pursuant to the 1981 Omnibus Budget Reconciliation Act, which were later consolidated into the JOBS program under the Family Support Act of 1988. Again, the story was familiar: only a small fraction of the recipients participated in these programs; there were large local variations in type and quality of the employment services; the local offices were plagued by funding shortfalls and administrative difficulties; and the impact of the programs on securing employment, improving earned income, and reducing welfare was at best modest.[10]

The Family Support Act of 1988

The Family Support Act's work program, called JOBS (Jobs Opportunities and Basic Skills Training Program), went into effect in 1990.[11] Again, notwithstanding the political rhetoric, JOBS delivered less than the promise. Many AFDC recipients were excused from participation—for example, for illness or disability. Others were excused because they were caring for one who was ill or incapacitated, or caring for a child under age three (or one, at state option), or under six if child care was not guaranteed.[12]

The overall scope of JOBS is quite modest. The 1994 minimum JOBS participation rate was set at 15 percent of all nonexempt adults. For fiscal year 1994, the average monthly participation rate was 593,137 persons.[13] This represents 21.6 percent of all AFDC recipients mandated to participate (and 13 percent of all adult recipients). There are great variations among states, with countable participation ranging from 8.6 percent in Oklahoma to 76.5 percent in Nebraska.[14] Nationally, on average, 43 percent of the participants were enrolled in educational activities (mostly high school, general equivalency diploma, or GED, and remedial education), 16 percent in training programs, 12 percent in assessment, 11 percent in job entry, 11 percent in job search or job readiness, and 4 percent in community work experience.[15] Again state variations are large. Overall average monthly expenditures (federal and state) for JOBS were $74 million for 1994. For fiscal year 1995, about $1 billion was awarded to the states, of which $875 million was actually expended.

The gap between the rhetoric accompanying the Family Support Act and the performance to date is unsurprising. Given the states' economies and fiscal problems and the level of recent funding, one could not have expected JOBS to do much of anything for the vast majority of welfare recipients. The problem of low participation will not be solved by granting more authority to require participation; the states need more resources to operate programs.

Preliminary findings about the implementation of JOBS in seven sites show considerable local variations. Overall, rates of participations are similar to those found in the mandatory welfare-to-work demonstration projects discussed below.[16] A survey of the participants showed that about a third of them reported inability to participate because they or a family member had a physical or emotional problem. In addition, the emphasis of JOBS on basic education or job search was not the type of activity the participants preferred. They wanted occupational-skills training programs. At the same time, at least a third of the participants had test scores which reflected achievement levels that would preclude them from jobs requiring more than minimal skills.[17] A survey by the General Accounting Office of a representative national sample of county JOBS administrators was not encouraging.[18] Most administrators reported that less than half of the participants who were job-ready found employment.

Preliminary findings of a two-year impact study of JOBS in six sites point to very modest outcomes.[19] Sites that emphasized up-front job search achieved an average earnings gain of $1,000 over two years. Sites that emphasized education and training achieved a gain of $600. There was also some reduction in months on AFDC, ranging from 2 months to 0.6 months over two years. Welfare savings ranged from $1,200 to $68. In most sites, the reduction in AFDC payments was equal to or greater than the gains in earnings. That is, financially, the recipients were not better off.

State Demonstration Programs

Under waivers from the U.S. Department of Health and Human Services and continuing under JOBS, many states instituted welfare-to-work demonstration programs.[20] These programs, particularly California's Greater Avenues for Independence (GAIN) program, provided the model for TANF and current state initiatives. The state projects vary considerably, not only at the state but also at the county level.[21] The programs are particularly sensitive to the local political economy. It influences both the number and characteristics of the welfare recipients the program will encounter. It also influences the types of jobs awaiting the recipients once they complete the program. As a result, welfare-to-work programs are caught in a vicious cycle; when economic conditions deteriorate, the welfare caseload and the political demands to cut welfare costs by forcing recipients into the paid labor market increase, while the opportunities to place recipients in jobs diminish. Not surprisingly, states with relatively strong economies tend to emphasize education, training, job placement, and supportive services. Economically depressed states, such as West Virginia, emphasize work-for-relief.

One of the most noteworthy programs is the Massachusetts Employment and Training (ET) program. When ET started in 1983, Massachusetts was already enjoying the lowest unemployment rate in the country—3.9 percent. In the three years before ET became operational, AFDC rolls had declined by 29 percent, and this decline continued while the economy remained robust. Under ET, recipients were required to register but not required to participate. Instead, ET provided incentives to participate through an array of services, including education, training, and child care, as well as transitional child care and health care for recipients who left welfare via employment. ET was expensive. State appropriations reached $68 million (1988), averaging approximately $2,000 per participant. Participation was high (67 percent of all adults); about 50 percent were active beyond the initial assessment and orientation. Of those who participated, 44 percent obtained jobs with a mean starting wage of $5.70 per hour. Of those who found jobs, about 49 percent stayed off welfare.[22]

There are criticisms of ET. It is claimed that voluntary participation and performance-based contracting resulted in selecting the most employable recipients and that costs rose and participation fell as ET exhausted this pool and began trying to recruit and train those who were harder to employ. Starting wages were higher for participants in areas with tighter labor markets and for participants who were either male, had previous work experience, had been on welfare for short spells, and participated in vocational training. In any event, the favorable economic conditions were a major influence on ET; in fact, one recent study argues that ET had no discernible independent effect on reducing the AFDC caseload; rather, it was local economic conditions.[23]

When the favorable conditions change, one would expect the program to change, and that is exactly what happened. As the Massachusetts economy declined and the budget deficit increased, political support for the expensive ET program disappeared. Welfare rolls increased but funding dropped. Despite the fact that welfare recipients who find work are also finding it increasingly difficult to stay off welfare, the program became mandatory. We will discuss the new Massachusetts welfare program shortly. The lesson is that as long as times are good and welfare rolls and costs are declining, the state will be generous. When times are hard, old-style work requirements come back.

Today, the most prominent example in terms of influencing welfare-to-work policies comes from California's GAIN program—particularly in Riverside County. The evolution of GAIN demonstrates the sensitivity of such programs to local political interests and ideologies, especially dominant attitudes toward poverty and welfare. Invariably, the programs come to incorporate these attitudes in the type of services they emphasize and in the manner in which services are provided. Moreover, because the program must accommodate contending ideologies and interests, it is beset by internal contradictions. The electoral and political changes at the state and local levels commonly manifest themselves in the management and services of the program.

The GAIN program emerged as a patchwork of compromises from contending ideological perspectives, fueled by continuous rises in AFDC rolls and declining public support for tax increases.[24] After much controversy, the liberals had to accept mandatory work, while the conservatives agreed to a package of services to help recipients become employable. Once again, the basic idea is that all eligible recipients are to participate in programs until they become employed or are off AFDC. Mothers whose children are three or older are required to participate. Recipients undergo orientation and appraisal, and are then slotted. For example, those with work experience go immediately into job search. Others might go to remedial education. Employment plans are developed for those unable to find jobs, and eventually, work-for-relief (workfare) is provided for those who complete the plan but fail to find a job within ninety days. Work-for-relief can last up to one year, and then the process starts over.[25]

The program was full of contradictions. It was expected to deter the able-bodied, yet it offered an attractive package of services. It was supposed to give priority to long-term recipients, yet performance-based contracts with vendors would encourage creaming. The program emphasized job search and placement but conceded the need for services for long-term recipients. Although the ultimate aim was to move recipients from welfare to jobs, numerous safeguards enabled recipients to refuse jobs that paid less than the monthly AFDC grant. With all the deductions and allowances, a mother with two children could refuse with good cause a job paying $1,100 per month. There were complicated procedural safeguards and numerous excuses for lack of participation (for example, emotional and mental problems, substance abuse, family crisis). The program was to provide extensive services but had a built-in disclaimer in case of lack of resources. Although the program is mandated by the state, implementation is left to county initiative. GAIN was to be funded from a combination of new federal funds, new state funds, and a redirection of existing state funds appropriated to state agencies that are mandated to serve welfare recipients, such as adult schools, community colleges, and employment programs. The device of reallocating existing state resources—called "maintenance of effort"—sets up conflicts at the local level for scarce resources.[26]

Almost immediately, because of the serious state fiscal difficulties, GAIN began to suffer budget reductions and the counties began to complain about underfunding. Familiar patterns of participation emerged. Only about a third of those who registered actually attended an initial program component (such as basic education and job search); almost two-thirds were deregistered or deferred.[27] Initial assessments revealed that much higher than expected proportions of registrants had basic literacy deficiencies, in effect changing GAIN from a jobs program to a massive compensatory education program.[28] This may have long-term benefits for recipients, but it also prolongs the stay of participants in the program, increases the costs, and increases the pressure to move registrants into job search rather than remedial education.

Not surprisingly, shortly after GAIN was enacted, California's (then) governor George Deukmejian stated that "GAIN should be transformed into a true 'workfare' program, where immediate priority is to remove people from the welfare rolls and put them on payrolls as quickly as possible." The governor especially objected to the extensive emphasis on education. After pointing to some rare misuses of education funds (as in graduate education), he proposed that participants be required to look for jobs before being diverted into education or training. As he put it, "Let the job marketplace, not caseworkers, determine who is employable."[29] Recent changes in the GAIN legislation, discussed shortly, echo these political sentiments.

There are considerable variations in how counties have implemented GAIN, pointing to the impact of the local environment on welfare-to-work programs. In addition to adequate funding, local welfare agencies have to have access to educational, training, employment, and other needed social services. In reality, funding is seldom available to serve any but a small fraction of the welfare caseload. States, facing fiscal difficulties, are unable to provide the matching funds that will enable them to fully draw down their federal allocation. One way in which state welfare agencies try to obtain additional resources is to gain access to existing educational, training, and employment services without reimbursing them for serving welfare recipients. The problem is that these other service agencies have no particular incentive to tailor their services to the special needs of the recipients.

At the county level, these issues manifest themselves in the decisions about how to structure and operate the local program. That is, local officials must decide how many recipients to serve, what services to offer, and how to negotiate the interorganizational network of services needed for the program, in light of the resources available to them. Not infrequently, the local program provides "side benefits" to other stakeholders that are not the recipients. These may include local educational and vocational vendors who can count on a steady stream of clients. Even when there is money to purchase services, however, it is never enough, and the welfare agency has to strike deals with other agencies and vendors. How these issues are played out and what consequences they have on the local program can be gleaned from the implementation of GAIN in Los Angeles.[30]

In planning the program, Los Angeles County made an early decision to rely extensively on contracting out every program component, particularly education and training. This strategy enabled the county to count on resources already allocated to adult basic education and the Job Training Partnership Act (JTPA) to serve the economically disadvantaged. At the same time, the strategy was fraught with political difficulties as various service providers tried to position themselves advantageously in order to optimize their bargaining position vis-à-vis the county. Because the county was dependent on the Los Angeles Unified School District (LAUSD) and the Los Angeles Community College District (LACCD) for adult basic education, it had to accept several unfavorable contractual arrangements, such as dropping its insistence on performance-based contracting, accepting the existing curriculum without modifying it to the specific needs of the GAIN population, and paying what the county thought were too high "excess costs" incurred by the providers in serving GAIN participants. For LAUSD and LACCD, the contract was seen as an important source of additional revenues because, in addition to the "excess costs" reimbursement, it would boost daily attendance counts that are used to compute the allocation of state educational funds. The county had far greater difficulties negotiating a contract with JTPA for job club (where participants learn various strategies for finding a job), job search, and vocational training services. Partly, JTPA officials were not particularly eager to serve welfare recipients because JTPA evaluations and payments are closely tied to client outcomes. Moreover, JTPA did not want to lose its autonomy by becoming accountable to the county. As a result, the county had to settle for a contract with the state employment development agency, even though county officials had a low opinion of the quality of its employment services.

In order to minimize the ability of the contractors to form a coalition, the county insisted on controlling all communication channels and avoided the development of any lateral relations among the service providers. These and other complex contractual relations resulted in a service delivery system that was plagued by serious problems of coordination.

The implementation of the county GAIN program was also impeded by the desire of certain politicians and officials to derive "side benefits" from the program. The conservative county supervisors and the county administrator saw an opportunity in GAIN to privatize county services by insisting that case management be contracted to a private for-profit organization rather than being performed by county welfare workers. This decision, justified on the basis of fiscal efficiency, plunged the program into a protracted political conflict pitting labor unions, state politicians, and county and state officials against each other. It resulted in major delays in the start of the program and the loss of state funding. Ultimately, county officials prevailed and the case management services were contracted out to a private for-profit organization. Because of the legal challenges and constraints, however, many of the innovations envisioned in the contract could not be implemented. Moreover, when after several years the political make-up of the county board of supervisors changed, the contract was canceled and case management was delegated back to the county welfare agency.

Finally, the county experienced fiscal shortfalls from the start. Its initial funding request was cut by half, and the county was never able to obtain a proportion of the state GAIN funds commensurate with its share of the state welfare caseload. As a result the county was never able to serve more than 8 percent of its welfare caseload.[31]

Similar patterns can be observed in the implementation of demonstration programs under JOBS in other states. Changes in political leadership, especially from Democratic to Republican, rapidly altered the course of the program. In Michigan and Mississippi, for example, newly elected Republican governors sought to reduce welfare costs by making dramatic changes in program policies and administration. In Michigan, in addition to eliminating aid and services to single adults, the welfare agency required all applicants to AFDC to sign a "social contract" in which the recipients agreed to spend twenty hours per week in a productive activity such as working, job search, or education. This meant that failure to comply would provide a reason for sanctions in the form of reduced benefits. In Mississippi, the governor replaced all the key staff administering JOBS, as well as direct contracting with local community action agencies. Even reelected governors may change the course of the program when they adopt the posture of "getting tough on welfare.[32]

The Effectiveness of Current Welfare-to-Work Programs

What do we know about the effectiveness of the state demonstration projects in placing recipients in jobs, increasing their earnings, and reducing welfare costs? The best data so far come from a three-year evaluation of the GAIN program in six counties in California.[33] This report is extremely significant for several reasons. The California GAIN program is the largest welfare-to-work program in the country; it combines an extensive amount of education and training with a traditional emphasis on job search and quick placement in entry-level jobs. Most significantly, the Riverside County GAIN program is becoming the standard-bearer or model for proposed changes not only in California but also in the rest of the country.

Although the Manpower Demonstration Research Corporation (MDRC) report examined the experience of six counties, to simplify the analysis, only three will be compared: Riverside, Alameda (Oakland), and Los Angeles. Riverside is a large county that includes both urban and rural areas. For the duration of the experiment, Riverside had the highest growth rate as measured by annual changes in employment. In 1990, its total AFDC caseload was about 24,000. More than half of the recipients were white non-Hispanic, 27.6 percent Hispanic, and 15.5 percent black. Riverside enrolled in GAIN all eligible AFDC recipients—applicants, short-term recipients, and long-term recipients (each roughly a third of the total caseload). Alameda County had a much larger proportion of long-term AFDC African American inner-city residents, with high proportions "in need of basic education." Alameda was distinctive in that it emphasized basic education and training to prepare recipients for higher-paying jobs. Los Angeles County had one-third of the state's welfare caseload as well as a large inner-city, long-term AFDC population, and it only enrolled those "in need of basic education." In addition, the Los Angeles welfare population had the highest proportion who were not proficient in English, the highest proportion who were of color, and the lowest proportion with recent work experience. The Los Angeles program had difficulty getting under way, and its caseload per GAIN case manager was the highest among the counties.

The MDRC study was based on 33,000 recipients, randomly assigned between experimentals and controls, who entered GAIN between 1988 and mid-1990. Although the report is appropriately cautious, it concludes that GAIN was successful, and, more important, that the Riverside program was a substantial success. The report states that Riverside had "unusually large . . . earnings gains and welfare savings. . . . These impacts were the largest in any of the six counties, and are larger than those found in previous large-scale experimental studies of state welfare-to-work programs."[34]

What was the Riverside "substantial success"? When we look at monthly differences in year 3, the Riverside recipients who worked averaged only $84 more per month in earnings than the controls, or less than $20 more per week.[35] Moreover, this average increase came about because more recipients began to work and for longer hours, rather than because of an improvement in wages. In fact, Riverside may merely be getting the experimentals to switch from the informal to the formal economy. In any event, the benefits to the recipients of the Riverside program—the best of the bunch—are very modest. In Alameda, in contrast, although fewer experimentals got jobs, more of the jobs were full-time and the wages were higher than those of the controls.[36]

In addition, there were reductions in welfare grants—not only AFDC but other programs such as food stamps as well. When the reductions are calculated, the difference in economic well-being between the experimentals and the controls is even smaller. In the last quarter of year 3, Riverside—again the "best"—experimentals were $77 better off than the controls (or $26 per month), and only 19 percent of the experimentals as compared to 16 percent of the controls had a total income above the poverty line for the year.[37]

What about the benefits to the public—that is, welfare savings as compared to the costs of GAIN? As the report notes, GAIN is expensive as compared to prior programs, primarily because of its emphasis on education and training. On average over a five-year period, the county departments and the other non-welfare agencies spent about $4,415 per experimental. The *net cost* per experimental varied widely, from less than $2,000 in Riverside to more than $5,500 in Alameda and Los Angeles.[38] In the latter two counties, more long-term recipients were enrolled in education and training. The report found a positive benefit-cost ratio in Riverside. "This return was exceptionally large in Riverside—$2.84 per every net $1 invested," but not in Alameda or Los Angeles.[39]

Despite the rhetoric about impressive results from the California GAIN program in general and Riverside's in particular, small differences run throughout the entire report. For example, the difference in employment between the experimentals and controls was only 6 percent for the entire sample; in Riverside it was only 9 percent, and this is for reported employment. But perhaps the most important statistic was that overall *about two-thirds of the experimentals were not working in the last quarter of year 3, and almost half never worked during the entire three-year period*. In Riverside, only 31 percent of the experimentals were employed in the last quarter of year 3 and about a third never worked during the entire three-year period.[40]

With the small amount of earnings and the nature of employment, most recipients who worked—whether experimentals or controls—also remained on welfare. For the entire sample, only about 19 percent worked and were off welfare during the last quarter of the follow-up as compared to 16 percent of the controls—a 3 percent difference. In both Riverside and Alameda, the differences were slightly larger. As to permanently leaving welfare, in Riverside there was a 4 percentage point difference (39 percent of experimentals versus 35 percent of controls).[41]

For experimentals who did not need basic education but did use vocational training and postsecondary education, Alameda County experimentals got better jobs and achieved the largest overall financial gains. However, this strategy was more costly for the government; in fact, there was a negative net investment per experimental from the standpoint of the government. Furthermore, in Riverside and San Diego, this subgroup also achieved large earnings and substantial welfare savings *without* vocational training and postsecondary education (as compared to the controls). Thus, the approaches in Riverside and San Diego may be more cost-effective, even though the recipients would not get better jobs.[42]

The MDRC GAIN study also examined the effects of basic education and training.[43] The programs were classes in adult basic education (ABE), which focused on reading and mathematics; preparation for the GED test; and English as a second language (ESL). The report emphasized, at the outset, that this was an evaluation of *mandatory* basic education services, and not "adult education services as they are normally delivered: to people who seek them out and participate in them voluntarily."

As to educational *attainment* (that is, achieving the GED or a high school diploma), GAIN was successful in most of the counties, especially for the recipients who were more literate to begin with.[44] Educational *achievement* was measured by the Test of Applied Literary Skills (TALS).[45] Here, in only one county (San Diego) were there large and significant improvements.[46] In the other counties, there was no improvement in basic math and literacy skills. However, even in those counties that improved either educational attainment or achievement, there was no impact on either employment or earnings within the two-year follow-up period. In three of the counties, for a small group, there were hints of a "possible growth in earnings impacts" in the third year.[47]

The MDRC finding as to basic education is troubling. Prior to the MDRC study, most thought that basic education *in the long run* would improve a recipient's prospects of economic independence. Now, that case has to be made. In the meantime, the up-front costs are high and the ultimate savings to the taxpayer are unclear. In the past, states have either been impatient or unconvinced and, after a relatively brief period of time, cut back on basic education and training. As will be discussed shortly, this is now happening not only in California but in welfare reforms in several other states. More of an emphasis will be placed on job search to move recipients into low-wage, entry-level jobs. This is the least expensive component and has the potential for the highest short-term payoff for the state, even though most recipients will be hardly better off.

The results of GAIN are also echoed in the evaluation of the JOBS demonstration program in nine counties in Florida, titled Project Independence.[48] The counties were randomly selected, and the participants were randomly assigned at point of application to AFDC or redetermination. Thus, they were less likely to be long-term recipients. Because the program was administered by a state-wide agency, the differences among the counties were far less pronounced than in GAIN. Still, some counties performed better than others. Similarly to Riverside, Project Independence emphasized job search and job club. Of those attending orientation, 42 percent participated in job search as compared to 23 percent who participated in any education or training activity. In terms of program impact, after one year, 55.3 percent of the experimental group were ever employed as compared to 52.5 percent of the control group, a difference of 2.8. Average total earnings for the experimental group were $2,540 and for the control group $2,383, a difference of $157. Of the experimental group, 85.1 percent received welfare as compared to 86.7 percent of the control group, and there was an average reduction of $157 in AFDC payments for the experimental group as compared to the control group. Results also varied by subgroups of recipients. The increase in first-year earnings was concentrated among those with no preschool children and those defined as job-ready. Those who had been on welfare for two or more years had larger increases in earnings and reductions in welfare payments.[49] It is important to note that the counties in Florida, despite their emphasis on job placement, were not able to replicate the results in Riverside.

Thus, the findings from Florida further confirm the very modest results that can be expected from welfare-to-work programs. Indeed, a national evaluation of JTPA similarly concluded that the program had no impact on the amount of welfare benefits received by the participants as compared to the control group.[50]

The Work-for-Relief Option

TANF requires adult recipients who fail to become self-sufficient after two years to participate in work activities. In addition, recipients must be participating in community service within two months of receiving benefits if they are not working. This approach—requiring work for the welfare grant—has historically been called "workfare." What is the viability of the workfare option? If history and current experience are any guide, it is unworkable, costly, and ineffective.

A study of unpaid work experience in several welfare-to-work programs evaluated by MDRC confirms the above conclusion.[51] First, with the exception of West Virginia, unpaid work experience operated on a very small scale and for a very limited time. There are many reasons why such an option is not common, including staff opposition, administrative difficulties, and insufficient resources. Indeed, it is not easy to place welfare recipients in jobs. Los Angeles County runs a workfare program for single men on general relief. Despite fairly aggressive marketing, the county cannot persuade other government agencies or nonprofits to take free labor for even the most menial jobs. Only 40 percent of recipients are placed. It's not that the men are "ne'er-do-wells"; rather, employers are reluctant to use welfare recipients because of union opposition and administrative costs.[52] Second, welfare recipients are not "free labor." Unpaid work experience is costly to administer when one takes into account the costs of developing the site, selecting and monitoring the participants, and providing support services such as child care. MDRC estimates that the costs of unpaid work experience per participant ranged from $700 to $2,100, and the annual cost per filled slot ranged from $700 to $8,200 (in 1993 dollars). Third, there is no evidence that unpaid work experience improves earning capacity or ability to obtain stable employment. Equally important, it does not lead to reduction in welfare receipt or welfare payments.[53]

The Utah Work Program

The latest program to be evaluated is the Utah welfare-to-work program—the Single Parent Employment Demonstration Project.[54] The lessons from the Utah experience provide a glimpse of the future. Utah policymakers, as is most common in the current welfare reform climate, announced that *all* welfare recipients in that state would either work or participate in work-related activities. The Utah experience is particularly valuable because that program has specifically focused attention on long-term, multiple-problem families. Even though Utah has a low proportion of its population relying on welfare, a low proportion who are long-term, relatively few who are of color, and a strong economy, the efforts to deal effectively with the long-term recipient proved to be especially problematic.

Eventually, the Utah program is expected to go statewide. So far, it has started in just a few counties—one serving part of Salt Lake City and the others rural, or containing small cities. The evaluation is based on the county serving part of Salt Lake City.

As stated, *all* adult recipients are required to participate. The only exceptions are children under sixteen. Although the ultimate aim of the program is to increase paid employment, participation is broadly defined. For example, participation includes education, training, part-time employment, mental health counseling, and substance abuse treatment. The staff is encouraged to develop strategies to engage recipients with multiple employment barriers. The assumption is that with appropriate help, multiple-problem families eventually can become self-sufficient.

The Utah program has a system of incentives and sanctions. Those who participate for at least twenty hours per week receive an additional $40. At first, the only sanction was a $100 deduction (the average grant was $414 for a family of three). However, many sanctioned families still did not participate. To strengthen the sanctions, Utah now provides that a family can refuse to participate for only a two-month period; if there is still no participation, welfare stops. A home visit is required before a family loses welfare. If a family loses welfare for nonparticipation, it can requalify only after participating in a structured program "designed to overcome recipient's fears of change."[55]

Other features of the Utah program are worth noting. Families applying for welfare for the first time meet with a "self-sufficiency" worker to develop a self-sufficiency plan. If there is a strong work history and an immediate job prospect, the family is "diverted" from welfare and given three months' cash assistance in a one-time payment. The diverted family is eligible for AFDC transitional assistance. AFDC families who do find unsubsidized employment have $100 per month plus 50 percent of earned income disregarded in calculating benefits. Under these more generous disregards, a family of three with one worker can receive welfare until he or she earns more than $4.92 per hour, as compared to $4.28 under current law. There are also more liberal asset and car limitations. There is no time limit on transitional child care; families can receive the subsidy as long as they are financially eligible. Transitional Medicaid is increased from four to twenty-four months as long as the family has earned income. Transitional support services (case management) are also available for one year after leaving AFDC. Finally, Utah has tried to simplify eligibility determinations to give the staff more time to devote to the employment program.

In the one county that was evaluated, after thirty months, there was a 12 percent decline in caseloads of experimentals over controls, although only a 2 percent decline in grant expenditures. A quarter of the recipients found jobs. The rest participated in education/training (26 percent), job search classes (11 percent), job readiness classes (6 percent), assessment (20 percent), counseling (8 percent), or were "temporarily excused" (5 percent). The hourly wages of those who found jobs were about $5.16; the average number of hours worked per week was thirty. As is true of almost all work programs, it is difficult to tell how much employment was due to the work program and how much to the general economy. Utah has a quite strong economy—in 1995, the state unemployment rate was 3.1 percent, as compared to national rate of 5.8 percent. Thus, as LaDonna Pavetti points out, it was not the lack of jobs that prevented recipients from making it into the paid labor force.

Twenty-eight percent of the Utah sample were long-term recipients. Generally speaking, the differences between the long-term recipients and the intermediate or short-term ones were predictable: the former were younger, tended to be teenagers at the time they first gave birth, and had more children. But there were no differences in terms of education, and the long-term recipients were somewhat more likely to be white. The longer time on welfare may have made a difference; the staff thought that this group had a harder time adjusting to the new program because they had more limited work experience and had never been required to do anything while on AFDC. The biggest difference, not surprisingly, between the long-termers and the rest was that they faced greater employment barriers. Long-termers were more likely to report children's behavioral problems, as well as health and disability problems. On the other hand, differences were less clear-cut in terms of substance abuse (except that it was very uncommon among short-termers), family violence, or homelessness. According to the staff, long-termers were more likely to suffer from lack of confidence and self-esteem. "Many of the recipients . . . have never been successful at anything and are afraid to try anything new."[56] The longer the time they had been on welfare, the more fearful the recipients were of losing their benefits.

One of the principal findings of the Utah study were the difficulties the staff encountered in trying to deal with the long-term, multiple-barrier families. Despite allocating considerable time, energy, and resources, including hiring special staff with smaller caseloads (thirty to thirty-five cases), providing home visits and one-on-one counseling, and conducting regular reviews, the staff felt that they were still in "uncharted territory, often having to rely on trial and error to identify the best strategy for helping a family overcome their barriers to employment."[57] The state has found that there is no proven method of dealing with the complex cases of the long-term dependent. Experimentation and, above all, patience are required—and, of course, commitment and resources on the part of the state.

The important points to note about the Utah experience are that:

- despite a tight labor market, only a quarter of the caseload was in paid employment;

- the bulk of the recipients were in various training, assessment, and job preparation programs;
- there was almost no difference (2 percent) in welfare savings between the experimentals and the controls;
- there was no cheap, quick fix for families facing multiple employment barriers.

Utah has recently enacted a time limit of thirty-six months, with exceptions for 15 percent of the caseload.

The Future

It seems clear that the states will be the principal players in the design and implementation of welfare-to-work programs. So far, there are two models at the state level. Both are strict in terms of time-limited welfare and work requirements, but one model—represented by Utah, Wisconsin, and Massachusetts—is expensive, and the other, represented by Riverside County, is cheap.

Wisconsin was granted a waiver that provides for a strict two-year time limit on eligible welfare recipients. The state promised the recipients assistance during the two years—job search, training, day care. If a recipient does not have a job at the end of the two years, the state will provide one, either in the private sector, with or without a subsidy, or in the public sector. There will also be day care subsidies and extended health benefits for a period of time. But the recipient has to work; there will be no more welfare.

So far, the Wisconsin program is in operation in only two rural counties, with small caseloads. The caseworkers in those two departments are providing intensive casework, and, significantly, are engaged in job development. In other words, the Wisconsin program is expensive—considerably more expensive than straight welfare or a stripped-down, quick job-search work program. Wisconsin has a low unemployment rate—in fact, welfare rolls had been declining substantially since the year *before* the Republican governor, Tommy Thompson, took office—so the chances are that the governor can claim "success" in these counties.

In anticipation of the conversion of AFDC into block grants, Wisconsin recently enacted legislation which, the state claims, will abolish AFDC cash grants and entitlements.[58] The focus of the proposed new program, called "Wisconsin Works," or W-2, is to move all participants as quickly as possible into unsubsidized employment. All participants are placed in one of four tiers of employment or employment experience. Payments are made by an employer for hours worked, or for "trial jobs," or as a monthly grant for community service jobs (workfare) and transitional placement (for those unable to work and who need services, rehabilitation, and so on). Two weeks of motivational and assessment training can be required for those assigned to community service jobs or the transitions program. There are provisions for short-term basic skills education and job training if it is directly linked to existing employment opportunities. The state provides for health care (replacing Medicaid for those on AFDC) and child care for many low-income working families. Minor teen parents are not eligible for cash assistance; to be eligible for W-2 child care and health insurance, they must live with their parents or in a supervised setting, and they must attend high school if they do not have a diploma. Mothers can qualify for benefits and choose not to work during the last two months of pregnancy and until the newborn reaches twelve weeks; then the work requirements apply. There are provisions for subsidized day care, extended health benefits, casework services, and, if necessary, community service jobs. All W-2 applicants must cooperate in establishing paternity and enforcing child support. Job search and training may be required during the application period. Recipients in community service or in transitional placements are sanctioned $4.25 per hour for every missed hour. Various time limits (three, six, or nine months) apply to specific jobs, and all recipients are expected to be in unsubsidized employment within two years. There is a five-year lifetime maximum time limit for any of the subsidized employment programs.

The Institute for Research on Poverty estimates that when W-2 is fully operational, 15 percent of the caseload will be in unsubsidized jobs; 10 percent in "trial jobs" (lasting up to two years); 50 percent in community service jobs (paying 75 percent of the minimum wage and lasting up two years); and 25 percent in transitional placement (counseling, training, and rehabilitation, also lasting up to two years). In other words, W-2 sounds something like the Utah program. Only a relatively small minority will be in the paid labor force; the bulk will be in various pre-employment placements; and the program will be costly.

The Center for Law and Social Policy has identified several troubling features of W-2 legislation.[59] The legislation explicitly states that "an individual is not entitled to services under Wisconsin Works," which means that there is no commitment to provide jobs, child care, or health care assistance to eligible families. In addition, families have no right to a fair hearing if they feel their aid has been wrongly denied or terminated. Recipients who play by the rules and cannot find a job are still subject to the strict time limits. Parents who work for their grant are not eligible for the Earned Income Tax Credit. Parents required to work thirty hours per week in a community service job who decline to participate in the required additional ten hours of education will have their grant reduced, and consequently earn less than the minimum wage. Because of the flat assistance structure of W-2, families with four or more persons and no other income will be poorer. Most ominously, although W-2 increases child care spending, "it sharply increases child care copayments in a way which makes licensed or regulated care unaffordable for working poor families."[60] The Center for Law and Policy concludes that "taken together, the child care, health care, tax, and other assistance policies of W-2 result in a system where a family earning $12 an hour may have less disposable income than a family where the parent earns $4.25 an hour."[61]

In the meantime, Massachusetts has taken the lead in tough welfare reforms. The Department of Welfare has been renamed the Department of Transitional Assistance. The state has adopted one of the most stringent time-limited welfare programs in the country. Among other provisions (such as retaining more money from earnings and imposing benefit cuts), all able-bodied recipients with no child under six must get a job or perform twenty hours of community service workfare per week within sixty days of going on welfare; subsequently, workfare recipients will have to work at least twenty-five hours per week, as well as spending fifteen hours per week searching for a job; drug or alcohol dependency is not considered a disability; recipients with children under age six must enroll in education or training until their youngest child reaches age six, when they must get jobs; and (with some exceptions) no able-bodied recipient will receive welfare benefits for more than twenty-four months in any sixty-month period regardless of whether he or she has found a job. Employers are to be encouraged to hire welfare recipients by using some welfare benefits as reimbursement for wages. There are large up-front costs in Massachusetts for education, training, day care, and casework services.[62]

Both the Massachusetts and the Wisconsin reforms are very tough, but they are also very expensive. Already, Utah is finding it costly, difficult, *and* time-consuming to deal with the hard-to-employ recipients and has recently enacted time limits. Patience and money quickly become scarce commodities among politicians, especially when local economies begin to decline. Thus far, Wisconsin has been able to finance a large part of its two-county demonstration project with a special allocation of federal funds, but these funds are quickly drying up, and where the administrative funds for W-2 will come from is uncertain.[63] Although politicians delegate welfare problems to the local level to avoid controversy, it is at this level that the conflicts are most keenly felt because of severe problems of horizontal equity. No one is paying child care subsidies or health benefits for the working poor, and they know it.

It seems safe to predict that the expensive parts of the state programs will not last and that the Riverside model will prevail. For example, in 1992 Michigan, under a welfare reform demonstration project, initiated the "social contract" as the cornerstone of it its reform. All recipients were to engage in productive activities that would lead to personal growth. Activities included education, training, substance abuse treatment, parenting classes, volunteer work, caring for the disabled, and so forth. Recipients were to submit activity reports that would be monitored on a random basis. However, because of huge caseloads, only a small number of noncompliant recipients were ever contacted, making compliance, in effect, voluntary. In 1994, Michigan altered its demonstration project by requiring all JOBS participants to enroll in "Work First," a seven-week job readiness/job search program. The emphasis now is on immediate employment and tougher sanctions.[64]

It is easy to see why past and present welfare-to-work programs sort out the way they have. It is cheaper to require welfare recipients to engage in job search and accept entry-level, low-wage jobs. Economically and politically, this strategy is preferable to an investment in education and training. The state saves money and upholds the politically popular norm of the work ethic.

Riverside is the future. In 1995, the GAIN legislation was amended (AB 1317) to require job club and job search as the first activity for most participants. It also tightened deferral provisions by modifying deferral due to being employed fifteen hours per week to deferral due to being employed fifteen hours per week *and* being enrolled in a GAIN activity (job search, education, or training) for an additional fifteen hours, for a total of thirty hours per week. It also required individuals deferred due to education to be in a program that *leads to employment*. Participants with children under six have to participate up to thirty-two hours per week, and parents with older children up to forty hours (compared to twenty hours per week under JOBS).

Other states, again as demonstration projects, are tightening their work programs by expanding the pool of mandatory participants, shifting the focus from education and training to more immediate job search and job placement. Although some work rules are liberalized—for example, income disregards, asset limits, and the provision of transitional child and health care—sanctions for nonparticipants are also strengthened.[65] Nevertheless, at least in the early stages of the demonstration projects, the states are reporting difficulties in increasing participation and "are still struggling to identify strategies for addressing this issue." Nonparticipating clients identify as reasons lack of child care and transportation, and physical abuse.[66]

Can Riverside's "success" be replicated? In many important respects, it is unique. Led by a charismatic director, Riverside emphasized a strong employment "message," inexpensive job search, and quick entry into the labor market pursuant to the philosophy that a low-paying, entry-level job was better than no job and could lead to a better job. The message was addressed to the staff as well as the recipients. The staff was specially recruited for commitment to the mission of the agency and tightly organized and monitored. *Recipient success was viewed as joint success by the case managers.* The staff closely monitored attendance and recipient job performance, as well as providing support services for employment or employment-related problems. Most significant, in our opinion, was that the staff engaged in extensive job development; in fact, workers were specifically hired for this task. The county was able to promise local employers job applicants "that afternoon." Employers cooperated to save the costs of screening large numbers of job applicants responding to general employment-available ads. Staff performance was rated, in large part, on job development and placement. Thus, the staff, in practice, emphasized their ability to find the participants jobs and to offer them needed services to get and keep the job. This was the Riverside commitment. Recall, too, that Riverside experienced a very strong job growth rate.

We think it highly unrealistic to expect large-scale replication of the Riverside experience. Florida, for example, failed to do so. Mary Jo Bane and David T. Ellwood argue that to achieve the goals of family self-sufficiency, there had to be a "dramatic shift" in the culture of AFDC from "eligibility and compliance to one in which clients and welfare workers are engaged in the common tasks of finding work, arranging child care, and so on."[67] The culture was changed in the Riverside office, and now "changing the culture" from one of writing checks to finding employment is the new buzzword in welfare reform. Riverside was able to change primarily because it had a highly dedicated, charismatic leader working in a very favorable economic climate. Charismatic leaders are not replicable; only "average" leaders are. And average leaders are not going to get welfare workers to engage in extensive job development, change their attitudes toward welfare recipients, view job placement in terms of a joint enterprise, and really work closely with recipients. Very favorable economic climates do not last, and when unemployment rises, no amount of dedication can produce job opportunities for a rising welfare caseload. It is a myth to think that welfare agencies across the country can be so transformed. In our opinion, this is another example of myth and ceremony, and of Washington hubris.

Transforming Welfare Departments into Employment Agencies

Much of the current rhetoric about welfare reform is fixated on the notion that the culture of the welfare department which emphasizes administration of relief can be changed to that of an employment agency which emphasizes job placement.[68] This idea strikes us as fanciful in light of the complex realities at the welfare offices. We have seen that there are very few successful work programs. We make three key points. First, there is vast incompatibility between administering welfare—determining income eligibility, setting a grant amount, and monitoring for cheating—and providing employment services—identifying client needs, locating appropriate services, and helping clients change their behavior. Second, as long as welfare is made contingent on participation in a work program, the work program becomes mired by the same bureaucratic rules and regulations that characterize welfare. Third and related, as long as the work programs exclusively target welfare recipients, they cannot escape the same political and economic forces that shape the culture of the welfare department.

The first thing to appreciate is that the term *welfare program* does not mean a single, uniform administrative system. Not only does each of the fifty states administer its own variation of a work program, but, as we have seen, there is considerable variation at the county offices. There are more than three thousand counties in the United States. Not all of them administer welfare programs, but in the larger, urban counties, there are several local offices. In many states, the programs are run by local state offices. In any event, the important point is that there are thousands of local variations in the actual day-to-day administration of the work program. States, counties, and local offices differ, sometimes in policies but always in details. And TANF will further accentuate these variations.

Scores of rules and regulations attempt to spell out almost every element in the work program: How is disability determined? When can a missed appointment or a class be excused? What happens when a recipient is fired from a job for misconduct? And on and on. There is an enormous amount of paperwork; everything has to be documented. But despite the quantity of rules, *a great many of the most crucial decisions require judgment or discretion on the part of the field-level workers.* The recipient who is claiming disability missed an appointment with a doctor because the bus was late. Does the worker believe the recipient is telling the truth? If yes, there is an excuse; if not, a warning or a sanction.

As we pointed out in Chapter 2, the work program is an add-on to the welfare office. By this we mean that the basic job of the welfare office is to administer the income-maintenance program, itself a formidable task. Now the welfare office is directed to run an employment program, but it is not an employment service. It doesn't have the expertise, and although it is often given additional resources, they are rarely sufficient.

Complicating matters for the welfare department is that in order to run a work program, it has to rely on others in the local area. The success of any program is clearly dependent on local employers. If they are not willing to hire welfare recipients, there is nothing the welfare agency can do. The welfare

agency is also dependent on other agencies. If the program provides for education and training, the agency will have to contract with other service providers
in the community—for example, community colleges or adult education agencies. We have seen the torturous negotiations that Los Angeles County had to
go through to line up service providers for its work program. The main
problem with these other service providers is that they are not particularly
interested in welfare recipients and rarely make adjustments for their special
needs. This is particularly true of local education services; they are geared to
adults who are eager, paying customers, whereas many welfare recipients have
had poor educational experiences and are doubtful, if not reluctant, about
more education. It is not surprising that the participation of welfare recipients
in education and training is problematic and rarely shows positive results. We
have seen the difference in results when education programs are specifically
tailored to the special needs of welfare recipients, but this kind of conscious
adaption is rare. All organizations—welfare agencies, community colleges,
adult education programs—seek legitimacy and support from their environments. They try to present themselves as efficient, capable institutions that are
fulfilling their mission. Community colleges and adult education programs are
interested in recruiting, educating, and graduating paying adults who want to
take advantage of their services. Employment agencies seek to build a reputation as a source of reliable labor; they are interested in prime-age white adults,
who are educated and have work experience. Welfare agencies are interested in
clients who fit the rules, who follow the rules, and who don't cause problems.

Welfare recipients suffer from two sets of disabilities. Although a great
many have labor-market experience, as a group they are hard to employ. Many
lack a high school diploma—now considered a virtual prerequisite for a job;
many have an uncertain work history; there is a fair amount of disability in the
group; and, of course, they are single parents with children, most of whom are
young, which means that there probably will be child care issues and other
distractions. It is a lot easier for an employer to hire a prime-age single white
adult with a high school diploma. In addition, welfare recipients suffer from
the negative stereotype, especially if they are of color. The ascribed moral
characteristics of welfare recipients affect the welfare agencies, other agencies
that the welfare has to deal with, employers, local politicians, and the local
community. The underlying premise of work programs is that able-bodied
welfare recipients suffer from either moral or personal deficiencies that prevent them from becoming productive members of society. By implication, they
also fail as parents. Making welfare contingent on participation in a work
program is seen as an effective strategy to change the negative values, attitudes,
and behavior of the recipients. The work program is designed to instill in them

the work ethic they are missing, the self-discipline they are lacking, and the human capital skills they need to make them competitive in the labor market. In other words, work programs are exercises in social control.

The importance of the negative stereotype lies in the fact that much of the work of welfare agencies involves decisions about the *moral* worth of the recipient. Cultural beliefs determine what values are legitimate and appropriate in working with clients. Workers are talking to recipients, teachers, other officials, and employers. Workers are making judgments based on these conversations. In turn, these judgments will greatly influence how the recipients are treated and how they come to experience the welfare department.

At the same time, one must appreciate the working conditions of AFDC field offices. Workers have large caseloads and deal with massive numbers of regulations and requirements. They are under great pressure to get the work out correctly. As Bane and Ellwood point out, this is the culture of eligibility and compliance. In large urban offices, workers talk to clients from behind bars or metal screens. There are also widespread accounts of negative attitudes on the part of workers toward recipients. Workers trained, socialized, and supervised in this manner will apply rules strictly and impose sanctions for poor attendance at job search meetings, failing to meet the required number of job searches per unit of time, and so forth. Many agencies take this approach. The job requires client placements in paid employment. Yet the staff is confronted with clients of variable capacities and personalities, as well as uncontrollable services (such as adult education) and local labor markets. Whatever the program demands, the staff response will be survival, not necessarily service to clients.

The response of staff to these pressures can be gleaned from a recent study of welfare demonstration projects in five states. The authors report on how difficult it is to change these offices, not only because of program rules but also because of the "attitudes and expectations of both the staff and the recipients."[69] Part of the problem comes from liberalizing the earnings disregard. Cases are now more complex, and income-maintenance workers in all of the five states report having to spend more time on financial matters, in addition to employment-related tasks.[70] The result was that although it was envisioned that income-maintenance workers would take on more case manager responsibilities, this did not usually happen. "In general, administrators report that it is difficult to change attitudes and expectations of the income maintenance staff. They were hired primarily because they were good at paying attention to details, managing deadlines and completing technical tasks. While some are interested in talking more with recipients about their plans for the future, not all of them are. In addition, because income-maintenance workers have so many deadlines to meet and carry large caseloads, it is often difficult for them to focus on activities other than those absolutely necessary."[71]

Some offices, according to the study, did change, but there are always exceptions, and policymakers are always eager to generalize from a few "hothouse" demonstration projects. The authors of the five-state study caution that it takes a "substantial amount of time to bring about change within the welfare system" and that planning efforts require the involvement of a broad spectrum of business and community groups, government employees, private citizens and recipients.[72]

The confluence of the external and internal forces that shape the implementation of work programs by welfare departments and the inherent incompatibility between the two can best be seen at the "street level." There is much talk about how in the "new" welfare office a contract is drawn between the welfare recipient and the agency which spells out the mutual obligations of both and makes them accountable to the terms of the contract. Yet, the idea of the "contract" is also an exercise in myth and ceremony. In her study of the implementation of JOBS in Chicago, Evelyn Brodkin showed how the state stacks the cards in such a way that the clients have few opportunities to influence the terms of the contract. Moreover, the caseworkers who draw up and implement the contracts are subject to forces that greatly reduce their ability to respond to the formal program obligations to their clients. Instead, they use their discretionary power to force the clients to comply with their interpretation of the contract.

In trying to reduce costs while maximizing federal reimbursement, Illinois shifted the work program from a voluntary program emphasizing education and training to a mandatory program emphasizing job search.[73] In doing so the state simply redefined its moral assumptions about welfare recipients and their service needs. Even with such an altered and reduced social service approach to welfare recipients, the department was ill equipped to implement the program. Because the department deprofessionalized its casework staff, it was unable to staff the work program with trained workers. Moreover, because of union rules, most workers were recruited from the income-eligibility and grant-determination units, which emphasize highly bureaucratic routines. The pressure to meet caseload quotas further eroded the attention paid to the specific service needs of the recipients. Finally, as we have seen in the case of the implementation of GAIN in Los Angeles, the welfare department is constrained by its contractual obligations with the various employment and education service providers.

How do these forces shape the interaction between the workers and the clients? As Brodkin shows, at orientation the workers constructed their own conception of the "welfare contract" which "excluded a client right to help in job-finding and denied a state obligation to assure that decent job opportunities existed or could be found."[74] During assessment of the client needs, the workers were motivated to fit the client into available slots and therefore ignored information about service needs they could not respond to. Not infrequently, caseworkers sent clients to job searches even though they did not meet the required level of education or literacy. Typical of street-level bureaucracies, workers make judgments about "favored" clients in allocating precious resources such as education or vocational training. Clients who try to assert their rights either may be threatened with sanctions or are given a "choice" to find their own training program, but without much assistance from the caseworker. Because job search was limited by federal regulations to eight weeks per year, the caseworkers needed alternatives to keep their clients in this low-cost activity. They created a new service category called "job readiness," and when it proved to consume too much time, they resorted to deferrals.

The welfare recipients had little recourse in trying to get the welfare department to meet its part of the contract. The ability of the workers to redefine the needs of the clients, to ignore information about client problems, and to interpret requests for additional services as indications of noncompliance made it extremely difficult for clients to exercise their rights.

In a broader sense, Brodkin's findings are not surprising and are replicated in many other instances. This is because when a welfare department undertakes to implement a work program, a process of structural isomorphism takes place in which the work program acquires the same structural attributes as its parent organization. There are several reasons for such isomorphism. First, the very same external and internal forces which produce the highly bureaucratic structure in the welfare department exist when it implements the work program. These include state pressures to reduce costs, accountability based on quantity rather than quality, deprofessionalization of the staff, pressure to process large numbers of cases, and limited availability of viable service options.

Second, the same client ideologies that pervade the welfare department are transferred to the work program. These ideologies tend to define the clients as morally deficient and justify treating them as unworthy recipients.

More important, the bureaucratic structure used to determine eligibility crowds out the professional structure needed to provide employment services. Welfare eligibility is (and should be) based on a service technology in which the decision rules are explicit and highly standardized, interaction with clients is brief and limited to eliciting information needed to determine eligibility, and workers' interest is limited to client attributes that affect eligibility. The organizational structure best suited to implement such a technology is based on a rational bureaucracy.

In contrast, the provision of social services, such as employment services, follows a professional model in which service decisions are based on assessing the particular attributes and problems presented by each client and judging the most effective way of responding to them. Interaction with clients is continuous and extensive, and the worker is interested in many of the clients' attributes that might affect their well-being. The effectiveness of the worker is based on problem-solving skills learned through extensive training, and is contingent on developing a sustained, trusting relationship with the clients. Organizationally, such a technology requires a professional structure in which staff are given considerable autonomy.

When the two functions—income eligibility and provision of services—are mixed, income eligibility invariably takes over. As Gordon Hamilton noted more than thirty years ago, "The money function disables or overwhelms the social services."[75] This crowding out of the professional structure is reinforced by the fact that program administrators and workers who come from the welfare department bring with them the organizational tools they know best. They are accustomed to use them and are rewarded for adhering to them.

It is not surprising, therefore, that combining welfare eligibility and social services has not worked.[76] In a welfare department oriented toward welfare eligibility, income verification, dispensation of cash aid, and prevention of fraud, and closely monitored for eligibility and disbursement errors, it is hard to see how social services can occupy more than a marginal position.

There is an analogous experience with the history of the public employment exchange system in both Great Britain and the United States. In both countries, . the employment exchange—linking job seekers with job opportunities—was coupled with the work test required for eligibility for unemployment benefits.[77] The institutional arrangement that put these two functions under one organizational umbrella reflected political compromises among contending interest groups. In the United States they included employers, who looked to the state to enforce the work ethic, trade unions, who did not want competition from nonunion workers, and southern politicians, who wanted to preserve their segregated employment system. Once the two functions were coupled, they had long-term and irreversible effects on the employment services. In effect, the employment exchange became subordinate to the work test function. Because of the primacy of the work test, the employment services were unable to attract either job seekers with skills or employers with good jobs. Consequently, the employment services became identified as serving the least skilled workers and providing a pool of cheap labor to employers. As Desmond King demonstrates, in both countries, the record of the employment services in placing job seekers in jobs was quite dismal. Worse yet, once the coupling between these two functions was institutionalized, it became almost impossible to separate them, except for brief periods of time when pro-labor and civil rights coalitions ascended to power. Hence, as long as employment services are required to administer the work test, they are likely to fulfill only a residual role in creating and promoting employment opportunities, and they will not be able to escape the stigma attached to the people they actually serve.

We conclude, therefore, that when either welfare eligibility or work test is coupled with the provision of social services, the idea of service provision or rehabilitation becomes a mere slogan.

Should Work Programs Be Mandatory?

As we have seen, throughout the long and varied history of welfare-to-work programs, one element remains constant: the programs are mandatory. It is taken as axiomatic that participation has to be required. We challenge that assumption. We argue that not only are sanctions unnecessary, they are also counterproductive to goals of moving the maximum number of welfare recipients into the paid labor force.

Advocates of mandatory work programs argue that welfare recipients, especially long-term recipients, do not have the necessary motivation and discipline to participate. Even when they are induced to enroll in the program, they lack the will and perseverance to successfully complete the program requirements.[78] Therefore, mandatory participation coupled with sanctions for noncompliance is viewed as essential to the success of the program. Clearly, the image of the welfare recipient as lazy, impulsive, and defeated by welfare dependency drives such a rationale. We have seen that this stereotype is part of welfare mythology.

Advocates of voluntary participation argue that a mandatory program reinforces the concept of punishment, just as welfare itself does, whereas a voluntary program gives the client a *choice*, and work becomes an asset rather than punishment.[79] Bane argued that the success of such programs depends on an organizational culture "that delivers a clear message that the goal is jobs, sets a clear expectation that clients can get jobs and that workers are obligated to make that happen, monitors performance, and provides necessary resources."[80] Although such a culture could be attained in a mandatory program, there is a danger that relations between staff and clients will become adversarial and that each will blame the other for failure and thus excuse themselves from taking positive actions. Thus, Bane concluded that a voluntary program is preferable.

We argue that in light of the political economy of welfare-to-work programs, mandatoriness and the use of sanctions are an exercise in myth and ceremony, divert precious resources from the actual services, undermine the program's ability to work with and change people, and usually lead to goal displacement. Advocates of mandatory participation argue that it is necessary to overcome the resistance of long-term welfare recipients to participate, but this is not persuasive. We have already noted that welfare-to-work programs are seldom capable of serving more than a small fraction of the eligible recipients. Indeed, as we have seen in the case of ET in Massachusetts, when programs have something to offer and jobs are available, the number of recipients likely to volunteer far outstrips the availability of services. Similarly, in the GAIN program, Alameda County, which targeted long-term inner-city welfare recipients, ran an effective program that was in effect voluntary, and the county did not seem to have any difficulty in recruiting participants or eliciting their compliance.[81] We should add that the evaluation of GAIN has shown no consistent relationship between the enforcement of mandatoriness through the use of sanctions and program outcomes.[82] Therefore, the insistence on mandatory participation and sanctions cannot be seen as necessary to elicit participation and compliance.

Still, state welfare reform initiatives typically resort to tougher mandatory requirements and stiffer sanctions in order to increase participation in their welfare-to-work programs. A study of five state welfare reform demonstration projects—in Colorado, Iowa, Michigan, Utah and Vermont—found that each state expanded its participation requirements by greatly limiting the number of exemptions and by strengthening the sanctions for noncompliance. The evaluation of these measures points again to the inherent difficulties in implementing such strategies.[83] To achieve the higher rate of participation, several of the states resorted to an expanded definition of participation. In Utah, for example, it included participation in any activity that could be seen as "preparation and support for employment," such as mental health counseling, parenting classes, drug and alcohol treatment. Similarly, in Michigan, the mandated recipient's social contract could be fulfilled with almost any useful social activity. Moreover, although failure to fulfill the contract meant placing the recipient in a JOBS activity, only a few who failed to comply were ever placed in such an activity, making the social contract de facto voluntary. Iowa included "monitored employment" as a legitimate program for recipients working twenty or more hours per week, even though it is not a countable activity under JOBS. In other words, the states expanded mandatory participation by defining a very broad range of activities as "participation." This is reminiscent of the "paper registration" in WIN II, discussed in Chapter 2.

The reliance on harsher penalties for nonparticipation also seemed to produce mixed results. The researchers found that many more sanctions were initiated, and "while a large fraction of those sanctioned eventually comply with program activities, the majority do not."[84] Moreover, those who fail to comply seem to be the more difficult cases—those with less than a high school education and limited work experience. Since work programs are less successful with such recipients, sanctions only make their already difficult life circumstances more miserable without much of an apparent benefit. It is also clear that when workers wanted to establish a close, trusting relationship with their clients, as in the case of Utah, some viewed the sanctions as an impediment.

In every program—that is, in every welfare population—some group cannot or will not participate. The evidence is reasonably consistent that sanctions make no difference for this group.[85] Behavior does not change; they only become poorer. Why, then, does welfare policy always insist that they be sanctioned? The example of the poorhouse provides the answer. There, it will be recalled, only the most desperate, those who *could not* work, suffered the poorhouse. They served the symbolic function of confirming the image of welfare recipients as lacking in self-motivation and the work ethic, and affirming the institutional rule of requiring able-bodied welfare recipients to work. Even though these unfortunates could not work, their incarceration would *deter* those who might be tempted to seek aid rather than work. In other words, as Michael Katz has stated, the poorhouse inmates were held hostage.[86] The same argument is made today. Sanctions, we are told, are necessary so that recipients understand that the program is "serious." Although this statement is constantly repeated, there is no evidence that the prospect of sanctions changes behavior.

On the other hand, insistence on mandatory participation and the use of sanctions as ceremony imposes considerable costs on the program. It requires the program to establish a costly system of rule enforcement that tends to dominate case management activities. A comparative study of four welfare-to-work programs in California found that in the programs which emphasized mandatoriness, the case managers were preoccupied with enforcing the rules with recalcitrant participants, and became mired by the paperwork needed to document rule infractions, warn the participants, determine cause, set up informal and formal conciliations, and impose sanctions.[87] Considerably less time was available for working closely with the participants to help them overcome problems affecting their participation. A kind of a Gresham's law took place in which preoccupation with rule enforcement and paperwork crowded out effective relations between the case managers and participants.

As a result, the goals of the welfare-to-work program become displaced. Instead of helping the participants obtain and use the educational and employment services they need, the emphasis is on processing paperwork, and determining and validating the participant's formal status in the program. One of the reasons for such a displacement is that case managers are evaluated less on their ability to assist the participant than on the timeliness and accuracy of their paperwork and adherence to the rules.[88]

There is an inherent incompatibility between the emphasis on mandatory participation and compliance through threats of sanctions and the importance of getting the participants to effectively use the educational, employment, and support services provided by the program. The success of any program that aims to change the behavior of its clients depends, first and foremost, on the development of a trusting relationship between the staff and the clients.[89] This in turn requires such things as close and frequent contact with the clients, establishment of an emphatic relationship between the staff and clients, active participation of the clients in the decisions about their treatment, assisting the clients in getting the resources they need, advocating on their behalf with various service providers, and providing them with personal counseling and support when they are in crisis. The threat of sanctions is least likely to produce such a trusting relationship.

Moreover, a voluntary relationship defines the client not as an "object" to work on but rather as a "consumer." Being consumers requires the workers to "market" their services, and to be closely attuned to the needs of their clients.[90] There is a subtle shift in the balance of power between the clients and the workers. In a voluntary program the clients have considerably more influence in getting the services they need. Therefore, they are also more motivated to reach successful outcomes. Describing the change from a mandatory (WTP) to a voluntary (ET) program in Massachussets, Robert Behn quotes one of the supervisors: "The attitude of the WTP workers was: 'I send out a letter. I expect clients to come to see me. If they don't show up, no big deal.' With ET, however, if [the] unit mailed out 'boring, dry old "you have been scheduled for an appointment on" or "you may continue to be eligible for"' letters, the recipient would not respond. They didn't have to." Also under ET the unit "had goals. So it was a big deal if they didn't show up. We knew they didn't have to show up. So we really had to change the way we were structured."[91] For the staff, selling the program means paying close attention to the quality of the services it provides.

There is a more insidious way in which the emphasis on mandatory participation and threats of sanction influence the behavior of welfare workers. They reinforce an image of welfare recipients as deviants, as persons out of control. In turn, these images justify the use of sanctions. Thus, a vicious cycle develops in which negative perceptions about welfare recipients encourage the use of sanctions. These, of course, evoke conflict and accentuate the client attributes the workers find offensive, thus reinforcing their negative images of the recipients.[92]

Another characteristic of mandatory participation is its legitimation of a "blaming the victim" ideology. It is a convenient way to shift the responsibility from the worker to the recipient. If the recipient refuses to participate, it is not because the program cannot offer a decent job, or because the educational component is of poor quality. Rather, it is because the recipient is unmotivated or mired in a welfare-dependency mentality. Put differently, failure need not be attributed to the worker or the program but rather to the recipient. It is not surprising that, inevitably, in programs that emphasize mandatoriness and sanctions, staff also tend to uphold negative images of their clients. These negative images not only justify the use of sanctions but also "rationalize" failures as a consequence of recalcitrant clients. In such programs, the workers need not reach out and invest themselves in developing a trusting relationship. At the same time, workers lose the intrinsic rewards that are inherent in a trusting relationship. Not surprisingly, participants are least satisfied in work programs that emphasize rule enforcement and sanctions.[93] Similarly, when workers are given the option, they prefer to work with voluntary participants.

It is argued, on the other hand, that when all else fails, staff occasionally need to use the threat of sanctions as a "therapeutic" device to jar highly resistant clients from their complacency. Staff who emphasize their role as counselors, brokers, and advocates and prefer to use persuasion will say that having sanctions in their arsenal is useful for the few particularly difficult clients, but they also recognize that its effectiveness hinges on their commitment to work closely with the client, and to be able to provide them with the services they need. Proponents of this view point to successful programs such as Riverside, where about 34 percent of the participants were threatened with sanctions, although only 6 percent were actually sanctioned.[94] We don't know what a sanction "threat" meant in practice. Were recipients who actually violated rules specifically warned that they would be sanctioned, or were sanctions mentioned only as part of the general description of the program? Or did the practice vary? After all, sanctions were also technically part of Massachusetts's ET program, even though the workers made it quite clear that the program was voluntary. In any event, the MDRC study concluded that there was no consistent relationship between use of sanctions and program effectiveness. Los Angeles County, for example, had a higher rate of sanctions but showed little effectiveness, whereas Butte County had a very low rate of sanctions and yet demonstrated effectiveness. More important, when one looks closely at Riverside, it turns out that sanctions—or, more accurately, the threat of sanctions—do not explain the success of the program at all. The explanation lies in a charismatic leader, the staff's commitment to work with clients, and, above all, job development. Sanctions were at best a minor part of this effort.[95]

In sum, the issue of mandatoriness is another of the apparent paradoxes in welfare policy. The evidence is both consistent and persuasive over a long period of time that there is no lack of work ethic among the vast majority of welfare recipients. Recent empirical work has shown that the majority of welfare recipients, against considerable odds, either work while they are on welfare or repeatedly try to find and keep jobs, and that, in fact, the majority do exit welfare via work. Laurie Udesky reports that when job training and other employment services were offered in the South, tens of thousands volunteered,[96] replicating a finding of Leonard Goodwin more than a decade ago.[97] Kathleen Mullen Harris puts the matter bluntly: "Parents rely on welfare simply because they cannot find jobs that pay enough to support their families."[98]

Yet, despite the evidence that not only do most welfare recipients prefer to work and try to work—it's not just a matter of subjective feelings—*and* that, invariably, work and training programs are repeatedly oversubscribed, policymakers insist that work programs be mandatory. Somehow, it is incumbent on politicians to "send a message." Lawrence Mead has long argued that welfare programs have to be made "authoritative," that welfare recipients have to be told that they have "responsibilities" along with entitlement; it is part of the social contract.[99] It is also argued that if most recipients are willing to participate, then mandatory sanctions will be relatively minor. Yet, as we have shown, mandatoriness has heavy costs and is counterproductive. It stands to reason that those who do try to leave welfare via work but fail, thus staying on welfare for longer periods, have greater difficulty entering the labor force. Harris reports that the least successful, or more dependent, welfare recipients have less human capital and larger families. They might also have more health or psychological problems. Whatever the reason, this minority of recipients is less susceptible to the cheap, quick fixes such as three-week job search or community service work relief. Sanctions, such as grant reductions or termination, only increase their hardship. Unless we are only interested in punishment, what these recipients need is more sustained, long-term investments.

These, then, are the contradictions of the very longstanding welfare-to-work programs. Recipients want to work, but even minimally adequate jobs aren't available. Politicians won't fund the costs of what at least a minority of recipients really need. Sanctions are ineffective. Yet the pressure is to reduce welfare costs through work programs. But work programs, even community service jobs for the welfare grant, will not reduce costs, at least in the short run, which unfortunately is the time frame for policymakers. The only sure way to cut welfare costs is to cut grants.

Probably the most fundamental reason why welfare-to-work programs fail is that they are seldom truly intended to respond to the needs of welfare recipients; indeed, welfare recipients are not their primary beneficiaries. Rather, they are used as symbolic institutions to distinguish between deserving and undeserving poor, to reaffirm the work ethic, to reinforce the legitimacy and primacy of the private labor market, and to justify poverty-level wages. As a subtext, they also confirm dominant belief systems about gender, family values, and ethnic hegemony.

The symbolic functions of such work programs can be gleaned from several inherent features. First, considerable effort and energy are devoted to identifying and demarcating the nonworking able-bodied poor, and in so doing set them apart from the rest of us and cast them as the "problem." Thus, the programs are driven by numerous eligibility-determination and participation requirements that are periodically revised to reflect changing attitudes toward the poor. Now that poor single mothers are expected to work, policymakers and program managers debate how low the age of the youngest child should be to justify exempting the mother from participating in the work program. It started at the age of six for WIN and fell to three under JOBS, with states having the discretion to reduce the age limit to one. Under TANF, states have the *option* of exempting single parents with a child under one year old. There are now pressures to further lower the age limits, even down to twelve weeks after birth.[100] Similarly, the programs are preoccupied with extensive concerns about the number of hours women must participate in the program, what constitutes a legitimate "work activity," and the conditions under which they might be exempt or deferred. The implementation of these ever-changing regulations occupies much of the energy of the program staff, and inevitably adds to the bureaucratic complexity that marks the administration of such programs.

Second, the "problem" of welfare recipients—their inability to find and hold regular jobs—is inevitably blamed on themselves. They are lacking either in work ethic or in human capital, or in both. Almost never is the problem blamed on the job market itself, or on the lack of stable jobs that provide living wages. As Gordon Lafer points out in the case of JPTA, policymakers and program managers take it for granted that jobs are available for the motivated clients. This assumption prevails even in the face of considerable evidence to the contrary.[101]

Third, despite their claims, these programs are seldom designed to be truly people-changing. By coupling income maintenance with work requirements and by making participation mandatory, the programs become mired in the enforcement of rules and regulations that takes precedence over the provision of services matched to the individual needs of the clients.

Fourth, only a very small fraction of the able-bodied poor are actually served by the work programs. To maintain the institutional symbols, it is more important that the programs identify and certify who is the "deviant" than to provide services to all of them. Services need to be provided only to a sufficient number (usually 20–25 percent) of the able-bodied poor in order to demonstrate to the nonpoor that the dominant values about work and family values are being upheld.

The relatively small number being served is coupled with a fifth characteristic of these programs: the very limited amount of resources that are actually allocated to them. Historically, no work program was ever allocated sufficient resources either to cover a substantial proportion of the able-bodied poor or to provide adequate services to those who enrolled. The reluctance to commit resources stems in part from the view of welfare recipients as undeserving. In the competition for public funds with programs that serve the middle class, work programs fare poorly. Moreover, there is an implicit recognition that for such programs to be truly effective in lifting the poor out of poverty, they would require substantial commitment of resources. Thus, it invariably becomes more expedient to resort to out-door relief.

Added to the uncertain benefit of such programs is the fact that, at best, they can demonstrate very modest results. Although they may increase the work efforts of the poor, they seldom reduce poverty, let alone the welfare rolls. Ultimately, policymakers, especially at the state and local levels, may come to realize that it is more effective to curb welfare costs and enrollment by reducing the public assistance grant, and by instituting tougher eligibility requirements. Indeed, that has been the response of most states to the rising costs of welfare in the face of declining or limited state resources. Adjusting for inflation, the average monthly AFDC grant declined by 40 percent between 1970 and 1992.[102] More recently, cuts in grant amount have been justified as an incentive to recipients to work, although there is little evidence to support such a claim.[103]

Localism is another earmark of work programs for the poor. Although guided and supported by federal legislation, state and local communities are given considerable discretion in the implementation and administration of the program. As long as the local program embodies in its structure the institutional norms and symbols it is supposed to uphold (for example, determining who the able-bodied poor are in establishing some employment services), it is given a great deal of leeway in the actual operation of the program, especially in determining the mix of services it will provide and how clients will be treated. There are several reasons for emphasizing localism. It buffers the symbols from the realities in the field, thus allowing policymakers to espouse and affirm the symbols without making them accountable to the difficulties such programs experience in the field. It shifts the responsibility for the control of the "deviant" poor to the locality, thus enabling the expression of local values and norms, while maintaining a broad and abstract national consensus. It enables local communities to design the program in light of their own political economies. That is, the program can reflect local labor market conditions, the attributes of the local welfare population, patterns of gender and ethnic relations, and the availability of local resources.

Finally, because welfare-to-work programs are essentially symbolic institutions existing in a moral environment with contentious values, they are fundamentally unstable and are subject to periodic changes. A typical cycle can be noted. In response to the increase in the welfare population and the costs of public assistance, a work program is introduced with great fervor and expectations. Once implemented, the program experiences serious substantive and administrative problems. Its limited ability to set the poor to work becomes evident over time, especially when the welfare rolls and costs continue to climb. The poor themselves come to realize that the rhetoric of the program does not match the reality. They cooperate reluctantly, if at all, and may actually resist passively (or occasionally actively) the restrictions imposed on them. General disappointment sets in. Confronted with a failure to solve the problem of the poor, coupled with normative changes toward work, family, and ethnicity, policymakers feel a need to reaffirm dominant values on these issues and to institute a new or a revised work program.

If we are serious about making work programs effective rather than exercises in myth and ceremony, the lessons are quite clear. Such programs must be universal and voluntary. They cannot be shackled by the stigma of serving only the "undeserving" deviants, or operate in the shadow of eligibility determination for public assistance. They must include an extensive array of employment-enhancing resources, such as education, vocational training, on-the-job training, and job opportunities. These must be coupled with adequate support services such as child care, transportation, and counseling. And the programs must be managed by highly trained and professional staff who have a long-term commitment to their clients. In Chapter 7 we will provide a blueprint for such programs. Simply put, effective programs require large economic and political investments. There are no proven cheap shortcuts to enabling the poor to earn living wages.

Part Two

New Directions

Chapter 5

Jobs, Income, and Employment Support

Although the long-term goal for our society should be a full-employment economy with well-paying jobs, the near future, at best, seems to promise a relatively full-employment economy with large numbers of low-wage jobs. Such an economy will probably reduce welfare rolls, but it will not reduce poverty. What has to be done is to make work pay.

Seven clusters of policy issues have to be addressed in order to improve the economic well-being of low-wage workers:

- There has to be job creation, because at present there are not enough jobs for all those who want to work.
- Income from work has to be improved, through either continued improvement of the Earned Income Tax Credit (EITC) or other forms of wage subsidies, coupled with modest raising of the minimum wage.
- Tax rates in related programs have to be adjusted so that people who either leave welfare for work or, as is increasingly common, combine work with income-maintenance programs, are not penalized. Various changes have to be made in AFDC and food stamps.
- Because so many low-wage workers are single mothers, child care has to be subsidized and continued efforts have to be made to improve child support.
- The lack of health insurance is a severe disincentive to leave welfare and enter the paid labor force. Clearly, health insurance has to be extended to the low-wage work force.
- The present unemployment insurance (UI) is based on the concept of a full-time worker involuntarily becoming unemployed. However, an increasingly large number of low-wage jobs are part-time, contingent, and seasonal. In addition, single mothers often cannot reconcile changes in shift work with child care. UI should be reformed to take account of these changing conditions of employment.
- Significant numbers of welfare recipients are disabled or care for disabled relatives; yet most are not on supplemental security income

disability (DI). In addition, the present DI rules discourage part-time employment. Here, too, reform is needed.

These reforms, we believe, will go a long way toward reducing both welfare rolls and poverty. In this chapter, we will discuss the first three policies.

Job Creation

As noted in Chapter 4, welfare recipients have considerable attachment to the labor force. While on welfare, the majority work and leave welfare via employment. Yet many return to welfare because they are unable to maintain steady employment. The problem is not work ethic but either the nature of the job itself or the life circumstances that make work difficult. Typically, many low-skill and low-paying jobs do not last or are seasonal, lack fringe benefits such as health insurance, and expose the workers to serious work hazards. The life circumstances of low-income and low-skilled workers, especially single parents, are such that unexpected events such as failure in child care, break-down in transportation, or illness of family members, which might normally be handled without disruption of daily life, quickly turn into crises.[1] A vivid example of how a fairly typical child care problem can escalate into a major family crisis is reported by Celia W. Dugger in a *New York Times* article entitled "Iowa Plan Tries to Cut off the Cash:"[2]

> The [welfare] mother had signed an agreement with the state to go to college, which she believed offered her the best route to a job that paid enough to support her three children. She was put on a waiting list. Her caseworker told her she would have to get a job in the meantime. A few weeks after she began working for $5.50 an hour, her 5-year-old got sick. The boy was running a fever and could not go to the day-care center. The worker then told the mother that the only acceptable excuse for missing work was a doctor's note saying that she herself was ill. So she left her son with a neighbor. When she came home, she found him alone and untended. She stayed home with him and was fired from her job. Her welfare benefits were then reduced because she had not done what her worker required. Unable to pay the rent, the family was evicted . . . and slept in friend's car. Because of the family homelessness, one of the children's teachers reported them to child-protection services. The child-protection worker told the mother that her children would be placed in foster care if she could not provide for them.

The story also illustrates what could happen when welfare eligibility is made contingent on efforts to obtain and keep a job, and what role the social workers must assume in such a setting.

The inability to maintain steady employment is not unique to welfare recipients but common to both poor men and women with limited education and employment skills. We can make work pay once we put into place adequate income support mechanisms that are attached to work such as EITC, wage subsidies, child care subsidies, and health and unemployment insurance. In Chapter 7, we argue that employment services need to be developed that would ensure that all those who want to work can find employment, and that the obstacles to stable employment can be reduced if not removed. We propose to replace existing welfare-to-work programs with community-based employment services that will be available to all members of the community who seek employment. However, here we argue that the effectiveness of both "making work pay" and employment services is predicated on a deliberate national policy of job creation.

The ultimate success of any program that tries to help able-bodied poor people become employable hinges on the availability of jobs, especially those that pay a living wage. If jobs are not available, no amount of job development and skill training will lead to employment. Roberta Spalter-Roth, Heidi Hartmann, and Linda Andrews found that for every one-percent increase in state unemployment rates there is a nine-percent decline in the probability that welfare mothers could have paid employment as part of their income package.[3] Similarly, for those women who combine welfare and work or recycle between welfare and work, every one-percent increase in the state unemployment rates reduces the probability that they will escape poverty by 31 percent. In short, the economic conditions of the local community have significant impact on the ability of welfare recipients to find jobs and escape poverty.

The precise extent of job availability is difficult to determine since no systematic data are being collected on job vacancies. We really do not know the actual number of jobs that are vacant at any point, whether they are full-time or part-time, whether they are permanent or temporary, and whether they pay decent wages. Similarly, the data on the job seekers is problematic because of difficulties in defining what constitutes participation in the labor force and what counts as unemployment. For example, persons working one or more hours per week for pay are counted as employed, whereas unemployed persons who want a job but are not actively looking for a job are not counted in the labor force. Persons who have not looked for work in the past four weeks are not counted as unemployed. As a result, we lack good estimates of the true dimensions of involuntary unemployment—that is, unemployment due to lack of jobs—which is probably higher, according to the current estimates by the Bureau of Labor Statistics.

Some argue that the potential discrepancy between the availability of jobs and the number of welfare recipients who might be forced into the labor market is not important because, in the long run, employers will be able to absorb all the welfare recipients. Gary Burtless, for example, suggests that market forces will encourage employers to change their production system to take advantage of the availability of low-wage workers.[4] Mostly, however, the abundance of low-wage workers will lead to a further decline in the hourly wage, resulting in "lousy" jobs that are irregular and dead-end, pay poverty wages, and have no benefits.

There are several difficulties with this line of argument. First, most unemployed cannot wait for the "long run," which may not come in their lifetime. In particular, we must consider the enormous social costs of being unemployed, especially the effects on their children. Second, it is not clear how much flexibility employers do have in adjusting their production systems to take advantage of these low-wage workers. There are also limits as to how many low-cost goods and services, such as fast food restaurants or cleaning services, a community can support, especially if many of its members cannot make a decent living. Third, as industries move their operations to communities or even shift their operations to other countries because these offer them a better competitive advantage, many of the unemployed lack the resources to migrate with the industries and are left behind in the high unemployment areas. Fourth, during periods of economic slow-down, employers who rely on low-skilled workers are often among the first to curtail production. Low-skilled workers are also the last to be hired when the economy experiences robust growth. Fifth, depressed wages, coupled with lack of benefits and uncertain employment, increase the attraction of nonwork or other alternatives to regular employment. Finally, from a societal perspective, the social and personal costs of working in "lousy" jobs or in the alternative underground economy may greatly outweigh their benefits.

The few studies we have on job availability suggest that many of the unemployed do not find jobs because they do not exist.[5] According to Philip Harvey, in New York City between 1987 and 1991 the jobless outnumbered available jobs by about seven to one.[6] In Milwaukee, the October 1994 Job Openings Survey found that in the central-city neighborhoods there were four unemployed workers for every vacant full-time job.[7] A study by the Illinois JOB GAP Project found that there were four job seekers for every entry-level job opening in the state. In Chicago the ratio was six to one, and in East St. Louis, nine to one. The report concluded that there was a severe shortage of entry-level jobs, especially ones paying a livable wage.[8] Other studies suggest that the problem is particularly acute in inner-city neighborhoods.[9] Harry Holzer, using a survey of employers, found that quite substantial cognitive and interactive skills were required in jobs in central cities that did not require a college degree, even non–white-collar jobs.[10] He further estimated that a very small fraction (5–10 percent) of the available jobs require minimal skills. If the only required credential is a high school degree and some general work experience, the percentage rises to 10–13. Among the service jobs, only 10 percent require just a high school diploma. Given the heavy concentration of persons with limited education, training, and work experience in the central cities, Holzer concluded that the supply of such workers far exceeds the availability of jobs they can qualify for.

The anthropologist Katherine Newman has been studying job availability for AFDC recipients in Harlem.[11] She found that in the fast food industry the rate of job seekers to each available job was approximately fourteen to one. The majority of those who were not hired remained unemployed a year later. The employers preferred to hire older workers and recent immigrants. Surprisingly, they also preferred hiring commuting workers rather than local job seekers. Especially disadvantaged were African American persons under age twenty and welfare recipients. Employers rely on network recruitment—using the social networks of their current employees to recruit new workers. One of the consequences of network recruitment is that the new hires replicate the characteristics of the current employees, such as age, gender, and ethnicity, leaving those lacking such characteristics at a disadvantage.

Conversely, we find that in a labor-shortage economy the employment opportunities of those most disadvantaged improve markedly. Paul Osterman found that when Boston experienced full employment in the mid-1980s, the poverty rate declined dramatically (and so did the number of people on AFDC), especially for white and black families and unrelated individuals.[12] Similarly, Freeman found that in a tight labor market (unemployment rate under 4 percent) the employment opportunities and the hourly wages for disadvantaged young men improve considerably.[13] Therefore, the availability of jobs is a key factor in the ability of low-skilled persons to become employed and earn a living, although many will still not escape poverty because of low wages.

In other words, the demand side of the welfare/work equation must be addressed. Unless there are sufficient jobs, welfare-to-work programs will simply amount to a game of musical chairs whereby those who get placed in jobs will shut out other similar job seekers who, for lack of jobs, will become impoverished and dependent on public assistance.[14] Put differently, unless jobs are created we engage in a zero-sum game in which one impoverished group benefits at the expense of another economically vulnerable group. This means that as long as unemployment remains high, job creation must be an essential starting point for the establishment of any employment program.

As a basic policy, we propose that all those who can work but cannot find a job on their own within a specified time period must be guaranteed a job paying at least the minimum wage in either the private or public sector. These jobs would provide either full-time employment to those who can work full-time or part-time employment to those who for health, child care, and other reasons cannot work full time.

Our approach recognizes that there are different sources of unemployment and that each may require different policy responses. Holzer distinguishes between three causes of unemployment—frictional, structural, and deficient-demand.[15] Frictional unemployment is due to the inability of people to find the jobs because of lack of information or access to available jobs. Our proposed job development and placement services (tier I in Chapter 7) would be an appropriate response. Structural unemployment is due to the mismatch between the job skills of the unemployed and the available jobs. It may arise as a result of technological, industrial, and product changes. Human capital investment programs, as we propose in tier II and III services (Chapter 7), that invest in education, training, and retraining of displaced workers could ease their transition to new occupational careers. Of course, for both frictional and structural unemployment the assumption is that jobs are available.

Far more vexing, however, is unemployment caused by deficient demand. The experience in pursuing a national policy of full employment is quite discouraging.[16] As we noted above, when jobs are unavailable, conventional manpower programs are doomed to fail. What is required is an aggressive public policy to stimulate new jobs in economically depressed areas. Such a policy may include programs such as economic incentives to industries to relocate to or remain in these areas; public investments in the infrastructure of the local community; and ultimately public service employment.[17] Harvey proposed a federal employment assurance program whereby the government will not only stimulate private employment but also supplement, as needed, the regular demand for labor with public employment.[18]

What has been our experience with policies specifically designed to create jobs? Job creation programs such as the Civil Works Administration (cwa) in 1933–34, and the Comprehensive Employment and Training Act (ceta) and the Youth Incentive Entitlement Pilot Projects (yiepp) in the 1970s, have proven quite effective in combating unemployment, despite political opposition by powerful business interest groups and exaggerated charges of "corruption." At the height of the Depression, the cwa was formally launched on November 9, 1933 and ended on February 15, 1934. In that short period of time, the program provided jobs to four million unemployed persons. cwa was strikingly different from typical work-for-relief programs. First, there were no means tests. Two million relief workers were transferred, and two million workers were selected on the basis of their skill, training, and experience. Second, the projects selected provided the workers with real jobs paying living wages. Moreover, the workers were entitled to the same medical and compensation benefits as federal employees.[19] Third, control over the administration of CWA was firmly in the hands of the federal government. Engineers and accountants, rather than the social workers, were given control over the program. Their chief concern was to manage the public employment program effectively and efficiently. The impact on the unemployed hired into CWA was dramatic. "In one stroke, 'clients' became wage earners who would receive cash for their labor to spend as they saw fit."[20] The program provided incentives to work and created pride in one's work.

The program was short-lived despite its undeniable and overwhelming success, and its popularity among the unemployed. President Roosevelt himself was afraid that the program would create permanent dependence on the state, and that it would be too costly. The business community saw in CWA unfair competition, driving up the wages of labor. In the South, the wage issue took on a racial overtone, since many black farm laborers earned higher wages than the farm owners had paid them. Although small businessmen feared the competition, corporate leaders feared the economic consequences of such an expensive program.[21]

CETA, enacted in 1973, provided for direct job creation in response to both cyclical and structural unemployment.[22] Although CETA acquired an unfavorable reputation as a result of a few isolated but highly publicized incidences of abuse and corruption, a careful review of the research on the effectiveness of the program suggests that such reputation is unwarranted. The record shows that a public service employment program (PSE), if well administered, can be quite effective in creating jobs during periods of high unemployment.[23] Yet, to be effective, there ought to be an automatic trigger mechanism to authorize federal funds whenever the unemployment rates exceeds a certain level. CETA lacked such a trigger and its funding was curtailed, providing employment to only a small fraction of the unemployed.

One of the arguments against PSE is job substitution—that is, that state and local public employers shift their regular employees to the federal payroll rather than create new jobs. However, research by the Brookings Institution following the 1976 CETA amendments found low rates of substitution. Indeed, when Congress tightened eligibility requirements and imposed wage and job-duration limits, the rate of substitution declined further to about 10 percent. Moreover, direct public job creation has been shown to be more cost-effective than indirect measures such as tax cuts.

As a strategy to combat structural unemployment, CETA has been shown to produce significant earnings gains, especially when it is targeted for highly disadvantaged populations.[24] Clifford Johnson concludes that "evidence suggests that public service employment programs under CETA enhanced the ability of participants to secure permanent jobs in the public sector, serving as a 'try-out' period and providing on-the-job training for adults with limited prior experience."[25] Moreover, the jobs themselves were shown to be useful and meaningful.

The demise of CETA as a job-creation program, despite its successes, was due to political antagonism fueled by implementation problems.[26] CETA was beset by conflicting aims: providing employment and training services to the unemployed, and giving an economic stimulus to communities hit by high rates of unemployment. Although CETA started with the former objective, rapidly rising unemployment shifted the program to the latter objective with the enactment of the Emergency Jobs and Unemployment Assistance Act of 1974. Yet, as it was a highly decentralized program, local communities were unprepared for the rapid influx of new resources and, not surprisingly, local elected officials greatly influenced the implementation of PSE. Indeed, according to Donald Baumer and Carl Van Horn, "local officials had carte blanche over money intended for public jobs."[27] A few highly visible instances of fraud and corruption created the political symbols needed to delegitimize the program. The reauthorization of CETA in 1978 curtailed the scope of the program, shifted its focus to the long-term unemployed, and imposed an extensive system of federal regulations that greatly diminished local discretion, resulting in withdrawal of local political support. The program became highly fragmented and, lacking a strong institutional base, it fell victim to the charges of corruption, as had previous job-creation programs.[28]

One of the legacies of CETA was the Youth Incentive Entitlement Pilot Projects, which represents one of the most ambitious efforts to test the feasibility and effectiveness of a job-creation program in reducing youth unemployment.[29] The project was designed in response to a dramatic rise in minority youth unemployment and school dropout rates.[30] YIEPP guaranteed young people from low-income and welfare families a part-time job during the school year and a full-time summer job on the condition that they remain in or return to high school and meet academic and job performance requirements. The demonstration was successfully implemented and created jobs for more than 76,000 youth in 11,000 work sites. Most jobs were of adequate quality and provided meaningful work experiences, not make-work. The program was very effective in attracting minority young people and had dramatic impact on their employment rates, particularly in the school year. Forty percent of young people were employed during the school year, as compared to 21 percent in the nondemonstration sites. Even in the summer, rates of employment in the demonstration sites were appreciably higher. YIEPP also closed the gap between black and white employment rates. The project belied the stereotype that minority young people are unmotivated or have unrealistic work expectations. It showed that a major reason for high minority youth unemployment is lack of jobs. Indeed, YIEPP created new jobs; for every 1⅔ jobs funded by YIEPP, one new job was created. What was particularly impressive about the project was its impact on postdemonstration employment. One year after the demonstration, the earnings of the African American youth were 40 percent higher than those in the nondemonstration sites.[31]

Reviewing the experience with these and other public employment programs Sar Levitan and Frank Gallo argue that if adequately funded, such programs could be quite effective. They calculate that if we set as a target an unemployment rate of 4.0 percent, then the federal employment programs at their peak (1979) reduced the job deficit by 43 percent.[32] The bottom line is that any successful strategy to reduce poverty and dependence on public assistance will require the assurance of employment to those who can work.

Although one would hope for an economy of well-paying jobs, the starting point is to try to increase the number of jobs, through both the market and job creation. Without even a plentiful supply of low-paying jobs, it is idle to talk about setting welfare recipients to work. If the jobs are not there, nationwide, not much will happen. To be sure, some programs may demonstrate some "modest" success, but even here, most recipients will remain on some form of welfare. Those recipients who do find work will displace other, similarly situated job seekers and, for the most part, will remain in poverty. Female heads of families will continue to recycle on and off welfare.

Thus, in order to reduce poverty and welfare, the available jobs have to be supplemented in terms of both earnings and benefits. In a comparative study of the poverty rates of working families in the United States and eight other industrialized countries, Lee Rainwater has shown that the United States is at the bottom end of the scale.[33] Although it has high proportions of families in work, it has the largest earnings differentials, the lowest social transfers, and the highest poverty rates. Working single mothers in the United States are much more dependent on their earnings than in the other countries. The conclusions that Rainwater draws follow the same logic as our proposals: (1) Poverty rates are dependent on the labor market—"the more solo mothers work, the lower their poverty rates"; (2) therefore, both jobs and returns (wages and benefits) from jobs have to be increased But (3) there also have to be transfers—what he calls a "social wage" (such as child allowances and child support payments).

We turn now to increasing the returns from paid labor.

Wages and Wage Subsidies

We have seen in Chapter 3 the poverty effects of the low-wage labor market. In this section, we consider the two principal mechanisms for increasing the earnings from work—wage subsidies, including the earned income tax credit, and raising the minimum wage.

The Earned Income Tax Credit

First enacted in 1975, the EITC has become a significant redistribution program, which, at least until recently, enjoyed strong bipartisan support. The EITC supplements earnings either through a tax reduction or, if the family owes no taxes, through a refundable tax credit.[34] Today, nearly fourteen million families receive the credit. For individual families, the benefits are substantial. For a family with two or more children, earning $8,500 per year, the benefit will be $3,370 (39.7 percent), which is just about the poverty line.[35] In 1996, the EITC rate was 40 percent of earnings for families with two or more children (a maximum credit of $3,370) and 34 percent for families with one child (a maximum of $2,040), and will also cover low-income childless taxpayers ($306).[36] For families with two or more children, the EITC increases a minimum-wage job to $5.95 per hour ($5.70 for a taxpayer with one child). More than six million working families with incomes below the poverty line will be eligible for benefits, the poverty gap will be decreased by $6.4 billion, and the incomes of one million taxpayers will be raised above the poverty line.[37]

As of 1994, the credit became available to low-wage adults without children, which substantially expands the number who qualify (and the cost). When fully phased in, it will be the largest cash program directed at low-income families.[38] By fiscal year 1998, the EITC is expected to cost $24.5 billion a year (the federal share of AFDC will be $16 billion). The rapid growth of the EITC is due primarily to policy decisions—to expand it to reduce the poverty of workers. Once the expansion is fully phased in, the growth will slow to about 4.5 percent a year, reflecting population growth and the changes in the Consumer Price Index.[39]

To illustrate the effects of the EITC on a welfare family, in Kathryn Edin and Christopher Jencks's study of working welfare mothers, the jobs they had paid about $5 per hour. If a mother worked twenty-five hours per week for forty-eight weeks at $5 per hour, she would earn $6,000, less $460 in payroll taxes, and receive and EITC of about $2,400. The total—$7,940—is $3,140 more than that family would get in Illinois (where AFDC plus food stamps comes to $4,800 per year). We have noted that a majority of welfare recipients are already working, and more than two-thirds will exit welfare via work. Over time, the changes in the EITC should greatly accelerate that process.

The EITC, thus far, has remained popular because it encourages work and provides income for the working poor. However, the EITC is not trouble-free.[40] First, there is the issue of work incentives. The credit increases with earnings up to a maximum amount; then there is a "phase-out" during which the amount of the credit decreases until the break-even point.[41] The question is, what are the incentive effects when a family enters the phase-out range? It is clear that incentives are positive and strong for the low-earners, but as earnings increase, the supplement decreases—which is, in effect, a tax. Critics of the EITC argue that many workers are in the phase-out range; these workers are potentially the more productive and it is bad policy to subject them to disincentives in order to provide a work incentive for a small number of welfare recipients.[42]

However, a family will always be better off working until the break-even point. A recent study has concluded that even though the poor face high marginal tax rates, the rates are not sufficiently high to offset the incentive effects of the EITC. In fact, with the EITC fully phased in, the effective tax rate will be reduced by 20 percentage points for an AFDC recipient who works significant hours at a minimum-wage job, and this should have a significant positive effect on labor market behavior.[43]

Besides, it may be more important, in the aggregate, to provide a large, strong work incentive to the welfare recipient.[44] Many economists, as well as the General Accounting Office, argue that the expansion of the EITC will induce single mothers to enter the labor force, with only a slight disincentive to other recipients.[45] In any event, as Rebecca Blank says, "There are no existing studies of the impact of EITC on work effort. Current recipients may be persons who would work even in the absence of the EITC."[46] The GAO estimated that the percentage reduction in hours worked as a result of the EITC is four times greater among wives in two-parent families than among husbands in such families. At the same time, there was little reduction in the work effort among single parents.[47] Besides, as Ann Alstott observes, it is not necessarily bad policy if the wife in a two-parent family reduces her work effort to spend more time with her children.[48]

There is a problem with the EITC participation rate. In order to receive the EITC, a family has to file a tax return. If a family does not owe any taxes, there is no requirement that a return be filed. In 1992, if a family did not earn $10,600, it would not owe any taxes but would be entitled to a refundable credit of

$1,384—but only if the family took the initiative and filed.[49] John Scholz estimates that between 10.4 and 11.2 million families are eligible for refunds and that the participation rate is between 80.5 and 86.4 percent—which is considerably higher than AFDC (62–72 percent) or food stamps (54–66 percent)—but which nevertheless means that between 1.3 and 2.0 million eligible taxpayers do *not* get refunds.[50]

By examining those who do file for the EITC refund, Scholz not surprisingly discovered that the greater the expected refund, the more likely a person was to file. The greater the self-employed income, the less likely he or she was to file. Taxpayers who fell in the following categories were more likely to be nonparticipants: receiving public assistance, working in private household occupations, child care workers, and laborers. Scholz thinks that the preference not "to formalize an informal working arrangement . . . may be a major hurdle to outreach efforts."[51]

There is also the issue of targeting. Once the EITC is fully phased in, the break-even level of income will be $27,000 for taxpayers with two or more children. This means that many will receive the credit who are above the poverty line. However, because of its progressive benefit structure, approximately half of the money will go to families with incomes below the poverty line, and approximately 1.4 million families will move over the line.[52]

Probably the most important problem right now with the EITC involves program integrity.[53] The IRS has estimated that in past years, more than 30 percent of EITC claimants were ineligible, amounting to nearly $2 billion in inappropriate claims.[54] With the increase in the EITC, there are now strong incentives to overreport income.[55] The IRS has difficulty detecting this kind of fraud, and because the individual amounts are small, monitoring is expensive.[56]

It is hard to know how many of the errors are due to fraud or ignorance. After all, a great deal of the population that is affected by the EITC lacks experience and skill in dealing with the IRS. A recent in-depth study by Lynn Olson of a small sample of thirty women in welfare-to-work transition programs presented two disturbing sets of findings.[57] On the one hand, there was considerable lack of knowledge, misunderstanding, and even apprehension on the part of the respondents. On the other hand, for-profit tax preparation agencies have mushroomed in low-income neighborhoods, especially during tax season. Ads appeared on buses, park benches, and television. The ads played on fears of making mistakes as well as inducements of quick refunds (by, for example, presenting images of vacations and new furniture). Virtually all of Olson's respondents paid a commercial preparer;[58] the fees were substantial, especially for those who wanted the "rapid" or "instant" refund instead of waiting four to six weeks for the IRS check.

Finally, there are incentives for both marriage and separation, which is also true for the income tax.[59] However, there is no empirical evidence as to whether people respond to these incentives.[60] And there are moderate, incremental reforms that can lessen the incentives.[61]

For more than ten years, taxpayers had the option of receiving in advance a portion of the EITC, but so far very few (less than 0.5 percent) take advantage of this option. It is not clear why the option is not used more.[62] No doubt there is a lack of awareness; in Olson's study, none of the respondents knew about the advance payment option.[63] In addition, there could be a preference for a lump sum, concern about burdening an employer, or concern about owing taxes at year's end. The low use of the option may indicate that it is not an important issue for most taxpayers; for example, when the advance payment option was explained to Olson's respondents, most preferred the year-end lump-sum payment.[64] However, advance payment would seem to be important for families moving from welfare to work. When welfare benefits are reduced, unless the EITC kicks in, after-tax incomes of newly working families are less than welfare, and this may discourage working. With incremental EITC benefits, employment income is higher than welfare.[65]

At the present time, there is extensive concern in Congress and the IRS about the problems of the EITC.[66] Many of the error-producing aspects of the EITC can be cured by changing the rules and the forms, although there will be tradeoffs.[67] At the same time, at least on the basis of Olson's findings, considerable attention has to be paid to the way the EITC is understood and used at the street level. She argues that it is unrealistic to think that the EITC can be self-administered for most filers. She recommends considerable outreach and education efforts. Since the IRS is not a "social service agency," this effort will have to be made by a variety of actors. Government will have to monitor commercial tax preparers, especially requiring disclosure of rates and fees (Wisconsin has passed such legislation). There are some community-level outreach campaigns—for example, the VITA staff of the IRS and the Earned Income Credit Campaign of the Center on Budget and Policy Priorities.

There are other proposals, however, that would significantly reduce EITC benefits—primarily by scaling back the benefit structure to 1995 levels. Approximately eight million families with two or more children, and two million families with one child, would receive reduced EITC benefits.[68] The combined effect of these proposals would erode the wages for low-skilled work.[69]

Granted that there are problems of program integrity that have to be addressed. It is still difficult to fathom why the EITC is now under attack. For more than two decades, it has enjoyed bipartisan support because it is an effective measure that both reduces poverty and rewards work.

Wage subsidies. Although the EITC has been praised for increasing the value of work, Haveman and Scholz argue that it does not go far enough in correcting the employment barriers facing low-wage, low-skilled workers.[70] In their view, EITC proponents wrongly assume that there is either strong excess demand for low-skilled workers or a high wage elasticity of demand; rather, they say, structural problems face the low-skilled worker. Despite high levels of employment, certain groups cannot get jobs primarily because they lack skills and education. Not only are such workers not profitable for business, but minimum-wage laws, union wage contracts, and fringe benefits and payroll taxes further compound the market disadvantages of the low-skilled. They propose, in combination with the EITC, a wage subsidy modeled on the New Jobs Tax Credit (NJTC) in 1977–78. Under that program, the subsidy (50 percent of the first $6,000) was sufficiently high that employers favored low-skilled workers. The program did, in fact, create jobs for low-skilled workers at a fairly low cost.[71]

Robert Haveman and John Scholz favor a permanent wage subsidy to increase the hiring incentives. In their opinion, the combination of employer-based (demand-side) and employee-based (supply-side) incentives would equalize the employment opportunities of the low-wage, low-skilled worker at a reasonable cost—certainly lower than providing jobs—and raise the incomes of the low-skilled workers.[72] There are other subsidy proposals.[73]

Family allowances; refundable tax credit. All industrialized countries—except the United States—have a child allowance.[74] The United States may be moving toward this direction by means of the refundable tax credit. Although similar to the child allowance as far as family economics is concerned, administration is different. With a child allowance, every family receives a weekly or monthly check. With the tax credit, the worker receives an offset to withholding. With no wage earners, the family would have to apply for the credit. The National Commission on Children proposed a refundable tax credit of $1,000 per child, at a cost of $40 billion a year.[75]

The simplest method would be a refundable tax credit to all families with children living in the home regardless of work or income status, the size of the credit varying with the number of children living at home. George Yin and his colleagues list a number of advantages. Benefits would be received in a timely fashion with each paycheck. Beneficiaries would not have to file complicated forms. Voluntary participation would not be an issue. Employers would not be burdened. Limiting the benefit to an exemption from taxes would eliminate the incentive to report fictitious income. The benefit would be automatically provided to middle- and upper-income taxpayers by adjusting the withholding amount. Low-income families could get advance payments, but there would not be the disincentives of the EITC advance-payment option (for example, all employees fill out the same, simple form indicating the number of children in the household). Requiring Social Security numbers for children would eliminate double-claiming. The principal disadvantage of the family allowance benefit lies in targeting, and for this reason there is considerable opposition to an across-the-board refundable tax credit.[76]

The cost of a $1,000 refundable tax credit would be $40 billion. But its antipoverty effects would be substantial. It is estimated that a $1,000 refundable tax credit (per child under eighteen), an assured child support benefit ($2,000 for the first eligible child), and national health insurance would reduce the poverty rate by 43 percent and the AFDC caseload by 22 percent, raise the annual incomes of poor families by $2,500, and enable AFDC recipients to work more hours.[77]

Although the expanded EITC or wage subsidies will make a significant improvement in the income of the working poor, it will still leave many families below the poverty line. It must be accompanied by further increases in the minimum wage.

Raising the Minimum Wage

In the decades prior to the 1980s, a full-time worker with a family of three, working at the minimum wage, was above the poverty line. During the 1980s, the Reagan administration refused to raise the minimum wage ($3.35 per hour) and its value fell sharply. In 1991 it was finally raised to $4.25 per hour, but since then its purchasing power has slipped; by 1996, the minimum wage had sunk to its lowest level in more than forty years.[78] Finally, new legislation was passed raising the minimum wages in two stages—to $4.75 in October 1996 and $5.15 on September 1, 1997. The Department of Labor estimates that when the full effect is in place, 9.7 million workers will have received a raise, and minimum-wage workers will receive an additional $1,800 per year in potential income.[79]

Not everyone is covered by the minimum wage. The Department of Labor estimates that only 30 percent of all employers and approximately 70 percent of the workforce are covered by the Fair Labor Standards Act (FLSA).[80] The most significant exemption is for small businesses; more than eleven million firms have gross annual incomes below the FLSA minimum of $500,000. Although most exempted employees are probably teenagers, it is likely that many exempted small retail businesses employ young welfare mothers. And these wages are often substantially below the federal minimum wage.

Given the low level of the minimum wage, the popular support for raising it,[81] and the fact that raising it would appear to be a more attractive policy option than redistributions financed through taxation, one would expect policymakers to seize upon this initiative. In fact, raising the minimum wage is quite controversial, especially in the business community and among professional economists.

Economists have long held to the proposition that raising the minimum wage would decrease employment; that it would reduce benefits; that it would raise prices; and that it is a blunt, if not ineffective, method of relieving poverty since most minimum-wage workers are teenagers who live in nonpoor families. The relationship between low wages and low household income is tenuous. Comparatively few workers are in minimum-wage jobs, and they quickly progress to higher-paying jobs. The EITC is a much more effective method of helping the poor.[82]

Many of these tenets are now being questioned. As to job mobility, teenagers move out of below–minimum-wage jobs fairly quickly as they gain experience, but at age twenty-one a fifth are still below minimum wage.[83] The same percentage—about 20 percent—of minimum-wage workers also remained trapped at that level. These tend to be part-time workers, older workers, minorities, and workers without high school diplomas.[84] As noted, recent research has shown that mobility is decreasing, especially at the lower wage levels.

The major argument against raising the minimum wage is that it will reduce employment; indeed, this hypothesis is an article of faith among most economists.[85] However, in several recent empirical studies, based on the 1990–91 increase in the federal minimum wage and the establishment of a teenage subminimum, the opposite was found—both employment and hourly and weekly earnings *increased*.[86] David Card and Alan Krueger, in their recent book summarizing the state of empirical research on the minimum wage, found no systematic evidence that employers reduced benefits to compensate for the increase in wages. As to redistribution effects, Card and Krueger found that minimum-wage workers were disproportionately members of families in lower earnings categories and that the increases in the federal minimum wage led to significant increases in the wages of workers at the bottom of the wage distribution. However, they emphasize that all of these effects are quite modest; in fact, the intensity of the debates both for and against raising the minimum wage is out of proportion to the modest impact on the national economy.[87]

Thus, it would seem that raising the minimum wage would perhaps (modestly) *increase* rather than decrease employment, and would have more distributional effects than previously acknowledged. These conclusions are vigorously disputed,[88] but at the very least there is little support for the conclusion that if there were adverse effects, they would be significant.[89] In any event, raising the minimum wage, *in combination* with the earned income tax credit, plus food stamps, will have a substantial effect in improving the returns from low-wage work and reducing poverty.[90] This combination should not only make work more attractive but also reduce the use of welfare by low-wage working mothers.

Integrating Related Income-Maintenance Programs

The above proposals increase the earnings from work. However, many workers combine work with various income-maintenance programs. Although the most common are food stamps and welfare, there are other means-tested programs. Of special importance will be Medicaid which, under the Personal Responsibility and Work Opportunity Reconciliation Act of 1996 (PRWOR), has its own, independent financial eligibility rules. There is a need to integrate these various means-tested programs with paid labor in order to lessen the disincentives to work.

For example, under the prior law, the tax rates of AFDC discouraged work. For the first three months of employment, the first $30 a month in earnings was disregarded, along with $90 a month to cover work-related expenses (such as transportation), and a deduction for child care costs that were in fact incurred. Thereafter, there was a 100 percent tax rate. Quite often, a family could be worse off working than on AFDC. The disincentive effects of AFDC were well known, and many states, under waivers, relaxed the rules in order to reward work.[91] For example, in Colorado, a family of three with one full-time worker can receive welfare until that worker's wage rate reaches $6.48 per hour.[92] This practice, in effect, raises the financial eligibility cut-off (families remain eligible with higher earned incomes), and thus increases the combination of work and welfare.

New York also experimented with a program that rewarded work by lowering the "tax rate" on earnings. Known as the Child Assistance Program (CAP), it was available to single-parent AFDC recipients with at least one child covered by a court order for child support from the noncustodial parent (this was designed to encourage child support enforcement).[93] Although the grant amount per child was lower than the AFDC grant, the parent could keep 90 percent of her earnings until her earnings reached the 1990 poverty level. Over that level, her grant was reduced by 67 cents for every dollar earned. There were no resource limits, food stamp benefits were given in cash, and the child care stipend was given in advance. The program was voluntary and administered separately from AFDC. For CAP to be financially advantageous, the mother had to earn more than $350 per month, which represents half-time employment at minimum wage. Thus, a parent with two children and two support orders earning $350 per month would have had a total gross income just about the same as if she had been on AFDC. But if her earnings increased to $500 per month, she would have a gross income gain of $102 per month. Since the program was available to all AFDC recipients, the treatment group included many who did not participate in CAP. In fact, only about 16 percent of those eligible for CAP actually took advantage of it at any time during the five years (which compares favorably to the participation rate in many mandatory programs). Therefore, the evaluation measured the impact of the *opportunity* to participate in CAP.[94]

The five-year evaluation found the following:

- CAP led to 20 percent higher earnings over the five years (an average of $2,613 more than the controls).
- There was a 4 percent reduction in public assistance payments (an average of $1,613 less in assistance over the five years).
- There was a modest overall financial gain to the participating families, but it was not statistically significant.
- Government saved, on average, $2,366 per family over the five years.
- The administration of CAP required a modest increase in government expenditures (an additional $237 per household).

The researchers concluded that CAP presents a viable alternative to mandatory welfare-to-work programs, especially since the results compare favorably with those of GAIN.[95] Indeed, one California county, Monroe, achieved comparable results to those in Riverside. Yet the program was not mandatory and did not require extensive government expenditures. From our perspective, CAP presents a potentially viable model of combining welfare and work that is relatively simple to administer and, most important, is not punitive. It offers sufficient incentives to work while providing the mothers with a basic income support.

The TANF does not provide a favorable context to implement programs such as CAP. Although the existing taxing and disregard rules are no longer applicable and the states have even more flexibility, the TANF and state cut-offs will discourage the longer-term combination of welfare and work.

There are also welfare asset limitations which have to be integrated. This will be discussed below.

Food stamps. Food stamps is an important source of additional income.[96] More than 87 percent of welfare recipients receive food stamps, providing an important supplement.[97] However, as part of PRWOR, food stamp benefits were reduced; among other things, the maximum benefit was reduced by 3 percent.[98] The question is, what happens to food stamp eligibility as more welfare recipients increase their earnings and either combine work with welfare or leave welfare altogether?

Food stamp benefits are a function of household size, countable net income, and maximum monthly benefit levels. Food stamp allotments cannot be counted against other welfare programs. Benefits are adjusted to inflation. The maximum monthly benefit for a three-person family (with some exceptions) is $313, now less 3 percent. In fiscal year 1995, monthly benefits averaged $71 a person and about $175 a household. In 1995, 26.6 million people used food stamps, down from the all-time high of 27.5 million in 1994. The average household size is 2.6.[99] In general, individuals living together are a single household unit and their income, expenses, and assets are normally aggregated in determining eligibility and benefits.[100] Except for households composed entirely of AFDC, SSI, or general assistance recipients, monthly cash income is the primary financial eligibility criterion. Rules govern what is includable, what is disregarded,[101] and what can be deducted.[102] Again, except for AFDC, SSI, or general assistance households, net monthly income cannot exceed 130 percent of the poverty line. For a three-person household (with some exceptions), the cut-off is $1,364 (gross) per month.[103] There are also asset limits.[104]

The current asset limitation with both food stamps and welfare should be changed. Under the prior AFDC rules, the limit was $1,000; for food stamps it was $2,000. In neither program has the limit been adjusted for inflation for a number of years. One issue regarding the asset limit involves the EITC. As noted, the overwhelming majority of EITC filers prefer the year-end lump-sum payment. At present, EITC payments are disregarded for both AFDC and food stamps, but only for the month during which the EITC payment is received and the following month. This means that a working family that receives a substantial EITC payment—the maximum benefit is $3,400—and wants to save it for education or training, or move, or for other purposes, would risk losing eligibility for AFDC and food stamps. The Clinton administration has proposed that EITC payments be exempt from the food stamp assets limit for twelve months. The same rule should apply to TANF recipients.[105]

An additional asset limitation change also should be made for designated purposes (such as self-employment enterprise, education, and homeownership). The Bush administration, in fact, proposed allowing AFDC families to accumulate assets up to $10,000 for designated purposes. Some states have increased the welfare asset limitation.

Another asset limitation problem, which has particular applicability for working families, involves the fair market value of a car. Set in 1977, the value of the car cannot exceed $4,500 regardless of the equity. There are no exceptions for cars that are needed for commuting. If the limit had been adjusted for inflation, it would be more than $10,000. Raising the vehicle limit would, of course, increase eligibility and raise food stamp costs. Still, cars are needed for work.[106]

There is a food stamp work requirement. Adult applicants must register for work and must accept a suitable offer, or engage in job search or training, as required by the welfare agency.[107] Those who are exempt are, among other things, already working at least thirty hours per week or earning the minimum wage equivalent, or are already complying with other program requirements (such as AFDC work and training requirements). There are numerous disqualifications for food stamps. For example, food stamp eligibility is lost if the family head voluntarily quits a job without good cause, or is on strike, or is not a permanent resident or citizen. All of these provisions need integration with employment. For example, we argue that mandatoriness in welfare is counterproductive; the same would apply to food stamps. Similarly, other food stamp disqualifications, such as quitting work, should be harmonized with unemployment insurance, discussed in the next chapter.

This chapter has spelled out the policy proposals that follow from our reconceptualization of the majority of AFDC recipients as part of the working poor. The proposals offered above and in the following chapter apply to all of the working poor, hence to the majority of recipients. The aim is to increase the earnings from work, while recognizing that some of the working poor will, from time to time, also have to rely on income-maintenance programs.

In the next chapter, we continue the discussion of other benefits that are necessary to make work pay.

Chapter 6

Employment-Related Benefits

If poor mothers, especially single mothers, are expected to work then it is obvious that they have to have child care and health care benefits. This chapter address these two pressing issues. We include a discussion of child support. Despite the energy that is going into increasing child support payments, it is not likely to be of much significance for most of the families that we are concerned with. The chapter then moves to benefits for people who are out of work, either because they have lost their job (unemployment insurance) or because they are disabled. Both programs are designed to be safety nets for the working population, but they need to be reformed to take account of the rise of mothers in the low-wage labor force and the changing nature of employment.

Child Care

Americans are in a state of denial about the crisis of child care. In a prior age—when the image of America was the two-parent family, with the husband earning a family wage and the wife as mother and homemaker—the world of Ozzie and Harriet—children were cared for by their mothers, at least until school age; families stayed together; relatives lived close by; and all lived in safe, supportive communities.[1] Child care was a private matter. Today, because of both the dramatic changes in family formation and the entry of mothers—both single and married—into the paid labor force, the issues of child care are dramatically different.

The crisis in child care cannot be stated more bluntly: the state of child care in America—especially for the working poor, the working near-poor, and welfare mothers trying to work or required to work—poses a significant danger to millions of infants, children, and adolescents. They are at high risk of being compromised both developmentally and in health status; they will suffer, and so will the rest of society.

The recent literature on child care is extensive. In this section, we summarize the following points: the risk factors of *mediocre* or inadequate child care; the demand for child care; the problems faced by consumers of child care; and the characteristics and costs of quality child care.

The risks of inadequate child care. Judith Musick starts her essay "The High-Stakes Challenge of Programs for Adolescent Mothers" with the following quote from the journal of an adolescent: "When I was about 11 or 12 I was very lonely, so then I went to having sex and then I got pregnant and that was my way of curing my loneliness [by] having kids. That's the best thing I have in this world and that's my kids."[2]

Musick is concerned with the question of why adolescent girls (and boys, for that matter) knowingly choose, often repeatedly, what amounts to self-destructive behavior—unprotected sex, repeating exploitive relationships with men, substance abuse, school failure, dropping out of special programs, and so forth. Her basic argument is that because of an impoverished early childhood, one in which these children were neither cared for nor protected, they are psychologically unprepared to negotiate the challenges of the teen years. Among other problems, they lack a sense of self and identity and a trust in adults. "In the search for the acceptance and love they crave, these girls will take many risks and few precautions. The capacity for self-care is, after all, *predicated on a history of being cared for and protected by others.*"[3]

Musick goes on: "Abusive or neglectful experiences in childhood do much more than foster bad attitudes and actions; they act to shape an inadequate adolescent sense of self and identity, one which prohibits forward movement in positive, self-enhancing ways, even when 'opportunities' present themselves." Although most studies focus on abusive adults—parents, stepfathers, boyfriends—Musick argues that "even relatively minor developmental damage can create vulnerabilities which diminish the ability to sense and actively avoid dangerous or risky situations and behavior, and in such environments danger and risk are the order of the day."[4] Life experiences in early childhood give these girls little or no foundation for resisting the internal and external pressures of the teen years. They are psychologically unprepared. For girls as well as boys, life in an impoverished environment can begin with a neglecting or abusive mother.[5]

Many children experience good-quality child care outside the home and do fine. And many children and adolescents who experience poor-quality child care are more resilient than others, and do grow up to become successful adults. As we will discuss below, much depends on the type of child care. *But the major policy issue is mediocre child care;* and mediocre child care has potentially harmful effects on school-age children left alone, preschoolers, toddlers, and infants. The growing numbers of *infants* in day care and the evidence of risks of harmful effects are especially disturbing.[6]

The point that Musick and many others make cannot be ignored. The daily nurturing, the warm, loving, human interaction that we (the readers of this book) experienced growing up and provided our own children, from the moment of birth, cannot be assumed in the exploding world of day care for large numbers of families today. It is the extent of mediocre day care that is the issue. "Child care can strengthen or undermine children's cognitive and social development. If child care quality is high, children learn rapidly, develop strong attachments to adults, and behave socially toward other children. If quality is low, children learn more slowly, develop less secure attachments, and demonstrate less sociability and consideration for others. These findings have held up in numerous settings, involving both group day care centers and family day care homes. In short, child care quality affects how children grow up, for better or worse."[7]

The National Commission on Children says: "Children are not inevitably impaired by out-of-home care during the first year. However, when they are in care for more than 20 hours per week, and when the quality of care is not sensitive and responsive to the special developmental needs of infants, the risks of problems are greatly increased."[8]

Inadequate child care also takes its toll on the parents. Child care problems, not surprisingly, contribute to family stress, depression, and ill health of the parents. Almost a third of employed parents are dissatisfied with their present child care arrangements and would change if they could; approximately the same percentage of women think that a mother should stay home with their children until school age. At the same time, a substantial number of women would like to work in the paid labor force but cannot because of the lack of child care. The General Accounting Office reports that reducing the costs of child care would substantially increase the likelihood that poor, near-poor, and nonpoor mothers would work.[9]

The quality of child care has significant impact on the work experiences of the parents (primarily mothers). Problematic child care can result in distractions, low morale, low productivity, absenteeism, quitting, and turnover. According to the Census Bureau, during a one-month survey, nearly 8 percent of mothers with the youngest child between one and two years of age lost work time because of a breakdown in child care; in a national survey, 15 percent of mothers had lost work time during the previous month because of a child care problem.[10] All of these factors add to the stress of these families.[11]

The demand for day care; the price of day care. The number of children who are either in day care or are potential consumers of day care is astronomical. In 1991, the National Commission on Children reported that nearly 20 million children are in the care of an adult other than a parent, grandparent, or sibling. And an estimated 1.3 million school-age children (ages five to fourteen) are left alone when not in school.[12] The mothers of most of the children in care or left alone are in the paid labor force. In 1994, 60 percent of mothers with preschool-age children and more than half of all mothers whose youngest child is under age two were in the paid labor force. The rise of single-parent families and their increased participation in the paid labor force contributes significantly to the demand for child care.[13] Child care is even more of an issue for low-income mothers, since they are more likely to be single parents.[14]

Given the stagnation of wages, and no signs of change in family formation, these trends are likely to continue for the foreseeable future. Both single and married mothers will have to participate in the paid labor force. Mothers will be working longer hours, there will be more shift and weekend work, parents will be spending less time with their children, and children will be spending more time in day care. Moreover, it seems likely that increasing numbers of very young children and infants (up to twelve months) will be placed in child care. As of 1992, the majority of mothers of *infants* were in the paid labor force.[15] Depending on the current and proposed welfare changes, mothers in some states will be required to seek work *three* or *four months* after the birth of their child.[16] This is the trend, despite the words of the National Commission on Children:

> The first years of life are a period of great vulnerability and opportunity. Infants and toddlers are wholly dependent on their parents (and other caregivers when parents are unavailable) to meet their basic needs. Without adequate nutrition and nurturing to fuel their rapid development, many children suffer delayed or stunted growth, impaired intellectual development, unresponsiveness, and low resistance to infection. . . . [In short], when parents, especially mothers, must return to work immediately following birth or adoption, the opportunities for establishing loving and trusting parent-child relationships are often compromised.[17]

Child care issues involve availability, cost, and quality. Group day care centers are increasingly preferred to family day care homes, if for no other reason than that formal arrangements tend to be far more stable than informal day care, and parents report a great amount of lost work time because of informal child care no-shows and other problems.[18] Yet centers are often filled to capacity. A 1990 government study reported that centers across the country were operating at almost 90 percent of capacity.[19] The problems of availability are more acute for infants and toddlers—almost half of all group day care centers require children to be toilet-trained; there are also restrictions against school-age children, children with disabilities, children who cannot speak English, who are ill, or who require evening or weekend care. Families of these children increasingly have to rely on family day care or kin-provided child care; and many school-age children are left on their own.[20]

The cost of child care is a major problem. Costs vary considerably. Estimates range from $3,300 per year per child (1991)[21] to $4,800 (1994).[22] Infants and toddlers are more expensive. William Gormley says that in 1993, the "average undiscounted fee for full-time infant care at a group day care center was $5,412 per year. In many parts of the country, however, infant care can cost as much as $200 per week or approximately $10,000 per year."[23] In a recent study of child care prices in six communities, the average price for full-time infant care at a center ranged from $3,276 per year to $8,076. As the report says, "To put these figures in perspective: a full-time minimum wage worker paying the average cost for care for an infant in a center would pay at least 50 percent of family earnings for child care in five of the six sites. If the worker could obtain care with the lowest-priced provider in their community (something which is not always possible and may not be desirable in terms of quality of care), the share of family earnings spent on child care still would be more than 35 percent of earnings in four of the six sites."[24]

Not surprisingly, the relatively high costs of child care effectively exclude many poor and near-poor children from formal child care, including Head Start and other public programs. Significant numbers of mothers use kin-provided child care.[25] Many parents, including middle-class parents, cannot afford to go to work because of child care costs.[26] The higher the cost of child care, the lower the probability of starting work and the higher the probability of leaving work. And parents with poor-quality child care are more likely to leave work than parents with higher-quality child care.

Working-class families, because of their low wages, can only afford low-cost care and are more likely to use relative care than center care.[27] Most centers do not offer sliding scale fees or accept subsidized children. However, even if a program is available, there may not be space.[28] Because increasing numbers of mothers with very young children are entering the paid labor market, more infants and toddlers are in family day care, sitter, or relative care rather than center-based care.

Then there is the issue of scheduling. One-third of working-poor and more than 25 percent of working-class mothers work weekends, which means that they cannot use most centers and family day care. Almost 10 percent of mothers work at night, and they are unlikely to use center care. Finally, almost half of working-poor parents work on rotating or shifting schedules, which also impacts on the stability of child care.[29]

Whether families pay for child care varies, of course, with socio-economic class. Whereas only 8 percent of nonworking poor pay for child care for their youngest child, the percentage jumps to 27 percent of the working poor, 32 percent of the working class, and 43 percent of the middle class (not all of these families have an employed mother).[30] Not surprisingly, with a single employed mother, the percentages increase markedly: 44 percent of the working poor, 69 percent of the working class, and 62 percent of the middle class. Dual-earner families also had high percentages paying for child care.

Most families receive subsidies for child care (at least through the tax system), but both the form and the amount make a difference. Direct child care assistance is usually limited to families below the poverty line.[31] In fiscal year 1993, the total federal amount for these programs was $1.74 billion; there are proposals for increases. Still, the largest source of federal support is the non-refundable dependent care tax credit. The credit offsets child care expenses for working parents up to a maximum. This program cost $2.5 billion in 1993, and most of the 6 million families that received the credit are middle- and upper-income.[32]

Given the incomplete data, it is hard to make reliable estimates as to how well these and the other federal programs are used.[33] It is estimated that 18 percent of working-poor and 12 percent of working-class families receive financial assistance. Single-parent families, regardless of income group, were more likely to receive child care assistance—about 20 percent. Families with children in center-based programs were more likely to be receiving financial assistance.[34] In any event, there is no doubt that many eligible families do not receive assistance. The General Accounting Office reports estimates of children waiting to receive subsidies ranging from 40,000 in Texas to 225,000 in California. Sandra Clark and Sharon Long say that "in San Francisco, a low-income working mother can wait up to two years to receive a subsidy for a toddler and one year for an infant."[35] "In helping a low-income working mother (earning 150 percent of poverty) find care for her children, the [child care resource and referral agency] . . . estimated that it would take 6 months to obtain funds to place an 8-year old in after care, 2 years to place a 3-year old in care, and 1 year to place an infant. [The agency] staff reported that, in the meantime, they would advise the mother to 'make do' as best she could."[36]

How much do families pay for child care? In 1990, the average weekly amount was $60 for a middle-class family, $45 for a working-class family, and $38 for a working-poor family. *However, the $38 per week represented 33 percent of the household income of the working-poor family as compared to 6 percent of the household income of the middle-class family and 13 percent of the working-class family's.*[37] How much does $38 a week buy? Even mediocre center-based care averaged $95 per week per child.

The quality of day care. What is the quality of the services that are purchased? Quality in child care comes down to the nature of the interactions between provider and child. Quality, like most items in this world, usually depends on cost. With child care, however, there is the idea, especially when it comes to subsidizing the poor, that the cheapest care—family care—may be good enough. States have great flexibility in setting the maximum payment for child care for working mothers. They use a variety of formulas that usually come out to a percentage of the "market rate."[38] There are no guarantees that these provisions will equal the actual cost of child care. At least in California, the "market rate" is the rate for family-member child care.

Family-member day care has an intuitive appeal—the image of the grandmother rather than a stranger looking after the child; it is cheaper than licensed care; and it is a way of employing additional poor families. In contrast to Europe, which also relies heavily on family care, in the United States almost all family day care—up to 90 percent—is unregulated. Licensing is costly, and as a consequence the vast majority of family day care providers avoid regulation. Either family care is exempt from regulation—because of the small number of children—or it is operating illegally.[39] Several studies have shown that regulated family day care provides better service in terms of physical setting, planning, basic care, and language, learning, and social development. The children in licensed homes are more likely to engage in group play.[40] Yet, since the great majority of day care for the working poor is unregulated, it is not surprising that lower-income families are less likely to use regulated family day care than upper- or middle-income families.

As more and more mothers enter the paid labor force, the clear trend is to favor formal center-based child care. By 1990, almost a third of the youngest preschool children of employed mothers were in center-based care, and most mothers who want to change their existing child care arrangements hope to move from relative care to center-based care.[41] Most center-based care (as well as licensed family day care homes) meet minimal state regulations, but not the higher standards of the National Association for the Education of Young Children, or of many experts in the field.[42] About a third of the centers are for-profit—and a sixth of these are run by chains—accounting for a similar percentage of children in child care. For-profits are cheaper than nonprofits, and chains are cheaper than the individually owned centers. According to Gormley, the lower price is not due to efficiency *but rather to a sacrifice in quality.* For-profits pay their staffs less, have higher turnover (which is harmful to children), have fewer teachers per child, and less-educated teachers. Within the for-profit sector, the chains have worse indicators than the independents. Quality of care is related to training and, more significant, commitments on the part of the child care providers.[43]

In any event, a recent study has shown that center-based child care, whether for-profit or nonprofit, can be quite problematic.[44] The study, conducted by four universities, collected data from 826 children in fifty nonprofit and fifty for-profit randomly chosen centers in California, Colorado, Connecticut, and North Carolina. The centers provided the services that the parents needed—that is, they met health and safety needs, and they were open long hours. Ninety percent of parents rated the programs as "very good." However, the parents overestimated the quality of care their children were receiving. Trained observers rated the same programs from "poor to mediocre."[45] The basic finding was that "child care at most centers in the United States is poor to mediocre, with almost half of the infants and toddlers in rooms having less than minimal quality." Minimal-quality care was defined as meeting "basic health and safety needs," although "little warmth and support" and "few learning experiences" were provided by adults. Only one in seven centers provided a level of care that "promotes healthy development and learning," the kind of warm relationships whereby children learn the trust and intellectual development necessary for school. Not surprisingly, the quality of child care was related to resources—higher staff/child ratios, staff education, training, and experience, and staff wages (97 percent of child care staff were female, with wages lower than even other female-dominated occupations).[46]

Providing quality day care. The task of providing quality day care is daunting. Very large numbers of children are spending considerable periods of time in child care in literally countless sites, ranging from center-based care (both for-profit and nonprofit) to family day care homes to kin-based care, most of which is unregulated. Large numbers of children are at risk because of high staff/child ratios, poorly trained and poorly paid providers who suffer from low esteem, lack of professionalism, and lack of commitment, and consequently, experience high turnover. There is a lack of monitoring by either the state or the parents. Parents find it difficult to either find or pay for high-quality child care; as a result, they also suffer in terms of employment and stress.[47]

The first issue in providing quality child care is to recognize the very large costs that are involved. Everyone is paying for cheap child care—the children, the parents, our society. What would good child care cost? In estimating the costs, Barbara Bergmann points out that subsidized child care cannot be restricted to women coming off of welfare, nor to one year per child, nor to half-day programs (such as Head Start), nor to single-parent families (which would not only discourage marriage but also ignore the needs of poor children in two-parent families). She also believes it important to extend the subsidy at least partially to middle-income groups to avoid "notch" problems and increase political support. There could be sliding-scale fees.

Bergmann estimates the costs of providing care to children of low- and middle-income families as follows: There are 19 million children under age five. Averaging the costs of providing care for infants and for older children, high-quality care for preschoolers costs approximately $4,800 per child per year. Providing the lowest-income fifth with free care and the next two-fifths with partially subsidized care on a sliding scale would cost $36 billion annually. There are 29 million children between ages five and twelve. Providing three-fifths of them care on the same basis before and after school, and in the summer, at a cost of $3,400 each, would cost an additional $39 billion. There would be other costs as well. As more mothers went to work, the cost of the EITC would rise. Also, unemployment insurance would rise as more qualified women workers would experience unemployment. On the other hand, there would be some savings in welfare and food stamps.[48]

Under President Clinton's proposed welfare reform, Gormley estimates that $1.8 billion additional dollars would have to be spent in 1999 for child care and related programs (such as an expanded at-risk program). If an additional one million children of working-poor parents were to receive child care subsidies, the cost would be an additional $1.7 billion, again in 1999.[49] On the other hand, the Congressional Budget Office estimates that under the TANF block grant for child care, federal funding would be reduced by $1 billion over fiscal years 1996–2000; furthermore, the states would no longer be required to match the federal funds; and previously eligible families would no longer have entitlements.[50]

In the meantime, current welfare reform is encountering the following dilemma: increasing the work requirements means increasing child care costs, which in turn means either reducing the work requirements or paying less per family for child care. So far, states have gone both ways. Under Wisconsin's W-2 plan, although child care benefits are extended to families up to 165 percent of the poverty line, the amount of the subsidy is considerably below the going rate. For licensed group and family day care centers and certified family day care providers, the maximum payments are set at 75 percent of the prevailing market rate. There is also to be a new category of provisionally certified family day care providers (with no training requirements); they are to be paid 50 percent of the licensed family day care center rate.[51]

In the five-state welfare reform demonstration projects report, each of the states saw an increase in the use of care assistance.[52] If the state could substantially reduce the welfare rolls, then the increase in child-care costs would be offset. On the other hand, in Iowa the shortage of child care funding forced the state, among other things, to change the focus of JOBS from education and training to immediate job placement and to establish waiting lists for recipients who wanted education and training. Michigan had to draw on its own funds after exhausting the federal allocation. Vermont was able to meet the increase in demand by having more recipients than anticipated use cheaper, unregulated providers. Because of the unexpected increase in demand, Colorado had to stop temporarily accepting applications for its low-income child care program. Even so, costs were higher than expected—in fact, twice as high for participants than for the control group. "Colorado state officials are extremely concerned that the child care costs associated with the demonstration project will 'break the bank' and make it impossible for the state to meet the cost neutrality requirement included in its waiver agreement with the Federal government."[53]

The plain fact is that child care is expensive relative to welfare costs. How expensive depends on state welfare benefits and local child care costs. In Vermont, a high-benefit state with low child care costs, child care (a day care center for a child under two) costs the state 72 percent as much as it costs to provide welfare to that family. In Colorado, a low-benefit state with high child care costs, it would cost the state almost 70 percent *more* for center child care than it costs to provide welfare to that family. Even with the cheapest care, it still costs 30 percent more than the welfare grant. The report concludes that even with reductions in the rolls, states with low to moderate benefits will have difficulty paying for child care costs unless the costs are low.[54]

But even assuming that the country was willing to spend large amounts of money for child care, what kind of structural arrangements should be in place so that parents would get what they are paying for? It should be recognized that as more money for child care becomes available, the for-profit market will expand—this certainly was the experience with nursing homes. As a result, child care may become more affordable, but unless quality-control mechanisms are improved, child care will also be more mediocre.[55]

Although the evidence shows that regulated care is better than unregulated care, it seems clear that it would be unfeasible to try to extend regulation—at least as traditionally practiced—to this vast, diverse industry. There should be some regulation—for example, standard setting, basic licensing of centers for health and safety—but on the whole quality child care ultimately will have to depend on the market. This means that parents, in addition to money, will have to have information and choice. Information will have to come from a variety of sources—government agencies, community-based institutions, local businesses, parent groups, and so forth.[56] In Chapter 7, we propose community-based social service agencies that would be employment-related. An important function of these agencies would be to provide a variety of child care services for families in the community—information, monitoring, advocacy, and back-up.

But whatever the reforms, it must still be recognized that there will be gaps. Day care will always vary in quality and availability; and parents and children will have special needs. For us, these inexorable facts lead to two conclusions. They strengthen our basic position that welfare-to-work programs should not be mandatory. Given the uncertain quality of child care and the potential harmful effects—especially for very young children and infants—child care decisions should be left to the individual family rather than a welfare department, which, as we pointed out in Chapter 4, is under a variety of pressures to get mothers into the paid labor market. The risks of mediocre child care are simply too high. Parents, of course, vary in their nurturing abilities, but if serious questions are raised about particular families, it is a matter for the child protection services, not welfare.

The second implication is that there should be paid parental leave to care for infants.[57] This is the European approach, which combines paid parental leave and government-funded centers.[58] It must be acknowledged, however, that the costs of paid parental leave are high. Gormley estimates that if all mothers stayed home for one year, at the minimum wage, the cost would be $27 billion per year (in 1999); at half the minimum wage, for intact families the cost would be approximately $18 billion per year.[59] For some families employers could pay part of the cost, but not for most, since we are talking about the working poor. In the end, there will be no substitute for *substantial* additional funding. At present, only a fraction of poor and near-poor children receive child care subsidies—estimates are as low as one-sixth. On the other hand, savings could be made by eliminating the child and dependent care tax credit for upper-income families (which cost $2.5 billion in 1993).[60]

Child Support

Reform of child support enforcement shares the policy characteristics of other reforms proposed in this chapter. Although clearly of concern to welfare, it is a much broader, long-standing issue and extends throughout all social classes. In 1990, approximately a quarter of all children lived with one parent (usually the mother); it is estimated that nearly half of all children born in the 1980s will live for a least part of the time with one parent.[61] Thus, reform efforts, if successful, will benefit a great many single mothers and their children who are not welfare recipients. As with the reform of low-wage work, health benefits, and child care, reform of child support enforcement breaks down the artificial distinctions between welfare mothers and other poor single mothers.

Concern about child support enforcement is justified. "Children who live with single mothers are five times more likely to be poor than children who live with both parents. When fathers leave the household, family income declines by about one-third. . . . Children born to unmarried parents suffer even more severe economic disadvantages. In 1993, about 66 percent of children who lived with never-married mothers were below the poverty line, compared to 38 percent of children who lived with divorced mothers."[62] Nevertheless, national concern to do something about child support arose only when welfare became a crisis. Public dollars were paying for dead-beat fathers. Part of current welfare reform is strengthening child support enforcement. In addition to the moral outrage, it is argued that if fathers of welfare children could be made to pay what they ought to pay, then welfare costs, welfare dependency, and poverty will be reduced.[63] Under the AFDC system, families received the first $50 of child support, with the rest going to the state for reimbursement for AFDC payments. In 1989, $1.5 billion was paid in child support, with most of it going to the government.

However, even under an ideal child support system—where realistic amounts would be set, collected, and paid to the custodial parent—poverty and welfare costs would decline only modestly. The reason, of course, is that between 13 and 26 percent of noncustodial fathers are themselves poor; for African Americans, the percentages ranged between 23 and 56. Virtually all (90 percent) poor noncustodial fathers did not work or worked only intermittently during 1990.[64] Under an ideal system—that is, one in which every noncustodial father had a support order, the order was set according to proposed realistic income guidelines (discussed below), and all orders were collected—welfare costs (including AFDC, food stamps, and Medicaid) would decline by $5 billion, AFDC rolls by 9 percent, and the poverty rate by 5 percent.[65] But an ideal system is a long way off.

Major reform of child support began in 1975, when a new part D was added to Title IV of the Social Security Act.[66] A Federal Office of Child Support Enforcement was established; the states were required to establish comparable offices. The federal government would pay three-quarters of the states' enforcement costs. The Family Support Act of 1988 imposed additional requirements on the states—minimum standards for the increases in proportion of legally identified fathers, improvements in collection rates, wage withholding for new support orders, adoption of federally approved uniform standards, and the mandatory updating of cases every three years. There has been a response, at least in some states—for example, computerized parent locator systems, paternity testing, garnishment of wages, and jail for defaulting fathers.[67] And there has been an increase in enforcement. Between 1982 and 1993, the ratio of amounts collected ($9 billion) per administrative expense improved by almost 40 percent. In 1993, more than 500,000 paternities were established, more than 4 million absent parents were located, more than 240,000 families left AFDC as a result of child support collections, and 12 percent of AFDC payments were reduced, again as a result of child support enforcement.[68] On the other hand, the real value of the awards declined 22 percent between 1978 and 1985; although there have been increases since then, in 1989 the average award was still 10 percent lower than in 1979.[69] One of the most serious problems is the matter of updating the awards. The Family Support Act requires awards in all AFDC cases to be reviewed every three years and all non-AFDC IV-D cases where either party requests a review. The results of five demonstration projects show that only about 20 percent of AFDC cases were reviewed, less than half that for non-AFDC cases, and that the review and modification process took approximately two hundred days. The updating problems argue in favor of support orders expressed as a percentage of income.[70] Under that system, the child support agency notifies the noncustodial parent's employer as to the percentage to be withheld, and as the income changes, the adjusted amount is withheld and paid over automatically.[71]

There are limits within the existing system; this is especially true with regard to welfare recipients. Georgia is one of the most aggressive and successful states in child support enforcement.[72] About a quarter of the welfare population receives at least some child support, a record far better than in most other states. The average support payment is about $100 per month. Although not nearly enough to eliminate AFDC, state officials estimate that with the combination of support payments and earned income, about eighteen thousand families left AFDC. Similarly, officials claim that AFDC rolls would have increased even more without aggressive support collections. However, there is only so much the state can do. The problem, say state officials, is usually not that the father cannot be located (most often he is named, or known, and easily found) but that a great many fathers are low-skilled and poorly educated, with low earnings; the money is simply not there. Then, some proportion of mothers either prefer "under-the-table" contributions or fear retaliation from absent fathers. Statewide, even under its aggressive approach, only 40 percent of fathers under orders to pay actually made payments, and that rate was even lower for welfare recipients.

Kathryn Edin amplifies these results in her study of 214 AFDC recipients in four cities (Chicago, Cambridge, Mass., San Antonio, and Charleston), supplemented by focus group interviews of seventy-one noncustodial fathers, collected by the Manpower Development Research Corporation.[73] Edin claims that the child support system is failing because although more than half of the women interviewed cooperate—at least with one of the fathers of their children—an equal proportion engage in what she calls "*covert non-compliance,* meaning that they had given false or misleading information to child support officials in order to protect the identity of one or more of their children's fathers."[74]

Although a majority of mothers (62 percent) cooperated with child support officials (for at least one of the fathers), less than a quarter of these received any money from the official system. A large part of the problem with the formal system is bureaucratic—the rules are complex, the lives of the fathers are often unstable, the process is lengthy, and, apparently, if the agency cannot find the father on the first attempt, the case simply languishes. In any event, the mothers believe that the system is unresponsive and compliance is not worth it, especially when they learn that the system keeps most of the money.[75]

More than half the mothers said that they either lied about the identity of the father of one of the children or failed to disclose crucial information (Social Security number, address, current employment). There were many reasons for covert noncompliance. About half of the women received "*covert support*"—on average $100 per month, which is twice the amount that they would have received under the formal system. Higher amounts were paid for younger children, and where the father secretly lived with the mother. These mothers preferred covert support because it paid more, they knew that the fathers' jobs were unstable and did not want them harassed or jailed (which would mean that they would get no support), and they thought that direct payments would be better for father-child relations. The informal system was also more flexible if the child had special needs (such as a winter coat) in any particular month. The mothers used the formal system for bargaining. Edin's findings were supported by the focus interviews of the fathers. Most were either unemployed or poorly employed. They knew that if they were involved with the formal system, not only would the family only get $50 but they would be exposed to penalties if they fell behind, including jail, which would further diminish their employment prospects.[76]

More than a third of the mothers did not pursue either avenue of support. The reasons varied. Some (25 percent) thought that their children's relationship with the father would be jeopardized. Others (33 percent) wanted to protect their control over their children. Others (24 percent) feared abuse. And others (18 percent) felt that there was no substantial relationship with the father.[77]

Although there is informal support, one must not exaggerate its importance. Judith Seltzer and Daniel Meyer report that most mothers (about 80 percent) who do not have a formal support order also do not receive informal support. Of those who do receive informal support, about half receive about $80 per month, on average (1987). Although not trivial (average annual family income in 1987 was about $9,200), informal payments "do not compensate for low levels of formal child support payments. Fathers who already pay formal child support are also more likely to make informal transfers than fathers who do not pay support."[78]

Edin draws the following conclusions: Current policy assumes that the primary reason for the lack of child support is lax enforcement. This may be true, she says, for the part of the population that is steadily employed at average wages, but it does not take into account the vast changes in labor markets for unskilled and semiskilled men. Nor does the present system take into account why welfare mothers would prefer an informal system; most are not interested in a system whose "main effects will be to make life miserable for absent fathers."[79] In the meantime, under TANF, states are required to reduce a family's grant by 25 percent if they fail to cooperate (without good cause) with efforts to establish paternity.

The more far-reaching proposal, spearheaded by Irwin Garfinkel, is a child support assurance (CSA), which is used in some European countries. This would be an addition to the Social Security menu of programs—an assured minimum level of child support, as with old age and disability. Child support awards would be set according to a nationally legislated formula based on a percentage of the noncustodial parent's income, and payments would be deducted from earnings, as Social Security deductions. The government would guarantee a minimum amount of benefit to those children legally entitled to private support. If the noncustodial parent paid less than the guaranteed minimum, the government would make up the difference. Thus, entitlement would depend not on the income of the noncustodial parent, or what was actually paid, but only upon the legal entitlement to private support. According to Garfinkel, an assured child support benefit would increase economic security and the establishment of paternity, substantially reduce both welfare and poverty, and mitigate the problem of low and irregular earned income. The benefit is not reduced as earnings increase. There are administrative costs, but Garfinkel argues that nationwide withholding and disbursement costs will be minimal, and certainly far less than the costs of redeterminations under the present system. Garfinkel believes that the costs would not be that great even though the benefits are not income-tested. The argument is that because most people marry others in the same socio-economic background, most expenditures would go to poor or near-poor families, and a large proportion of these families are already receiving welfare. He estimates that an assured benefit of $2,000 per year for one child would cost between $1 and $2 billion.

Health Care
AFDC recipients used to be automatically covered by Medicaid. Now, separate eligibility determinations have to be made for Medicaid. Although Medi-

caid is a troubled program, it is certainly far better than no insurance at all, which is the plight of vast numbers of the working poor. Reforming health care by extending coverage to the working poor dramatically illustrates our basic approach: the majority of welfare recipients are, and ought to be considered as, part of the working poor. Yet to a considerable extent they cannot leave welfare and fully enter the paid labor force because of the lack of health coverage. Childless adults, especially when they are young, can gamble (many have no choice); mothers cannot risk the health of their children.

There are two major problems with the U.S. health care system—its increasing cost and its lack of accessibility to lower-income populations.[80] Accessibility and cost are related; if access is increased, utilization and costs will be as well. The United States is already spending more per capita on health care than any other country—in 1990, the total bill was $666.2 billion—and these costs are rising.

Most Americans (about three-quarters) are covered by private insurance, mostly through their employment. There is a tax subsidy for this—the employer's contribution (5.1 percent of wages and salaries) is not taxable income to the employee. In 1992, the estimated value of the subsidy was $270 for taxpayers in the lowest quintile, $525 for the next quintile, and $1,560 for the highest.[81] The value of the tax subsidy is of no benefit to the poor. Very few poor are covered by employment-based insurance—in 1989, 2.7 percent of those 50 percent below the poverty line, 6.2 percent of those between 50 and 100 percent of the poverty line, and 13 percent of those between 100 and 150 percent of the poverty line.[82]

Medicare and Medicaid are the major public health care programs. Medicare covers the aged and those who qualify for Social Security benefits because of disability. Medicaid is the program for the poor. It covers about 10 percent of the population, including about 61 percent of all poor children. Medicaid is a joint federal-state program and states have been cutting back on eligibility, services, and access.

Rising health care costs are having a serious impact on business, and firms are increasingly cutting back coverage. Not only are more costs being imposed on workers (in the form of deductibles and coinsurance, for example) but, increasingly, firms are reducing coverage for workers' dependents, as well as for part-time and temporary employees.

As a result of incomplete federal programs, gaps and changes in employer-based insurance, fluctuations in employment, and increasing numbers of people working in jobs that do not provide health care insurance, "between thirty-three million and thirty-seven million U.S. citizens do not have any health insurance coverage at a point in time, including perhaps twenty to twenty-five million who were uninsured throughout the year. Another twenty million have too little health insurance to protect them from the financial burdens of a major illness."[83] The probability of being uninsured varies by class, race, age, and family composition. About 60 percent of the uninsured are in families with incomes below 200 percent of the poverty line; about 30 percent in families with incomes below the poverty line. Those who are poor (or near-poor) are more likely to experience longer spells without health insurance. Latinos are more likely to be without insurance than whites, with African Americans in the middle. Single-parent families are more likely to be without insurance than childless couples. And those without insurance are less likely to use health care; they are less likely to have a regular source of care, they have fewer contacts, they are more likely to delay care, and they receive different care.[84]

Not surprising, poverty and health problems go together. Survey data show that more reports of physical limitations and poor and fair health among low-income people as compared to those in middle or higher incomes. Poor health impacts on the ability to work—both the type of work one can do and the hours that one can work. Moreover, poor health of children limits the employment ability of mothers.[85] Low-income people are more likely to suffer from high blood pressure, obesity, cancer, infectious disease, heart disease (25 percent higher than average-income people), and violence. Low-income children are more likely to be exposed to lead and to contract AIDS, cancer, heart disease, congenital anomalies, and infectious diseases than children in higher-income families.[86] Because higher proportions of African Americans are poor, and they have a higher rate of teen births, they suffer a higher incidence of illness and poor health.

Because they have poorer health, low-income people tend to use more health care than higher-income people; yet the poor have greater difficulty in getting health insurance and health care. States are restricting Medicaid; in addition, many physicians refuse to take Medicaid patients because of the low reimbursement rates. Moreover, says Barbara Wolfe, access problems for the poor are likely to get worse. In addition to the AIDS and substance abuse epidemics, private insurance is becoming increasingly resistant to cross-subsidization (that is, charging paying patients an excess to cover the costs of provider deficits), there is a shortage of physicians in both the inner cities and rural areas, and preventive health care for the poor is declining (as evidenced by the lower rates of immunization in large urban areas).

At present, the difficulties in reforming the health care system for the poor seem truly daunting. Some of the health problems of the poor can be ad-dressed, at least in part, through information, education, and community-based programs. These would cover substance abuse (including alcohol and smoking), immunization, and prenatal care, as well as the location and availability of providers. Other problems are more intractable—for example, time and wages lost from work, transportation, child care, and the hassles of negotiating daily living in the inner cities.[87]

The major problem, by far, is the issue of costs and financing. Medicaid is already seriously inadequate. It covers fewer than half of those below the poverty line, and fewer than 20 percent of those up to 133 percent of the poverty line. Welfare recipients account for about a quarter of the Medicaid enrollees, but the big-cost increases are for the disabled, blind, and aged—particularly for long-term care (which is not covered by Medicare). In addition to these populations, all poor pregnant women and children born after September 30, 1983 are covered.[88]

A basic problem with Medicaid is its "bright-line" eligibility—one dollar above the financial line and the family loses coverage. This, of course, creates a strong disincentive to take a job (at least on the books) and to remain on welfare. And, indeed, many recipients who leave work give this reason. Covering poor pregnant women and children and, at least until PRWOR, the provision for continuing Medicaid coverage for one year after leaving welfare lessens this problem somewhat (now it is up to the states whether to continue this provision). Other problems with Medicaid include variations in coverage and services by state, lack of coverage for the working poor and adults that do not have dependent children, low reimbursement rates for providers, and the inability to combine Medicaid with private insurance.[89]

There are other sources of care for the poor—federal block grants for maternal and child health services, community health centers (providing primary care on a sliding-fee schedule), migrant health centers, and the Indian Health Service. In addition, hospitals provide more than $3 billion in "uncompensated care" (1988 figures). But most of these programs, especially the hospitals, are under increasing pressures.[90]

Given the recent debacle of comprehensive health care reform, it is difficult to recommend what should be done. Most Americans, and both major political parties, are reluctant to embrace systemic, costly reform. Yet there seems to be no alternative if we are to "make work pay" for the vast majority of low-income workers. Unless health care benefits are made available for this group, it is both idle and reckless to talk about moving substantial numbers of poor single mothers into the paid labor force. They simply cannot risk the health of their children.

A number of alternatives have been proposed for health care reform.[91] The dilemma, though, remains: expanding health care coverage will dramatically increase health care costs. For example, under the Clinton administration's ill-fated plan, which would have relied considerably on mandated employer coverage, federal subsidies would have amounted to $82 billion in 1998, $108 billion in 2000, and $173 billion in 2004, according to the Congressional Budget Office.[92] Some of these expenditures, it was argued, would have been offset by slowing the rate of growth in health care expenditures and in actual cost savings; however, it has proven extremely difficult to enact major changes that will significantly reduce health care costs. In addition to the extremely powerful interests in favor of the status quo, most Americans are reasonably satisfied with existing arrangements, or, not sufficiently dissatisfied that they favor major change.[93]

Barbara Wolfe suggests one set of reforms—covering *all* children under age nineteen for a specific set of services. This "Healthy-Kid" program would provide primary care in community care centers. Certain kinds of basic care would be provided free; others would be subject to copayments (on a sliding scale). If further care were needed, there would be referrals to private providers, but the community center would remain the case manager. The plan would be operated by the Health Care Financing Administration (HCFA), which currently runs Medicare. Financing would be by capitation or salaried physicians. This plan, argues Wolfe, could "go a long way" toward providing preventive care in low-income areas, a place of continuing care, and a place for at-risk teens, as well as enabling a number of current programs to be consolidated.

There are other advantages to the plan. Children are relatively inexpensive in terms of health care and this would avoid a dual-quality system. It would reduce the cost of employer-based insurance. Location would encourage appropriate utilization and reduce the use of emergency rooms.

Wolfe estimates the plan would cost between $40 and $45 billion, based on the current Medicaid average expenditure per child (approximately $800 per participant). To help finance the plan, Wolfe would cap the tax subsidy on employer-based insurance—for an estimated saving of between $26 and $36 billion. Loan forgiveness could also be used for professional staffing.[94]

Some of the poor would still be left out—singles, childless couples, parents in two-parent families. Wolfe would expand the coverage of the community health center network on a sliding-scale basis (many already do this). Another alternative would be refundable tax credits (vouchers) to allow poor families to buy basic coverage. The credit would be graduated and would extend to families with incomes up to twice the poverty level. States would require insurance companies to join a pool offering basic coverage. The disadvantage with this plan is the high tax rate. These programs, Wolfe argues, would be limited first steps to improving the health care system for the poor. Among other things, it would reduce the disincentive effects of Medicaid on labor-force participation and it would not have large negative employment effects.[95] There are other proposals for small steps. For example, Henry Aaron thinks that there might be bipartisan support for the direct delivery of health services though neighborhood clinics or schools.[96]

As with child care, providing adequate health care is a serious policy issue that must be confronted. Lower-income people get sick; they cannot be expected to be self-supporting in the paid labor market unless they have adequate health care. And adequate health care is very costly.

Reforming Unemployment Insurance

Benefits derived from work—whether earnings or wage subsidies, child care, or health insurance—depend on time spent working. We have seen, however, that the low-wage labor market has become increasingly characterized by contingent or part-time work. Moreover, the population that we are concerned with—mothers—often have to take time off from work because of family responsibilities.[97] The unemployment rate among single mothers averages 10 percent.[98] This raises the question of income support during periods of unemployment.

Insurance for death, illness, and involuntary unemployment is considered the pillar of the developed welfare state. Yet, as discussed in Chapter 2, in the United States unemployment insurance (UI) has always proved controversial. Although coverage has been gradually extended, the UI still remains a system of state programs under federal standards. Eligibility conditions and benefits vary.

At present, about 90 percent of employed workers are technically covered, although only about 30 percent of the unemployed actually receive benefits. Moreover, despite the steady increase in coverage, this fraction has been falling more or less steadily since the late 1950s, from roughly 50 percent of the unemployed.[99]

Unemployment insurance has three requirements for eligibility: (1) The claimant must have lost a covered job and be currently available and actively searching for work. In all but a few states, an employee who has been fired or quit is disqualified. (2) The claimant must be unemployed for a period greater than a minimum waiting period (usually one week) and less than the maximum duration (usually twenty-six weeks). In other words, UI benefits usually last only twenty-six weeks. In states that do pay benefits to quitters, there is a longer waiting period—usually ten to twelve weeks. And (3) the claimant must have received a minimal level of earnings or worked a minimum number of weeks during a "base period" prior to becoming unemployed. With some variation, most states calculate the base period as the first four completed calendar quarters prior to the quarter in which the person became unemployed.[100]

The UI system contemplates the full-time, male, year-round workers in relatively stable jobs. It is ill designed for the current changes in the workforce—the transformation from manufacturing to service, the decline in unionization, the rise of low-skilled, low-paying, no-benefits, contingent, and part-time work, and the huge increase in women in the paid labor force. Younger, nonunionized workers, females, workers with shorter unemployment spells are less likely to apply for benefits.[101] With women, especially mothers, there is more part-time employment (although a majority of mothers are in the paid labor force, only about a third are full-time workers), more dropping out, less availability for weekend or shift employment, and continued job segregation in jobs with lower pay, less security, and fewer benefits.[102] Moreover, to the extent that women might have to take night work, or work in isolated sites or in private homes, they are more likely subject to higher risks of sexual harassment and sexual violence, and thus more likely to quit "voluntarily."[103] It is no surprise that fewer unemployed women receive benefits than men.[104]

The UI eligibility requirements create the following problems for women workers, especially welfare recipients who are trying to work their way off of welfare or low-wage workers who are trying to avoid welfare:[105] First, the claimant must have worked sufficient hours or earned a sufficient amount. Workers who are in and out of the labor market because of the nature of the jobs or for family reasons may not satisfy this work test. Some states provide for more flexible ways of counting the base periods—for example, returning to work after a period of disability—but so far, there are no provisions making adjustments for birth or child care.

Second, if the mother has to quit work because of a breakdown in child care or for another family reason, she may be disqualified as having quit voluntarily. All states disqualify voluntary quits "without good cause." In about half of the states, "good cause" has to be "connected with work" or "attributable to the employer"—for example, the mother quits because of poor working conditions rather than family reasons. A common problem arises when an employer changes the terms of employment, making it impossible for the mother to work because of child care problems. Courts go both ways in deciding whether quitting under these circumstances is due to working conditions or family reasons.[106] Courts do recognize that medical reasons can constitute "good cause," but, as Deborah Maranville points out, these reasons are usually beyond the control of the claimant. Moreover, according to Maranville, the trend during the 1980s has been to make disqualification of the voluntary quit without good cause grounds for an absolute bar rather than a longer waiting period.

The voluntary-quit disqualification also causes problems with people taking multiple jobs or temporary work. Does the voluntary-quit disqualification apply to one or both jobs—for example, the claimant loses the full-time job and cannot afford the part-time job? There are conflicting interpretations concerning temporary agency workers—some courts hold that merely accepting temporary work is, in effect, a voluntary quit.

Third, individuals have to be "able and available for work" or fourth, they cannot refuse an offer of "suitable" work. As Maranville observes, this provision again assumes a male breadwinner who has full-time, year-round work, regardless of the shift. We have noted that most mothers are not full-time workers. Are part-time workers available for work? Again, there are splits. A few states expressly insist that part-time workers are available for part-time work. Some courts will allow part-timers to qualify if the restrictions are because of health, family matters, or school, but other courts require claimants to be available for generally accepted working hours. Maranville notes that mothers may not be available for weekend or nighttime hours. She says that although the courts are split here as well, the trend seems to be in favor of recognizing family responsibilities as good-cause refusal.[107]

Given the present state of UI, it is no surprise that the great majority of welfare recipients do not receive any UI benefits despite considerable work effort.[108] A study conducted by Roberta Spalter-Roth, Heidi Hartmann, and Beverly Burr found that over a two-year period, although 43 percent of AFDC recipients worked—about half-time—only 11 percent received any UI benefits. As might be expected, those who did not receive UI benefits worked at jobs with lower wages; and they had fewer jobs, fewer hours of work, and fewer weeks of full-time work than those who did receive UI benefits. But the former still engaged in considerable work effort. Almost 80 percent of the "non-UI" recipients had about the same work effort as the UI recipients, that is, the number of hours worked over the two-year period. The only significant difference was that the UI recipient held more jobs during the two-year period. Those who did not receive UI benefits tended to work in food service, cleaning, and personal service, spent more time on AFDC (combining AFDC with work), and were more likely to be a minority. Those who received benefits worked in sales, in clerical or administrative support positions, or as operators, handlers, and laborers, but not in service jobs. Those who received UI benefits were more likely to live in more generous states.[109]

Spalter-Roth, Hartmann, and Burr conclude that both UI and AFDC have a role to play in providing income support to poor mothers who are in and out of the paid labor force.[110] UI has to be made more responsive to those who display a high work effort but who have low, sporadic earnings. There should be a movable base period—that is, earnings should be computed in the four most recently completed quarters of work instead of the first four of the last five quarters. Some states already do this. States should also be required to set the base-period earnings requirement so that part-time or low-wage workers (who have a substantial tie to the labor market) are not disqualified for insufficient base-period earnings, or insufficiently high quarter earnings. The voluntary-quit and availability-of-work disqualifications have to be liberalized. Five states extend temporary disability insurance to cover family emergencies; this should be extended. The authors favor paid family leave during periods of non-employment. States should be required to consider part-time workers or previously full-time workers who now have child care constraints and are looking for part-time work as actively seeking work. Similarly, the requirement that recipients actively seek work should be satisfied when a mother has to restrict her search to shifts in which child care is available; similarly, refusal of a job that requires shift work when child care is unavailable should be considered good-cause. Claimants should not be disqualified when a seasonal job ends as long as the claimant has met the other UI requirements. The voluntary-quit disqualification should not apply if workers have to quit due to an employer decision that becomes inconsistent with parenting responsibilities, or is due to fleeing domestic violence, sexual harassment on the job, or other compelling family responsibilities.

Disability

The ability of poor men and women, especially welfare recipients, to work is partly determined by their own health status and those they have to care for. Disabled people are restricted in the kind of work they can do; employers are reluctant to hire people with disabilities; and family care problems are more difficult when the person to be cared for is disabled. Poverty is associated with high rates of ill health and disability of both adults and children.[111] Several studies using self-reported health status of single parents have shown that poor health inhibits the capacity to work and increases welfare dependency.[112]

Because self reports of disability may overstate its prevalence, some studies measure disability by using activities of daily living (ADL) and instrumental activities of daily living (IADL), which should provide a more accurate picture of the prevalence and consequences of disability among welfare recipients and their employability. Acs and Loprest, using the 1990 Survey of Income and Program Participation (SIPP), measured disability in terms of having some difficulty performing activities of daily living (walking, climbing stairs, bathing, dressing) or instrumental activities (doing light housework, lifting ten pounds, preparing meals, walking up stairs, using the telephone, keeping track of money and bills) or as having sensory/physical difficulties (hearing, seeing, speaking). They found that 20.1 percent of welfare recipients reported some limitation in the above activities, and 8.4 percent reported that they needed help or were unable to perform one of those activities. A substantial percentage had more than one limitation. Recipients with a disability were more likely to be older and married, less likely to have a high school education or have young children, and more likely to have been longer on welfare.[113]

Respondents were also asked whether their children had any disabilities and, if so, whether the children received special education or any therapy or diagnostic services designed to meet developmental needs. More than 11 percent of the families had a child with some limitation. Combined, more than a quarter (27.4 percent) of AFDC families have either a mother or a child with a disability.[114] Not surprisingly, having a disability affects the probability of leaving welfare for work. On the other hand, very few recipients (fewer than 1 percent) leave AFDC for SSI.[115]

Welfare recipients were also more likely to care for disabled children or other adults. The disability rate of children whose mothers were between fifteen and forty-five was 6.3 percent, while among children of welfare recipients it was 8.5 percent. More disabled women on AFDC had a disabled child (22.6 percent) than AFDC recipients without disability (10.4 percent). In addition, welfare recipients were more likely to care for another disabled adult (7 percent). If we assume that AFDC recipients who are disabled or care for a disabled person are exempt from work, then the number of welfare recipients eligible for work drops by a third.[116]

Finally, Barbara Wolfe and Steven Hill, using the 1984 SIPP data, tried to estimate the net impact (independent of other demographic and economic factors) of health status and caring for a disabled child on the likelihood that a single mother will be employed. They found that both factors significantly inhibited the ability of the mothers to be employed and limited the hours they could work when they were employed. On the other hand, Acs and Loprest were not able to find that the presence of a disabled child affected exits from welfare via work.[117]

Even these studies that rely on ADL may not adequately address other disabilities that single mothers may have to manage, especially mental illness and addiction. We do know that these conditions are more prevalent among poor people. Thus we suspect that the prevalence of disabling physical and mental conditions among welfare recipients may be underestimated. Nonetheless, these studies confirm that disability is an important contributor to poverty and the need for income support. Disability, either of the primary wage earners or of a dependent, is a significant factor in limiting the ability of welfare recipients to work. Thus, it is unrealistic to expect welfare recipients who have to manage their own or their dependent's disabilities to work full-time, and they cannot be expected to leave welfare as a result of earnings. At the same time, the data show that such recipients do work, to the best of their abilities, when on aid.

How, then, should social policy respond to the income needs of disabled welfare recipients? Prior to PRWOR, needy families who were deprived of parental support because of "physical or mental incapacity" were eligible for AFDC-Incapacitated (AFDC-I). However, that program was apparently underused. As a percentage of all AFDC cases, AFDC-I declined from 22 percent in the 1950s to less than 3 percent in 1983; since then the percentage has fluctuated around 3 percent.[118] In part, the declining fraction of incapacity cases is due to the increase in SSI disability.[119]

The mainstay income support program for the disabled poor has been supplemental security income (SSI), enacted in 1972. In some respects SSI has been quite successful in providing a national minimum income to the disabled poor. Federal benefits are currently set at 75 percent of the poverty line for individuals and 89.5 percent for couples.[120] With state supplementation, the maximum benefit in most states is close to the poverty line. These benefits, per person, are considerably more generous that those set by most states for AFDC. Moreover, the federal benefits are indexed to the consumer price index.[121]

The obvious question, then, is why disabled mothers or mothers who are caring for disabled relatives are on AFDC instead of disability? We noted that Acs and Loprest found that fewer than 1 percent of AFDC recipients leave welfare for SSI. The answer lies in the history and present administration of SSI disability. Enactment of SSI has created a class of "deserving poor," that is, poor people who, because of aging or disabling conditions beyond their control, cannot be expected to work and provide for themselves.[122] Initially, most of the deserving poor were elderly, but with the expansion of Social Security, larger numbers have become disabled.

Under SSI, a disabled person is defined as an individual who cannot engage in any substantial gainful activity (SGA) as a result of a medically determined physical or mental impairment which has lasted or is expected to last at least twelve months or lead to death.[123] Such a person becomes eligible if his or her countable income is less than $5,352 per year. Earnings averaging more than $500 a month are presumed to represent substantial gainful activity. In 1993, 56 percent of the disabled had a diagnosis of either mental illness or mental retardation, 11 percent had diseases of the nervous system and sense organs, 7 percent had musculoskeletal diseases, and 6 percent had circulatory diseases.[124] Among the children, 61 percent had mental disorders, mostly retardation.

The disability rolls expanded dramatically during the 1970s. Fearing that employers were using the program for early retirement, the federal government began imposing a series of reforms designed to restrict the program to the "truly" disabled. Attempts were made to classify disabling conditions, review and restrict the discretion of administrative law judges, and require periodic determinations.[125] Disability quickly became mired in administrative regulations. At present, eligibility criteria for determining both disability and resources are strict and complex. As stated, disability is defined as the inability to engage in gainful activity for a period of at least one year. With some exceptions, "gainful activity" means *any* gainful activity, and not the work one was formerly doing. For example, an injured construction worker would not be eligible if he could work as a sedentary night watchman. Furthermore, with some exceptions, it is irrelevant whether night watchman jobs are available or an employer would hire a disabled person. It is a hypothetical test.

Both eligibility and benefit amounts are affected by the income and in-kind support and maintenance available to the recipient; yet the determination and treatment of in-kind support and maintenance have been an administrative nightmare. Also, a recipient who lives in another person's household and is getting support from the household is eligible for only two-thirds of the basic SSI grant. Similarly, until the Supreme Court decision in 1990, SSI did not recognize functional disabilities in children.[126]

Most important is the earnings definition of the inability to engage in substantial gainful activity, which is currently set at $500 a month. Such a definition fails to recognize that many disabled persons do work or could work if adequate job-related support services were provided. Not unlike the case with AFDC, the demarcation between disability and work is untenable; it overlooks the fact that many disabled have extensive attachment to the labor market, and it discourages the disabled who could work if they were permitted to combine earnings with disability payments. Indeed, Charles Scott found that 79 percent of disabled SSI recipients had pre-application work experience, and 20 percent had some postapplication work experience.[127]

The line between disability and the ability to work is further complicated by the Americans with Disabilities Act of 1990 (ADA), which has implications for welfare-to-work programs. The primary purpose of the ADA was to eliminate the barriers that prevent disabled people from working and to provide equal employment opportunities to the disabled.[128] In brief, the ADA prohibits discrimination against qualified individuals with disabilities and requires employers to make reasonable accommodations unless those accommodations would create undue hardships on the employer. As Frank Ravitch points out, many issues require interpretation—what constitutes a "disability" under the

ADA, "reasonable accommodation," "undue hardship," and so forth. Still, the ADA has the potential significantly to increase the employment opportunities for the disabled. The question he raises concerns the potential conflict between the ADA and SSI's determination whether an individual can perform substantial gainful employment. To what extent can or will SSI take into account the possibilities for employment under the ADA and deny claims? (Or to what extent would a welfare office take the same position with respect to enforcing work requirements on a recipient who is disabled?) SSI, it will be recalled, uses general presumptions about the availability of jobs, regardless of whether those jobs exist or whether employers would hire the particular claimant. Would SSI (and welfare agencies) now expand their view of the availability of jobs under the reasonable-accommodations requirements of the ADA; that is, would SSI (and welfare) now *assume* that employers will make these accommodations? Furthermore, the ADA contemplates *individualized* determinations. Disabilities, and reasonable accommodations, are not static; and an employee who needs only minor modifications at one time may need more extensive ones later. SSI thinks in terms of generalities, and "millions of disabled individuals would be denied benefits based on the blanket assumption that they can perform jobs with reasonable accommodations, and that employers will immediately provide such accommodations."[129] None of the ADA requirements for employers are clear-cut.[130] Ravitch argues that SSI should not take into account the ADA reasonable accommodations in deciding disability decisions. That agency lacks the experience to understand or predict how these requirements would operate in fact. The only exception would be where the claimant is actually engaged in substantial gainful activity.[131] The same restrictions should apply to welfare agencies.[132]

Starting in 1990, as a result of a U.S. Supreme Court case, the number of children receiving SSI has more than doubled to 890,000.[133] In addition, the Social Security Administration revised and expanded the list of mental impairments that would qualify children for SSI. Awards based on the mental impairment listings tripled, while those based on physical impairments doubled.

The SSI program for children became extremely controversial. It was claimed that the standards are complex, subjective, and easily manipulated. Reports of fraud and abuse mounted.[134]

Despite its many limitations, SSI, with appropriate modifications, could provide an effective response to the economic needs of welfare recipients who are disabled or who care for disabled children. If such recipients were to be covered by SSI, their economic situation could improve significantly, and they would escape the stigma associated with welfare. To do so, several changes in SSI would have to occur, including those recommended by the SSI Modernization Project experts. First, the definition of disability, especially "substantial gainful activity," needs to be relaxed so that most recipients defined as disabled by ADL will be covered. Second, calculation of benefits needs to take into account the number of dependent children the disabled recipient must support, and the level of the basic support for the entire family unit should be set at or above the poverty line. Third, the proposed changes in the work incentives of SSI should be enacted, thus enabling the disabled recipients to increase and maintain their attachment to work. For disabled working mothers, these incentives should also include assurance of child care and exclusion of child care costs. Fourth, like other SSI recipients, disabled welfare recipients should also qualify for the various rehabilitation incentives offered by SSI, specifically (a) participation in plans for achieving self-support (PASS) which allow the participants to set aside earned or unearned income for a work goal; and (b) impairment-related work expenses (IRWE) which are excluded from earnings. Fifth, serious consideration should be given to expanding supported employment programs to disabled welfare recipients. These programs, initially organized for the developmentally disabled and later extended to the mentally and physically disabled, provide employment in *integrated* work sites at or above the minimum wage through the provision of *support* services.[135] We discuss some of these programs in Chapter 7.

Unfortunately, the 1996 reforms move in the opposite direction. With regard to children, the definition of disability has been sharply restricted, and it is estimated that more than 300,000 children could be denied benefits by 2002.[136] In addition, SSI recipients whose primary disability is alcohol and/or substance abuse were no longer eligible for benefits as of January 1, 1997. Recipients who have been incarcerated for more than thirty days, as well as most noncitizens, will no longer be eligible for benefits.[137] It is estimated that 850,000 families (15 percent) will lose benefits.[138]

Targeted Universalism

The major underlying point of our key proposals—improving returns from earned income; reforming unemployment insurance, welfare, food stamps, and disability insurance; improving child care and child support; and providing health benefits—is that they apply to the *low-wage worker*. By focusing our proposals on the relatively short-term AFDC recipients—who happen to be the majority of the caseload—we are reasserting their proper definition: They are low-wage workers who, from time to time, have to package additional social support with earned income. They are working, or trying to work, or have recently lost a job primarily because of the structural conditions of the low-wage labor market—low wages, lack of benefits, lack of child care support—

rather than lack of work effort. Moreover, even when these people are back on welfare, welfare only provides, on average, about a third of their monthly budgets.

Recasting the majority of AFDC recipients as low-wage workers has many advantages. Aid to low-wage workers rewards work—not dependency—which has been the source of political support for the EITC. Although minority workers are disproportionately poor, the vast majority of the working poor and near-poor are white. Thus, aid to low-wage workers, although of great benefit to minorities, is both race- and gender-neutral. Moreover, these proposals extend above the poverty line, into the moderate-income working class.[139] Thus, aid to low-wage workers is more "universal" than "targeted,"[140] in the same sense that Social Security retirement is considered universal in that all workers will eventually benefit, even though the poor aged workers and their families are blanketed in. So far, the EITC has enjoyed this kind of political support—tied to work effort rather than dependency or minority status. The principle of providing health benefits enjoys popular support, although reaching a consensus on how to provide health care to the working poor will, unfortunately, prove difficult for some time to come.

The hope is that by reasserting what we believe is the more accurate definition of the majority of AFDC recipients, by including them in programs designed to help the working poor and thereby reducing the size of the AFDC population, at least this group—again, the majority of the caseload—will shed the unjustified stigma of dependency. Attention then should be paid to the more difficult cases—the subject of the next two chapters.

Chapter 7
Employment Services

The inability to maintain steady employment is not unique to welfare recipients; it is common to both poor men and women with limited education and employment skills. As suggested in Chapters 5 and 6, we can make work pay once we put into place adequate income-support mechanisms that are attached to work such as the earned income tax credit, wage subsidies, child care subsidies, and health and unemployment insurance. Employment services need to be developed to ensure that all those who want to work can find employment, and that the obstacles to stable employment can be reduced if not removed. As we showed in Chapter 4, current welfare-to-work programs fail to achieve these goals. We propose to replace them with community-based employment services that will be available to all members of the community who seek employment. However, the effectiveness of such services is predicated on a deliberate national policy of relatively full employment and, if necessary, job creation.[1]

The proposed community-based employment services will be markedly different from existing welfare-to-work programs in several ways. First, they will be universally accessible and organizationally distinct from the local welfare offices. As we argued in Chapter 4, they must be completely decoupled from income maintenance. Second, participation will be voluntary, because a mandatory program is inconsistent with the kind of organization that is needed for an effective employment service. People changing programs require a cooperative relationship based on information and trust, developing into a partnership between the worker and the client. This relationship is founded on a *moral* conception of the client as a subject, rather than an object, as a person who is worthy of trust and support. Both the client and the worker have to believe that the client is there because she wants to be there, that she wants to participate, and that even though there may be setbacks, she will succeed. This moral conception is inconsistent with the threat of sanctions, and with the belief that the client is there not because she wants to but because the welfare department is threatening her family's well-being. The most successful programs are based on this kind of voluntary relationship. Third, the services will consolidate the plethora of employment placement and training programs under one organizational umbrella, thus making it possible to tailor services to the needs of the clients.

By proposing the new model of employment services, we also want to make clear that the ultimate decision as to whether mothers with young children should be employed is better left to them. The employability of parents, especially single parents, depends not only on the availability of employment services of the type we suggest below but crucially on family responsibilities.

Most welfare-to-work programs excuse recipients who are caretakers of disabled family members. Whether mothers of young children should also be excused is controversial. Prior to Temporary Aid to Needy Families, most welfare-to-work programs excused mothers of preschool children. Over the years, the upper age limit for welfare children has been lowered, first to two years, then on occasion one year, and now in some state initiatives to four months for the second child. We regard state-imposed rules in this area as a great mistake. The parent-child relationship, especially for the very young child, is one of the most intimate, personal, individualized relationships imaginable. Absent evidence of serious deviance, our society believes that parents should have maximum responsibility. As pointed out in Chapter 6, serious questions are being raised about effective childrearing when parents are working long hours and quality child care is either unaffordable or unavailable. Although the majority of nonwelfare mothers are in the paid labor force, most do not work full-time. The problems of balancing work with family responsibilities are exacerbated with single poor mothers. These mothers should be offered support and opportunities to enter the paid labor force, but they must be allowed to make their own decisions based on their own needs. For some good child care will be available, but not for others. Some will live in secure neighborhoods; others will have to supervise their children closely. Judging from past experience, most of these mothers will move into the paid labor force. The availability of jobs with decent earnings and benefits and an effective employment service will open up their choices.

An Integrated Model of Employment Services

A troubling feature of existing employment and training programs for the economically disadvantaged is that they are organized to serve specific target populations, resulting in overlapping jurisdiction, fragmentation of services, and administrative inefficiency.[2] There are currently more than 160 federally funded employment training programs, providing about $20 billion in employment training assistance. These range from Food Stamp Employment and Training to Women's Business Ownership Assistance.[3] There are 9 programs with funding of about \$2.7 billion in 1994 specifically targeted to the economically disadvantaged. These range from the Job Training Partnership Act (JTPA) to Student Literacy and Mentoring Corps. Similarly, there are 9 programs for dislocated workers, 4 for older workers, and 16 for young people. The General Accounting Office found that many of these programs serve the same clients and have similar goals.[4] Most provide the same type of service, and many clients enroll in several different programs. This is clearly an inefficient way to deliver services.

The model we are proposing is community-based employment services to be available to all who need them. It is predicated on a concept of a neighborhood service center which (a) promotes access through outreach, dissemination of information, and case advocacy; (b) provides a one-stop, integrated array of basic social services; (c) is staffed by an interdisciplinary team of service workers; (d) recruits many of the staff from the local community; (e) encourages the clients to be active participants in decision making; and (f) sets clear criteria of accountability and staff rewards on the basis of service outcomes.[5] Thus, the community-based employment services will provide a single entry point to a wide array of employment services, many of which will be housed in the center. It will assign the client a case manager responsible for accessing and coordinating the various services the client needs. The employment services offered by the center will be structured to reflect the particular employment needs of the community it serves. Thus, it calls for the consolidation of all the disparate employment training programs, especially those targeted to the economically disadvantaged, into a common funding stream, allowing each community to establish the mix of services most suitable to its circumstances.

The model we propose builds on the best experiences and lessons learned from various employment programs, including welfare-to-work, that have proven successful, especially with regard to poor single mothers. Two key features of these employment services are their universal accessibility and their complete separation from welfare. This enables the employment services to avoid the stigma attached to welfare. Equally important, they open their doors to men, including the fathers who could contribute to the support of their children if they were gainfully employed. By completely separating such services from welfare, they can concentrate on what they can do best—helping people find and keep jobs.

We envision such centers to provide three tiers of services. The first tier consists primarily of job development and placement, and postplacement support services. The second tier provides short-term remedial education and skill training, and the third tier offers an intensive and integrated educational and vocational training program. Each tier represents a higher level of intervention responding to the different needs of the potential clients. Each tier has been shown to be effective for the population it targets.

There are three key features to the three-tier model. First, the boundaries among the tiers are highly permeable and the interrelations flexible. Clients can move back and forth across tiers as their needs and circumstances change. Second, there is a major emphasis throughout on job development. That is, the agency will be staffed with job developers whose primary task is to ensure that jobs are available to the clients who are ready to enter the labor market. Traditionally, employment services have assumed a passive role in linking job seekers with employers. They have relied on employers to post jobs with the agency. As a result, the agency served as a "residual" employment placement service. In the new model, the agency will take a far more proactive approach, reaching out to employers, soliciting and ensuring job opportunities for their clients, and becoming an integral part of the hiring networks used by employers. Third, the employment centers will offer support services whose purpose is to keep the workers employed once they are placed in a job, and to help them cope with life events before they turn into debilitating crises. These support services may include child care, transportation, loans to meet unexpected expenses, referrals to treatment programs, peer support groups, and counseling.

The rationale for the three-tier model follows the dynamics of poverty, unemployment, and welfare. Lawrence Summers, who studied the dynamics of unemployment, has shown that the patterns of unemployment spells are not dissimilar to welfare dynamics.[6] First, he noted that even in a tight labor market, "over half of the joblessness is traceable to persons out of work for more than six months in a year." Second, the longer a person remains unemployed, the lower the probability of exit. Thus a substantial portion of the unemployed are not workers who are temporarily laid off or are between jobs. Rather, they are workers who want to work but cannot find a job, and the longer they stay unemployed, the worse the chances are that they will get a job. The best predictor of length of unemployment or welfare spell is human capital. The less the human capital (as measured in education, work experience, skill training), the longer the spell.

The three-tier model is directed, first, at providing immediate job opportunities to the unemployed in order to reduce their length of unemployment. For those who cannot obtain a job due to some educational or training deficiencies, the second tier is used to provide the necessary remedial services. Finally, for the small group with very limited work experience and education, third-tier services provide an intensive and coordinated program of education, training, and work experience. Thus, each tier of services attempts to compensate for the corresponding lack in human capital resources, while at the same time generating the needed job opportunities.

In proposing each tier in the model, we rely on notable field experiments that have demonstrated their relative effectiveness. We also take into account the costs and benefits associated with each tier, and some of the examples we cite have positive net values for both clients and government. Some, however, benefit the clients more than the government. As Daniel Friedlander and Gary Burtless note, there seems to be "a tradeoff between savings for government and income gains for the enrollees."[7] We subscribe to the principle that the long-term objective of social policy is to provide stable employment and improve earnings. Our three-tier model tailors the intensity and scope of services to the relative disadvantage of the client.

Tier I: Employment Development and Placement

The majority of welfare recipients, especially those with a high school diploma or some work experience, need, first and foremost, a job that provides a living wage (in conjunction with the appropriate income supplementation). When such jobs are available, recipients need help in connecting to the employers and presenting themselves in a way that increases their chances of being hired. The objective for these recipients is to shorten the time they remain unemployed, which will also reduce their time on welfare.

Therefore, a primary function of the employment services must be *job development*. The current emphasis of most broad-coverage programs is job club and job search. These are low-cost services aimed at serving as many recipients as possible by teaching them basic job search skills over a short period. However, much of the onus of finding a job falls on the recipients themselves. It is hard to tell whether job club and job search gives the participants job-hunting skills they lack or merely motivates them to go look for a job. The participants tend to rate them less favorably than other program activities, such as education and training.[8] Although job club and job search are useful, reliance on them without corresponding emphasis on job development could displace what should be the major emphasis of the employment services. Instead of focusing on the key problem facing welfare recipients—lack of jobs—these "motivational" services redefine the unemployment problem as residing in the recipients themselves and not in the labor market. In doing so, they divert attention from the real problem and shift precious resources away from the real task of job development. Undoubtedly, it is easier organizationally to focus on the deficiencies in the recipients than on developing job opportunities. Yet every successful employment program we are aware of has a strong job development and placement component.

Most people find jobs through informal networks. Evidence suggests that in the low-skill labor market, employers resort to network recruitment—referrals from their own employees.[9] Harry Holzer estimated that 35–40 percent of new hires were made via informal referral mechanisms. Other studies suggest that more than half of employees obtain their jobs through informal networks. From the employer's perspective, network recruitment saves costs by weeding out potentially undesirable employees. As Roger Waldinger points out, relying on current employees to recruit new workers capitalizes on the existing social structure in the workplace; the employees know who will make a good recruit and whom they do not want as coworkers.[10] When the employers tap into the social network of the employees for new workers, they also capitalize on that network to socialize and discipline the worker. Moreover, evidence suggests that for low-skilled jobs employers value workers' attitudes and demeanor more than their job skills. Because these traits are not readily observable, using current employees as recruiters ensures that persons with the right "attitude" will be hired.

Joleen Kirschenman and Katherine Neckerman found that for sales and customer service jobs, appearance, communication skills, and personality, but not education, were the key factors employers looked for. The preference for demeanor associated with white middle-class behavior was quite apparent. For clerical jobs, employers typically administered a basic skill test in language and mathematics, but also placed a premium on interpersonal skills and appearance that are also closely associated with white middle-class behavior. Finally, for low skilled blue-collar and service jobs, employers looked for dependability and willingness to work hard and cooperate with others, and they used race, locality, and class as markers for such traits. When employers emphasize personality traits over job skills, they are more likely to engage in statistical discrimination—use of group membership on the basis of race, ethnicity, class, and residence as proxies for desirable work traits. One of the consequences of statistical discrimination and the resultant network recruitment is that it reproduces the characteristics of the existing workforce, including race, ethnicity, and gender.[11]

Given these patterns of hiring, one can see how many welfare recipients will find it difficult to obtain employment because they carry with them "negative" markers such as being on welfare, being a single mother, living in an undesirable neighborhood, or being an ethnic minority. In addition to and because of statistical discrimination, welfare recipients lack access to hiring networks, such as coworkers who know of job openings and can vouch for their "good" behavior. For these reasons, welfare recipients will benefit from employment services that can provide the functional equivalent of recruitment networks.

This can be accomplished when the employment services become proactive at job development by maintaining close contacts with local employers who come to see the employment services as a reliable source of good workers.

To be effective at job development, the employment services will have to provide services that reduce the cost to employers of hiring and retaining workers. This can be accomplished in several ways. First, the employment services will have to work closely with the employers in order to understand their particular employment needs. As community-based agencies, the employment services have the capacity to develop inside knowledge of the local employers and their hiring needs and practices. Second, they have to recruit and orient the potential employees to meet the employer's behavioral expectations. As we have seen, these expectations often have less to do with specific job skills than with attitudes and communication skills. The job clubs may be a good vehicle to convey these expectations. Third, employers need to know that when they do have job vacancies, the employment services can respond quickly by referring appropriate applicants who most likely will meet their needs. Fourth, the employment services need to follow up and monitor the newly placed workers in order to handle whatever adjustment problems they may experience and to assist them in the transition to work. Finally, and most critically, they must provide the new workers with continuing support services such as child care and transportation assistance in order to minimize crises that might lead to tardiness or absenteeism. These services are particularly crucial to single parents who face the onerous task of reconciling family responsibilities with work requirements. The availability, for example, of emergency child care in case the child is sick or when normal child care arrangements break down can make the difference between leaving the job and risking being fired and maintaining steady employment. Similarly, the availability of transportation assistance may enable the workers to continue to work when other means of transportation fail.

As we will discuss below, an important advantage that employment services have over informal networks is their ability to provide additional human capital investments to potential employees who need them through such programs as supported work experience, remedial education, and skill training. Employers become aware that the pool of potential workers reached through the employment services may be more qualified, more skilled, and thus more productive than the one reached through the informal network.

When employers experience an added value in relying on the employment services rather than on informal networks to meet their hiring needs, they are more likely to turn to them when job vacancies occur. Similarly, prospective workers, such as welfare recipients, knowing that the employment services have the inside track on many jobs and that they offer support services to keep them employed, are more likely to turn to them. This, in turn, increases the pool of potential workers available to the employers.

Indirect evidence suggests that welfare-to-work programs which emphasize job development coupled with support services can be quite effective. One of the unique features of the Massachusetts Employment and Training (ET) program was that it was marketed to potential employers.[12] Businesses received letters, including one from the governor, encouraging them to turn to ET. In addition, an aggressive media campaign was launched to advertise the program to the business community. One of the components of the services provided by ET was an employment network that involved job development and job placement by the local employment services (ES) staff, who were housed in the same location as the welfare office. Such physical proximity was designed to make these services more accessible to welfare recipients. To reinforce the importance of helping the recipients get good jobs, performance contracts were issued in which the contractors, such as ES, were paid in part according to the number of participants who obtained jobs that were full-time, lasted more than thirty days, and paid at least $5 per hour.[13]

Another important feature of ET was the emphasis on support services, especially child care. ET offered extended child care subsidies for twelve months after participants obtained a job. They received vouchers that could be used for certified or licensed child care providers. Health care benefits were also extended to twelve months after leaving AFDC. In addition, other support services such as education and training were available to recipients even after leaving the program.

A stronger case for job development and placement can be made on the basis of the GAIN program in Riverside, California, which has had the most impressive impact of all welfare-to-work programs evaluated by the Manpower Development Research Corporation. One of its features is the emphasis on job development and placement. More than other programs, Riverside emphasizes quick entry into the job market, and the performance of case managers is closely related to their success in placing their clients in jobs. Staff compete for rewards on the basis of their placement record. Each case manager, for example, is expected to have a minimum of twelve employment placements per month. Therefore, the case managers have an incentive to contact employers and to seek out job opportunities. It is not uncommon in Riverside to have jobs lined up for participants to consider while they are still in job club. More important, however, is that each local office has its own job developer whose role is to establish contacts with employers and to encourage them to call the program when they have vacancies.[14]

Riverside aggressively markets its services by making presentations at various business forums. The job developers offer employers such services as pools of applicants, initial screening of the applicants, and follow-up on new hires. One of the regional managers recalled how an employer phoned early one morning looking for nine applicants by that afternoon. The staff mobilized and screened potential applicants from their client caseload and, to the surprise of the employer, by that afternoon had eleven GAIN participants ready to be interviewed. The employer was impressed by the prompt response and the prescreening done by the staff, and ended up hiring all eleven applicants.[15] One of the workers in Riverside describes the success of job development as follows: "[Employers] know we have a work force for them. We're not just 'welfare.' Our job development is doing a lot of public relations. Also, this is something done by the counselors and supervisors—letting employers know we're here and have a skilled and unskilled work force for them. We've been proactive. Employers are calling us for more people."[16]

The lesson to be learned from Riverside is that an aggressive job development and placement program in which staff performance is measured and rewarded on the basis of the number of clients placed in jobs can go a long way in speeding the entry of welfare recipients into the job market. However, job development can only succeed if jobs are available.

Less is currently known about the effectiveness of postplacement support services.[17] In four experimental sites, the following services are being evaluated: assistance in child care, income maintenance and transitional benefits, EITC, reimbursement of work-related expenses, and counseling.[18] If such support services are implemented well, their importance should not be underestimated. It is extremely important to find ways to assist the newly hired workers, especially single parents, to remain employed by preventing and reducing work-related stresses they are surely going to experience. The employers too need to know that they can obtain assistance when they experience difficulties with the workers.

Accordingly, we believe that the job development and placement services should be accompanied by proactive postplacement case management, for at least the first year of employment, that has some of the following characteristics. First, case managers need to monitor the newly placed workers so that they can respond early and quickly to emerging problems. Initially, the monitoring may focus on such things as ensuring that child care arrangements are in place, that transportation has been secured, that the workers have the appropriate attire, that they arrive at work on time, and that they understand and comply with the expectations of their employers. Second, the new workers may need transitional income support as their income shifts from welfare to wages. Third, the case managers should have at their disposal the resources and services needed to address problems that may arise which could impede the ability of the worker to stay on the job. These may range from back-up child care resources to emergency cash assistance. Finally, the case managers need to have counseling and mediation skills to handle interpersonal issues that may arise in the workplace between their clients and supervisors and coworkers.

Tier II: Individualized Employment Services

Those who experience greater human capital deficits, such as intermittent work experience, lack of specific work skills, or some educational deficiencies that prevent them from getting a steady job, can benefit from participation in remedial education, work experience, on-the-job training, or vocational training. At this tier, the approach is more individualized and the range of remedial resources is wider and geared to the specific needs of the client. For some, the goal may be removing certain educational deficiencies in reading or computation; for others, it may be having a structured work experience in a particular setting or job. Still others may need to strengthen certain vocational skills to master the job they aspire to.

A key feature of this tier is that the clients continue to receive the needed income support while they are in a particular service component. Thus, they are given the opportunity to complete their training without adverse financial burden. Upon completion, the clients are referred to the job development and placement services to try to get a job. Although many of the needed services, such as remedial education, might seem to be available in the community, these services must be geared to the needs of the particular clients. In Chapter 4, it will be recalled, adult education was not suitable for many welfare recipients, who had already had negative educational experiences. The one exception was San Diego, which specially tailored its educational program to welfare recipients.

The choice as to the most suitable service component should rest with the clients after careful assessment and consultation with their employment counselors. We view this relationship as essential to the success of this approach. The employment counselors, in addition to their expertise about vocational assessment and the services, must be able to develop a trusting relationship with their clients. They must be proactive in maintaining close contact with their clients, engaging the clients in the decisions, mobilizing the necessary services for them, advocating on their behalf with service providers, and handling emergencies and crises that might disrupt the learning process.[19] Again, the importance of the support services cannot be overstated.

An example of such a model might be found in the Options Program in

Baltimore, a Work Incentive (WIN) Demonstration project initiated in 1982. Operated by a well-established and respected local employment agency, the program benefited from considerable organizational expertise and experience in job development.[20] Options, targeting AFDC recipients with no children under age six, emphasized enhancing the participants' long-term employability through education and training.[21] It offered an array of services including job search, unpaid work experience, basic skill and GED instruction, vocational training, and on-the-job training. A key feature of the program was the individualization of services: On the basis of the participants' background and needs, the staff determined the type of services best suited for them. Essential to this process was a careful assessment of the participants' educational background, employment history, skills, attitudes, goals, and barriers to employment.[22] Moreover, staff emphasized the importance of actively involving the participants in the program assignment decisions. Although the program was mandatory, the staff tried hard to gain the participants' cooperation and seldom threatened them with sanctions. In general, participants assigned to job search were judged to be more job-ready, while those referred to work experience tended to have less education and work experience, and had been off AFDC longer. Similarly, those assigned to education and training were judged to be less employable because of limited education and work experience and long duration on welfare. Although the program emphasized human capital investment, most program activities were of modest duration.[23]

Options, as well as three other welfare-to-work programs in Virginia, Arkansas, and San Diego (Saturation Work Initiatives Model, or SWIM) were evaluated using experimental-design and long-term (five-year) data.[24] For Options, the experimental group showed a five-year earning gain of $2,119 over the control group but very little increase in AFDC savings ($62). The lack of impact on AFDC payments is understandable in light of the program's emphasis on long-term employability rather than rapid entry into the labor market. The net program cost was $953 per participant. Thus, in a cost-benefit analysis there was net gain to the participants and society but not to government.

What is most remarkable about Options, in contrast to the other three programs that emphasized job placement, is the persistence of the treatment effect. After five years, the experimentals were earning significantly more than the controls ($475). In the other programs, there was a convergence between the experimentals and controls such that no earning differences persisted by year five.[25] In other words, the human capital investments in the participants seem to have paid off in terms of higher earnings, although the gains were quite modest.[26]

Tier III: Intensive Employment Services

Tier III services are to be targeted at those who experience serious human capital deficits, in particular, a combination of lack of education, training, and work experience. For such persons, neither remedial education nor skill training nor work experience alone will suffice. They will need a combination of these and other services in order to have an impact on their employability and earning capacity. It is not clear how much basic education alone can improve their employability. Particularly worrisome are findings that getting the GED alone may not improve the earning capacity of those who dropped out of high school. Stephen Cameron and James Heckman show that persons with a GED "are statistically indistinguishable in their labor market outcomes from high school dropouts."[27] In contrast, the best route to higher-wage jobs seems to be a combination of education *and* postschool training.[28] Therefore, it seems to us that for persons with serious human capital deficits, an integrated approach will be necessary that combines education, skill training, and job development in ways that are mutually reinforcing.

One successful example of such a model is the Center for Employment Training (CET) in San Jose, California. The CET Represents a relatively effective employment training program for poor women who face the greatest barriers to employment, especially women who have very young children, lack recent work experience, and are on welfare.[29] By integrating into one program skill training, remedial education, job development, child care, and support services, the CET is able to attain impressive results. The evaluation of the program showed that it improved the average monthly earnings of the experimental group in the fourth quarter of the experiment by $133. By way of comparison, the GAIN program in Riverside improved the average monthly earnings in the fourth quarter by $76.

What makes the CET a model program? The answer seems to lie in its guiding philosophy and the design and delivery of its services. The philosophy of the program enumerates the following principles:[30]

Anyone can improve his or her employment skills and go to work; access to occupational skill training need not be predicated on aptitude or prior mastery of specific basic educational skills.

Practical skill training in demand occupations is the activity that responds best to the goals and motivations of persons who face employment problems.

The benefits of practical skill training are accessible to all applicants, even though many need to improve their basic literacy, math and English language skills while pursuing job training.

Trainees learn and master skills at different speeds and thus require the flexibility of courses structured to permit "open entry" and "open exit."

Support services and a supportive "family" environment at the program are essential to help trainees overcome logistical, emotional, and motivational problems that could undermine their success in training and finding and keeping employment.

This philosophy is manifested in the special ways in which the CET organizes and operationalizes its services. Participants are recruited through active community outreach, which includes contacts with agencies and presentations to community groups. When they sign up for the program, prospective participants identify the occupational skills they are interested in. An interview with the appropriate instructor is followed by a three-day trial period in the training class to ensure that the prospective participant understood the nature and requirements of the training course.[31]

The training classes offered by the CET answer the needs expressed by potential employers. Indeed, a special feature of the CET is the close relationship it develops with local employers, who come to rely on the program for trained employees. Courses are developed or dropped to reflect changes in market conditions. The instructional staff have extensive experience in their trade, and they keep current with recent developments in it.[32] During the time of the study, the CET offered courses in basic office skills, data entry and word processing, bookkeeping, shipping and receiving, electronic assembly, industrial maintenance mechanics, and custodial services.

The training course focused on mastery of the actual skills needed for the particular job. It combined instruction in both technical job skills and "feeder" skills—the specific reading and math skills needed for the job. That is, educational remediation was directly linked to the skill training itself. When the skill required a certain knowledge of math that the participant lacked, she took the necessary math module, and when she had mastered it, she returned to the skill training. The participant might also spend one or two hours a day in a supplementary class to receive a certificate in GED or English as a second language.[33] The key to the effectiveness of the training program, then, is the integration of the skill training with the remedial education. Participants can see the value and importance of the educational component as it relates directly to their vocational interest. This is in sharp contrast to the conventional training approach, in which remedial education precedes skill training.

Moreover, the instruction does not follow a conventional classroom pattern. Rather, it is based on individual coaching. Because of an open-entry policy, each class may include participants at different stages of training, with the advanced trainees helping the less advanced.[34] On average, participants spent twenty-six weeks in training and education.

The CET is also unusual in the support services it provides its participants. First, there is a child care center at the training site especially designated for infant and toddler care. Second, the CET expends considerable effort in job development. A cadre of job developers is assigned to cultivate relations with employers, identify job openings, prepare the participants to enter the job market, refer the participants to employers, and follow up after employment placement. The CET has an Industrial Advisory Board, which consists of representatives of the major employers in the community. In addition, the job developers actively scan the labor market, visit potential employers, and promote close relations between them and the program. As a result, the CET regularly gets job orders from employers.[35] The job developers are also responsible for job placement, which is greatly facilitated by their knowledge of the employers. Indeed, one of the attractions of the program to potential participants is the recognition that the program provides access to jobs.

Such a program does not come cheaply. Sharon Handwerger and Craig Thornton estimated the average cost per enrolled to be $3,573, while the average cost per woman entering education and training was $5,232 (in 1986 dollars).[36] Yet the costs of CET are not unusually high, especially if one keeps in mind that the program provided on-site child care services. On average, child care costs represented 28 percent of the total costs of the program.

Still, the CET is cost-effective. From a social perspective, it produced a net benefit of $1,200 per treatment group member over five years, or a return of $1.28 to society for every dollar of costs. From the participant perspective, the CET generated a net benefit of $2,371 per treatment-group member over five years.[37]

An alternative model to consider for long-term welfare recipients with no work experience is based on the positive impact of the National Supported Work (NSW) demonstration-experiment on AFDC recipients conducted in the mid-1970s in several cities.[38] The target group were recipients who had been on aid for thirty of the preceding thirty-six months, whose youngest child was six years of age or older, and who were currently unemployed and had spent no more than three months in a job during the past six months.[39] The majority had less than a twelfth-grade education and were predominantly African American. Thus, the program targeted the potential long-term welfare recipients. The intervention was a transitional direct work experience with tangible outputs. That is, the work projects had to be suitable to the general skill levels of the participants, yet produce tangible products or community service. The projects also had to provide "graduated stress"—a gradual increase in the level of work expectations and complexity and close supervision, and work had to be done in crews in order to provide peer support. Wages were slightly below the estimated prevailing market wage for low-skilled workers in that city.[40] Generally, participation was limited to twelve or eighteen months; the average was nine months.[41] Most of the projects were in service occupations. The participants relied heavily on the program to place them in a job after completion of their work experience.

The impact analysis showed that those in the experimental group made significant improvements in their employability. More were employed, worked more hours, and earned more. The gains, though modest, were long-term.[42]

The experience with NSW suggests that such a program, coupled with appropriate support services, might be useful to long-term welfare recipients with little work experience and limited education. It provides them with an opportunity to enter the workplace through a gradual and controlled process without overwhelming them, and yet leads them toward acquiring work habits and skills that can make them employable.

Thus far, we have described what we believe should be the substance of employment services, that is, the work they should do. We now to turn to how the employment services should be organized to carry out that work.

Successful Organization of Employment Services

The most effective employment service programs have the following characteristics:

- Clients have different needs, and the services reflect this variation.
- Services are individualized and flexible.
- Workers and clients enter into mutually supportive, trusting, cooperative relationships.
- Services are geared to work with clients who have long-term needs.

What are some of the organizational prerequisites for such employment services? As we have seen, the road from the enactment of social policy to its implementation is often littered with so many obstacles and side issues that the ultimate services, at best, loosely echo the intents of the policy, and at worse subvert it. As Richard Nathan puts it, there is a "shadow land between policy and its execution."[43] Effective implementation of social programs hinges, first, on the mobilization of external political and economic resources to support the program, and second, on the internal allocation of power and the selection of a service technology that is consonant with the desired outputs of the program. Tying the external and internal political economies into a coherent whole is a set of clear and explicit organizational objectives that emanate from an overarching organizational ideology.

Successful implementation requires, first and foremost, an articulate mission that can be translated into a set of clear objectives. As Robert Behn writes, "The public manager needs to know *what* results he or she wants to produce and *how* they might be produced."[44] Common to such disparate, yet successful, programs as ET or the CET was the fact that each was driven by a coherent and unambiguous mission that was institutionalized throughout the organization and manifested in every service component. In ET, for example, it was the idea that welfare recipients want to work; that they will if provided with basic education, job-skill training, and placement services; and that recipients must make their own choices in a noncoercive environment. In the CET it is the conviction that every client can improve her employment skills provided she receives practical skill training in demand occupations, and does so at a speed appropriate to her needs.

As these examples show, when the mission defines the desired outcomes, it also constructs, explicitly or implicitly, a *moral conception of the clients*. This moral conception is a critical dimension of the mission because it crucially defines the program's commitment to its clients, the expectations it sets for them and for its staff, and the relations the staff will develop with their clients. When the moral conception of the clients is negative and stigmatizing, the program is likely to circumscribe its investment in the clients and lower its expectations about what results can be achieved, and the staff will develop a distrusting relationship with their clients. A self-fulfilling prophecy is likely to be set in motion in which the staff in their behavior and the clients in their response will confirm the negative moral conception. Not surprisingly, there is ample evidence to suggest that to be successful as a people-changing organization, the program must ascribe to its clients a high social worth, assume that they are amenable to change, and grant them the capacity to be active participants in the decisions affecting their future.

To adopt a mission with a clear vision of service outcomes requires political support from the external environment that gives it legitimacy. We have noted from our own research on welfare-to-work programs that the local political climate, as reflected by the elected officials, has considerable influence on the type of mission and ideology espoused by the programs. Hence, to attain legitimacy for the mission depends, in part, on the ability of the program leaders to link to and mobilize supporting political constituencies and interest groups. They may include not only important political officeholders but also stakeholders in such sectors as the business community, civic organizations, and educational and training programs.[45]

At the same time, the program also needs to be buffered from political interference by interest groups that may wish to use it obtain side-benefits such as political patronage, or for a supply of cheap labor. We have seen that such side-benefits subvert and corrupt the mission of the program. Thus, the legitimation of the program must be based on and acknowledge the professionalism of its staff.

Similarly, for such programs to have more than symbolic impact, they must obtain sufficient external resources to operationalize their service technologies and reach their target population. We have seen that many work programs fail to have much of an impact because, among other things, they lack resources to do the job. In contrast, all the successful programs we have cited were adequately funded to meet their objectives. Not only the amount of resources committed to the program but also their stability are crucial. A program that struggles year in and year out with the uncertainty of resources cannot take a long-term view of its mission, which is clearly needed if the program is to have any lasting effects.

As Jan Hagen and Irene Lurie note, the development of an interorganizational network to provide the complementary and possibly some of the core services needed by a comprehensive employment service is indispensable to its success.[46] We have already indicated the vital importance of linkages with employers, but the network must also include educational and training programs, child care services, mental health and counseling services, and the like. The relations must be such that clients referred to them are assured of obtaining the necessary services. This can be accomplished only if each of the exchanging organizations perceives that a distinct benefit will be derived from the relationship. That is, an educational program will respond favorably to referrals of clients if, for example, it obtains additional resources or its legitimacy is enhanced. Again, considerable research on interorganizational relations points to the importance of such an exchange network to the effectiveness of the organizations.[47]

Finally, the program must be embedded and integrated into the local community, not only through the community's formal structures but also through its numerous informal networks. Residents of the community, especially those who might need its services, should have a stake in the program. The program must reach out to them through various neighborhood organizations, the use of indigenous workers and former clients, and other grass-roots activities. Behn defines such outreach activities as being "close to the customer." He describes, for example, how ET used focus groups consisting of current and former welfare recipients, teen parents, and residents of public housing to try to identify the most effective ways to reach out to these potential clients. The program managers discovered through these groups that one effective way to recruit welfare recipients was through the testimonials of the children of the participants in ET about the impact of the program on them and their mothers. When the residents of the community develop a sense of ownership in the program rather than seeing it as an alien organization, they are much more likely to come forward and use its services.[48]

Turning to the internal structure, there is considerable agreement among researchers that the mission of the employment services must be translated into a set of concrete and measurable outcome objectives. These objectives may include increasing the number of clients with limited work experience who are placed in jobs lasting more than three months, the number of clients whose reading and computational skills have been raised above a certain level, and the proportion of clients needing child care who are able to enroll their children in licensed child care facilities. The idea is to make the program and its staff accountable to very specific and concrete outcome measures. Once such accountability is established, the staff who work with the clients can be given considerable autonomy, relying on their professional knowledge and experience in accomplishing these objectives. The combination of clarity and specificity of outcomes and internal flexibility of how to attain them is essential to organizational effectiveness in people-changing organizations.

Moreover, to institutionalize accountability in the organization, it is vital that staff rewards be made contingent on successful attainment of the outcome objectives. That is, compensation and promotion of the staff who work with the clients must be linked directly to the service outcomes they accomplish. Indeed, the success of the staff must be tied to the success of the clients. In other words, the more successful the clients are in becoming employable and self-sufficient, the greater the rewards the staff will obtain. To avoid creaming, the rewards should be weighted by the degree of difficulty the clients present.

By granting staff discretion in deciding how best to serve their individual clients, the organization must encourage individualized attention so that the staff can tailor the services to the specific needs of the clients. The clients must become active participants in the service-delivery process. They must be given a real voice in deciding what services they need, and they must be given choices if they are to have a stake in getting successful outcomes. When clients are given choices and an active voice, they also share with their workers the responsibility for the consequences. Being given such responsibility means that the clients as well as their workers must bear the costs of failing to fulfill their obligations in the service-delivery process. Moreover, since the rewards of the staff are contingent on the success of the clients, the relationship between them becomes interdependent. It is through such interdependence that a trusting relationship, so fundamental to the success of the program, can begin to emerge. It is for this reason—the importance of the interdependent, trusting relationship, founded on the moral conception of the client—that a successful, effective employment service cannot be mixed up with welfare eligibility. A service technology predicated on individualized attention and staff discretion requires staff with professional training and expertise. Professionalism signals not only technical skills, indispensable to successful operation of the technology, but also adherence to a code of conduct which treats clients as subjects and not objects, which grants them high moral worth, which acknowledges their potential to succeed, and which respects and protects their rights.

The organizational model we propose, in which the service objectives are externally defined by an explicit set of concrete and measurable outcomes, while internally the organization and its staff have considerable discretion in selecting the means to attain them, also addresses the problem of localism we have alluded to in Chapter 4. That is, traditionally, local communities have been given considerable discretion in how to implement their work programs, having to adhere only to very broad and often vague outcome goals. Consequently, work programs face the danger of becoming "corrupted" by local political and economic forces which push the program to pursue objectives that benefit various local interest groups rather than serving the needs of the clients. Our model recognizes that for the program to be effective it must adjust and adapt to the local political economy. But by requiring the program to adhere closely to very explicit outcome objectives, and making the resources available to the program contingent on attaining these objectives, the program is prevented from subverting or displacing its service goals.

Moreover, we believe that the organizational design we propose reduces the bureaucratization of the employment services. A program organized around achievement of discernible outcomes encourages flexibility, initiative, and creativity in selecting the appropriate means to attain them.

Replication

A major failing in social policy is the blind replication of seemingly successful programs, which are more often than not demonstration projects. The present example is Riverside. First California and now the rest of the country wants to apply the Riverside model as *the* welfare-to-work program. However, Riverside crucially depended on some features that were probably unique to that agency. As stated above, the first and most obvious feature is the charismatic head of the agency. Lawrence Townsend had a missionary zeal which he was able to impart to his staff. Even though there is some evidence of staff dissatisfaction, it surely is unusual for the average welfare bureaucracy to experience this kind of totally committed leadership and staff organization. Second, as discussed, the staff developed a cooperative relationship with the clients rather than a bureaucratic one. And third, the staff engaged in extensive job development.

As compared to the average welfare agency, Riverside has made profound changes. David Ellwood and Mary Jo Bane, for example, in proposing changing welfare-to-work from an eligibility condition to a joint enterprise, use the words "change in culture."[49] It is precisely for this reason—the depth and extent of the change required—that the Riverside model is so problematic when applied throughout the country. This is not to say that some welfare offices may not be able to become professional employment services, but surely it is idle to think that a far-flung, decentralized, field-level bureaucracy will be able to change meaningfully. Yet this is the road that we are currently embarked upon.

To some extent, the same objection also applies to our proposal. There are mitigating factors. Our proposal does not call for a restructuring of welfare; we prefer that local welfare offices concentrate on income maintenance and apply the rules bureaucratically, with minimal interference in the lives of their clients. Our proposal also assumes a much smaller population, since the vast majority should be able to get jobs on their own. However, we do call for a network of community-based, professional service agencies, based on a few exceptional models. Furthermore, our proposal, although voluntary, is designed to target the more difficult cases, which means that the failure rate (however defined) is bound to be high and that the agencies will always feel under pressure.

In the end, one has to admit that replication will be problematic. At present, good, systematic knowledge about the important conditions of replications is lacking. We do not even have good outcome measures; many variables, in addition to effective services, will affect the employment of particular individuals as the years go by. Patience and experimentation are needed. We hope that they will be easier to come by when services are divorced from welfare, are community-based, are universal, and are designed to help those who want to help themselves.

The problems that most welfare recipients face in getting and keeping a job are not substantially different from those faced by many poor and low-skilled workers, both men and women. In common with other single parents, welfare recipients bear the heavy burden of having to care for young children without the resources available in a two-parent family. What they all need is, above all, access to jobs that offer decent wages and benefits, and second, support services to handle life crises and workplace stresses in order to keep them employed.

Any employment strategy must be based on the availability of jobs. We have noted that most employment programs tend to assume that jobs are available and that joblessness is due to deficits, of either human or moral capital, in the unemployed. We have shown that lack of jobs is a fundamental cause of unemployment among vulnerable populations, welfare recipients included. Therefore, the success of the employment services we propose hinges on the existence of a policy that ensures employment to those who can work.

We believe that targeting employment services only to welfare recipients is the wrong strategy and may actually make it more difficult for them to enter the labor market. We suspect that employers tend to discriminate against welfare recipients since they are not immune from the negative stereotypes associated with such a status. This is one reason why we feel that the employment services we have proposed should be totally divorced from the welfare agency and available to all members of the community who need a job. The second reason for separating such services from welfare eligibility is that the two functions are incompatible with each other. A welfare agency is inherently a people-processing organization that is preoccupied with enforcing rules and regulations. Effective employment services must be people-changing organizations that rely on the trust and quality of the relations between the staff and their clients to deliver their services.

We also believe that making participation in the employment services mandatory through threat of sanctions is an exercise in symbolic politics. It somehow seems important to show that majoritarian society is in control, that it is asserting its values, that it is sending a message. But a message to whom? Not to those who are being sanctioned—the welfare abusers are outside the system— but a message to the majority. This is the age-old "hostage" theory of welfare reform.[50] The clearest example was the nineteenth-century poorhouse. There, those who were truly out of the labor force (children, the sick, and the disabled) were nevertheless confined under appalling conditions as a threat to the able-bodied. As we have argued throughout this book, we need a new approach.

Chapter 8

Teenage Parents and Welfare

Every era selects its own category of poor to be singled out as the "outsiders" and as a threat to its moral order. As we have seen, in a prior age working single mothers were seen as a threat to the patriarchal order in general, and to the well-being of their children in particular. In the 1960s single mothers on welfare who stayed home to care for their children became the "dangerous class" because they undermined the work ethic. In the 1990s teenage parents have been targeted as the great threat to the moral order and the cause of some of our most serious social ills—welfare dependency, child abuse, crime, violence, and drug abuse. The Personal Responsibility and Work Opportunity Reconciliation Act of 1996 was fueled by images of "kids having kids" who will grow up to become future teenage parents and dependent on welfare. The "findings" section of Temporary Assistance to Needy Families (TANF) is quite instructive. Here are some examples:

> An effective strategy to combat teenage pregnancy must address the issue of male responsibility, including statutory rape culpability and prevention. . . .
>
> The increase of teenage pregnancies among the youngest girls is particularly severe and is linked to predatory sexual practices by men who are significantly older. . . .
>
> The negative consequences of an out-of-wedlock birth on the mother, the child, the family, and society are well documented as follows: (A) Young women 17 and under who give birth outside of marriage are more likely to go on public assistance and to spend more years on welfare once enrolled. These combined effects of "younger and longer" increase total AFDC costs per household by 25 percent to 30 percent for 17-year-olds. (B) Children born out-of-wedlock have a substantially higher risk of being born at a very low or moderately low birth weight. (C) Children born out-of-wedlock are more likely to experience low verbal cognitive attainment, as well as more child abuse, and neglect. . . .
>
> Between 1985 and 1990, the public cost of births to teenage mothers under the aid to families with dependent children program, the food stamp program, and the medicaid program has been estimated at $120,000,000,000. . . .

Therefore, in light of this demonstration of the crisis in our Nation, it is the sense of the Congress that prevention of out-of-wedlock pregnancy and reduction in out-of-wedlock birth are very important Government interests and the policy contained in [TANF] is intended to address the crisis.[1]

As we shall see, these "findings" present a very selective, biased, and alarmist view of the scope, causes, and consequences of teenage parenthood. Still, in response to this "crisis" the legislation prohibits support for minor single teen parents who do not live in an adult-supervised setting; requires teen mothers to stay in school; and imposes the five-year lifelong time limit on receipt of assistance.[2] There is no longer a guarantee of child care when needed to participate in mandated activities. In addition, TANF requires state plans to have provisions to reduce teenage pregnancies, and a program of education and training regarding statutory rape. It provides a "bonus" to five states who have shown decreased rates of illegitimacy and abortions. However, no funds are set aside for family planning, except for $50 million each year for abstinence education.[3]

Teenage mothers have become the quintessential symbol of what is wrong with the welfare system. As a powerful moral symbol, teenage mothers on welfare signify the terrible social costs of the breakdown in family values and discipline, of rampant and irresponsible sexual behavior, and of a life mired in dependence on public assistance. By casting teenage mothers as the ultimate failure of the welfare state, dominant values are reinforced—abstinence from premarital sex, the sanctity of marriage, and the importance of hard work and self-reliance. Again, as a symbol, teenage parenthood also has a strong racial subtext. Since teenage mothers are overrepresented among blacks and Hispanics, the category is also an implicit condemnation of the culture, values, and way of life of these ethnic groups. As Ann Phoenix put it, "In societies in which black family structures are considered responsible for producing inner-city problems of poverty and crime, associating blackness with another stigmatized group (teenage mothers) produces moral panic."[4]

We begin this chapter by examining the scope and dimensions of the problem showing that the rhetoric does not match the empirical reality. Teenage parents represent a very small fraction of mothers on AFDC. Moreover, the rate of teenage childbearing has not changed dramatically over time. What has changed is the *marital status* of teenage mothers. They are much less likely to be married. The chapter then discusses the causes of teenage childbearing. We begin by recognizing that we are dealing with a very complex and multifaceted issue that defies simple explanations. Therefore, we focus on the most powerful forces that can be amenable to social policy intervention. We show that there is little empirical evidence that the welfare system itself encourages teenage childbearing. Most of the research, especially studies based on longitudinal data, points unequivocally to poverty and lack of opportunities as key determinants of teenage childbearing. Still, the majority of poor teenagers do not become pregnant, and we lack good understanding of the processes by which some of them make that choice. Yet poverty immeasurably increases the risk of teenage childbearing, especially when the fathers are included in the picture. We show that the majority of fathers are not teenagers but adults, and that they come from highly impoverished environments that discourage marriage because the men lack the resources to support a family. We conclude this section by showing that, related to poverty, lack of access to health care and, particularly, family planning resources adds to the risk of childbearing by teenagers.

Next we take up the issue of the consequences of teenage childbearing. We show that the supposedly terrible social and economic costs of teenage childbearing are overstated. The majority of teenage mothers become productive citizens and good parents. This is especially true for older teenage mothers between ages eighteen and twenty-one, who constitute the largest cohort of teenage parents. Younger teenage mothers, especially under age seventeen, and their children do incur appreciable costs. They are less likely to graduate from high school and more likely to remain longer as single parents and to have larger families. They also stay longer on welfare. The children of younger teenage mothers are more likely to have a higher rate of behavioral problems, especially during adolescence. Yet it is important to remember that these young mothers constitute a small fraction of all teenage mothers.

Finally, we address the question of policies and programs to prevent and mitigate the effects of teenage childbearing. We show that public policies and programs have focused on "rehabilitation" of teenage mothers, and that these have shown, at best, modest success. We point out that despite the legislative rhetoric, little has been done to prevent teenage pregnancies, though prevention is a far more effective strategy. Yet prevention means addressing the root causes of teenage childbearing—the poverty and lack of opportunities that such women and their families experience. Put differently, we argue that the most effective way to reduce teenage childbearing is to reduce poverty, especially by increasing educational, employment, and income opportunities for both men and women. Coupled with this strategy, teenagers must have ready access to family planning resources that can best be achieved through a universal health care system. TANF clearly fails both of these tests.

Trends and Patterns of Teenage Parenthood

The reality of teenage parenthood and welfare belies the validity of the public image. Of all AFDC mothers in 1994, only 2.6 percent were under age nineteen. Moreover, the notion that welfare encourages teenage mothers to form independent households is exaggerated. Only 18 percent of all AFDC mothers under age eighteen in 1990 lived in an independent household. The majority lived either with their parents (58 percent) or with their spouse (12 percent).

We do not imply that the problems encountered by teenage mothers are not serious; indeed, current and former teenage mothers make up a sizable proportion of the AFDC caseloads.[5] Still, as we will show below, teenage mothers do not overwhelm the welfare system. A majority leave AFDC, provide good care for their children, and lead a productive life. Yet, like many other single mothers, they find it difficult to escape poverty.

The alarming concern about teenage mothers is also not matched by the demographic trends. As Frank Furstenberg notes,[6] thirty years ago teenage childbearing rates were 50 percent higher than they are today. In 1955 the birth rate per 1,000 for women between ages fifteen and nineteen was 90. In 1992 the rate was 61, and it declined further to 58.9 in 1994.[7] Even in absolute numbers, more children were born to women under age twenty in 1972 than in 1994. Most of the sensational accounts of "children having children" are also unwarranted. The birth rate for women age fourteen or less has remained essentially unchanged over the past forty years, standing at 1 per 1,000.[8]

The debate about teenage mothers has been fueled by the dramatic change in patterns of marriage. In 1955 only 15 percent of mothers under age twenty were unmarried. That number climbed to 40 percent in 1975, and to 71 percent in 1992.[9] For whites, the rate rose from less than 20 percent in 1970 to more than 60 percent in 1992. For blacks the rate rose from more than 60 percent to more than 90 percent. Thus, teenage childbearing came to be viewed as a serious social problem when marriage no longer accompanied the birth of the child. It is mostly this demographic transformation, which has occurred in a context of rising economic insecurity, ethnic polarization, and increasing fear of the "underclass," that has challenged dominant values about marriage and family, reproductive rights, transition to adulthood, and the role of public assistance.

Causes of Teenage Childbearing

Teenage childbearing is the culmination of a complex series of decisions, events, and behaviors, including engagement in sexual activity, use of contraception, pregnancy, resolution of the pregnancy, and marriage. Moreover, the teenage population at risk is very heterogenous. The causes of teenage childbearing are equally complex and multifaceted, ranging from broad socioeconomic predisposing conditions to specific, and often unknown, psychosocial processes affecting individual behaviors. To put the question of the causes of teenage childbearing in an appropriate context, it is important to bear in mind that the combination of earlier sex and delayed marriage has produced a long interval of risk of teenage parenthood.[10] There has also been a shift in resolving pregnancy from abortion to birth.[11] Moreover, many female teenage sexual experiences are nonvoluntary, and up to 25 percent of such teenagers indicated forced sexual behavior. Thus, it is not surprising that most teenage pregnancies are unintended.

In this context, Kristin Moore and her colleagues, after a comprehensive review of existing research, reached the following conclusion: "Youth most at risk of becoming parents during their teenage years are those least well-situated to raise a healthy, well-adjusted and high-achieving child. Youth from economically disadvantaged families and communities, youth with substance abuse and behavior problems, youth who are behind in school and youth who have low aspirations for their own educational attainment are found more likely to initiate sexual intercourse at a young age, less likely to contracept consistently and more likely to bear a child, particularly outside of marriage."[12] Brent Miller reaches a similar conclusion, stating that "teenagers who do poorly in school, who have low future expectations, and who come from disadvantaged families and communities are more likely to initiate sex at a young age, are less likely to contracept effectively, and once pregnant, are more likely to bear a child, particularly to bear a child outside of marriage."[13]

Yet these findings do not tell us about the conditions that expose the teenagers to these risk factors. Our concern is to identify the most powerful and persistent forces that increase the risk of teenage childbearing and yet can be alleviated by social policy. We will show that the overwhelming evidence points to poverty and lack of economic and social opportunities as the primary candidates because these factors create the social settings that put teenagers at a high risk. Therefore, poverty and lack of opportunity must be addressed first if we are to do anything effective to reduce teenage childbearing.

By focusing on poverty, we are not implying that there is a simple and straightforward "cause" of teenage childbearing. In fact, we know that the majority of young women living in poverty will not become teenage parents, so clearly many other factors mediate between living in an impoverished environment and becoming a teenage parent. That is, within such a deprived environment there are complex and dynamic social and developmental processes, not fully understood, that encourage some of these adolescents to engage in high-risk behavior, including childbearing. Some of these processes emanate from growing up in families that fail to provide the values, support, and nurturing adolescents need; some are triggered by experiences of physical and sexual abuse; others spring from peer relations and culture that reinforce deviant behavior; and still others may arise from school environments that are dull and unchallenging. Judith Musick,[14] for example, argues that teenagers who persistently and knowingly expose themselves to high-risk behavior have experienced family and other environments that provide too little protection and care to their children and youth. By failing to provide "good enough" child rearing environments, "they poison the lives of [society's] youngest, most vulnerable members, thwarting their development, blocking their paths to success in school and work, and diminishing their capacities for health, self-enhancing interpersonal relations."[15] As a result, these young women have an inadequate sense of self and identity that fosters dysfunctional relationships with men.

We do not dispute that this may be the experience of some teenage mothers, especially the very young. Yet our main argument is that social policies and programs have had little success in intervening and repairing these damaging social and developmental processes. We do not think that such programs can be very successful unless the underlying conditions of poverty that trigger and magnify these damaging developmental processes are addressed. If the young women and men have no economic future, they are not likely to get married and form "healthy" families. When the young mothers are forced into low-paying jobs, having to rely on wholly inadequate child care arrangements, we are still exposing their children to child-rearing environments that are not "good enough," and we are repeating the vicious cycle of poverty. Finally, we need to move toward a policy of prevention rather than a policy of rehabilitation that focuses on the difficult cases but ignores most of the teenagers living in high-risk environments. A policy of prevention that addresses the poverty that creates most of these high-risk environments is likely to influence the lives of most poor teenagers and be far more effective.

There is, of course, a counterargument that antipoverty policies, especially welfare, are actually to blame for the rise in teenage childbearing. We, therefore, begin by examining the evidence. We go on to review studies, especially those based on longitudinal data, that try to identify the conditions that increase the risk of teenage childbearing. We also bring the fathers who are often ignored in such studies into the picture. Finally, we examine availability and access to contraceptives as a contributing factor.

Is Welfare to Blame?

Conservatives have put the blame for the rise in single teenage mothers squarely on welfare. Charles Murray, for example, argued that welfare benefits, especially for black women, greatly reduce the costs of illegitimacy.[16] Therefore, eliminating welfare benefits would be an effective policy response to the rise in out-of-wedlock births, including teenage childbearing. Yet Robert Moffitt, in his extensive review of studies on the effect of welfare on family structure, concluded that the effects are small in magnitude and could not explain the rapid rise in single-parenthood during the 1960s and early 1970s.[17] In a more recent review of the effects of welfare on nonmarital childbearing, Moffitt pointed to the difficult methodological issues of imputing causality. He suggested that although the welfare system may increase nonmarital childbearing, its effect is small in comparison to other contributing factors, such as the availability of employed men.[18]

Focusing specifically on black female teenagers, Greg Duncan and Saul Hoffman used data from the Panel Study of Income Dynamics (PSID) to estimate the effects of AFDC benefit levels as compared with future economic opportunities on out-of-wedlock births. They found "that AFDC benefit levels have a modest but statistically insignificant positive effect on the incidence of teenage out-of-wedlock birth, whereas future economic opportunities have a larger and statistically significant negative effect."[19] They estimated that a 25 percent increase in AFDC benefits will result in a 1 percent increase in out-of-wedlock births. Kristin Moore and her colleagues,[20] using data from the National Longitudinal Survey of Youth (NLSY), did not find a relationship between AFDC benefits levels and age at first birth. Shelly Lundberg, Robert Plotnick, Martha Hill, and June O'Neill, using data from the NLSY, did find that the combined benefits of AFDC and food stamps affect the probability of a teenage nonmarital birth among white but not black females.[21] In contrast, Robert Haveman and Barbara Wolfe,[22] using the PSID data, found no effect of maximum welfare benefits when measured to include AFDC, food stamps, and Medicaid.

Alternatively, it can be argued that it is not welfare generosity that induces teenagers to become parents but rather living with a parent who is a welfare recipient. That is, having a parent who is a welfare recipient creates a role model that encourages the daughter to have an out-of-wedlock child and to use welfare to support her family. To answer this question, Haveman and Wolfe used the PSID data, consisting of twenty-one years' follow-up of families and their children. They found that females whose families received welfare at any time during their childhoods were no more likely to become teenage parents, controlling for other factors. Thus, they found "no evidence of a significant role of intergenerational transmission of welfare on the probability of a teenage marital birth. None of the variables of parental receipt of welfare, the proportion of female-headed families in the area, the mother having had a nonmarital birth or her having a birth as a teenager (based on her age at first birth), nor the state generosity of welfare benefits—are even marginally significant."[23]

Thus, the best available data makes it clear that welfare, so vehemently vilified as the cause of our most pressing social problem—single teenage parent-hood—plays at best a small role in explaining it. Therefore, reducing welfare benefits to discourage out-of-wedlock births is likely to have a small impact, while increasing the poverty of the children of welfare recipients. Again, pro-ponents of such policies play on their symbolic rather than substantive value.

Family and Neighborhood Factors

Next we examine the impact of the environment—family and neighbor-hood—on the risk that teenagers will have out-of-wedlock births. An early study by Dennis Hogan and Evelyn Kitagawa on a sample of black adolescents in Chicago found that the following variables significantly predicted rates of first pregnancy: living in a poor neighborhood, parents being in the lower social class, the mother being unmarried, and parents having low control over dating. Mark Hayward and his colleagues found that the mother's education was an important factor in inhibiting pregnancy by delaying the onset of sexual activity and in reducing the risk among sexually experienced teenagers. One reason may be that children of more educated mothers were more likely to use contraceptives. They also found that living in a central city increased the risk for blacks but not for whites. Nevertheless, in contrast to other research, they did not find that living in a single-parent household increased the risk of becoming pregnant.[24]

More recently, Haveman and Wolfe tried to assess the effects of these back-ground variables.[25] Recognizing that the decision to have a child and the subsequent decision to go on welfare are interrelated, the researchers devel-oped a statistical model that considers these related choices. Using this model, they found that teenagers are more likely to have a nonmarital birth if their family experiences economic hardship; if there are stresses in the family due to parental separations or remarriages; if the teenagers have more siblings; if their mothers did not graduate from high school; if the mothers have no religious preference; and if they are African American.[26] Haveman and Wolfe identified only two significant variables affecting the likelihood that the teenage mother will subsequently receive welfare—number of years living in the South and the family's economic hardship.

Although Haveman and Wolfe did not find neighborhood influence on teenage out-of-wedlock births, Hogan and Kitagawa and Jeanne Brooks-Gunn and her colleagues did find such an effect.[27] Jonathan Crane, using a measure of proportion of adult workers holding professional or managerial jobs in the census tract, found that there is a large increase in teenage nonmarital births when one moves from a "bad" neighborhood to the worst neighborhood.[28]

Looking more directly at the employment opportunities available to teenagers, Randall Olsen and George Farkas used the experimental data from the Youth Incentive Entitlement Pilot Projects (YIEPP), discussed in Chapter 5, to assess their effect on teenage nonmarital births.[29] Restricting the data to African Americans, they used the employment rate of their peers at age seventeen and estimated its effect on the rate of births at age eighteen and two months. They found a significantly strong effect such that if the employment rate rose by 20 percent (the typical impact of YIEPP), the rate of births would decline between 8 and 24 percent.

Similarly, a study by Haveman, Wolfe, and Elaine Peterson, using the PSID data, followed girls who were one to six years old in 1968 for the next twenty-one years.[30] Controlling for variables such as family structure, ethnicity, and poverty level, they found that the adult unemployment rate in the neighborhood is associated with the probability of nonmarital birth. Per capita expenditures on family planning resources also affect the risk of nonmarital births. Other studies show that neighborhood factors such as census tract median family income, racial dispersion, proportion of women employed full-time, rate of residential turnover, and divorce/separation rates affect teenage sexual activity and risk of pregnancy.[31]

Neighborhoods that expose youth to high-risk behavior, besides their distressed economic and demographic attributes, are also marked by impoverished social institutions, such as schools, that play a crucial role in the socialization of children and adolescents. Research shows that school failures and dropouts are associated with earlier sexual activity and higher rates of pregnancy. In particular, students who fail and are held back are far more likely to exhibit high-risk behavior, and the rates of failure are especially high among young people living in economically impoverished and ethnically segregated neighborhoods. Moreover, young women who drop out of school have a greater probability of giving birth than of returning to school and graduating.[32]

School failure is a culmination of a process conditioned by both individual characteristics and the quality of the school. From a policy perspective, it is important to recognize that poor schools, by failing to offer a nurturing and stimulating educational environment, cannot protect youth from such risk behavior as early sexual behavior, pregnancy, and childbearing. Schools in poor neighborhoods are appreciably different from schools in more affluent neighborhoods. They are characterized by lower expenditures per pupil, which translates into inadequate and low-quality educational resources.[33] Students in such schools are less likely to interact with highly qualified and better-paid teachers; they are less likely to have access to enriched curricular and extracurricular activities; and they are more likely to be tracked into vocational and remedial classes that set lower expectations for academic achievement. For many young people who already face serious developmental disadvantages, a good school with caring teachers and counselors can provide an alternative and an opportunity for self-growth despite the other obstacles in their environment. Indeed, studies of resilient youth show that such schools can be life-saving.[34] In contrast, low-quality schools, rather than compensating for impoverished family environments, reinforce them. This is particularly important for teenage mothers, because having a baby *while in school* is not a significant hindrance to completion of high school.[35] Therefore, being in a high-quality school will make a great deal of difference for such mothers and the future of their children.

The Role of the Fathers

To better understand the conditions that encourage young poor women to engage in risk-taking behavior, especially childbearing, we need to bring the men into the picture. They are clearly a very important part of the story, and yet we have considerably fewer studies about them. In part, studying the fathers is much more difficult, since their identity is often not known; they are less likely to admit fatherhood and their relations with their children are more tenuous.[36] Still, these factors cannot fully explain the limited attention given to them. More probably, it reflects the normative bias we have against the women and the double standard we apply to them.

When the men are added to the picture, the impact of poverty and lack of economic opportunities becomes even more magnified. It is important to recognize, in this context, that the fathers of children born to teenage mothers are older than the women. According to David Landry and Jacqueline Darroch Forrest, the fathers of babies born to mothers between ages fifteen and seventeen were, on average, 3.6 years older. About half were twenty years of age or older, and only 35 percent of the fathers of babies born to women ages fifteen to nineteen were under twenty.[37] It is reasonable to impute from the data, and as indicated by some of the available clinical evidence, that the adult men use their experience and power to pressure teenage women into sexual relations.[38] The potential for coercive sexual relations is particularly high for mothers fifteen years of age. About a third of them have had partners who were at least six years older. We have also noted that younger women are more likely to report having had involuntary sex. What is not in doubt is that many of the fathers lack the economic resources to sustain a family.

Because researchers often assume that the fathers are also adolescent, the few available surveys focus on teenage fathers. Robert Lerman, using the National Longitudinal Survey of Labor Market Behavior, attempted to present a profile of young unwed fathers by following them from their late teenage years to their late twenties.[39] He found that unwed fathers were much more likely to be unemployed and without a high school degree. Looking at personal and family background, he found that higher family income reduced the chances of unwed fatherhood, while living in a welfare family increased them, and that blacks were four times more likely than whites to become unwed fathers. He did not find that county rate of unemployment has any effect, but this variable may not present a true picture of the employment opportunities the young men encountered.

Looking at the life chances of poor men in general, William Julius Wilson advanced the hypothesis that the decline of marriage among low-income African American women is due to the deterioration of the economic opportunities available to their male counterparts.[40] The males, facing high unemployment and lack of job opportunities because of the decline in low-skill manufacturing jobs, can no longer provide the economic resources that would make marriage economically attractive. Wilson developed a "male marriageable pool index" based on the proportion of employed civilian men to women of the same race and age groups.[41] He showed that since 1960 for the age group sixteen to twenty-four there has been a steady decline in the index for blacks as compared with white men. Mark Fossett and K. Jill Kiecolt did find that for African Americans, family formation and family structure are influenced by the sex ratio and the socio-economic status of the men and the women.[42] Similarly, Greg Duncan proposed that the marriage market does influence nonmarital fertility decisions, but the number of available men is less important than their ability to support the family.[43]

Frank Furstenberg and his colleagues, in their study of conditions in Baltimore, found that marriage contributed little to the mother's subsequent economic well-being.[44] Only those who completed high school and entered an enduring marriage managed to improve their economic status. Several ethnographic studies confirm this overall thesis. Mercer Sullivan studied two very poor neighborhoods in New York, one predominantly black and the other Puerto Rican.[45] He found that in the black community negotiations took place about the father's rights and responsibilities. Yet they were not likely to involve marriage because of the uncertainty of employment for the men, and the general feeling that both parents should continue their education. In the Puerto Rican's neighborhood greater pressure existed for marriage and cohabitation, but the newly formed households were very unstable because of lack of jobs and greater reliance on criminal activities. The men often became unemployed or, when working, did not earn enough to support the family. Elijah Anderson confirmed these observations in his own ethnographic study of poor black neighborhoods.[46] As he put it, "In this environment, where hard economic times are a fact of daily life for many, some young men are not interested in 'taking care of somebody else,' when to do so means having less. In this social context of persistent poverty young men have to devalue the conventional marital relationship, easily viewing women as a burden and children as even more so."[47] Moreover, in such a deprived environment, denial of paternity helped the mother obtain AFDC that was more reliable than the irregular support from the sporadically employed father.

Furstenberg followed for about five years a small group of black young adults who were the offspring of the teenage mothers in the Baltimore study.[48] He noted that the men's commitment to paternity was fragile because of the cultural and economic conditions they experienced. Most of the young men grew up in households where the father was absent. They acknowledged that their family life had ill prepared them to become parents, yet they were aware of the high expectations the women had of them as fathers. Their precarious economic status and lack of resources made it difficult for them to enter a marriagelike relationship. As Furstenberg put it, "When ill-timed pregnancies occur in unstable partnerships to men who have few material resources for managing unplanned parenthood, they challenge, to say the least, the commitment of young fathers. Fatherhood occurs to men who often have a personal biography that poorly equips them to act out their intentions . . . and fatherhood takes place in a culture where the gap between good intentions and good performance is large and widely recognized."[49]

Still, contrary to the popular belief, the fathers do have appreciable involvement with their children in their earlier years. Frank Furstenberg and Kathleen Mullen Harris,[50] in a twenty-year follow up of their Baltimore study, found that about half the children lived with their biological father at some time during their first eighteen years, mostly during early childhood. As babies, more than 80 percent received child support from their fathers, but by the time the children reached age four, only a third received financial support. Rebecca Maynard and her colleagues also found that although two-thirds of the teenage mothers had some contact with the fathers early on, within two years of the birth of the child only a fourth of the teenage mothers on welfare received support from the fathers.[51] Only fathers who married the child's mother continued to support them. Furstenberg and Harris found that the more frequent the contact between the father and the child, the greater the bonding between them. Of particular importance was the fact that early contact did not ensure bonding, unless it was sustained in later years. They also found that it was not just the father's presence in the child's life but the closeness of the relationship between them that affected the child's future well-being, as indicated by educational attainment and the potential of teenage birth and depression. That is, the children are better off if they have sustained and frequent contact with their fathers, especially when they live with them.

The Impact of an Impoverished Environment

Taking all these studies together, it seems to us an inescapable conclusion that poverty and lack of economic resources and opportunities increase significantly the risk of single teenage parenthood. Several of the significant risk factors identified by Haveman and Wolfe—low income, mother's low level of education, and parental separations—are direct and indirect indicators of the impoverished familial environment in which the teenagers live. As noted by Sara McLanahan and Gary Sandefur, parental separations create tremendous economic hardships on the family.[52] The lack of education of the teenagers' mothers is surely another sign of an impoverished opportunity structure. Haveman and Wolfe estimated that if all the mothers completed high school, the rate of teenage nonmarital births would decline by 48 percent. If there were one less parental separation, the rate would decline by 27 percent, and if there were a 20 percent increase in the average ratio of income to the poverty line, the rate would decline by 10 percent.[53]

When we look at the life circumstances of *both* teenage mothers and the fathers of their children, we can begin to appreciate the profound impact of growing up and living in poverty on the decisions and choices they make about sexuality, pregnancy, marriage, and birth. Growing up in a poor single-parent family, living in an economically bleak environment that lacks opportunities and a future, attending poor-quality schools, lacking access to family planning, and relying on welfare as the only source of stable financial support exposes young women and men to greater risk of early sexual activity and delayed marriage, ineffective use of contraceptives, failure in school, deviant behavior, unwanted pregnancies, and early childbearing. For ethnic minority teenagers, especially African Americans, residential segregation further exacerbates the economic and social deprivation they encounter and heightens their risk.[54] A vicious cycle develops in which both the men and the women, in response to economically harsh life circumstances, engage in mutually reinforcing risk-taking behaviors that are likely to result in single parenthood and further poverty.

Arline Geronimus has gone further, suggesting that the harsh economic and labor market conditions facing poor black women may actually encourage early births as an adaptive strategy.[55] By the time they reach age twenty, the women must work full-time and remain employed. Poor black women have far greater difficulty balancing work with caring for their children because of lack of adequate child care resources and the infeasibility of suspending their employment temporarily. Therefore, according to Geronimus, the only time they have to fully invest in the care of their children is during their teenage years, when they cannot work and when they can live with their families of origin and receive the protection and care of their own mothers. By the time they reach their twenties and must work, their children are old enough to be in school, and they need less attention. Geronimus further proposed that the progressive effects of living in a very disadvantaged environment could leave older women at greater risk of poor pregnancy outcomes, thus encouraging earlier childbirths.

Still, most teenage women and their children would be better off delaying childbearing. For many of the teenagers who do become pregnant, it is a culmination of risk-taking behaviors whose potential consequences are not fully understood or appreciated when living in an environment with a high level of poverty and limited opportunities. Retrospective studies show that very few teenagers wanted to become pregnant when they initiated sexual activity.[56] Thus, teenagers may fail to grasp fully the costs involved, not because the costs are small but because it is hard to appreciate them in the context of an environment that seems to offer little of a future. For example, dropping out of school may not seem much of a cost at a time when the value of education is not visible in such a deprived environment, and when other inducements such as having a boyfriend, playing out a dream of forming a loving household and hoping that having a child will solidify the affection of the man,[57] or exchanging sexual favors for gifts and promises of financial support become more attractive. Put differently, in such a restricted social and economic environment, the young woman may perceive that she has little to lose if she becomes pregnant, and may gain in status as an "adult" if she has a baby. Only after the fact do teenage mothers realize the costs they have to bear, and they certainly do not want their children to go through a similar experience.[58] As Musick emphasizes, many teenagers, despite being aware of the costs involved, are driven to such risk-taking behavior by "emotional discontinuities—breaks between present and past, between thought and feeling, and between actions and intentions."[59]

The implications of these studies to social policy are clear. A policy directed at reducing teenage childbearing must, first and foremost, be an antipoverty policy that significantly reduces the economic deprivation experienced by both the young men and the women. In particular, an effective strategy to prevent teenage pregnancies and childbearing must include strategies to reduce the poverty of the families in which the teenagers grow up. In addition,

considerable investments must be made to improve the educational opportunities for poor youth.

The Panel on High-Risk Youth reached a similar conclusion, pointing
out how high-risk young people encounter settings—families, neighborhood,
schools, health services, and employment and training opportunities—that are
unable to give them the resources, the support, and the opportunities they
need to grow up to become productive citizens.[60] The panel singled out family
income as a key factor because it affects the family's ability to provide them
with a nurturing neighborhood, school, and economic opportunities.

Availability of Contraceptives

So far we have said little about the availability of contraceptives as an
important factor in affecting the risk of pregnancy and childbirth. The United
States has the highest rate of teenage childbearing among the highly industrialized countries: in 1992 it was 61 per 1,000 women under age twenty. The
comparable rate for England was 33, for Spain and Sweden 13, and for France
and Denmark 9. In part, the difference is due to differential access to effective
family planning services. In an international comparative study, Elise F. Jones
and her colleagues found that countries with few unplanned pregnancies are
characterized by wide access to very inexpensive, if not free, effective contraceptives provided by family physicians in primary health care services.
The lack of universal health care in the United States, the reliance on special-
ists, and the unequal distribution of medical services by income deprives
poor young women and, in particular, the near-poor from access to effective
contraceptives.[61]

Young people living in an economically deprived environment also experience greater difficulty in obtaining effective contraceptives because of limited
access to primary health care services. As Sara Brown and Leon Eisenberg note,
many women cannot obtain family planning services because of high costs,
unless they live close to publicly funded clinics.[62] In addition, many women
lack knowledge of the services, have no transportation to get to them, or fear
that their anonymity will not be protected. In this context, Moore and her
colleagues reported that, other things being equal, states with coordinated
pregnancy-prevention programs have lower pregnancy rates, and states with
restrictive policies about the distribution of contraceptives have higher pregnancy rates.[63]

There is also evidence to suggest that access to effective contraceptives that
require a contact with a health care agent may be constrained, especially in the
public sector.[64] Although Medicaid is the principal source of public funding
for contraceptives, poor adolescents may find it difficult to rely on Medicaid to

pay for contraception. In addition, teenagers may find it difficult to establish eligibility to Medicaid independently of their parents.[65]

We have also noted that the abortion rate for teenagers who have had intercourse has declined since 1980, possibly due, in part, to the more restrictive policies enacted by the federal government and many states, the dwindling number of providers, and increased harassment of clinics.[66] These policies, including the prohibition of using Medicaid for abortion services in a number of states, are likely to erect greater barriers to low-income young women in preventing unwanted births.

The Consequences of Teenage Childbearing

A main concern about teenage parenthood is the assumed high social costs to the mothers and their children and to society in general. We are particularly concerned about the impact on the children who are more often than not the silent victims of our social policies. In this section we examine the available evidence. There is reason to believe that the costs may have been exaggerated for two reasons. First, when teenage mothers are compared to nonparenting teenagers, there always remains the distinct possibility that the differences are due to unobserved factors, even after controlling for obvious sociodemographic differences. As we will see, this is true even when sisters are compared, because parents may make different investments in their offspring. The second problem relates to the length of time the two groups are followed over their life-cycle. Differences greatly diminish as the teenagers reach midadulthood.

Impact on the Mothers

In a classic study of teenage mothers, Frank Furstenberg, Jeanne Brooks-Gunn, and S. Philip Morgan followed a group of 404 pregnant teenagers who received care at Sinai Hospital in Baltimore between 1966 and 1968.[67] They were interviewed in 1972 and again in 1984. Because most of the mothers were African American, the analysis was restricted to them. For comparison, the researchers used three national surveys of urban women between ages twenty-nine and thirty-six with at least one child, who were interviewed in 1982 or 1983. Overall, the researchers found that "a substantial majority completed high school, found regular employment, and, even if they had at some point been on welfare, eventually managed to escape dependence on public assistance. Relatively few ended up with large families."[68]

Kathleen Harris took a more detailed look at the welfare and work experience of these women.[69] As discussed in Chapter 3, she found that the mothers had extensive work experience *combined* with welfare. Women who left welfare through a new job were more likely to graduate from high school, had fewer than three children, and did not have previous work experience. Women with work experience seemed to substitute work for education, and this put them at a disadvantage. Thus, teenage mothers who remain on welfare to complete their high school education are actually making a more effective choice if they want to become self-sufficient.

Furstenberg, Brooks-Gunn, and Morgan concluded that about 25 percent of the teenage mothers could be identified as a high-risk group, as manifested by their continued reliance on welfare and inability to escape poverty. It is this group that requires an extensive array of economic support and social services, especially in their early childbearing years.

Although the Baltimore study is rich in data and longitudinal in scope, and provides invaluable insight into the life circumstances and experiences of teenage mothers, its limitations are obvious. Its sample is not random and the comparison groups are not truly comparable. Thus, it is possible that the study misstates the consequences of teenage parenthood. Arline Geronimus and Sanders Korenman used three longitudinal data sets to compare teenage mothers with their sisters who did not give birth or delayed it.[70] Using such outcomes as income-need ratio, family income, poverty, high school completion, postsecondary schooling, and being currently married, they showed that although the teenage mothers are worse off then their sisters, using the fixed-effect model reduces the size of the difference. Indeed, in one data set (the National Longitudinal Survey Young Women's Sample, or NLSYW) few appreciable differences in outcomes between the teenage mothers and their sisters were found. The authors suggested that even using this mode of analysis, differences might be overstated because the sisters of the teenage mothers may be more endowed by their parents. Saul Hoffman, Michael Foster, and Frank Furstenberg, replicating the fixed-effect model on the PSID data, concurred that differences are overstated when cross-sectional models are used.[71] Still, they found important adverse consequences.[72]

Nevertheless, these findings must be viewed with caution, given the possibility of important unobserved differences between the teenage mothers and their sisters. A recent study by Joseph Hotz, Susan McElroy, and Seth Sanders suggests that this may be the case.[73] They employed a different strategy, comparing teenage mothers with women whose first teenage pregnancy ends with a miscarriage, arguing that the miscarriage is a random event and, therefore, the two groups are as close to an experimental design as one could get. Using the National Longitudinal Survey of Youth since 1979, they selected all women who were teenagers between 1970 and 1985. They estimated the effects of a teenage birth on the mothers relative to what would have happened to them had they experienced a miscarriage. They employed several statistical procedures to adjust for the fact that some of the women who miscarried might have chosen to abort the pregnancy. They also divided their teenagers into three pregnancy cohorts—age fifteen or less, ages sixteen to seventeen, and ages eighteen to nineteen.

The researchers found that teenage mothers, especially under age sixteen, were likely to have 0.5 to 1.0 more children over their lifetimes. With the exception of those in the oldest cohort, they were also more likely to have children out of wedlock. The rate differed by race, being higher for blacks and Hispanics than for white women. The women were also more likely to remain single, especially in the youngest cohort.

Except for those in the eighteen-to-nineteen cohort, the women were 30–50 percent less likely to complete high school. However, they were more likely to obtain a GED certificate. Especially interesting were the findings about patterns of work. Although the teenage mothers worked 45–100 hours less per year when their children were young, they increased their labor participation when the first-born got older. By their late twenties, these mothers worked 100–200 hours more than if they had delayed their childbirth. Thus, although early childbirth initially reduced earnings by $1,000–$4,000 per year, by the time the women reached their mid-twenties, their earnings increased by $2,000–$8,000 more than if they had postponed childbearing. There is little evidence that early childbearing affects work behavior or annual earnings.

Mothers in the two younger cohorts received about $1,600 more per year in public assistance until they reached their mid-twenties. By age thirty-two, the differences disappeared. There were also differences by race—the effects were much larger for Hispanic than for black or white women.[74]

Hotz and his colleagues also attempted to calculate the costs to government of early childbirth. They estimated that the total annual public assistance costs of early childbirth, controlling for taxes the mothers pay, are only $665 per mother. If the women delayed giving birth by three to four years, however, the net cost to government would be more than $1,200 per teen mother. This is due to the loss in earnings and taxes paid by the women for delaying their first birth.

This study shows that many adverse consequences of teenage childbirth on the mothers are indeed overstated, especially regarding participation in the labor force and costs to government. It also points out that some adverse consequences are transitory and disappear when the women reach their mid-twenties. Moreover, for all practical purposes, the mothers in the age cohort eighteen to nineteen are not appreciably different from women who postpone childbearing. Only the mothers in the age cohort fifteen and younger incur significant costs to themselves and society.[75]

Impact on the Children

Furstenberg, Brooks-Gunn, and Morgan in their longitudinal study found significant adverse consequences on the children of the teenage mothers who experienced much more educational and behavioral problems. Fifty three percent of the children had to repeat a grade, as compared with only 20 percent of the children whose mothers delayed birth. Grade failure was associated with behavioral problems and earlier sexual activity. The researchers found that the children's family environment has an appreciable impact on their well-being. Thus, in the five-year follow-up, children who grew up with a mother who had three children, was unmarried, received welfare, and did not go back to school did worse than those whose mother married, had no other children, returned to school, and did not receive welfare. Similarly, teenage children whose mothers were on welfare, unmarried, or did not graduate from high school were more likely to fail a grade.[76]

Moore and her colleagues compared children born to teenage mothers to children born to mothers who delayed childbirth until their early twenties.[77] The researchers distinguished between children born to teenage mothers seventeen years old or younger and children born to older teenage mothers (eighteen to nineteen years old). The findings indicate that the younger the mother at birth of the child, the greater the likelihood that the child will experience cognitive and behavioral difficulties. On the other hand, children born to the older teenage mothers are not appreciably different from children born to women in their early twenties. Although these findings should be interpreted with caution, given the difficulties in controlling for all the relevant background variables, they do support the notion, noted by Hotz and his colleagues, that the most deleterious effects of teenage childbearing occur among the youngest mothers.

Sara McLanahan, in her review of current research, also concluded that, especially for younger teenage mothers, the adverse effects on the children are substantial, particularly in terms of cognitive development and quality of home environment. Yet there is no evidence of adverse health consequences.[78] A troubling finding is that remarriage does not seem to improve the social development of the child, except among African Americans, whose rate of remarriage is quite low. One possibility, as noted by Furstenberg, Brooks-Gunn, and Morgan, might be the lack of strong bonding between the stepfather and the child.[79]

Although more careful research needs to be done to control for differences among the women, on balance the evidence points to significant adverse cognitive and behavioral effects on the children of younger teenage mothers. But we must remember that they constitute a relatively small group among all teenage parents.

Programs for Teenage Parents: What Does and Doesn't Work?

In this section we review some of the educational, employment, and treatment programs targeted at poor teenage parents. There is a plethora of such programs, and we have selected a few that have been carefully evaluated using an experimental design, and that have become models for various state and local initiatives.[80] We begin by examining programs that focus on the provision of educational and employment opportunities normally not available to poor teenagers. Next, we review the merit of voluntary versus mandatory educational and social service programs for teenage parents on welfare, and show that the results are very modest, but that in general voluntary programs perform better. These findings do not bode well for the current rush to legislate mandatory educational programs for teenage parents on welfare. Finally, we discuss the results of some intensive treatment programs.

Provision of Educational and Employment Opportunities

A key emphasis of such programs is to make education and posteducation employment opportunities a more attractive option. One example of such an effective program is the Youth Incentive Entitlement Pilot Project described in Chapter 5, which provided employment opportunities to young people while in school and during the summer. We have seen that such a program was also effective in reducing teenage childbearing.

The second example is the Quantum Opportunity Program (QOP), which was a small demonstration project aimed at improving the educational achievement and success among high school students from families on welfare.[81] It did so by providing additional educational activities such as tutoring, community service activities, and developmental activities such as life/family skills. QOP guaranteed up to 250 hours in each of these activities starting in the ninth grade through high school graduation for in-school youth or anytime for youth who dropped out, transferred, or left their original neighborhood. Students received hourly stipends starting at $1.00 per hour and rising to $1.33. After completing a hundred hours of programing, the students received a $100 bonus, and an equal amount was put into a savings account to be used for future college or training. Staff also received bonus payments and incentives. In each of the five sites—San Antonio, Philadelphia, Milwaukee, Saginaw (Michigan), and Oklahoma City—twenty-five young people entering the ninth grade and living in families receiving public assistance were randomly assigned to the experimental and control groups. The program began in 1989 and the students were followed through 1993. The evaluation showed that the young people in the experimental group were much more likely to graduate from high school, more likely to be in college, less likely to drop out of school, and less likely to have children. They were also more hopeful about the future and more likely to consider their lives a success. From a cost-benefit perspective, assuming those in college will complete their education, the expected total benefit per person was $32,244. The total cost was $10,000, with a net benefit of $21,644. Thus, an investment of an additional $10,000 in the education of these high-risk youth produced a threefold return in benefits. Of course, although QOP seems a highly promising program, attaining its impressive results may not be possible on a broader scale.

In this context, we need also to consider the importance of school-to-work programs that resulted in the School-to-Work Opportunities Act of 1994. As we noted earlier, low-income youth have fewer opportunities to study in high-quality schools and to be adequately prepared for either postsecondary education or the workplace. Although we still lack evaluation of the impact of such programs, several promising models have been initiated and implemented.[82]

Common to all these programs is an attempt to move away from the traditional and often ineffective vocational education to a model that provides much closer integration between school and work. By bringing the workplace into the classroom, both the academic curriculum and the vocational preparation are more attuned to the skills needed in the workplace, and the students are better prepared to meet the workplace requirements.

Voluntary Educational and Social Service Programs

For teenagers who do become mothers, a human capital strategy that enhances their employability and parenting skills is particularly important. That is, programs and services must be developed to keep the mothers in school, improve their family planning capabilities, enhance their parenting skills, and ensure adequate support systems to protect the well being of their children. Several such programs (for example, Project Redirection and New Chance) have been evaluated and have shown modest positive results.

Project Redirection was a multisite voluntary comprehensive intervention operating between 1980 and 1986 for mothers under age seventeen who were on or eligible for AFDC, and did not have a high school diploma or GED certificate.[83] Besides providing education and job, parenting, and life-skills training, the program actively encouraged the participants to delay further childbearing. Building trusting relationships with and enhancing the self-esteem of the participants was a primary program focus. The project provided services both on site and through existing community organizations. Services included medical care for the mother and her baby, educational and employment services, and "life management," such as family planning, nutrition, child-rearing, budgeting, and assertiveness training. The participants' link to outside services was strengthened through workshops, peer support groups, and individual counseling, and by pairing each participant with a mentor—adult women from the community who volunteered to provide ongoing support, guidance, and friendship outside and within the formal program structure. "They served as the teenagers' friends and confidants, reinforced the program messages, monitored the teenagers' scheduled activities, relayed problems and progress back to staff, and taught participants, by their own example, how to be effective parents."[84]

Overall, the five-year follow-up found that Redirection participants had higher employment rates than the comparison group (34 percent compared with 28 percent), and higher weekly earnings ($68 per week versus $45 per week). Nevertheless, the program did not have an impact on total household income. Ten percent fewer women in the experimental group were receiving AFDC than those in the comparison group (49 percent versus 59 percent). Although the Redirection women had fewer repeat pregnancies at year one than the comparison group, by year five they had slightly larger families (2.4 children compared to 2.0 children). Further, the Redirection participants scored higher on parenting skills and a larger percentage had children enrolled in Head Start. Independent of the effect Head Start might have had, the children of these mothers scored higher on vocabulary tests than their counterparts. Unfortunately, however, even among these children skills remained below the national average (in the twentieth percentile). Finally, lower problem-behavior scores were obtained by the project children than among the comparisons, although maladjustment was not an attribute of either group.

The program did *not* affect the education, employment, or welfare dependence of those who either were *not in school* at time of enrollment or had *never worked,* although it did positively influence their parenting and child development outcomes. Overall, it seems clear that the effects the program was able to achieve were positive and enduring. Nevertheless, most of these women and their children remained disadvantaged and poor. Fewer than half had completed high school or received a GED certificate, only a third were employed, and more than 50 percent were still receiving AFDC.

New Chance was also a voluntary comprehensive service demonstration for young, unmarried, welfare-dependent women who had children as teenagers and were high school dropouts.[85] The overall goal of New Chance was to enhance the long-term self-sufficiency and well-being of the participants by preparing them "for their dual roles as productive earners and effective parents." In addition, the program hoped to strengthen the cognitive, emotional, and social development of the participants' children. Findings from the interim evaluation are mixed.

In an attempt to foster a "warm and supportive—but demanding—environment," New Chance program components had small caseloads and the services were intensive (twenty to thirty hours per week). Although participation was limited to eighteen months, a follow-up year of case management (which included individual counseling) was offered. Free child care (most of which was on-site), parenting education, and pediatric health services were provided throughout the program. The education and employment components were delivered in two phases. In phase 1, the women were offered basic education and GED preparation, employability development classes, and personal development classes (including health and life-skills education and family planning information). Phase 2 services were more intensively employment oriented. These components were offered after a participant had either earned a GED certificate or been in the program for five months. Many of these services, which included skills training, paid and unpaid internships, and job placement assistance, were provided off site.

The interim evaluation was conducted eighteen months after enrollment. Although the program was able to increase GED receipt and high school completion by 13 percent for the experimental group (43 percent as compared to 30 percent), reading skills remained similar for both groups (7.8 grade level). During the follow-up period, the experimentals were more likely to engage in education (85 percent versus 60 percent) and averaged twice as many weeks of participation.

Although both groups had similar birth rates at follow-up (about 27 percent), the women in the experimental group were less likely to be regular contraceptors. The New Chance participants were also more likely to have been pregnant at some time after random assignment (57 percent compared to 53 percent). A higher percentage of women in the experimental group (21 percent) than in the control group (13 percent) obtained a GED certificate despite having a pregnancy during the follow-up period. [86]

As a result of spending more time in education and training, the experimental group was less likely to have been employed in the first six months following random assignment; however, employment rates began to converge over time. After eighteen months in the program, "61 percent of the sample had not yet obtained their GED or high school diplomas; 65 percent were neither employed nor in an education or training program; and 82 percent were still on welfare."[87] The interim results of New Chance are somewhat disappointing but may also reflect the short duration of the follow-up period.

Mandatory Educational and Social Service Programs

Both Project Redirection and New Chance were voluntary programs. We now have experience with similar programs that are *mandatory* and are targeted specifically at teenage parents who are active welfare recipients—the Learning, Earning and Parenting Program (LEAP) and the Teenage Parent Demonstration project. They are prototypes of the programs, combining services with sanctions and inducements, that are being implemented on a wide scale in many states.

In 1989, Ohio established its Learning, Earning, and Parenting Program, one of the first mandatory, large-scale demonstrations for all adolescent mothers (under age twenty) receiving AFDC who have not had a high school diploma or GED certificate.[88] The main goal of the program was to increase school completion. This applied both to teenagers who were in school and to dropouts. Teenagers who were enrolled in a school or program received a bonus of $62. They also received an additional $62 in their welfare check for each month in which they met the attendance requirements. Teenagers who failed to enroll without good cause or had too many unexcused absences were sanctioned $62 each month until they complied.[89] In addition, the program used case managers to explain the program rules, help the students in overcoming barriers to attendance, and monitor compliance. Child care and transportation subsidies were also provided. Besides case management, transportation, and child care assistance, the education system was expected to provide all services.[90]

Within eighteen months of eligibility, 93 percent of the eligible teenagers were scheduled for either a sanction or a bonus—18 percent were scheduled for sanctions only, 38 percent for both sanctions and bonuses, and 37 percent for bonuses only. The Manpower Demonstration Research Corporation estimated that the rate of sanctioning requests was more than three times higher than for mandatory welfare-to-work programs for adults. Twenty two percent of the LEAP teenagers were *repeatedly* sanctioned, most of whom dropped out school for more than a year prior to entering LEAP, and 13 percent were subject to four or more sanctions but never cooperated with the program. This is an important lesson about the relative effectiveness of sanctions in such programs. These findings suggest that staff may be spending considerable efforts to force recalcitrant young people, who are less likely to benefit or succeed in the program, to participate, and in so doing may divert energy and resources from the more promising participants.

The three-year evaluation shows that although LEAP was successful, the gains have been quite modest. LEAP did increase school retention.[91] Among those already enrolled, retention increased by 10.3 percent in the first twelve months following entry to LEAP. Among teenagers who dropped out, there was a 13.4 percent increase in the return to school. Still, less than 20 percent of the dropouts who otherwise would not have enrolled in school actually enrolled because of LEAP. Overall, 21.1 percent of LEAP teenagers, compared with 15.5 percent of the controls, either completed high school or received a GED.[92]

To determine whether additional support services would enhance LEAP's effects, the Cleveland Student Parent Demonstration was mounted. In this special program, students in six of the city's twelve high schools received an enhanced package of services.[93] About the Cleveland program, the evaluators concluded: "All impacts appear small, and are statistically insignificant. . . . The estimated impacts on high school attendance, high school credits, and GED completion are all near zero."[94]

The Teenage Parent Demonstration Project was a large-scale mandatory program mounted as Project Advance in Chicago and as Teenage Progress in Newark and Camden, New Jersey, between 1987 and 1991.[95] The program had three main mandates for pregnant and parenting teenagers who had one child and were receiving AFDC.[96] These requirements were: (1) if they were attending school at the time they enrolled in the program, they were required to stay in school; (2) if they did not have a high school diploma or GED and were not in school, they were required either to return to high school or to register for an adult education program; (3) if they had earned a high school diploma or a GED, they were to enroll in postsecondary education, enter a skills-training program, or look for employment as an alternative to or after completing their education or training. As a group, participants had substantial educational deficits. Only 33 percent completed high school or GED, and about 30 percent dropped out of school.

In all the sites the education, training, and employment services in the community were heavily relied on. Therefore, the effectiveness of the program was dependent, in part, on the availability and quality of these services. Case management figured prominently in the program's design and was supplemented with child care and transportation assistance, counseling, and various workshops designed to develop the mothers' personal life skills, motivation, and readiness to pursue education, training, and employment. The average program cost per participant was about $1,400 per year, plus about $800 in community-provided services (less than half the costs of Project Redirection).

Because the Teenage Parent Demonstration Project was a mandatory program, persistent failure to comply resulted in sanctions—reduction in the AFDC grant by the amount normally allocated to cover the needs of the mother— $160 in New Jersey and $166 in Chicago. Sanctions remained in force until the mothers complied.

Over the two-year period, the experimentals had a significantly higher participation rate in program activities, ranging from an increase of 4 percent in job training to 18 percent in job clubs. Most of the impact in participation was due to the large impact (12 percent) on rate of participation in school. The higher participation rate resulted in an average of 0.7 to 1.6 months of more education, but there were few statistically significant gains in basic skills.

The program had a modest impact on employment and earnings: a 6.5 percent gain in participants who were employed at some time, a 2.4 months' gain in the total months employed, and a $21.10 increase in the average monthly earnings. In both the experimental and control groups, patterns of job tenure and job characteristics were essentially the same. As to AFDC benefits, the experimental group, in comparison to the control group, showed a decline of $19 in the average monthly grant, but not much in the average number of months on AFDC. However, sanctions played an important role in lowering the benefit amounts.[97] As expected, participants with more education and greater work experience showed the greatest reduction in AFDC benefits. More important, however, the program did not improve the overall economic well-being of the participants, as measured by their total income.

Finally, the program had little impact on key social and demographic outcomes. It did not encourage living with a spouse or male partner, or reduce repeated pregnancies. In fact, it increased the number of new births. Its only positive achievement was a significant increase in establishing paternity.

It is difficult to get excited about low-cost mandatory programs such as the Teenage Parents Demonstration Project. Its chief weakness is reliance on existing educational, training, and employment services that are essentially designed to serve adults. Many of these services have a poor track record in meeting the special needs of teenagers in general, and teenage parents in particular. None of these programs make the investments that we have seen in more successful programs such as Project Redirection or the Quantum Opportunity Program. Most important, no appreciable investments are made by such programs to ensure that job opportunities will be available or will be created for the participants after finishing their education or training, as was the case in YIEPP. Making such programs mandatory, then, may make us feel better that we require teenage mothers on welfare to participate, and that we enforce discipline and a sense of responsibility in these teenagers. Yet this hardly seems to contribute to the program's effectiveness, especially when the needed resources and the job opportunities are not there. Therefore, we do not believe that programs such as the Teenage Parents Demonstration Project and possibly LEAP are the answer.

Intensive Service Programs

The rationale behind intensive service programs is the notion that early intervention and close monitoring of the teenage parent, both during pregnancy and after the birth of the child, are more effective in preventing maladaptive behavior by the mothers, protecting the well-being of the baby, and motivating the mother to use educational and employment resources. An example of such a program is the Nurse Home Visitation program.[98] It typically involves pre- and postnatal home visitations by a professionally trained counselor, usually a nurse. During pregnancy the nurse visits every two weeks for about one hour. Following delivery, the visits are weekly for six weeks, gradually tapering off to once a month when the infant is more than one year old. The nurse attempts to develop a therapeutic relationship to help the women plan to complete their education, return to work, and avoid repeated pregnancies. This is accomplished through linking the mothers to appropriate services, and assisting the women and their partners to use effective family planning methods. The nurse uses the visits to develop a trusting relationship with the young mothers, to give them information and knowledge about the care of their infants, to mobilize needed services, and to provide social support. The persistence of the visits, even in the face of initial reluctance by the mothers, seems essential to gaining the confidence of the mothers.

In the successful programs, a comprehensive array of services is provided.[99] These include health and parenting education, parent cognitive stimulation of the child, toys and books for the child, involvement of family and friends, and linkage to other needed services. The focus of the visits is on family planning, educational achievement, and participation in the workforce. The effectiveness of the relationship seems to increase if the professional also assumes a therapeutic role to address the mental health needs of the mothers by providing counseling and emotional support.

The evaluation of such programs, based on experimental designs, points to promising results. Parental caregiving shows significant improvement, with positive effects on the child's health and cognitive development. There are also indications that the mothers are more likely to reduce subsequent pregnancies, continue their education, and ultimately have greater participation in the labor force. In one site (Elmira, New York), by the fourth year after the birth of the child, the mothers in the experimental group showed an 82 percent increase in the number of months they worked, and a 43 percent reduction in subsequent pregnancies.[100] David Olds and his colleagues estimated that the annual costs of such programs were about $1,280, or a total of $3,200 for more than two and a half years of home visiting. They estimated that the families receiving home visitations would use $3,300 less in other government services over the first four years of the child's life than families in the comparison group.[101]

Several lessons can be gleaned from the review of all these programs. First, there are no "magic bullets" that can readily alter the life trajectories of high-risk youth, especially young teeenage mothers. Second, programs that are preventive in nature, offering enriched educational and employment opportunities, show particular promise of reducing the risk of teenage childbearing. Third, programs for teenage mothers are far more effective as long as the mothers remain enrolled in school. Therefore, investment in programs that prevent school drop-out would be highly cost-effective. Fourth, voluntary programs that center around the development of a trusting and close relationship between the teenage mothers and professional service providers, who have access to a wide array of needed services, are more promising than mandatory programs that try to coerce young mothers to remain or return to school, or seek employment.

Still, we must bear in mind that the most effective response is to prevent teenage pregnancies in the first place. To do so requires a four-pronged attack on the conditions of poverty these young women experience; the lack of access to health care and family planning; the failures of the schools to provide enriching and rewarding educational experiences; and the paucity of effective sex-education programs. Yet, as we shall see shortly, current social policies fail on all four counts.

Policies Targeted at Teenage Parents

Not unlike our policies toward older welfare recipients, our current policies—and TANF is no exception—are driven by a mixture of "moralistic" and "human capital" remedies. The moralistic solution is based on the assumption that the causes of teenage pregnancy are immorality, decline in parental authority, and weakening of community sanctions against illegitimacy. The "human capital" solution assumes that the causes are personal deficiencies due mostly to parental failure to invest in their children adequately and properly.[102] What is patently clear is that policies which attempt to legislate morality are doomed to fail. They try to reverse the trajectory of very powerful long-term demographic, economic, and cultural trends. These include earlier puberty and sexual activity, a long period of adolescence, delayed marriage, changing economic opportunities for young men and women, decline in religiosity, and changes in attitudes toward nonmarital sexual behavior—all of which have increased the risk of nonmarital pregnancies. The effectiveness of programs that try to inculcate "family values" has been nothing short of dismal. Moreover, such remedies reframe the underlying structural conditions—mainly poverty and lack of opportunities—that put certain teenagers at high risk of becoming parents as manifestations of immorality. In doing so, policymakers are absolved of the need to address the causes of poverty.

As we have seen, the "human capital" solutions, in and of themselves, are likely to produce modest success at best. Although they recognize that the deficiencies they try to remedy may be a manifestation of more serious structural problems, no serious effort is made to address them. As a result, a remarkable feature of most current policies and programs addressing the problem of teenage parents is that they focus primarily on changing the behavior of the teenage women themselves, especially after they become parents, rather than on improving their life chances. Also, social policy tends to ignore the employment status and economic well-being of the men. Third and related, there is little emphasis on effective strategies to prevent teenage childbearing.

None of these approaches give serious attention to the needs of the children. Nowhere in the debate about reforming welfare to combat teenage childbearing is there any serious discussion about the potential consequences of the proposed policies—such as a family cap, time-limited welfare, or the required work for aid—on the children. The mandatory programs being implemented to move teenage parents into the labor market cover some of the costs of child care. They may also make available such services as parenting classes, family planning, and counseling, but their accessibility and especially their quality are tangential to the programs' primary objectives. The welfare and well-being of the children themselves are seldom, if ever, a central focus or a measure of the success of such programs. They seldom appear in the cost-benefit calculations. As always, the children become the silent victims of welfare reform.

What should be our policy strategy? As we have seen, compelling evidence points to poverty and lack of educational and employment opportunities as the major correlates of out-of-wedlock teenage parenthood. Unless these are addressed, programs targeted at changing the behavior of teenage mothers are likely to have little success. We can achieve some modest success through small and service-intensive demonstration projects, but the chances that these can effectively be implemented on a broad scale are remote. Moreover, as suggested earlier, such programs have limited success because none of them does anything about the conditions of poverty that these teenagers live in. Instead, we tend to blame the teenage mothers for the failure of such programs. Put differently, programs for teenage mothers serve a symbolic function. They reaffirm our moral condemnation of teenage childbearing. They demonstrate to the concerned public our resolve to deal with this pressing social problem, and in so doing they divert attention from the more fundamental issue of poverty and income inequality.

We do think that teenage mothers need services. However, a more effective way to prevent single teenage parenthood is through education, employment, and income-support strategies that lift the parents and the young men out of poverty. Similarly, enhancing posteducation employment opportunities will increase the value of education and improve the likelihood that teenagers will complete their high school education and delay childbearing. Finally, if we are truly serious about the well-being of the children, we must above all reduce the poverty of the environment in which they grow up.

We also must increase availability and accessibility to contraceptives and family planning services.[103] Young women growing up in economically deprived environments also lack adequate access to these vitally important resources. One of the greatest impediments, besides the prevailing moral ambivalence toward family planning, is the lack of a universal health care system. Therefore, a policy that provides universal and low-cost health care, in which young women have easy access to primary care physicians providing free contraceptives, will immeasurably reduce unplanned pregnancies. Coupled with access to contraceptives, there is a need to combat the extensive ignorance, misinformation, and fears about contraceptives found among high-risk teenagers. There is a consensus that much of the current school-based sex education curriculum, while increasing knowledge about sexual behavior and contraceptive options, does little to alter behavior. The only curriculum found effective is one based on a model that combines "information, discussion of reasons for delay or protection, opportunities to practice interpersonal and decision-making skills, and opportunities to understand the risks of even one or two unprotected acts."[104] However, few teenagers are currently exposed to such a curriculum.

Thus, rather than focus our social policies and programs on teenagers *after* they become parents and expect very modest results, it would be far better to emphasize *preventive* policies and programs, along the principles we have enunciated, that address the underlying structural determinants of high-risk behavior. In doing so, we would appreciably reduce the size of the population at risk and possibly the relentless demonization of teenage parents that only exacerbates their problems. Of course, such an approach will require allocation of resources far greater than what we currently spend on poor teenage mothers. And this is the rub. The rhetoric about the terrible social costs of teenage parenthood is not matched by an adequate commitment of resources to reduce the scope and consequences of the problem. Keeping the young women on welfare, and offering essentially symbolic services while condemning them, is cheaper for government than making a sustained investment in preventive policies. As a result, the young women and their children bear the costs of such shortsighted policies.

Within the general policy approach we propose, we must also recognize that specific policies must take into account that we are addressing a highly heterogenous population. As with other moral categories, there is a tendency to undifferentiate among those labeled teenage mothers. As the studies by Kristin Moore, Donna Ruane Morrison, and Angela Dungee Green and by Joseph

Hotz, Susan McElroy, and Seth Sanders show, we need to distinguish among three groups each representing a different set of life circumstances requiring a distinct policy response.[105]

Older Teenage Mothers

The first group includes women eighteen to nineteen years old, who make up the bulk of the so-called teenage mothers (56.8 percent of all unmarried mothers under age twenty in 1991). It is arguable whether these women, having reached the age of majority, should now be viewed as adults. In many communities, women in this age category are expected to assume full adult responsibilities; these include establishing a family, raising children, and becoming economically productive. For all practical purposes, these women are not much different from other women who fall on hard times because, for whatever reason, they have lost the economic support of their male partners, and they cannot remain economically self-sufficient. In their reliance on AFDC and the problems they experience, they are not substantially different from the older women we have been discussing all along. Most, as we have seen, have considerable attachment to the world of work and will provide effective socialization for their children. The problems they experience emanate from their inability to find a job that will provide a living wage while also trying to care for their children. Thus, most of them use AFDC to supplement their earned income, especially during periods of unemployment. As we have proposed in previous chapters, an effective response to the needs of these women is a job strategy coupled with adequate income supplementation, subsidized child care, and health benefits.

Middle Teenage Mothers

The second group consists of single mothers sixteen to seventeen years old. They account for 33.4 percent of all unmarried mothers under age twenty. Undoubtedly, these mothers encumber most of the social costs associated with teenage parenthood. Their ability to participate in the labor market at such an age is exceedingly limited. They face a high risk of not graduating from high school. Moreover, they may experience greater difficulties caring for their children because they themselves are caught in the difficult transition from adolescence to adulthood.

What these mothers need, first and foremost, are services that will enable them to remain in school and complete their education. Therefore, they need strong inducements to remain in school. This requires the development of innovative education and employment programs not unlike the Quantum Opportunity Program, YIEPP, or Project Redirection. A key to the success of such programs is the availability of trusting mentors to which these young women can turn to for help, support, and role modeling. The programs also require access to a wide array of health and social services such as family planning, child care, and counseling that are sensitive to particular needs of the mothers.

Young Teenage Mothers

The third distinct group are teenage mothers under age sixteen, who constitute 9.8 percent of all teenage mothers under age twenty. As we have seen, they are at great disadvantage and are likely to produce most of the social costs we typically associate with teenage parents. They are more likely to have repeated pregnancies, fail in school, and stay on welfare longer, and their children are more likely to experience greater cognitive and behavioral problems. A significant proportion of these teenagers may be victims of physical and sexual abuse. They tend to fit the Judith Musick's description of adolescents who grew up in "damaged and damaging family situations" and therefore have unresolved childhood developmental needs.[106]

Young teenage mothers and their children undoubtedly need very extensive and intensive social services that, first and foremost, protect the well-being of *both* the children and the mothers, and, second, attend to the serious psychological needs of the mothers. As Musick argues, most service programs for such teenagers have limited success because they fail to address the special developmental needs of these young mothers. In particular, they need highly skilled, caring mentors with whom they can develop trusting and therapeutic relations that enable them to explore and resolve interpersonal, sexual, and self-identity issues impeding their developmental progress. Such programs must provide close contact and monitoring of these families coupled with access to an extensive array of health, family planning, educational, and social services. As we have seen, the Nurse Home Visitation Program is a possible prototype.

One cannot escape the conclusion that in order to uphold dominant values about sexual behavior, marriage, and family, teenage mothers have been demonized as the Willie Horton of the 1990s. They have come to symbolize middle-class fears of the "underclass," violent youth gangs, sexual promiscuity, and substance abuse. The idea of "kids having kids" conjures up images of teenagers parenting children who will grow up to become a threat to society. As a subtext, they also epitomize the racial hostility toward ethnic minorities and immigrants who are viewed as a threat to dominant values and the social order. Current and proposed policies are driven by images that are astonishingly far removed from the facts. Although teenage mothers are a very small fraction of the welfare caseload, many policymakers have portrayed them as a menacing social problem. In doing so, they have exaggerated the consequences of teenage childbearing, thus justifying such policies as family cap on benefits, time-limited welfare, and mandatory enrollment in schools or work programs. They blame welfare itself for the rise of out-of-wedlock teenage childbearing, though there is little evidence to support such an assertion.

When teenage mothers are viewed as a threat, there is a tendency to formulate exclusionary rather than inclusionary policies and programs. We react only *after* the young women have children and become dependent on welfare, but we invest little in policies and programs that reduce the risk of teenage childbearing. Moreover, we target for treatment the worse cases—teenage mothers who have dropped out of school and are probably living in independent households—and we ignore most of the young women who live in high-risk conditions. We do so because of the symbolic value of such programs. They demonstrate our commitment to uphold dominant family values while showing that we are doing something about the worst offenders. In fact, we design policies and programs with built-in self-fulfilling prophecies. Such programs that target the difficult cases, as we have seen, produce little success and reinforce the image of teenage mothers as incorrigible deviants.

Even more remarkable is the fact that our current policies and programs generally ignore the fathers. Except for legislating symbolic policies to establish paternity and collect child support that are difficult to enforce, the men have been written off. Partly, this may reflect our historic tolerance of men's sexual exploits, but mostly it is because we do not depend on the men as we do on the women to care for their offspring. Moreover, to consider the men will require policymakers to address the inability of many fathers to support a family financially.

In the final analysis, our policies and programs serve as a diversion from the real issue behind teenage childbearing—poverty and lack of economic and social opportunities. Let us be clear that most of the young men and women living in poverty do not become teenage parents. Yet the studies we have reviewed point unequivocally to the fact that an impoverished environment immeasurably increases their risk-taking behaviors. Most important, even if these young men and women experience faulty parenting, in itself a pernicious result of poverty, living in an economically deprived environment only magnifies their developmental difficulties and reduces their ability to buffer themselves against the risks they face.

It is clear that if we seriously want to reduce out-of-wedlock childbearing, we must design policies that decrease poverty and increase economic and social opportunities. These policies must be inclusive. That is, they have to alleviate the poverty of both men and women, parents and children. We must develop enriched educational and employment opportunities that make schooling an attractive option. We must also greatly expand the availability and accessibility of family planning services. Finally, we must overcome our moral ambivalence about sex education and offer curricula that provide not only information but opportunities to practice interpersonal and decision-making skills, to understand the risks of unprotected sex, and to discuss reasons for delay and protection.

Chapter 9
Conclusions

The United States, in the closing decade of the century, presents something of a paradox. Since the 1980s, the economy has been creating jobs—millions of jobs—making it the envy of Western Europe, now struggling with historically high unemployment. At the same time, poverty has remained stubbornly high and far more severe than in Western Europe, despite its much higher unemployment. If the economy is doing so well, if millions of people are working, how do we explain the persistence of poverty? Policymakers take two approaches. "Be patient; if we all work hard, the rising tide will lift all boats." If it doesn't, they blame the individual. If millions of people have jobs, those who fail to find employment or remain poor are said to lack a work ethic. Poverty is not caused by structural conditions in the economy, such as low wages or the lack of full-time jobs; rather, poverty is an individual *moral* fault. Blaming the individual, or the victim, has a number of advantages. It affirms the moral worth of those who are working, who believe that they are making sacrifices for themselves and their families, who are "playing by the rules." At the same time, it diverts attention from the tough structural reforms that are controversial and costly, such as reforming labor markets, that pit capital against labor, the rich against the poor.

Assigning moral fault invariably includes race and ethnicity, gender and family relationships. Today, the stereotypes of the moral deviants are inner-city African Americans and illegal Hispanic immigrants. In the last century, it was the Chinese, the Irish, the Italians, other people from the Mediterranean, and Catholics. The moral fault of poverty invariably includes the outcasts of society.

It is this approach to poverty—avoiding the larger structural issues in the economy and the polity by assigning individual moral fault—that explains not only the extraordinary continuity of welfare policies throughout history but also the *repeated failures* of welfare policy. For more than a half millennium, dependency has been held as a conscious choice made by the individual. That individual could support himself or herself and the family by getting a job, like everyone else. Jobs are available—everybody else is working. But aid gives that person an alternative to work; therefore, welfare *causes* poverty. In the fourteenth century, the Statute of Laborers prohibited the giving of alms to sturdy beggars. The Elizabethean Poor Laws required the able-bodied to work as a condition of aid. In the nineteenth century, out-door relief was to be abolished. Today, work is required and welfare is time-limited. The theory of welfare and poverty remains the same. It is the indiscriminate giving of aid that destroys the moral fiber. It is soul that the poor need, not soup.

Of course, not all the poor can work. Some are disabled, some are too young, and some are too old. The task then of welfare administration is to separate the "deserving poor"—those who are poor through no fault of their own—from the "undeserving poor." Four strategies, or clusters of strategies, developed to separate the deserving from the undeserving. These strategies interact and reinforce each other, and they have always been present through welfare history, although emphasis may vary from time to time.

The first strategy is known as "less eligibility," setting the grant amount to be less than the lowest prevailing wage in the community. It ensures that welfare does not become a viable alternative to work. Setting the grant level as low as possible also ensures that the undeserving do not flock to the community. It is a way of avoiding the "welfare magnates." Moreover, when officials become concerned with rising welfare rolls and costs, they find it expeditious to reduce the assistance level, thus forcing the more "able-bodied" poor either to seek work or to find other ways of fending for themselves. It is easy to rationalize such reductions as providing incentives to work or saving resources for worthier causes. Of course, the poor who somehow manage to survive with less only confirm to the officials that they were right and that the poor are not deserving of more generous support.

The second strategy can be called local administration. When a person applies for aid, someone—in the old days a charity worker, today a local government worker—has to decide whether that person qualifies, fits within the rules. Is the person an able-bodied "sturdy beggar" or disabled? Is the supplicant a morally responsible person? Quite often, in practice, these are not easy decisions. Local officials can be very harsh, especially with strangers, since it is in the community that symbolic antagonisms are often most keenly felt. On the other hand, supplicants can evoke sympathy—the worthy widow, or the neighbor or relative who lost a job. When times are hard and welfare rolls and costs rise, central government politicians always feel that local officials are too generous, they are letting too many people have aid. Consequently, the top seeks to control the bottom with more and more rules and regulations designed to separate the worthy from the unworthy and to control costs and taxes.

Whatever the reaction from the top, it has always been proved difficult to administer welfare in the field. There were local objections to the poorhouses. Neighbors did not want neighbors institutionalized. There were objections from local vendors to cutting off out-door relief. Local labor markets are variable. Sometimes employers need labor, sometimes they don't. If times get hard enough, there is the threat of crime and disorder. Local administrators are under a lot of pressure and have always had a difficult time balancing the competing forces and making the fine distinctions between the worthy and the unworthy. Consequently, two additional strategies have been used to enforce welfare policy.

The third strategy is requiring work as a condition of aid. The stone pile and the woodyard are self-acting tests of necessity; if the applicant is willing to work for relief rather than seek work in the paid labor force, then that proves the need. Relief recipients, at least those considered to be able-bodied, have always been set to work.

But what of those who cannot work? It still may be too difficult or problematic to try to separate them out administratively at the local level. When times get tough enough, when welfare becomes a political "crisis," then the fourth strategy is used—what Michael Katz calls the hostage strategy.[1] As discussed in Chapter 2, the classic example was the nineteenth-century poorhouse. Frustrated by the failure of out-door relief, both England and the United States tried to limit relief to those who were forced to accept institutionalization, that is, the destitute who could not work. Not only would institutionalization "prove" necessity, but the miserable conditions of the poorhouse would deter the able-bodied from choosing relief instead of work. The loss of liberty, the forced segregation from society, the criminalization of poverty, stigmatized the rest of the poor. Today, the stereotype welfare recipient is the hostage—the young inner-city African American woman who has children to stay on welfare and whose teenage children will repeat the pattern, with a subtext of neglect, substance abuse, and crime. It is this stereotype that stigmatizes the rest of the poor.

As we discussed in Part 1 of this book, the four welfare strategies are alive and well in contemporary America. Welfare grants have been drastically reduced. Welfare offices are run by undertrained eligibility clerks, trying to cope with a massively complex regulatory system, obsessed with avoiding errors and fraud. The bureaucratic task is to limit entry, minimize payments, and purge rolls. For those who have to rely on welfare, benefits are sufficiently low; thus most recipients combine welfare with informal paid work. Participation in work programs has been increasingly required for the past thirty years. Recipients are no longer forced into poorhouses—that proved to be too expensive and unworkable; instead, they are stigmatized and demonized. Accepting welfare, whatever the circumstances, is shameful. The consistent ideological themes are that welfare dependency causes poverty, that individuals choose welfare rather than work, and that therefore the task of welfare policy is moral reformation by denying aid, reducing aid, requiring work, and stigmatizing recipients.

The Lessons We Refuse to Learn

What are the lessons that we collectively refuse to learn from this history?

The problem of poverty—and welfare—is not the lack of a work ethic. It is the lack of support for those not in the paid labor market (primarily children; mothers of young children, the disabled, and the unemployable). Western Europe, despite high unemployment, is not experiencing a growth in inequality and a high level of poverty because a developed social safety net is still in place.[2] The problem is also the lack of decent jobs for those who want to work. As we pointed out in Chapter 5, the evidence is clear and consistent that there are always more people—usually many more—looking for work than there are available vacancies. Not only is there a lack of jobs, but there is also a lack of decent-paying jobs. The principal reason for the high level of poverty and inequality in America, despite the growth in jobs, is that the real wages of low-skilled workers have stagnated or declined, even with the more recent modest growth in productivity. More people in the United States are working more—there are two, sometimes three jobs per family—yet the middle class is barely keeping even, the less-skilled workers are earning less, and single-parent families are sinking. And this same analysis applies to welfare recipients. Contrary to the stereotype, the majority of recipients are working, or trying to work, and will leave welfare via work in a relatively short time. There is no lack of work ethic on the part of the majority of AFDC recipients. What they do lack is decent-paying jobs, with benefits, that will either prevent them from resorting to welfare in the first place or facilitate a quick, permanent exit from welfare.

Poor people cannot move out of poverty and they cannot avoid welfare unless they have sufficient earned income. It has repeatedly been shown that welfare rolls track employment rates; when employment goes down, the rolls go up; when employment goes up, the rolls go down. This is true historically, and is true today. This means that, in the final analysis, the state of the local labor market will determine the "success" or "failure" of local welfare work programs. *But welfare reforms do not create jobs.* And this explains why even the so-called best welfare work programs have only "modest" results.

Instead of confronting the issues of poverty, policy continues to demonize welfare recipients. Despite the fact that the majority of welfare recipients are adults, have small families, are working or trying to work, are on welfare a relatively short time, and leave via work, the stereotype dominates the public imagination. The welfare poor are the "dangerous class." Stereotyping the adults allows us collectively to ignore the terrible consequences for the children. Very large numbers of children are poor; and we know the damaging effects of poverty on children and teenagers—poor health, dangerous neighborhoods, inferior schools, and a high risk of failing as adults. Indeed, no other Western democracy tolerates as high a level of poverty among its children as we do.

Despite the continued futility of welfare policy, and despite the great harm that these policies cause parents and children, there is no real change. The Family Support Act of 1988 was not fundamentally different. To be sure, at least in its initial rhetoric, there was much talk about (but little money for) increasing education and training, but the emphasis was still on reforming the individual rather than reforming the labor market. Predictably, after a brief period, when welfare rolls remained unaffected, and when the costs of education and training were calculated, the talk about education and training disappeared, and the emphasis shifted to quick job search, movement into low-paying, entry-level jobs, and time-limited welfare. These are the same old "remedies"; they have failed before and they will fail again. A modest few get jobs (which they probably would have gotten anyway) but remain in poverty.

"Ending Welfare as We Know It": The Personal Responsibility and Work Opportunity Reconciliation Act of 1996 (H.R. 3734)

The welfare reform legislation enacted in August 1996 is complex, affects a number of programs in addition to AFDC, and is quite ambiguous in many key features. The most far-reaching provisions are delegations to the states, permissions to enact certain requirements, and increasing state flexibility with regard to both state and federal funds. In other words, H.R. 3734, for the most part, is a vague charter for the future. State and local control will be much more pronounced under H.R. 3734. This means that the future direction of welfare will be even more varied than in the past. So much will depend on local conditions—local economies, the politics of race, ethnicity, immigration, crime, substance abuse; the politics of religion, family values, and on and on.

In this section, we will first present a brief overview of most of the key sections of H.R. 3734, especially the ones that either directly affect welfare or impact on the economic well-being of families. Then we will discuss the key welfare features: (a) the conversion of AFDC to TANF block grants; (b) the two major provisions—work requirements and time-limited welfare; and (c) the family-values provisions. We will present some views of how the reforms might play out. We will argue that it is highly unlikely that this reform will "succeed" in terms of the usual political rhetoric—that is, it is unlikely that as a *result of these reforms* significant numbers of welfare recipients will leave welfare for the paid labor market. To be sure, if employment continues to grow, welfare rolls may continue to decline, as they have recently; as we have repeatedly emphasized, most recipients work and leave welfare via work. But these reforms, like all previous reforms, do not deal with the low-wage labor market; they do not deal with the poverty of mothers and children; instead, they perpetuate the failed policies and programs of punishing the poor. We conclude this section with our—very cautious—predictions as to how the reforms will play out.

Summary of Key Provisions

AFDC. H.R. 3734 repeals AFDC, the Job Opportunities and Basic Skills (JOBS) program, and the emergency assistance program and replaces them with the Temporary Assistance for Needy Families (TANF) program. Federal funding for these programs is consolidated into one TANF block grant for each state. Basically, the block grant is calculated on the basis of the state's AFDC caseload in 1994.[3] There are two sets of time limits. There is a cumulative five-year limit on cash assistance (with limited exceptions for no more than 20 percent of the caseload).[4] Adults are expected to participate in work activities after receiving assistance for two years. States must meet a minimum participation rate for single-parent families that increases from 25 percent in 1997 to 50 percent by 2002. Work participation rates are higher for two-parent families.[5] States are required to reduce grant amounts for recipients who refuse to participate in "work or work activities." States have the option to exempt for one year parents with a child under age one. These welfare-to-work requirements are to be enforced by funding cuts in the block grants.

TANF prohibits the use of federal funds for parents under eighteen years of age who are not in school or other specified educational activities or living in an adult-supervised setting. States are required to reduce a family's grant by 25 percent if they fail to cooperate (without good cause) with efforts to establish paternity.[6]

States may eliminate cash assistance to families altogether, or provide any mix of cash or in-kind benefits they choose. They can deny aid to all teen parents or other selected groups; deny aid to children born to parents receiving aid;[7] deny aid to legal immigrants; or establish their own or lower time limits for receipt of aid. States can provide newcomers benefits at the level they would have received in their former states for up to one year. States may choose to deny cash assistance for life to persons convicted of a drug-related felony after August 1996 (pregnant women and individuals participating satisfactorily in rehabilitation programs are exempted).

Medicaid. The basic funding and financial eligibility structure of Medicaid remains intact. However, TANF families will no longer be automatically eligible; they will have to apply separately for Medicaid, and no doubt some percentage will not enroll. States may terminate all legal immigrants as of January, 1, 1997 (except veterans, military personnel, refugees, political asylum cases, and those with a ten-year work history in the United States). Immigrants arriving after August 22, 1996 will be barred from Medicaid and other federal means-tested programs for five years after arrival (the same exemptions apply). After five years, many legal immigrants will be disqualified through the deeming of sponsors' income. Emergency treatment will still be covered by Medicaid.

Supplemental security income (ssi). The definition of disability for children is substantially narrowed. As stated in Chapter 6, it is estimated that more 300,000 children could be denied benefits by 2002.[8] A prior law (P.L. 104–121, March 1996) denies eligibility to recipients whose primary disability is alcohol and/or substance abuse. Current cases are to be redetermined; benefits for those found to be ineligible were denied beginning July 1, 1997. Recipients incarcerated for more than thirty days are denied eligibility. Most noncitizens (with the same exceptions as above) will no longer be eligible. Legal immigrants were required to have their cases reevaluated by August 22, 1997.[9]

Food stamps. Benefits are to be reduced in a number of ways. First, the formula for calculating families' eligibility is tightened by including a cap on the deduction for housing costs at 50 percent of income. Second, the maximum benefit level will be reduced by 3 percent across the board. Third, childless able-bodied adults will be limited to benefits for three months within every three-year period, unless they are working or in training more than twenty hours per week. Last, legal immigrants (with the same exceptions) were no longer eligible beginning August 22, 1997.

Other provisions. Various child care programs (Title IV-A, AFDC Child Care, At-Risk Child Care, Transitional Child Care) are consolidated into the Child Care and Development Block Grant. Although child care funding has been increased, it still falls far short of what is needed, and there is no longer a federal guarantee of child care for welfare recipients who are trying to move into the workforce. Several provisions are aimed at bolstering current child support enforcement efforts. The $50 pass-through (stipulating that the mother receives only $50, the balance going to the state) is eliminated, but former welfare recipients will be given priority over the state in receiving collected child support arrearages. Several provisions will reduce or eliminate the funding for child nutrition and meals programs, including programs in family day care, the Summer Food Program, the School Breakfast Program, and other meal services. States may deny all federal food assistance, except school lunch and breakfast, to undocumented immigrants. Finally, states are allowed to transfer up to 30 percent of their TANF block grants to Child Care and Development Block Grants and Title XX Social Services Block Grants, but transferred funds have to be used for children and families below 200 percent of the poverty level. In the meantime, funding for the Title XX Block Grant has been cut 15 percent.

Devolution; Work; Family Values

Devolution to the states. We have argued that a favorite device for managing political conflict in the United States is delegation to lower units of government. The structure of the U.S. welfare state demonstrates this pattern: when there is agreement on the "deserving poor," programs are relatively transparent and administered at upper levels of government. The most prominent example is the Social Security pension system. Conversely, when programs are conflictual and morally ambiguous—for the "undeserving poor," they are usually at lower levels of government, such as AFDC, unemployment, and general assistance. This arrangement suits upper-level politicians who want to avoid conflict; they prefer a symbolic "solution" but, in effect, delegate administration; a successful delegation is one that stays delegated. The welfare-to-work programs are prime examples. Upper-level politicians promise to get welfare recipients to work. It is the field-level officials who have to resolve the conflicts between the demands of local labor markets, the employability of recipients, and need. TANF continues the delegation process of WIN, WIN II, the *Family Responsibility Act of 1988*, and the state waivers granted under the Bush and Clinton administrations.

At the state level, the same patterns are repeated. We noted that prior to H.R. 3734, a great deal of the decisionmaking in AFDC was at the local level, especially administration of the work requirements. In California, the welfare proposals advanced by Gov. Pete Wilson contain some new state requirements,[10] but the basic approach is to have the counties "experiment" with the work requirements. They will be "rewarded" by being allowed to keep at least a quarter of any savings based on putting recipients to work. Simultaneously, county obligations to provide general relief are reduced.[11] We expect this pattern of devolution to be repeated in other states. Indeed, similar proposals have been made in Colorado, Indiana, New York, and Ohio.[12] Counties may compete with each other to provide the lowest benefits in order to discourage "welfare magnates," thus setting off a race to the bottom.

The devolution to the states and counties is likely to result in severe limitations on the availability of data on welfare. Most states do not have *longitudinal* data; moreover, they have neither the computational nor the human resources to produce these data.[13] Local offices decide who satisfies eligibility, who gets sanctioned, and who leaves welfare because of "work" or other reasons, and counties cannot readily exchange data. Federal and state monitoring will be very uncertain; quality control, after all, applies primarily to *overpayments;* there is very little, if any, monitoring of denials.[14] Both the states and the counties now have even stronger incentives to make negative decisions. The smaller the total caseload, the smaller the number of recipients subject to the work requirements and, as we have pointed out, the smaller the burden on the already underfunded, undertrained welfare offices.[15] The amount of the block grant to the state is not reduced when the caseload declines; therefore, the state has more money. And, at least in states like California, the counties can keep part of the savings. Both incentives to restrict aid and control the data will become even more pronounced if welfare becomes privatized through contracting out, as is being seriously considered in some states.[16] The major recipient advocacy services—Legal Services—have been seriously crippled both in terms of funding and restrictions on the type of cases they can take. In short, there will be very serious problems in finding out what is happening—that is, assessing accountability—at the local level. This is no accident. A successful delegation is one that stays invisible, thus allowing politicians to continue to provide symbolic reassurance.

The Work Requirements

TANF sets up strict work requirements, both as a condition for receiving welfare after twenty-four months and through a lifetime limit of sixty months. Are the federal or state goals realistic? In 1994, only 13 percent of all AFDC families participated in the JOBS program. States are supposed to double this figure by next year. Work programs require additional up-front money. Besides child care, there are costs of administration and supervision. And as the percentage requirements increase, so will the proportion of recipients who are harder to employ, thus increasing the costs. Aside from the projected shortfalls in child care expenses, the Congressional Budget Office estimates that even if the states maintain their fiscal year 1994 level of spending for work programs, there will be a $13 billion shortfall for the next six years.[17] The record of even the best state demonstration projects—reviewed in Chapter 4—is not a cause for optimism. Moreover, will there be sufficient available jobs to accommodate all the recipients who will be required to work? In California, it is estimated that one million people not on welfare are currently looking for low-wage work; in addition, one million people are not counted in the labor force but want to work, and nearly a half a million part-time workers would like to work more hours. And California is expected to move nearly one million recipients off of welfare into work.[18] President Clinton has called on the private sector to hire welfare recipients, but by all accounts this is a rhetorical request not matched by the reality of hiring practices of firms. The five giant companies hailed by the President for their pioneering efforts have so far managed to hire only a few hundred welfare recipients into their workforce of nearly 700,000.[19] Monsanto, also singled out by the President, has 15,000 employees and has managed to hire only five recipients.[20] It is worth recalling that almost half of all welfare recipients do not graduate from high school, and that long-term recipients face daunting employment barriers, including disabilities. In short, "it seems safe to predict that rates of nonemployment among current long-term recipients will be quite high, and wages and benefits for those who obtain work will generally be very low."[21]

On the other hand, TANF does give the states alternative ways of meeting the work requirements—by reducing the caseloads. States receive a "caseload reduction credit" that provides for a reduction in the applicable participation requirement if their welfare caseloads are reduced, regardless of whether the reduction is the result of increased employment or, because of a strong economy, the state has imposed new eligibility requirements or has cut off new applications or simply is taking longer to process them.[22] It is cheaper to deny aid than to find a mother a job or a work program slot.[23]

If the work requirements are carried out as intended, the most likely result is that substantial numbers of welfare families will be subject to the time limits. Long-term recipients, although a distinct minority of the welfare population, cumulate and at any one time constitute a significant proportion of the caseload. States can exempt up to 20 percent of the long-termers, but it is not clear how far states will take advantage of this provision. Exempting families rather than terminating does not affect the TANF grant; besides, states can shift up to 30 percent of the TANF grant to other programs. In any event, the numbers of affected families can be quite high. The Urban Institute, making fairly optimistic assumptions—that states will use the full exemption and that about two-thirds of long-term recipients will find jobs, half at full-time—estimates that when TANF is fully implemented, nearly one million families will lose all AFDC (TANF) assistance.[24]

Family Values[25]

As noted, despite the lack of evidence, there is the strongly held belief that welfare encourages teen birth, discourages male responsibility, and encourages school failure and the formation of separate households.[26] As described in Chapter 8, state plans must describe the "special emphasis" they will give to reducing teen pregnancy and out-of-wedlock births.[27] States have options to develop special paternity procedures for teens and to establish "grandparent liability." There are no separate child care provisions for teen parents; as with adults, there are no guarantees of child care when it is needed for recipients to participate in mandated activities. On the other hand, states are prohibited from denying TANF funds to an individual who refuses to work if the reason is a demonstrated lack of child care.

States will vary as to which options will be taken and how rigorously they are enforced. Many states have proposed a variety of sanctions beyond what is required in the federal legislation.[28] Again, the numbers of children affected can be quite significant. In California, for example, it is estimated—assuming present cash-assistance growth rates—that by 2005, 588,000 children will have benefits reduced for failure to establish paternity, and benefits will be denied to 13,770 children because they were born to mothers under eighteen and to 433,000 children because they were born to mothers on welfare.

Poverty Effects of H.R. 3734

Taking all of the provisions together—time limits, work requirements, SSI and food stamp cuts, and so forth—the Urban Institute estimated the impact on America's poor.[29] The institute included cash and "near cash" income (less taxes) but excluded changes in Medicaid eligibility. When fully phased in, government assistance to low-income families will be reduced by $16 billion per year. An estimated 2.6 million additional people will fall into poverty, including 1.1 million children—a 12 percent increase in poverty for children. More than 20 percent of all families with children will feel some reductions in income, averaging $1,300 per year. Almost half of these families are currently working, and 80 percent of these families have incomes below 150 percent of the poverty line.[30] Most long-term recipients who leave welfare for jobs will remain poor.

Likely Future

There already is a "race to the bottom" at the political, rhetorical level. Eighteen states have set time limits that are more stringent than the five-year lifetime limit authorized by H.R. 3734.[31] Connecticut has instituted an 18-month time limit. Most recently, Governor Wilson of California has proposed a one-year time limit; recipients would then have to wait another year before getting back on aid (with a five year cumulative total). Several states require work participation immediately after enrolling.[32] Michigan cuts benefits by 25 percent if participants fail to participate in work activities within two months. At least nineteen states have a family cap, stipulating no increase in payments

for having additional children while on assistance.[33] There is also a reaction—
at least to some parts of the legislation.[34] However, no state at this point is
either predicting significantly more federal money or easing many of the requirements on TANF families. Of course, many of the states enacting tough
legislation do not have to face the consequences of their political rhetoric for a
while. On the other hand, some governors are fearful of the impact of the
immediate cuts concerning legal immigrants.[35] Indeed, thirty-six states said
that they would continue welfare to legal immigrants who arrived before
August 22, 1996 (the date the President signed the bill).[36]

Nevertheless, there are brakes on sudden, draconian changes in welfare for
families. A great many of these families are living on the edge. Although cash
assistance accounts for only about 60 percent of their budgets, on average, they
have very little to spare, and significant reductions can result in considerable hardship. Moreover, this hardship is likely to be *visible*—families become
homeless, sleep in cars, show up in shelters, and beg on the streets—which is
certain to arouse the liberal community, the traditional children's advocates,
and other political groups and concerned citizens. The problem for political
leaders—both state and local—is that alternatives to the status quo are more
expensive. We have discussed the costs of trying to implement work requirements, especially with respect to child care, and how some of the more progressive states have had to scale back. Nothing in the new legislation will
change this pattern. The increased federal funding is still far short of what is
needed to enroll a significant number of new participants and pay for the
increased child care costs. The CBO estimates that the new legislation will result in a $1.4 billion shortfall in the child care needed for welfare families.[37]
The new legislation does nothing about changing the low-wage labor market.
There are still many more people looking for these jobs, and most welfare
recipients are in a poor competitive position.[38] And the vast majority of those
who can find work will remain in poverty. On the other hand, local political
leaders know that the costs of deep cuts in welfare can also be very costly,
especially at the local level. This is particularly true if there is any appreciable
rise in homelessness—and there certainly will be. Sheltering families and the
inevitable increase in the need for foster care are much more expensive than
welfare.[39] These are direct costs that will have to be paid.

In the past, welfare officials faced with these alternatives, especially at the
local level, somehow managed to blunt or deflect the more serious, more
immediate impacts of welfare reform—whether poorhouses, abolition of outdoor relief, or tests. Our guess is that the same will happen with the time limits.
States will be under great local pressure to use the exemptions and to be
creative in defining what counts as participation in work activities and educa-

tion. This is not necessarily good news. The present dismal trends will continue. Families not only will not receive much-needed help but benefits will continue to decline, eligibility will continue to become more restrictive, and more sanctions will be imposed. The changes will be gradual. They will be largely invisible, but the suffering will increase. It is time to change direction.

Our Approach

We start with the proposition that the problem is poverty, not welfare. Many more people are in poverty than are on welfare. And poverty is the single most important predictor of the harmful family effects commonly associated with welfare.

Our approach is to attack poverty, and in the process reform welfare, by reforming the low-wage labor market.[40] This is no small task. Part 2 of this book details the reforms that are needed. The first issue that must be confronted is job creation. Despite the growth in jobs, and despite the low "official" unemployment rate, there is consistent empirical evidence that many people are looking for work and cannot find jobs, or want to work more hours. Therefore, a national policy which ensures that every person who wants to work can obtain a job must be in place. Existing jobs and jobs that are to be created will most likely be low-wage, low-benefit jobs. Therefore, we propose the following:

- supplementing income through the earned income tax credit or other forms of wage subsidies;
- another moderate raise of the minimum wage;
- integrating other income-maintenance programs, such as TANF and food stamps, with earned income;
- providing child care support as well as improving the quality of child care;
- continuing to improve the child support system;
- providing health insurance;
- reforming unemployment insurance;
- reforming disability insurance and supplemental security income.

The earned income tax credit (EITC), although not trouble-free, rewards work and significantly reduces poverty. Raising the minimum wage is controversial (at least among professional economists), but it seems to us that another modest raise would be worth the risk. A dollar more for the minimum wage, plus the EITC, would lift millions of working families above the poverty line.

Integrating TANF and food stamps with earned income may at first seem puzzling. If people are working, why do they need income maintenance? We have seen that the majority of welfare recipients engage in income packaging, that is, they combine welfare with earned income or cycling—they cycle back and forth between welfare and work until they eventually leave welfare permanently through work. In other words, cash assistance functions somewhat like unemployment insurance, and various provisions, such as earned-income disregards, assets, and allowable savings, should be recalculated to eliminate disincentives to work.[41] The same is true of food stamps. They have always applied to the working poor as well as the welfare poor. The H.R. 3734 cutbacks should be repealed and adjustments should be made in the various accounting rules with regard to income, assets, and expenses.

In addition to the EITC, the major issues with low-wage work are child care and health insurance. How ominous developments in both of these areas have become cannot be overemphasized. Millions of adults in two-parent households and single mothers are now working, and working longer hours. Millions of children—including infants—are in child care, and decent child care—not great child care, but child care that is better than *mediocre*—is very costly. It is estimated that the working poor are already spending about a third of their income on child care, and the quality of care that they are purchasing is very doubtful. No other industrialized country relies so extensively on unregulated, informal child care. Yet the current welfare reforms in the more "generous" states only provide for child care subsidies at a proportion (for example, 75 percent) of the market rate for low-cost care (unregulated family day care). The developmental consequences for children who spend long hours in *mediocre* child care are very troublesome. By ignoring this issue, by refusing to face up to the significant costs involved—and here we are talking about billions of dollars—our society is in danger of significantly increasing the risks of compromising the lives of these children.

A similar analysis applies to health insurance. It is now estimated that more than 40 million people lack health insurance, either permanently or during any given year. The recent debacle of health care reform illustrates the great difficulty and huge costs involved in extending adequate health insurance to the working poor. Nevertheless, we are, as a society, paying for the cost of an inadequate health care system. Families who lack health insurance have to rely on public hospital emergency rooms, which are becoming more difficult to use, or welfare to qualify for Medicaid, which is also becoming much more restrictive. Thus, it is no surprise that families who lack health insurance are less likely to engage in preventive health or to get health care for nonemergency reasons. Lack of health care, it need hardly be emphasized, compromises work effort. It also has serious consequences for children. Children who have hearing deficits because of the failure to promptly treat infections, or sight problems, or decaying, painful teeth, or other low-visibility disabilities that are often undiagnosed, in addition to suffering, are at much higher risk of school failure.

Adequate child care and health care are the essential employment-related benefits that must be provided, and they involve major costs; it is simply dishonest and cruel to expect and require millions of Americans to engage in low-wage work without providing these benefits.

We also propose other reforms for low-wage work. The unemployment insurance (UI) system was designed for a different type of working family, in which the father earned a family wage in a full-time job and the mother stayed home taking care of the children. Today, many workers, especially single mothers, do not qualify for UI because of part-time or contingent work, and because, quite often, child care or other family responsibilities interfere with changes in employment—for example, shift or weekend hours. Disability programs also need to be reformed. Many disabled people are on welfare rather than on disability, primarily because of restrictions, especially the substantial gainful activity (SGA) requirement. These are people who can work at least part-time, in limited kinds of jobs, but cannot earn enough; yet they are disqualified for disability. There are also conflicts between disability and laws prohibiting discrimination against the disabled.

The costs of reforming the low-wage labor market are significant. The EITC already costs more than TANF, and decent child care and health care are very expensive. This raises the question of whether reforming the low-wage labor market is a sensible path to follow.

The Basic Income Guarantee Alternative

An alternative approach, principally coming out of Europe, looks at the low-wage labor market and sees two alternatives, neither of them very sanguine. One is that when the technological revolution hits the service sector, there will be massive unemployment.[42] The other view is that, even if there are jobs, the restructuring of the global economy will cause continuing significant amounts of both unemployment and low-wage, low-benefit, contingent work. The creation of lower-end jobs should not be encouraged because of the degrading working conditions and the harmful consequences to families, primarily women and children.[43] Work, as traditionally conceived, in addition to being drudgery, is also gendered, and single mothers will never be able to compete successfully. Jobs for people such as TANF recipients will never be able to move these families out of poverty. Therefore, the emphasis should be on expanding the social benefits for people who are, in effect, out of the labor market. This argument stresses that instead of forcing single mothers into low-wage work, the value of home care should be recognized and paid for. The alternative to spreading poverty should not be labor-market reforms; rather, it should be a broad-based basic income guarantee.

In a recent paper, Fred Block and Jeff Manza reopened the case for a negative income tax.[44] They propose, for an additional $70 to 83 billion (1990 dollars), to bring all citizens to within 90 percent of the poverty line and raise two-parent families well above the line. All adults would have a firm income guarantee of $6,000 whether or not they had earned income. The same guarantee would be available for emancipated eighteen-to-twenty-year-olds and teen mothers living on their own. Dependent children would have a guarantee of $2,500 for the first child, $2,000 for the second, and $1,500 for each additional child. The benefits would bring a single-parent family with one child to 94.3 percent of the poverty line; two parents and two children would be substantially above the poverty line, thus creating incentives for families to stay together. There would be a 50 percent tax rate until the household received twice its benefit level.[45]

There is truth in many of the arguments in favor of a basic income—the workplace clearly is gendered; there are huge numbers of lousy jobs; there is strong downward pressure on the returns from paid labor; workers would be better able to resist exploitation; people would have real choice in work options;[46] and a basic income would value the nonmonetized work of human and social reproduction. Yet we reject the basic income guarantee approach because we believe it runs counter to the strongly held beliefs about the value of work for both economic and social reasons, for both families and community. We believe that most people would prefer to support themselves and their families through paid labor, and we think that they are right to hold these views. At least at this point in history, work is held to be morally important by the vast majority of people. The evidence is overwhelming that most people prefer to work in the paid labor force, are willing to work even at poor jobs, and want the independence and sense of contribution that come from paid employment. Perhaps this strong preference for work is fueled, at least in part, by the alternative—the miserly, conditioned welfare state. This may be true in the United States, but it is not true in Western Europe. Even with a much more generous and humane social welfare state, people still feel alienated when they lack a stable connection to the labor market. Indeed, most social benefits in Western Europe are tied to participation in the paid labor force. People want the independence that they feel comes from their own labor. Transfer payments perpetuate the historic separation of the welfare poor and the working poor, thus subjecting the former to moral condemnation. We think that, as unrealistic as our proposals may be, generous transfer payments to nonworking adults are even more unrealistic. Those not participating in the labor market would be subject to what Nancy Fraser calls two kinds of injustice—economic and cultural.[47]

We also take our position for pragmatic reasons. One need not belabor the point that the climate in the United States—and increasingly in Western Europe—does not favor expanded, generous provisions for welfare recipients. We are sympathetic with reformers who take a more fundamental view and work for the long term, but our book is focused on the near future, and in the short term the dominant policy emphasis must be on moving single mothers into the paid labor force. This is what most of these mothers want at present. The question is how can we change policy so that the desire to work is fulfilled in a more satisfactory manner.[48]

We recognize that a work strategy has serious risks. We are assuming the present labor market. This means that existing jobs, as well as those created, would be low-wage, many would be without benefits or with only minimal benefits, and many would be contingent. Women, and especially mothers, although employed in large numbers, have not fared well in this market. They suffer from race and gender discrimination, poor working conditions (including sexual harassment), poor wages, and serious child care problems. It is because of these poor working conditions that arguments are made for basic income transfers: Wouldn't everyone—parents, children, and society—be better off if we recognized the value and importance of home care, compensated caretaking adults accordingly, and encouraged mothers to stay home with their children, or at least offered them the option of doing so?

These are powerful arguments, but, in addition to doubting whether home care would be sufficiently recognized by society, at least in the near future, we believe that our alternative—reforming the low-wage labor market—is still preferable. Although gainful employment is no guarantee of the good life, as the existing labor market attests, it is still the surest method of achieving not only economic viability but also moral recognition and societal inclusion—in short, social citizenship. It is no accident, we believe, that the most significant benefits of the European social safety net are employment-related. Reforming the low-wage labor market incorporates the welfare poor into the working poor, where they belong. They are no longer a separated, stigmatized minority. This is the path that the vast majority of the poor prefer. They prefer the autonomy and the moral status of employment. However we may deplore the conditions of the low-wage labor market, the preference for work rather than welfare is widespread, long-standing, and consistent. Reforming the low-wage labor market will be far more expensive than welfare, but we think that self-sufficiency through labor market activity not only comports with fundamental societal norms but, for that reason, is essential for the effective socialization of children.

Objection: Universalism versus Targeted Programs

Reducing poverty and reforming welfare by reforming the low-wage labor market reconceptualizes the welfare poor as the working poor. Our proposals apply to all the working poor, which includes the majority of welfare recipients. Proposals to reform the low-wage labor market are sometimes called "universalism" or "targeted universalism," to distinguish them from proposals targeted toward specific poverty populations, such as welfare recipients.[49] Each type of program has its pros and cons. Targeted programs, it is claimed, are more efficient and allow for consciousness-raising and political mobilization. Conversely, it is argued that because targeted programs identify groups that have always been considered morally problematic by majoritarian society, these programs invariably become stigmatized, underfunded, and restrictive, as well as reinforcing the image of moral fault—witness welfare, affirmative action, and so on. It is also claimed that universal programs mask or otherwise ignore the underlying discrimination that often operates within so-called universal programs to the disadvantage of people of color and women. This claim can certainly be made with regard to our proposals. Expanding the EITC, raising the minimum wage, providing child care and health care benefits, and reforming UI, by themselves, do nothing about the serious problems of gender and race discrimination in labor markets. Our proposals are aimed primarily at reducing poverty by reforming the low-wage labor market, but, as we have pointed out, poverty among the working poor is also caused by employment practices that discriminate on the basis of race and gender.

In our view, the choice between universalism and targeted programs is not self-evident. Clearly, both approaches ought to be pursued simultaneously. In this book, we have chosen to emphasize universal programs not because we are unmindful of the serious issues of discrimination, but because we think that the rhetoric and political sloganeering about welfare reform—with its obvious racial and gender subtext—continues to divert attention from the poverty issues of the working poor, which includes large numbers of women and minorities.

The traditional approach, including H.R. 3734, is to concentrate on the hard cases—those who are more likely to be, or are already, the long-term dependent. The justification is based on a cost-benefit analysis. The long-term dependent is, by definition, the least likely to exit welfare via work and, for that reason, the most expensive consumer of welfare. Therefore, human capital investments (welfare-to-work programs) are more likely to have the largest payoff when these recipients leave welfare via work.

The problem with this argument is that these targeted programs do not work. Despite repeated efforts, most of the long-term dependents neither leave welfare as a result of these programs nor escape deep poverty. Yet policymakers and the public continue to believe in programs with this focus. After every cycle, the proponents of targeted welfare-to-work argue that we have never really tried the programs; the programs were never adequately funded, or lasted long enough, or were tough enough. When the programs continue to fail, the response is to make them tougher. The continued popularity of this approach—indeed, the fixation on it—we believe, is explained less by a desire to move recipients off of welfare than by a need to satisfy the symbolic needs of victim blaming. Targeting, along with repeated failures, reinforces the negative stereotype of the welfare mother. It allows policymakers to avoid the more controversial and difficult problems of labor market reforms.

Today, the argument is that the most recent welfare-to-work demonstration projects have shown that moving hard cases into paid work can be done. Yet the results of the current demonstration projects are, despite the rhetoric, exceedingly meager; despite modest reductions in welfare costs, the vast majority of participants remain both on welfare and in poverty; and there is serious question as to whether even the better programs are replicable.

Our approach starts from the opposite perspective. Policy should concentrate on preventing single mothers who are already in the labor market from falling into welfare and on making it easier for those who are trying to leave welfare via work. The advantages of this approach are the largest reduction in the number of people who will need welfare and, most importantly, the reduction of poverty among single-mother families. Stabilizing earned income and benefits from earned income, including health care and child care, should reduce the number of mothers who have to return to welfare when jobs collapse. For those trying to exit, similar work-related benefits are necessary. In addition, postemployment services should be used to help new entrants into the workforce overcome unexpected problems with, for example, child care or transportation. It is true that the great bulk of these mothers will eventually leave welfare, but reforms that focus on the jobs rather than individuals will help the exit process and reduce poverty.

Our approach—for both the bulk of the recipients and the more dependent—concentrates on work. Yet we have noted that the moral condemnation of the welfare poor involves more than threats to the work ethic; there is always the subtext of race, gender, and family values. Race and gender discrimination remain deep-seated, pervasive problems in American society. It can be argued that when the welfare recipients move into the paid labor force, they will still suffer from racial and gender discrimination on the job. This is absolutely true. However, the current approaches to welfare reform not only do not address race and gender discrimination, they exacerbate discrimination by perpetuating the welfare stereotype. Low-wage work can be hazardous. There are serious issues of gender discrimination and sexual abuse.[50] Current policies, including our own proposals, create strong incentives for women to enter the low-wage labor market. Historically, female wages have been depressed; and despite the apparent gains for women workers, at least relative to men, the future does not look good for the female low-wage worker.[51] This is all the more reason to supplement earnings and benefits. It is vital that social policy address working conditions.

Similar concerns are raised with regard to child care. There is a very serious argument that increasing work incentives for mothers without paying attention to child care issues—particularly the quality of child care—is, to say the least, not in the best interests of children. As with race and gender discrimination, this is a much broader societal issue than welfare reform; it involves no less than the massive entry of mothers into the paid labor force. The child care issue is especially critical for the working poor because of the costs and lack of accessible, high-quality care. The current welfare reform proposals clearly exacerbate the problem of child care. The same can be said about our proposals to increase employment incentives. Accordingly, we spell out the critical importance of subsidizing and improving child care.

At the same time, because of the importance of child care, we oppose forcing mothers to work. Absent traditional standards of abuse and neglect, child care decisions should remain in the family. We present what we think are persuasive arguments that mandatory work programs are counterproductive; they merely make sanctioned families even more poor; there is no evidence that sanctions increase work effort; and there is strong evidence that sanctions are inconsistent with good welfare-to-work programs. However, our proposals do encourage paid labor, and if mothers are to work, serious attention must be paid to the availability of quality child care. We have noted that despite the rhetoric, welfare reform is rarely concerned with the children. This is clearly true with the current reforms that seek to force welfare mothers into the paid labor force, with little if any support services. Poverty is the single most important determinant of at-risk children and youth—poor mental and physical health, abuse, violence, school failure, delinquency, and crime. Our proposals, to the extent that they increase the income and benefits of the mothers, will help the children. But adequate child care subsidies must be provided.

We concentrate on the working poor. By moving into the paid labor force in greater numbers, single mothers join in common cause with the rest of the working poor, especially working mothers, rather than remaining a separate class, suffering additional discrimination. The welfare system has *always* divided the poor by stigmatizing the dependents. Our proposals do not offer an answer to the more pervasive conditions of discrimination, but they do try to lessen the additional burdens of the welfare mother. Without these provisions, or at least those that increase earnings and provide health benefits and day care, it is hard to see any possibility of significant progress in making low-wage work feasible for single mothers. These policies are addressed to the working poor. But since most welfare mothers are part of the working poor, unless the returns from low-wage labor are improved, discussions of welfare reform are not serious.

Significantly, those who argue for concentrating on the long-term dependent leave the men out of the equation. Except for efforts to increase support payments, social policy tries to ignore the men. This is a serious mistake. Whatever one believes as to the causes of the decline of marriage and single parenthood, surely a significant factor has to be the dismal employment prospects of less-skilled, undereducated males, especially minorities. Many welfare families suffer from domestic violence and child abuse, evidence of the rage among the desperately poor. The concern about family values, role models for children, family stability, marriage formation, and decreases in poverty must include improving the employment prospects of men.[52]

For all of the above reasons, we argue that welfare reform should start at the other end—those who are relatively short-term recipients, who are trying to exit via work, and who eventually do so. This includes not only the recipients who are more likely to exit welfare via work in a relatively short time, but also those who already have a connection to the paid labor market, or are more likely to have recent work experience. There is no secret to the method; as many others have said, it is to "make work pay." With better jobs, fewer single mothers will be forced to rely on welfare in the first place and those who are on welfare will be more successful in leaving more quickly and permanently via work.

The advantages of this approach are obvious. Since this group comprises the largest number of AFDC recipients by far, welfare rolls will be reduced, and they ought to be reduced substantially. Welfare *costs* may not be reduced—the long-term dependents absorb most welfare costs—but, as we have argued, welfare costs are not really the issue; they are a proxy for symbolic concerns about threats to moral values. We hope that, as the size of the welfare population becomes significantly smaller, society will be able to deal with the long-term dependents in a less visible, punitive, and counterproductive manner.

Very important—in fact, most important from our point of view—is that our approach will reduce *poverty*. This is a crucial issue that should not be lost sight of. The current approaches to welfare reform define "self-sufficiency" as the absence of welfare, *not the reduction of poverty*. It is worth repeating that the failure to address poverty has serious social consequences for children, adolescents, and adults. Thus, we regard the lack of targeting as an advantage. Sooner or later, our country must address the problems of growing inequality and the spread of poverty among the working poor. The majority of present and potential welfare recipients will be incorporated into these more universalized programs. They will become part of the growing numbers of mothers in the paid labor force, some of whom work full-time, but most of whom combine part-time work with family responsibilities. Work and work-related supports and other kinds of social supports will be merged. These recipients will lose their identity as a separate, stigmatized class. They will be part of the working poor, as they already are.

The specific policy options that we favor are not new. In fact, one of the most important—the Earned Income Tax Credit—has been in place for two decades, and others, such as health care, child support, and child care, have been on the policy agenda for some time. In Europe, various provisions are designed to mitigate both job and income instability, as well as provide a better social safety net, apparently without adverse effects on flexibility of employment.[53] Universal approaches to welfare have also been proposed. What we are trying to do is to combine the potential of the universal policies with a demonstration of the futility, indeed the cruelty, of the traditional approach. The package we present is the way to attack welfare dependency. Welfare recipients are incorporated into the more broadly based programs for the working poor; thus, rather than separating welfare from work, we combine work with income redistribution. Whatever the disguise, the EITC, subsidized health care, and child care are redistributive policies.

Universal proposals avoid using the welfare bureaucracy. The EITC, the minimum wage, child care, health insurance, and UI operate through their own administrative systems. Welfare offices should handle the functions that they are equipped to handle—providing income assistance when a family's income falls below the poverty line for such reasons as a family emergency, inability to work full-time, loss of a job, or during enrollment in an education or skill-training program.

Targeted Employment-Related Services

Recognizing what welfare offices can and cannot do leads to our proposals for a separate, employment-related social service system. Although reforming the low-wage labor market will help the majority of welfare recipients find their way more quickly and permanently into the paid labor force, there will be those who will not be able to make this transition. There could be a variety of reasons, ranging from a lack of information or networks to more serious problems of education and training deficits or physical or psychological problems. This, of course, is the group that welfare reform policy focuses on—the long-term recipients. Although this would be a minority of present welfare recipients, it would not be a trivial number.

We do know certain things about helping at least some of this group. Some need relatively simple support—information, contacts, material support (for example, transportation, child care), and sometimes postemployment support. With others, however, what to do and how to do it present more difficult issues. It is not easy to get adults back into education when they have a history of bad educational experiences, lack self-esteem, and do not have a clear sense of the advantages of going back to school. It is not easy to get people to seek work and stay on the job when they have suffered repeated blows. And, as we discussed in Chapter 8 dealing with teen parents, we only know that the processes by which young girls make compromising decisions are complex, elusive, and not amenable to simple answers and solutions.

At this stage of our knowledge, it seems clear that whatever efforts are needed to help these people, they will not come out of welfare offices. Programs for the hard to employ and for teenagers require patience, professionalism, and the slow building of trust and confidence. These characteristics are noticeably absent in public welfare agencies. What kinds of agencies are best suited to undertake these tasks is not clear. There are many different kinds of programs. Some claim success, but in truth there is not much careful evaluation, and there is always the difficult problem of replication. We favor these programs as part of separate social services not necessarily because of a firm conviction in their success in achieving results, but primarily for humanitarian reasons: the people served by these programs need help, a just society tries to provide that help, and we have to keep experimenting with different approaches.

Our approach, of course, means that participation must be voluntary. The issue of mandatoriness, it need hardly be said, is a major part of all welfare reform. We know that the majority of welfare recipients do not need welfare reform as currently conceived. They are more than ready, willing, and able to leave welfare on their own for the paid labor market; all they need is for the road out of welfare to be made easier. They also do not need mandatory requirements for work participation, family caps, and time limits. It is time to recognize that the majority of welfare recipients are not deviants, they are not in need of moral rehabilitation; they are just the same as ordinary working people trying to make a living and raise a family.

We also know that sanctions are ineffective for recipients at the other end of the spectrum. Sanctions do not get teenagers back in school; there is no evidence that sanctions reduce sex and childbirth; and there is no reliable evidence that sanctions affect work behavior, other than anecdotal stories by workers and recipients. On the other hand, we know that making sanctions part of welfare programs entails serious organizational costs.

Nevertheless, welfare policy is fixated on sanctions. The idea of a young woman who is doing nothing to help herself or her children—especially with the racial, ghetto, crime, substance-abuse, and child neglect overtones—is intolerable. To the extent that this situation is true—and, sadly, there are such situations—this is a matter for the child protection service. These cases—or, more accurately, the image of these cases—should not drive welfare policy; they should not divert attention from the serious, poverty issues of the working poor. Yet they always seem to. An analogy can be drawn with the death penalty. Despite the evidence, despite the moral issues, executing a few people somehow conveys a sense of control, but it is only an illusion. Sanctioning the few who fit the welfare stereotype somehow conveys the same sense—despite the evidence, despite the moral issues of increasing harm by increasing poverty, and despite the diversion from confronting more humane, more fundamental reforms, there is the illusion of control. No matter the cost, to the family, to the children, to society, that woman will pay.

Costs and Choices

The proposals in this book are costly. But, as we have emphasized throughout, the issue is poverty, not welfare reform. We know the tragic costs of poverty on the working poor, on single parents, on millions of children—on all of us. We must face reality: there is no cheap way to reduce welfare and poverty through work without major expenditures. Invoking "costs" in the context of the welfare reform debates is the usual ruse for avoiding the issue. We must start talking about the politics of major income redistribution.

We return to the questions that we raised at the end of Chapter 1. After the very long history of myths and delusions and failed policies to deal with welfare or, more broadly, poverty, we do not have to look far to see what choices we face in the next century. We see societies in which there is growing inequality, divisions between the rich and poor have become increasing pronounced and hostile, and the wealthy live in armed, gated communities. We also see societies that have made other choices, in which social divisions and inequalities are lessened, commonalities and community are emphasized, and children—all children—are valued and cared for. These societies, too, are under stress. There are serious problems of unemployment, immigration, and global competition. Societies with developed welfare states are confronting difficult choices in balancing the claims of the poor, the working poor, and the unemployed with stimulating employment and managing deficits. America refuses to confront these difficult issues. Despite the spread of low-wage work and underemployment, despite the unprecedented inequalities between the rich and the poor, despite the deepening poverty among single mothers and their children, among people of color, among the inhabitants of our inner cities, American policy refuses to confront the structural causes of poverty. It's time to stop the age-old practice of blaming the poor and welfare for poverty. It's time to reform the low-wage labor market.

Notes

CHAPTER 1

1. Fernand Braudel, *The Structures of Everyday Life: The Limits of the Possible*, trans. Sian Reynolds (London: Collins, 1981), 74–76. Emphasis in original.

2. U.S. Congress, H.R. 3734, *The Personal Responsibility and Work Opportunity Reconciliation Act of 1996*.

3. In addition to AFDC, the legislation affects food stamps, SSI, alien restrictions, child care, child support enforcement, child protection, and child nutrition programs. Center on Social Welfare Policy and Law, *Welfare News*, Aug. 20, 1996: 2.

4. Under current law, AFDC is a grant-in-aid; thus, states are always free to refuse to have an AFDC program—as long as they are willing to forgo federal financial participation, covering roughly half the costs. However, as a condition of participation, all eligible applicants for AFDC must be enrolled; the states and the federal government are obligated to appropriate the necessary funds. Under the block grant proposal, states would be given a fixed amount of money by the federal government. If the federal money was exhausted before the end of the fiscal year, a state could either enroll new applicants with its own money or deny aid until the next fiscal year. Or the states could go farther. For example, they could end AFDC as a cash program and use the block grant money for other programs (e.g., child care, training) or for vouchers, and so forth. Under these options, AFDC would no longer be an "entitlement"; poor single mothers and their children would no longer have a guarantee of subsistence.

5. The federal formula is based on the highest of 1992–94 spending, 1994 spending, or 1995 spending for AFDC, JOBS, and emergency assistance. For most states the TANF block grant amount will be frozen through FY 2002. A minority of states will receive an annual 2.5 percent adjustment. The maintenance-of-effort requirement is reduced to 75 percent if the state meets the work participation requirements. If the state does not meet the required spending level, it risks a dollar-for-dollar reduction in the federal grant. Mark Greenberg and Steve Savner, *A Detailed Summary of Key Provisions of the Temporary Assistance for Needy Families Block Grant of H.R. 3734* (Washington, D.C.: Center for Law and Social Policy, 1996), 2.

6. The annual rate is based on the average monthly rates for the year. The hours per week required to count as participation starts at 20 and increases to 30 by FY 2000. See Greenberg and Savner, *Detailed Summary,* 39.

7. There is a third work requirement: Unless a state opts out, adults who are not exempt or participating in work activities must participate in community service after having received assistance for two months. Ibid., 3.

8. Urban Institute, "Potential Effects of Congressional Welfare Legislation on Family Incomes" (Aug. 8, 1996).

9. U.S. House of Representatives, Committee on Ways and Means, *1994 Green Book: Background Material and Data on Programs within the Jurisdiction of the Committee on Ways and Means* (Washington, D.C.: U.S. Government Printing Office, 1994), 324–25, 5, 125, 325. Hereinafter cited as *1994 Green Book*.

10. Charles Murray, *Losing Ground: American Social Policy, 1950–1980* (New York: Basic Books, 1984).

11. Probably the most noteworthy statement is Lawrence Mead, *Beyond Entitlement: The Social Obligations of Citizenship* (New York: Free Press, 1988).

12. Irwin Garfinkel and Sara McLanahan, *Single Mothers and Their Children: A New American Dilemma* (Washington, D.C.: Urban Institute Press, 1986); David Ellwood, *Poor Support: Poverty in the American Family* (New York: Basic Books, 1988).

13. Karl De Schweinitz, *England's Road to Social Security, 1349–1947* (Philadelphia: University of Pennsylvania Press, 1947).

14. Lawrence Mishel, "Rising Tides, Sinking Wages," *American Prospect* 23 (1995): 60–5.

15. U.S. Census Bureau Report, discussed in Steven Holmes, "Income Disparity Between Poorest and Richest Rises," *New York Times,* June 20, 1996: 1.

16. Keith Bradsher, "Ideas and Trends: More on the Wealth of Nations," *New York Times,* Aug. 20, 1995: section 4, 6.

17. William Julius Wilson, "The New Urban Poverty and the Problem of Race," *Michigan Quarterly Review* 33 (1993): 95–108.

18. Mishel, "Rising Tides," 64.

19. Jeff Faux, "A New Conversation: How to Rebuild the Democratic Party," *American Prospect* 21 (1995): 35; Richard Freeman, "Are Your Wages Set in Beijing?" *Journal of Economic Perspectives* 9 (1995): 15–32.

20. Rebecca Blank, "Does a Larger Social Safety Net Mean Less Economic Flexibility?" in Richard B. Freeman, ed., *Working Under Different Rules* (New York: Russell Sage Foundation, 1994).

21. See, for example, the experience of Utah in trying to cope with the long-term welfare dependent, in LaDonna Pavetti, " . . . And Employment for All: Lessons from Utah's Single Parent Employment Demonstration Project" (paper delivered at the Seventeenth Annual Research Conference of the Association for Public Policy Analysis and Management, Washington, D.C., Nov. 2–4, 1995).

22. Annette Bernhardt, Martina Morris, and Mark S. Handcock, "Women's Gains or Men's Losses?" *American Journal of Sociology* 302 (1995): 304.

23. Tamar Lewin, "Parents Poll Finds Child Abuse to Be More Common," *New York Times,* Dec. 7, 1995: A17.

CHAPTER 2

1. Gosta Esping-Andersen, *The Three Worlds of Welfare Capitalism* (Princeton, N.J.: Princeton University Press, 1990).

2. Karl De Schweinitz, *England's Road to Social Security, 1349 to 1947* (Philadelphia: University of Pennsylvania Press, 1947).

3. Ibid.

4. For a recent argument that panhandling should be restricted to designated areas, see Robert Ellickson, "Controlling Chronic Misconduct in City Spaces: Of Panhandlers, Skid Rows, and Public-Space Zoning," *Yale Law Journal* 105 (1996): 1165.

5. De Schweinitz, *England's Road to Social Security.*

6. Michael B. Katz, *In the Shadow of the Poorhouse: A Social History of Welfare in America* (New York: Basic, 1986).

7. Walter I. Trattner, *From Poor Law to Welfare State: A History of Social Welfare in America,* 4th ed. (New York: Free Press, 1984), 18.

8. Ibid., 20–21.

9. Ibid., 23.

10. Katz, *In the Shadow of the Poorhouse,* 11.

11. "Paupers were living proof that a modestly comfortable life could be had without hard labor." Ibid., 11.

12. Trattner, *From Poor Law to Welfare State,* 51–52.

13. Gertrude Himmelfarb, *The Idea of Poverty: England in the Early Industrial Age* (New York: Knopf, 1983), 149.

14. Trattner, *From Poor Law to Welfare State,* 17–18.

15. Himmelfarb, *Idea of Poverty,* 165.

16. Trattner, *From Poor Law to Welfare State,* 59.

17. Ibid., 32.

18. Himmelfarb, *Idea of Poverty,* 175–6.

19. Katz, *In the Shadow of the Poorhouse.*

20. Trattner, *From Poor Law to Welfare State,* 21.

21. Ibid., 54–55.

22. Ibid., 56, 69. An earlier (1840s) but influential view of the advantages of private charity was exemplified by the New York Association for Improving the Condition of the Poor (AICP), which warned that the poor would "over-run the city as thieves and beggars and endanger the security of property and life—tax the community for their support and entail upon it an inheritance of vice and pauperism." The leading causes of poverty, in the AICP's view, were extravagance, improvidence, indolence, and, above all, intemperance—all noneconomic factors. Drink was clearly the leading cause of want and woe. The "environmental causes of poverty" were "filth, crime, sexual promiscuity, drunkenness, disease, improvidence, and indolence"—these were the "serious obstacles to morality." In Trattner's view, the New York AICP "probably loved the poor less than they feared or perhaps even hated them. . . . The A.I.C.P. was no more a charitable agency than an instrument for reducing relief costs and keeping society orderly, stable, and quiet."

23. Katz, *In the Shadow of the Poorhouse.*

24. Trattner, *From Poor Law to Welfare State,* 95, n. 14.

25. Katz, *In the Shadow of the Poorhouse,* 56.

26. There is a small component of AFDC for intact families—where the principal earner is unemployed. AFDC is 90 percent female-headed.

27. Theda Skocpol, *Protecting Soldiers and Mothers: The Political Origins of Social Policy in the United States* (Cambridge: Harvard University Press, 1992).

28. Ibid., 102–51.

29. Alice Kessler-Harris, *Out to Work: A History of Wage-Earning Women in the United States* (New York: Oxford University Press, 1982).

30. See Nancy Fraser and Linda Gordon, "A Genealogy of Dependency: Tracing a Keyword of the U.S. Welfare State," *Signs* 19 (1994): 309–36.

31. Linda Gordon, *Pitied But Not Entitled: Single Mothers and the History of Welfare, 1890–1935* (New York: Free Press, 1994).

32. Ibid.; Kessler-Harris, *Out to Work.*

33. Gordon, *Pitied But Not Entitled,* 84–87.

34. Linda Gordon, *Heroes of Their Own Lives: The Politics and History of Family Violence, Boston, 1880–1960* (New York: Viking, 1988), 82–108.

35. Ibid., 82–115.

36. Ibid.

37. Winifred Bell, *Aid to Dependent Children* (New York: Columbia University Press, 1965), 6–7; Mark Leff, "Consensus for Reform: The Mothers'-Pension Movement in the Progressive Era," *Social Service Review* 47 (1983): 397–417.

38. Only about 15 percent of the state statutes used the term *mothers' pensions.* The rest of the statutes either said "aid to dependent children" or "aid to mothers of dependent

children." The statutes are listed in U.S. Department of Labor, Children's Bureau, "Chart No. 3: A Tabular Summary of State Laws Relating to Public Aid to Children in Their Own Homes, in Effect January 1, 1934" (1934).

39. Gordon, *Pitied But Not Entitled.*

40. Bell, *Aid to Dependent Children,* 4.

41. See, for example, Irwin Garfinkel and Sara McLanahan, *Single Mothers and Their Children: A New American Dilemma* (Washington, D.C.: Urban Institute Press, 1986), 99.

42. Bell, *Aid to Dependent Children,* 6–8; Leff, "Consensus for Reform"; Joel F. Handler and Yeheskel Hasenfeld, *The Moral Construction of Poverty: Welfare Reform in America* (Newbury Park, Calif.: Sage, 1991), 63–74; Margaret Rosenheim, "Vagrancy Concepts in Welfare Law" in Jacobus ten Broek, ed., *Law of the Poor* (Berkeley: School of Law, University of California, 1966), 187–242.

43. Handler and Hasenfeld, *Moral Construction of Poverty,* 68–70; Gordon, *Pitied But Not Entitled,* 129.

44. Joel Handler and Ellen J. Hollingsworth, *The "Deserving Poor": A Study of Welfare Administration* (New York: Academic Press, 1971), 20–26.

45. Ibid., 25–26. Workers' compensation, another important social reform, had yet a different legal and administrative structure. By the beginning of the twentieth century, prominent capitalists, organized labor, and social reformers began to express alarm at the rise and costs of accidents, primarily in the steel, railroad, and mining industries. Traditional common law defenses began to crumble under pressure of public outrage and increasing negative publicity about the uncompensated losses suffered by working people. In order to stabilize costs and avoid the ever more unpredictable common law tort recoveries, employers pushed through an administrative compensation scheme whereby employees would receive benefits according to fixed tables for calculating wage replacement, the extent of disability, and medical expenses. Programs were run through separate administrative agencies; with few exceptions, employees lost the right to sue. Employees still bore most of the costs of injuries. Handler and Hasenfeld, *Moral Construction of Poverty,* 76–79.

46. Katz, *In the Shadow of the Poorhouse,* 207.

47. Nancy Rose, "The Political Economy of Welfare," *Journal of Sociology and Social Welfare* 16 (1989): 96.

48. Katz, *In the Shadow of the Poorhouse,* 225.

49. Ibid., 233. As Bremer put it, "The New Dealers' desire to preserve the morale of the unemployed eventually collided with their assumption that they must maintain the capitalist system on which work relief depended for many of its distinguished features." William Bremer, "Along the 'American Way': The New Deal's Work Relief Programs for the Unemployed," *Journal of American History* 42 (1975): 638.

50. Nancy Cauthen and Edwin Amenta, "Not for Widows Only: Institutional Politics and the Formative Years of Aid to Dependent Children," *American Sociological Review* 61 (1996): 427–48.

51. Bell, *Aid to Dependent Children,* 14; Handler and Hasenfeld, *Moral Construction of Poverty,* 71; Rosenheim, "Vagrancy Concepts," 187.

52. Handler and Hasenfeld, *Moral Construction of Poverty,* 113.

53. Garfinkel and McLanahan, *Single Mothers and Their Children;* Frances Piven and Richard Cloward, *Regulating the Poor: The Functions of Public Welfare* (New York: Pantheon, 1971).

54. James Patterson, *America's Struggle Against Poverty, 1900–1980* (Cambridge: Harvard University Press, 1981).

55. Frances Fox Piven and Richard A. Cloward, *Poor People's Movements: Why They Succeed, How They Fail* (New York: Pantheon, 1977), chap. 5; Handler and Hasenfeld, *Moral Construction of Poverty,* 118–19.

56. Mimi Abramovitz, *Regulating the Lives of Women: Social Welfare Policy from Colonial Times to the Present* (Boston: South End, 1988).

57. Ibid., 321–22.

58. Ibid., 329–32.

59. David Ellwood, *Poor Support: Poverty in the American Family* (New York: Basic, 1988); Garfinkel and McLanahan, *Single Mothers and Their Children.*

60. The chief sponsor and person most identified with the *Family Support Act of 1988* is Sen. Patrick Moynihan.

61. Joel Handler and Michael Sosin, *Last Resort: Emergency Assistance and Special Needs Programs in Public Welfare* (New York: Academic, 1983), 3.

62. Abramovitz, *Regulating the Lives of Women.*

63. Handler and Sosin, *Last Resort,* 3–4.

64. Evelyn Brodkin and Michael Lipsky, "Quality Control in AFDC as an Administrative Strategy," *Social Service Review* 57 (1983): 1–34; Frederica D. Kramer, ed., *From Quality Control to Quality Improvement in AFDC and Medicaid* (Washington, D.C.: National Academy Press, 1988).

65. Brodkin and Lipsky, "Quality Control in AFDC."

66. Michael Lipsky, "Bureaucratic Disentitlement in Social Welfare Programs," *Social Service Review* 58 (1984): 3–27.

67. Kramer, *From Quality Control to Quality Improvement.*

68. Alvin Schorr, "Welfare Reform, Once (or Twice) Again," *Tikkun,* November–December 1987: 18.

CHAPTER 3

1. Monica D. Castillo, *A Profile of the Working Poor, 1993* (Washington, D.C.: U.S. Department of Labor, Bureau of Labor Statistics, Report 896, 1995).

2. Ibid.

3. See, for example, Annette Bernhardt, Martina Morris, and Mark Handcock, "Women's Gains or Men's Losses? A Closer Look at the Shrinking Gender Gap in Earnings," *American Journal of Sociology* 101 (1995): 302–28; U.S. Bureau of National Affairs, *Daily Labor Report* (Washington, D.C.: Bureau of National Affairs, 1994), chap. 3; McKinley Blackburn, David Bloom, and Richard Freeman, "The Declining Economic Position of Less Skilled American Men," in Gary Burtless, ed., *A Future of Lousy Jobs? The Changing Structure of U.S. Wages* (Washington, D.C.: Brookings Institution, 1990), 31–76; Rebecca Blank, "The Employment Strategy: Public Policies to Increase Work and Earnings," in Sheldon Danziger, Gary Sandefur, and Daniel Weinberg, eds., *Confronting Poverty: Prescriptions for Change* (Cambridge: Harvard University Press, 1994), 168–204; Lawrence Mishel and David Frankel, *The State of Working America, 1990–91* (Armonk, N.Y.: M. E. Sharpe, 1991). It has recently been noted that even with the rise in productivity, wages have remained stagnant or declined. Steven Pearlstein, "Recovery's Weak Spot Is Wages," *Washington Post,* March 9, 1994: 1.

Recently, an argument is being made that if the CPI were adjusted (primarily to take account of increasing quality of goods), it would show a modest rise in the wages of low-skilled workers. Even so, the dramatic rise in inequality would not be affected.

4. Robert Haveman and John Sholz, "Transfers, Taxes, and Welfare Reform," *National Tax Journal* 47 (1994): 419, table 1.

5. Richard Freeman, "How Labor Fares in Advanced Economies," in Richard Freeman, ed., *Working Under Different Rules* (New York: Russell Sage Foundation, 1994), 13.

6. Bernhardt, Morris, and Handcock, "Women's Gains or Men's Losses?" 314, 323; Blank, "Employment Strategy," 173.

7. Bernhardt, Morris, and Handcock, "Women's Gains or Men's Losses?" 325.

8. Panel on High-Risk Youth, Commission on Behavioral and Social Sciences and Education, National Research Council, *Losing Generations: Adolescents in High-Risk Settings* (Washington, D.C.: National Academy Press, 1993), chap. 2; see also U.S. Bureau of National Affairs, *Daily Labor Report*, 25–26.

9. U.S. House of Representatives, Committee on Ways and Means, *1996 Green Book. Background Material and Data on Programs Within the Jurisdiction of the Committee on Ways and Means* (Washington, D.C.: U.S. Government Printing Office, 1996), table H-1, 1223.

10. Panel on High-Risk Youth, *Losing Generations*, chap. 2.

11. Aimee Dechter and Pamela Smock, "The Fading Breadwinner Role and the Economic Implications for Young Couples" (Madison, Wis.: Institute for Research on Poverty, DP 1051–94, 1994).

12. Ibid.

13. Louis Uchitelle, "Moonlighting Plus: Three-Job Families on the Rise," *New York Times*, Aug. 16, 1994: A1.

14. Panel on High-Risk Youth, *Losing Generations*, chap. 2.

15. Robert H. Haveman and Barbara Wolfe, *Succeeding Generations: On the Effects of Investments in Children* (New York: Russell Sage Foundation, 1994), 2.

16. Jason DeParle, "Sharp Increase Along the Borders of Poverty," *New York Times*, March 31, 1994: A8.

17. U.S. Bureau of National Affairs, *Daily Labor Report*.

18. Moshe Buchinsky and Jennifer Hunt, "Wage Mobility in the United States," Working Paper 5455 (Washington, D.C.: National Bureau of Economic Research, 1996), 2.

19. Roger Waldinger, "Black/Immigrant Competition Re-Assessed: New Evidence from Los Angeles" (unpublished manuscript, 1994).

20. Blank, "Employment Strategy," table 3.

21. U.S. House of Representatives, Committee on Ways and Means, *1992 Green Book: Background Material and Data on Programs within the Jurisdiction of the Committee on Ways and Means* (Washington, D.C.: U.S. Government Printing Office, 1992), 555–56. Hereinafter cited as *1992 Green Book*.

22. U.S. Government Accounting Office, *Workers at Risk: Increased Numbers in Contingent Employment Lack Insurance, Other Benefits*, report to the chairman, Subcommittee on Employment and Housing, Committee on Government Operations, 1991; U.S. Bureau of National Affairs, *Daily Labor Report*, 28–29.

23. Rebecca Blank, "Are Part-Time Jobs Bad Jobs?" in Burtless, *Future of Lousy Jobs?* 123–64.

24. David Lewin, "Institute of Industrial Relations, UCLA," *Time*, Feb. 1, 1993: 53.

25. Karen Holden, "Comment," in Burtless, *Future of Lousy Jobs?* 156.

26. Holden, "Comment."

27. Chris Tilly, *Short Hours, Short Shrift: Causes and Consequences of Part-Time Work* (Washington D.C.: Economic Policy Institute, 1990), 5–6; David Lewin and Daniel Mitchell, *Alternative Approaches to Workplace Flexibility in the U.S.A.* (Los Angeles: UCLA Institute of Industrial Relations, 1992).

28. Tilly, *Short Hours, Short Shrift*, 9; U.S. Bureau of National Affairs, *Daily Labor Report*, 28.

29. General Accounting Office, *Workers at Risk*, 5–6.

30. Panel on High-Risk Youth, *Losing Generations*, chap. 2.

31. Gary Burtless, "Worsening American Income Inequality: Is World Trade to Blame?" *Brookings Review* 14 (1996): 26–31; Richard Freeman, "Are Your Wages Set in Beijing?" *Journal of Economic Perspectives* 9 (1995): 15–32.

32. U.S. Bureau of National Affairs, *Daily Labor Report*, 25.

33. Panel on High-Risk Youth, *Losing Generations,* chap. 2. A recent study, consisting of open-ended interviews with 56 employers in Los Angeles and Detroit, concluded that African Americans with only a high school education suffer employment discrimination from employers for a variety of reasons. Employers are relocating from the inner city to save money but also to target a non–inner city and primarily white workforce. They are also moving because of a growing need for literacy and numeracy skills, especially "people" skills (communication, demeanor, motivation, attitudes, etc.); word-of-mouth and employee referral networks to generate applicants as well as personal interviews; and strong negative perceptions of the work habits of African American men, fear, and concerns about relations with coworkers and customers. Philip Moss and Chris Tilly, "Raised Hurdles for Black Men: Evidence from Interviews with Employers" (New York: Russell Sage Foundation, Working Paper 81, November 1995).

34. Panel on High-Risk Youth, *Losing Generations,* chap. 2.; U.S. Bureau of National Affairs, *Daily Labor Report,* 14.

35. According to Richard Freeman, at any one time, 18 percent of all 18–24-year-old dropouts and 30 percent of 25–34-year-old dropouts are under the supervision of the criminal justice system. For blacks, the figures are 42 percent of the 18–24-year-old dropouts, and more than three-quarters of the 24–34-year-old dropouts. Richard Freeman, "Employment and Earnings of Disadvantaged Young Men in a Labor Shortage Economy," in Christopher Jencks and Paul E. Peterson, eds., *The Urban Underclass* (Washington, D.C.: Brookings Institution, 1991), 103–21.

36. *1996 Green Book,* 385.

37. *1994 Green Book,* 399.

38. *1993 Green Book,* 615.

39. *1996 Green Book,* 385.

40. Ibid., 4, 134, 874, 861, 896.

41. Ibid., 385.

42. Center on Social Welfare Policy and Law, *Living at the Bottom: An Analysis of 1994 AFDC Benefit Levels* (Washington, D.C.: Center on Social Welfare Policy and Law, 1994), 10.

43. Gary Sandefur and Tom Wells, *Trends in AFDC Participation Rates: The Implications for Welfare Reform* (Madison, Wis.: Institute for Research on Poverty, DP 1116–96, 1996).

44. *1994 Green Book,* 399.

45. *1996 Green Book,* 472–73.

46. Ibid., 386.

47. Maris Vinoskis, "Historical Perspectives on Adolescent Pregnancy," in Margaret Rosenheim and Mark Testa, eds., *Early Parenthood and Coming of Age in the 1990s* (New Brunswick, N.J.: Rutgers University Press, 1992), 136–49.

48. Gary Burtless, "Paychecks or Welfare Checks: Can AFDC Recipients Support Themselves?" *Brookings Review* (Fall 1994): 35–37.

49. Mark Greenberg, *Beyond Stereotypes: What State AFDC Studies on Length of Stay Tell Us About Welfare as a "Way of Life"* (Washington, D.C.: Center for Law and Social Policy, 1993), i; LaDonna Pavetti, "The Dynamics of Welfare and Work: Exploring the Process by Which Women Work Their Way off Welfare" (Ph.D. diss., John F. Kennedy School of Government, Harvard University, 1993). Monthly data studies are limited to about five states, plus several work demonstration projects; although there is variation, they are consistent in overall patterns. They are also consistent with the Census Bureau's Survey of Income and Program Participation (SIPP), which reported that 53.5 percent of AFDC entrants exited with one year, and 71.5 percent within two years. The median length of welfare spell was seven months for " 'AFDC or other cash assistance' " (e.g., general assistance). Quoted in Greenberg, *Beyond Stereotypes,* 17.

50. Greenberg, *Beyond Stereotypes;* Pavetti, "The Dynamics of Welfare and Work." What,

then, accounts for the commonly held view of the long-term welfare recipient? Despite the fact that most welfare spells are relatively short, at any one time a majority (65 percent) of persons enrolled are in the midst of what will be long periods of welfare receipt. This is because the probability of being on welfare at a given time is necessarily higher for longer-term recipients than for those who have shorter welfare spells. Thus, even though the typical recipient is a short-term user, the welfare population at any point is composed predominantly of long-term users. The example that the House Ways and Means Committee uses to illustrate this point is as follows: "Consider a 13-bed hospital in which 12 beds are occupied for an entire year by 12 chronically ill patients, while the other bed is used by 52 patients, each of whom stays exactly 1 week. On any given day, a hospital census would find that about 85 percent of the patients (12/13) were in the midst of long spells of hospitalization. Nevertheless, viewed over the course of a year, short-term use clearly dominates: out of 64 patients using hospital services, about 80 percent (52/64) spent only 1 week in the hospital" (U.S. House of Representatives, Committee on Ways and Means, *1992 Green Book: Background Material and Data on Programs within the Jurisdiction of the Committee on Ways and Means* [Washington, D.C.: U.S. Government Printing Office, 1994], 686. Hereinafter cited as *1992 Green Book*).

51. Mary Jo Bane and David T. Ellwood, *Welfare Realities: From Rhetoric to Reform* (Cambridge: Harvard University Press, 1994), 51.

52. Kathleen Harris, "Work and Welfare Among Single Mothers in Poverty," *American Journal of Sociology* 99 (1993): 317–52; Greenberg, *Beyond Stereotypes;* Pavetti, "The Dynamics of Welfare and Work."

53. Changes in marital status or the youngest child reaching 18, each account for just over 10 percent of all exits. Greenberg, *Beyond Stereotypes,* 2.

54. Frank Furstenberg, Jr., "The Next Generation: The Children of Teenage Mothers Grow Up," in Rosenheim and Testa, *Early Parenthood,* 113–35.

55. Ibid.

56. Peter Gottschalk, Sara McLanahan, and Gary Sandefur, "The Dynamics and Inter-generational Transmission of Poverty," in Danziger, Sandefur, and Weinberg, *Confronting Poverty,* 107. See also Robert Haveman and Barbara Wolfe, *Succeeding Generations: On the Effects of Investments in Children* (New York: Russell Sage Foundation, 1994), 210. See also Phillip Levine and David Zimmerman, *The Intergenerational Correlation in AFDC Participation: Welfare Trap or Poverty Trap?* (Madison, Wis.: Institute for Research on Poverty, DP 1100–96, July 1996).

57. Christopher Jencks, *Rethinking Social Policy: Race, Poverty, and the Underclass* (Cambridge: Harvard University Press, 1992), 204.

58. The sampling technique is described in Jencks, *Rethinking Social Policy,* 206. Edin basically relied on introductions and recommendations to minimize refusals and evasions. She also had to oversample to get enough whites. The final sample was 46 percent African American, 38 percent European, 10 percent Latin American, and 6 percent Asian, which is similar to national figures. She also oversampled from subsidized housing so that the rents actually paid would more closely resemble rents paid nationwide.

59. *1996 Greenbook,* 1241.

60. Christopher Jencks, *The Homeless* (Cambridge: Harvard University Press, 1994), 110.

61. For example, in 1984–85, rents for low-budget families averaged $240 per month in the San Francisco Bay area and Los Angeles, $220 in New York and Philadelphia, and $175 in Chicago and Detroit. Jencks, *Rethinking Social Policy,* 212.

62. Jencks, *Rethinking Social Policy,* 204.

63. Harris, "Work and Welfare Among Single Mothers."

64. Greg J. Duncan, *Years of Poverty, Years of Plenty: The Changing Economic Fortunes of American Workers and Families* (Ann Arbor: Survey Research Center, Institute for Social Research, University of Michigan, 1984).

65. Roberta Spalter-Roth, Heidi Hartmann, and Linda Andrews, *Combining Work and Welfare: An Alternative Anti-Poverty Strategy* (Washington, D.C.: Institute for Women's Policy Research, A Report of the Ford Foundation, 1992), iii.

66. Roberta Spalter-Roth, *Making Work Pay: The Real Employment Opportunities of Single Mothers Participating in the AFDC Program* (Washington, D.C.: Institute for Women's Policy Research, 1994). The report is based on a Census Bureau survey of AFDC recipients during a two-year period.

67. Ibid., 4.

68. Harris, "Work and Welfare Among Single Mothers," 333. See also Bane and Ellwood, *Welfare Realities,* 55–59.

69. Burtless, "Pay Checks or Welfare Checks," 35.

70. Gary Burtless, "Employment Prospects of Welfare Recipients," in Demetra Nightingale and Robert Haveman, eds. *The Work Alternative* (Washington, D.C.: Urban Institute, 1995), 71, 77.

71. Harris, "Work and Welfare Among Single Mothers," 349. See also Bane and Ellwood, *Welfare Realities;* Greenberg, *Beyond Stereotypes;* and Pavetti, "Dynamics of Welfare and Work."

72. Kathleen Harris, "Teenage Mothers and Welfare Dependency: Working off Welfare," *Journal of Family Issues* 12 (1991): 496.

73. Ibid.

74. Ibid., 498.

75. Ibid., 502.

76. Ibid., 503.

77. The probability of a woman who completes her education and does not work being able to exit welfare via work is 0.19; this drops to 0.01 if the teenager drops out of school and combines welfare with work. Stated in other terms, "Women worked their way off welfare when they finished their high school education or through cumulative work experience. Working welfare mothers who attained a high school diploma increased their chances of welfare exit by 75% compared to welfare mothers who did not finish high school. Each additional year of labor market activity improved the likelihood of working off welfare by 8%. [On the other hand] women with preschool children . . . faced 43% lower odds of leaving welfare while working than did working mothers with older children" (ibid., 512).

78. Ibid.

79. Kathleen Harris, "Life After Welfare: Women, Work, and Repeat Dependency" (paper delivered at the annual meeting of the American Sociological Association, Aug. 5–9, 1994).

80. Ibid., 35.

81. "For the majority of women who manage to remain self-sufficient, life after welfare involves work at some point in time, regardless of the route of exit. . . . Work and the conditions of work among the poor remain the best opportunity for policy to reduce repeat dependency among the women who manage to end welfare receipt. The solution, however, is not as simple as moving women into the labor force. Clearly, they are already there, working primarily at low-wage or part-time jobs. Despite the fact that a majority of women exit welfare through work, more than half return to welfare because of work instability, and work exits appear more likely to lead to a revolving poor pattern of welfare dependency. Though many women travel the work route, it is a rocky one. There is qualitative evidence that many women who move off welfare by entering the labor force do not fully understand nor anticipate the demands of single parenthood and full-time work, and the loss of Medicaid benefits, and quickly return to welfare once they experience the full implications of the work transition . . . . Many women, and especially young women, are unprepared for the world of work and are quickly overwhelmed by the hardships and conflicts involved in

juggling work and family, especially in the deprived environment with [many] fewer resources than in middle-class communities. Many do not foresee any hope of job advancement and decide that work is just not worth it . . . . While the potential for work to replace
welfare dependency among poor women is certainly founded in this research, its promise
lies in a policy vision that extends beyond the welfare exit to reinforce and sustain the
obvious efforts of poor women to support themselves and their children through their own
earnings." Ibid., 36–37.

82. "The HHS Poverty Guidelines: One Version of the [U.S.] Federal Poverty Measure,"
Federal Register 60, no. 27 (Feb. 9, 1995), 7772–74, table 6.

83. Denton Vaughan, "Exploring the Use of the Public's Views to Set Income Poverty
Thresholds and Adjust Them Over Time," *Social Security Bulletin* 56 (1993): 22–46.

84. Hugh Heclo, "Poverty Politics," in Danziger, Sandefur, and Weinberg, *Confronting
Poverty*, 420.

85. "Measuring Poverty: A New Approach," *Focus* (Madison, Wis.: Institute for Research
on Poverty) 17, no. 1 (1995): 2.

86. Constance Citro and Robert Michael, eds., *Measuring Poverty: A New Approach*
(Washington, D.C.: National Academy Press, 1995). The panel felt that the present measure
is outmoded primarily because it is based on gross income alone; thus, it fails to take
account of the fact that tax payments and other nondiscretionary expenses can put families
below the poverty line; at the same time, it fails to include in-kind assistance that can put
families above the poverty line. Some of the more specific reasons for proposing revisions of
the official measure were child care costs because of the increasing participation of women
in the labor force; differences in medical costs that families incurred because of the differences in health status and insurance; differences in disposable income because of the
increase in the payroll tax and the growth of food stamps and the earned income tax credit.
Other reasons included the need for regional variation, family size adjustments in view of
the changing demographic and family characteristics, and changing concepts of what constitutes minimum needs—for example, food expenditures are now a lower proportion of a
family's budget and housing costs are higher. "Measuring Poverty: A New Approach," 4.

87. Ibid., 6. There were many other recommendations by the panel—variations for
differences in family composition, age of children, cost-of-living adjustments, regional
variations in housing costs, and so forth. Although some of the recommendations of the
panel are controversial (such as calculating health care expenditures), there is general
agreement on others—for example, deducting taxes and work expenditures and adding in-
kind expenditures that support consumption.

88. David Betson, "Consequences of the Panel's Recommendations," *Focus* 17 (1995): 11.
The report did not calculate the composition of people receiving assistance that would
move above the poverty line. It is hard to believe that many would be AFDC recipients.
Benefits vary by state, but the national average, including food stamps, is 70–80 percent
of the poverty line. In some very high benefit states—for example, Alaska—some AFDC
recipients would no longer be considered in poverty.

89. Ibid., 12.

90. Sheldon Danziger and Daniel Weinberger, "The Historical Record: Trends in Family
Income, Inequality, and Poverty," in Danziger, Sandefur, and Weinberger, *Confronting Poverty*, 33.

91. *1993 Green Book,* 1308. See also Joan Kahn and Rosalind Berkowitz, "Sources of
Support for Young Latina Mothers" (Washington, D.C.: Urban Institute, 1995).

92. Panel on High-Risk Youth, *Losing Generations,* chap. 2; U.S. National Commission
on Children, *Beyond Rhetoric: A New Agenda for Children and Families* (Washington, D.C.:
U.S. National Commission on Children, 1991).

93. David T. Ellwood, *Poor Support: Poverty in the American Family* (New York: Basic
Books, 1988), chap. 4.

94. Haveman and Wolfe, *Succeeding Generations*, 3.

95. Sara McLanahan and Gary Sandefur, *Growing up with a Single Parent* (Cambridge: Harvard University Press, 1994), 154.

96. Panel on High-Risk Youth, *Losing Generations*.

97. S. M. Dornbusch et al., "Single Parents, Extended Households, and the Control of Adolescents," *Child Development* 56 (1985): 326–41.

98. U.S. National Commission on Children, *Beyond Rhetoric*.

99. McLanahan and Sandefur, *Growing up with a Single Parent*, 33–34.

100. Controlling for income, approximately the same percentages of white, black, and Latino students will have neither a high school diploma nor a general equivalency diploma by the time they are 24. Panel on High-Risk Youth, *Losing Generations*, chap. 6.

101. Uri Bronfenbrenner, "What Do Families Do?" *Family Affairs* 1–2 (1991): 1–6.

102. Mark Testa, "Racial Variation in the Early Life Course of Adolescent Welfare Mothers," in Rosenheim and Testa, *Early Parenthood*, 89–112.

103. Hugh Heclo, "Poverty Politics," in Danziger, Sandefur, and Weinberg, *Confronting Poverty*, 428–29.

CHAPTER 4

1. A review of the history of WIN can be found in Mildred Rein, *Dilemmas of Welfare Policy: Why Work Strategies Haven't Worked* (New York: Praeger, 1982) and Joel F. Handler and Yeheskel Hasenfeld, *The Moral Construction of Poverty: Welfare Reform in America* (Newbury Park, Calif.: Sage, 1991).

2. Mimi Abramovitz, *Regulating the Lives of Women: Social Welfare Policy from Colonial Times to the Present* (Boston: South End Press, 1988), 321–22.

3. Gertrude Himmelfarb, *The Idea of Poverty: England in the Early Industrial Age* (New York: Knopf, 1983), 175–76; Michael B. Katz, *In the Shadow of the Poorhouse: A Social History of Welfare in America* (New York: Basic Books, 1986), 33.

4. Handler and Hasenfeld, *Moral Construction of Poverty*.

5. Ibid., 141.

6. Ibid., 146–54.

7. Ibid., 138–46.

8. WIN II budget grew to more than $300 million and stayed at that level until 1981, when it began to decline. Still, this was wholly inadequate for the more than 1 million recipients now required to register. This was still only 40 percent of AFDC recipients. Registration turned out to be a "paper" requirement. Only half of the registrants were selected to participate and the rest were put on "hold." Of those who participated, 25 percent became employed, but 70 percent of these claimed to have obtained their jobs on their own. Under the best scenario, WIN II was able to remove less than 2 percent of the AFDC recipients from the rolls and reduce grants by an additional 2 percent. Ibid., 156–57.

9. Ibid., 154–58.

10. Judith Gueron and Edward Pauly, *From Welfare to Work* (New York: Russell Sage Foundation, 1991).

11. Handler and Hasenfeld, *Moral Construction of Poverty*.

12. Only about 45 percent of AFDC recipients are actually subject to participation requirements, and of these, states are only required to enroll 20 percent of the mandatory caseload in JOBS activities. With all the exemptions, it is estimated that only 9 percent of all recipients are required to participate. See LaDonna Pavetti and Amy-Ellen Duke, *Increasing Participation in Work and Work-Related Activities: Lessons from Five State Welfare Reform Demonstration Projects*, final report, vol. 1 (Washington, D.C.: Urban Institute, 1995), 26. The five states are Colorado, Iowa, Michigan, Vermont, and Utah.

13. U.S. House of Representatives, Committee on Ways and Means, *1996 Green Book. Background Material and Data on Programs Within the Jurisdiction of the Committee on Ways and Means* (Washington, D.C.: U.S. Government Printing Office, 1996), tables 8–9, 426–27.

14. No state has yet been penalized for failing to meet the minimum participation requirements.

15. *1996 Green Book,* 419.

16. Gayle Hamilton and Thomas Brock, *The JOBS Evaluation: Early Lessons from Seven Sites* (New York: Manpower Demonstration Research Corporation, December 1994).

17. Ibid., xii. According to Mark Greenberg, some states are reporting bits of data—for example, average entry wages vary from about $6.75 per hour to $4.44—but most do not report hours worked. Retention rates vary. Because of the lack of uniform reporting requirements, it is very difficult to generalize, but many appear to lose their jobs within a few months, and many of the jobs still leave the families in poverty. Greenberg reports substantial job loss. Nine states reported entry-level wage data. The range of reported entry-level wages is $4.44 to $6.57. Assuming a 35-hour week, this translates into monthly wages of $6.68 to $989. Thus, in only one state would a family escape poverty ($964/month). See Mark Greenberg, *Welfare Reform on a Budget. What's Happening in JOBS* (Washington, D.C.: Center for Law and Social Policy, 1992).

18. U.S. General Accounting Office, *Welfare to Work: Most AFDC Training Programs Not Emphasizing Job Placements* (Washington, D.C.: GAO, 1995).

19. Stephen Freedman, Daniel Friedlander, Kristen Harknett, and Jean Knab, *Preliminary Impacts on Employment, Earnings, and AFDC Receipt in Six Sites in the JOBS Evaluation* (New York: Manpower Demonstration Research Corporation, 1997).

20. For the state waiver process, see Joel Handler, *The Poverty of Welfare Reform* (New Haven: Yale University Press, 1995), chap. 5; Michael Wiseman, *State Strategies for Welfare Reform: The Wisconsin Story,* (Washington, D.C.: Institute for Research on Poverty, DP 1066–95, revised 1995).

21. Handler and Hasenfeld, *Moral Construction of Poverty,* 179–86; J. L. Hagan and I. Lurie, *Implementing Jobs: Progress and Promise* (Albany: Nelson A. Rockefeller Institute of Government, State University of New York, 1994); James Riccio et al., *GAIN: Early Implementation Experiences and Lessons* (New York: Manpower Demonstration Research Corporation, 1989).

22. June O'Neill, *Work and Welfare in Massachusetts: An Evaluation of the ET Program* (Boston: Pioneer Institute for Public Policy Research, 1990); Stephen Savner, L. Williams, and M. Halas, "The Massachusetts Employment Training Program," *Clearinghouse Review* 20 (1986): 123–31; Handler and Hasenfeld, *Moral Construction of Poverty,* 186–90.

23. O'Neill, *Work and Welfare in Massachusetts.*

24. David Kirp, "The California Work/Welfare Scheme," *Public Interest* 83 (1986): 34–48.

25. Handler and Hasenfeld, *Moral Construction of Poverty,* 190–92.

26. Ibid., 190–96.

27. Riccio et al., *GAIN* (1989).

28. John Wallace and David Long, *GAIN: Planning and Early Implementation* (New York: Manpower Demonstration Research Corporation, 1987).

29. Handler and Hasenfeld, *Moral Construction of Poverty,* 196.

30. Yeheskel Hasenfeld, *The Implementation of GAIN in Los Angeles County: 1988–1990* (Los Angeles: Center for Child and Family Policy Studies, UCLA, 1991).

31. James Riccio et al., *GAIN: Benefits, Costs, and Three-Year Impacts of a Welfare-to-Work Program* (New York: Manpower Demonstration Research Corporation, 1994).

32. Hagan and Lurie, *Implementing Jobs,* 17–18.

33. Riccio et al., *GAIN* (1994).

34. Ibid., xxx.

35. In year 3, the experimentals earned $1,010 more than the controls (an increase of 40 percent). In year 1, the difference was $920 and in year 2, $1,183. Ibid., table 1.

36. Ibid., xxxi.

37. Ibid., 156–60.

38. The net cost is the government's net expenditures after adding the costs of education and training that the experimentals undertook on their own after leaving GAIN and subtracting the education and training costs that control groups received on their own. Ibid., xliii–xlvi.

39. Ibid., xlvii.

40. Ibid., table 4.1. Among all the counties, whites and African Americans experienced the largest gains. The increase for Latinos and for Asians/others was small and not statistically significant. Alameda produced significant and relatively large earnings for African Americans—and its sample was almost entirely long-term and inner-city. Moreover, these gains applied to registrants who were in need of basic education. Three counties had large numbers of Latinos in the sample, but only in Riverside were there a significant earnings gain and welfare reductions for Latinos, as well as for whites and African Americans. Finally, except in Riverside, the earnings effects were "weak" for the most disadvantaged recipients, defined as those who had spent more than two years on AFDC, who had no employment in the year preceding GAIN, and who were high school dropouts. See Daniel Friedlander, *The Impacts of California's GAIN Program on Different Ethnic Groups: Two-Year Findings on Earnings and AFDC Payments* (New York: Manpower Demonstration Research Corporation, 1994).

41. Ibid., table 4.8.

42. Ibid., xlvii–xlviii.

43. Karen Martinson and Daniel Friedlander, *GAIN: Basic Education in a Welfare-to-Work Program* (New York: Manpower Demonstration Research Corporation, 1994). The report is based on a sample of more then 2,500 welfare recipients, xviii.

44. Recipients generally received the GED rather than the high school diploma. Ibid., xxxiii.

45. TALS uses written materials encountered in everyday life—e.g., schedules, maps, want ads—to assess understanding and problem-solving ability. MDRC used TALS on the basis of expert opinion that it is an appropriate test for disadvantaged adults, has a high statistical reliability, and has been used nationally, thus affording an ability to compare GAIN recipients with other groups. Ibid., xxiii.

46. San Diego was the only county that established a new county-wide program exclusively for GAIN recipients. It provided a network of centers (classrooms) including computer-assisted learning combined with classroom instruction, integrated academic and life skills instruction, off-campus instructional sites, a new teaching staff, classes for learning disabled adults, and a more intense program than the other counties. In addition, the program offered special services, such as counseling, attendance monitoring, and support. San Diego provided special case managers who spent a significant part of each week at the schools, helping the participants, especially in resolving attendance problems.

47. Ibid., xx, xxxix. MDRC plans an analysis of the longer-term impacts. Pavetti found that merely enrolling in GED classes was not effective. She concludes that education has to be more than standard adult classes.

48. J. Kemple and J. Haimson, *Florida's Project Independence* (New York: Manpower Demonstration Research Corporation, 1994).

49. Ibid., table 2.

50. Howard Bloom et al., *The National JTPA Study: Overview, Impacts, Benefits, and Costs of Title II-A* (Bethesda, Md.: Abt Associates, 1994).

51. Thomas Brock, David Butler, and David Long, *Unpaid Work Experience for Welfare*

Recipients: Findings and Lessons from MDRC *Research* (New York: Manpower Demonstration Research Corporation, 1994).

52. Tracy Kaplan, "Jobs Scarce for Recipients of 'Workfare,' " *Los Angeles Times,* June 24, 1994: B1.

53. Brock, Butler, and Long, *Unpaid Work Experience,* 3–4.

54. LaDonna Pavetti, " . . . And Employment for All: Lessons from Utah's Single Parent Employment Demonstration Project" (paper delivered at the Seventeenth Annual Research Conference of the Association for Public Policy Analysis and Management, Washington, D.C., Nov. 2–4, 1995).

55. Ibid., 3.

56. Ibid., 12.

57. Ibid.

58. "Welfare Reform Under Construction: W-2 Wisconsin Works," prepared by Karen Folk, UWEX Extension, Family Living Programs. Assembly Substitute Amendment 3 to Assembly Bill 591, April 1, 1996.

59. Center for Law and Social Policy, "Wisconsin Works: Significant Experiment, Troubling Features" (June 13, 1996).

60. Ibid., 11.

61. Ibid., 12.

62. Handler, *Poverty of Welfare Reform,* 107.

63. Michael Wiseman, *State Strategies for Welfare Reform: The Wisconsin Story* (Washington, D.C.: Institute for Research on Poverty, DP 1066–95, revised 1995).

64. Pavetti and Duke, *Increasing Participation in Work and Work-Related Activities,* 20–21. Two of the other states, Iowa and Utah, have also shifted from education and training to immediate job search and placement.

65. Ibid. The five states are Colorado, Iowa, Michigan, Vermont, and Utah. The report is preliminary and bases its conclusions, in part, on the demonstration participants only, without looking at the controls. More detailed evaluation studies are under way.

66. Ibid., 49.

67. Mary Jo Bane and David T. Ellwood, *Welfare Realities: From Rhetoric to Reform* (Cambridge: Harvard University Press, 1994), 2.

68. See, for example, Bane and Ellwood, *Welfare Realities.*

69. Pavetti and Duke, *Increasing Participation in Work and Work-Related Activities,* 84–85.

70. Ibid., 87.

71. Ibid., iii.

72. Ibid., 90.

73. Evelyn Brodkin, *The State Side of the "Welfare Contract": Discretion and Accountability in Policy Delivery,* University of Chicago, School of Social Service Administration, Working Paper 6 (1995).

74. Ibid., 15.

75. Gordon Hamilton, "Editorial," *Social Work* (1962): 128.

76. A study by Handler and Hollingsworth in Wisconsin found that the social workers visited families once every three months, provided few concrete services, and did little to enable the families to get additional resources. See Joel Handler and Ellen Jane Hollingsworth, *The "Deserving Poor": A Study of Welfare Administration* (Chicago: Markham, 1971).

77. Desmond King, *Actively Seeking Work?* (Chicago: University of Chicago Press, 1995).

78. Lawrence Mead, *Beyond Entitlement: The Social Obligations of Citizenship* (New York: Free Press, 1986); Charles Murray, *Losing Ground: American Social Policy, 1950–1980* (New York: Basic Books, 1984).

79. Robert Leon and Michael O'Hare, "Welfare Reform and Work," *Journal of Policy Analysis and Management* 8 (1989): 293–98.

80. Mary Jo Bane, "Welfare Reform and Mandatory Versus Voluntary Work: Policy Issues or Management Problem?" *Journal of Policy Analysis and Management* 8 (1989): 287.

81. Riccio et al., GAIN (1994).

82. Ibid., 292.

83. Pavetti and Duke, *Increasing Participation in Work and Work-Related Activities*.

84. Ibid., 39.

85. This is also true for learnfare—sanctions make no difference for students who drop out. Handler, *Poverty of Welfare Reform*, 105–9.

86. Katz, *In the Shadow of the Poorhouse*.

87. Yeheskel Hasenfeld and Dale Weaver, "Enforcement, Compliance, and Disputes in Welfare-to-Work Programs," *Social Service Review* 70 (1996): 235–56.

88. It is interesting to note that in the five state demonstration projects, all of the states, thus far, have instituted tough new sanctions for nonparticipation, but, at the same time, elaborate procedures to avoid the imposition of the sanctions, including an extensive conciliation and review process. Pavetti and Duke, *Increasing Participation in Work and Work-Related Activities*, 35–38. These demonstration projects are in the early stages. In demonstration projects farther along, such as GAIN, the sanctioning process has been streamlined.

89. Yeheskel Hasenfeld, *Human Service Organizations* (Englewood Cliffs, N.J.: Prentice Hall, 1983); Joel F. Handler, *The Conditions of Discretion: Autonomy, Community, Bureaucracy* (New York: Russell Sage Foundation, 1986); John Mitchell, Mark Chadwin, and Demetra Nightingale, *Implementing Welfare-Employment Programs: An Institutional Analysis of the Work Incentive (WIN) Program* (Washington, D.C.: U.S. Department of Labor, Employment and Training Administration, 1979).

90. Robert D. Behn, *Leadership Counts: Lessons for Public Managers from the Massachusetts Welfare, Training, and Employment Program* (Cambridge: Harvard University Press, 1991).

91. Ibid., 94.

92. Hasenfeld and Weaver, "Enforcement, Compliance and Disputes."

93. Ibid.

94. Riccio et al., GAIN (1994), table 2.12.

95. It is quite telling that the JOBS program in Florida, called Project Independence, employed a Riverside-like model statewide. That is, the primary emphasis of the program is up-front job search followed by job club, and the state agency established job placement goals and placement competitions among the counties. Use of threats of sanctions was fairly high, with 24 percent of the participants receiving sanction notices, although only 3 percent were deregistered with a sanction enforced. Nonetheless, the effectiveness of the program was exceedingly modest, and no county came even close to the achievements of Riverside.

96. Laurie Udesky, "Punishing the Poor," *Southern Exposure* (Summer 1991): 12–13.

97. Leonard Goodwin, *Causes and Cures of Welfare: New Evidence on the Social Psychology of the Poor* (Lexington, Mass.: Lexington Books, 1983).

98. Kathleen Mullan Harris, "Work and Welfare among Single Mothers in Poverty," *American Journal of Sociology* 99 (1993): 345.

99. Mead, *Beyond Entitlement*.

100. In Wisconsin's proposed W-2 program.

101. Gordon Lafer, "The Politics of Job Training: Urban Poverty and the False Promise of JTPA," *Politics and Society* 22 (1994): 349–88.

102. U.S. House of Representatives, Committee on Ways and Means, *1993 Green Book: Background Material and Data on Programs within the Jurisdiction of the Committee on Ways and Means* (Washington, D.C.: U.S. Government Printing Office, 1993).

103. See, for example, Rosina Becerra, Alisa Lewin, Michael Mitchell, and Hiromi Ono, *California Work Pay Demonstration Project: January 1993–June 1995* (Los Angeles: UCLA, School of Public Policy and Social Research, 1996).

1. Mark Rank, *Living on the Edge: The Realities of Welfare in America* (New York: Columbia University Press, 1994).

2. Celia W. Dugger, "Iowa Plan Tries to Cut off the Cash," *New York Times,* April 7, 1995: A1.

3. Roberta Spalter-Roth, Heidi Hartmann, and Linda Andrews, *Combining Work and Welfare: An Alternative Anti-Poverty Strategy* (Washington, D.C.: Institute for Women's Policy Research, 1992).

4. Gary Burtless, "Employment Prospects of Welfare Recipients," in Demetra Smith Nightingale and Robert Haveman, eds. *The Work Alternative* (Washington, D.C.: Urban Institute Press, 1994), 71–106.

5. Abraham found that in the mid-1960s, when the unemployment rate averaged about 4.5 percent, there were 2.5 unemployed for every vacant job. In the early 1970s, when the unemployment rate rose to 4.5 percent, there were four unemployed for every vacant job, and when unemployment continued to rise to 9.5 percent in 1982, there were an average of 8.4 unemployed persons for every vacant job. Katherine G. Abraham, "Structural/Frictional vs. Deficient Demand Unemployment: Some New Evidence," *American Economic Review* 73 (1983): 709–10.

6. Philip Harvey, "Welfare Reform, Human Rights, and the Future of Capitalism," Joanne Woodward Lecture, Sarah Lawrence College, April 6, 1994.

7. Employment and Training Institute, University of Wisconsin, Milwaukee, Fall 1994.

8. Illinois JOB GAP Project, *Are There Enough Jobs? Welfare Reform and Labor Market Reality* (DeKalb: Northern Illinois University, Office for Social Policy Research, 1996.)

9. E.g., Haya Stier and Marta Tienda, "Are Men Marginal to the Family? Insights from Chicago's Inner City," in Jane C. Hood, ed., *Men, Work, and Family, Research on Men and Masculinities Series,* (Newbury Park, Calif.: Sage, Annual Meetings of the American Sociological Association, 1992), 4: 23–44; William Julius Wilson, *The Truly Disadvantaged: The Inner City, the Underclass, and Public Policy* (Chicago: University of Chicago Press, 1987).

10. Harry Holzer, *What Employers Want: Job Prospects for Less-Educated Workers* (New York: Russell Sage Foundation, 1996).

11. Katherine Newman and Chauncy Lennon, "The Job Ghetto," *American Prospect,* Summer 1995: 66–67.

12. Between 1980 and 1988, the poverty rate for white families declined from 10.6 percent to 5.6 percent. For African Americans it declined from 29.1 percent to 13.4 percent, and for Hispanics from 42.9 percent to 24.8 percent. Paul Osterman, "Welfare Participation in a Full Employment Economy," *Social Problems* 38 (November 1991): 475–91.

13. In metropolitan statistical areas with a tight labor market in 1987, for African American youth with 12 years of education or less, the unemployment rate declined from 40.5 percent in 1983 to 7.2 in 1987. Richard Freeman, "Employment and Earnings of Disadvantaged Youth in a Labor Shortage Economy," in Christopher Jencks and Paul E. Peterson, eds., *The Urban Underclass* (Washington, D.C.: Brookings Institution, 1991), 103–21.

14. Philip Harvey, *Securing the Right to Employment* (Princeton, N.J.: Princeton University Press, 1989); David R. Riemer, *The Prisoners of Welfare* (New York: Praeger, 1988).

15. Harry Holzer, *Unemployment, Vacancies, and Local Labor Markets* (Kalamazoo, Mich.: W. E. Upjohn Institute for Employment Research, 1989).

16. Margaret Weir, *Politics and Jobs: The Boundaries of Employment Policy in the United States* (Princeton, N.J.: Princeton University Press, 1992).

17. Full discussion of these options is beyond the scope of this book, but see Sheila D. Collins, Helen Lachs Ginsburg, and Gertrude Schaffner Goldberg, *Jobs for All: A Plan for the Revitalization of America* (New York: New Initiatives for Full Employment, 1994). Spalter-Roth, Hartmann, and Andrews, *Combining Work and Welfare,* using a conservative esti-

mate, suggested that the creation of 500,000 public service jobs targeted to welfare recipients would cost $6.6 billion (1990 dollars), affect 800,000 women, and save $1.7 billion.

18. Harvey, *Securing the Right to Employment*.

19. Bonnie Fox Schwartz, *The Civil Works Administration, 1933–1934: The Business of Emergency Employment in the New Deal* (Princeton, N.J.: Princeton University Press, 1984).

20. Ibid., 42.

21. Ibid.

22. Much of the discussion that follows is based on the report written by Clifford Johnson (1985), titled "Direct Federal Job Creation: Key Issues," for the National Committee for Full Employment, Job Creation Education Project.

23. Sar Levitan and Frank Gallo, *Spending to Save: Expanding Employment Opportunities* (Washington, D.C.: Center for Social Policy Studies, Georgetown University, 1991).

24. Most evaluation studies on the impact of CETA report that one year of PSE raised the earnings of women classified as disadvantaged or on welfare by $1,000 to $1,600 per year. The gains for men were generally much smaller. Burt S. Barnow, "The Impact of CETA Programs on Earnings," *Journal of Human Resources* 22 (1987): 157–93.

25. Johnson, "Direct Federal Job Creation," 16.

26. Donald Baumer and Carl Van Horn, *The Politics of Unemployment* (Washington, D.C.: CQ Press, 1985).

27. Ibid., 76.

28. Weir, *Politics and Jobs*.

29. The findings reported here on YIEPP rely extensively on Judith Gueron, *Lessons from a Job Guarantee: The Youth Incentive Entitlement Pilot Projects* (New York: Manpower Demonstration Research Corporation, 1984).

30. In the demonstration period (1977–1981), unemployment among African American male youth between ages 16 to 19 reached close to 80 percent, and school dropout rates ranged from 20 to 26 percent.

31. At the same time, YIEPP did not have an effect on school enrollment, graduation, and dropout rates. In particular, it was not able to attract back to school those who had already dropped out. We discuss the problems of reaching teens who drop out of school in Chap. 8.

32. Levitan and Gallo, *Spending to Save,* 15–16.

33. Lee Rainwater, "Poverty and the Income Package of Working Parents: The United States in Comparative Perspective," *Children and Youth Services Review* 17 (1995): 11–41.

34. Rebecca Blank, "The Employment Strategy: Public Policies to Increase Work and Earnings," in Sheldon Danziger, Gary Sandefur, and Daniel Weinberg, eds., *Confronting Poverty: Prescriptions for Change* (Cambridge: Harvard University Press, 1994), 192. Three very important changes have been made in the earned income tax credit: (1) it now applies to welfare recipients—previously, at least 50 percent of income had to be from "earnings"; (2) benefits have been raised significantly; and (3) EITC receipts are not counted against welfare income.

How these changes came about and their importance for AFDC recipients is a little-known story. When Nixon's Family Support Act was defeated in the 1970s, Sen. Russell Long, no friend of welfare, introduced the earned income tax credit (EITC) to help the working poor. Consistent with historic traditions, welfare recipients, even if they worked, were not eligible. A working parent had to have a legal dependent *and* provide more than half the support through earnings. Because the earnings requirement caused a lot of errors, the Internal Revenue Service wanted that requirement dropped, but the Reagan administration, which had already passed many AFDC reforms designed to strengthen the distinction between the working poor and welfare recipients, refused. The Bush administration didn't care. The 50 percent requirement was dropped. This meant that AFDC mothers who worked would be eligible. The Clinton administration made other changes. The amount of the credit is to be significantly increased and the credit is not to be deducted from welfare benefits. For a short political history of the EITC, see Christopher Howard, "Happy Returns: How the Working Poor Got Tax Relief," *American Prospect* 17 (Spring 1994): 46.

35. Robert Greenstein, *The Earned Income Tax Credit: A Target for Budget Cuts?* (Washington, D.C.: Center on Budget and Policy Priorities, 1995), 10.

36. John Scholz, "Tax Policy and the Working Poor: The Earned Income Tax Credit," *Focus* 15, no. 3 (1993–94): 2.

37. Robert Haveman and John Scholz, "Transfers, Taxes, and Welfare Reform," *National Tax Journal* 7, no. 2, (1994): 17; John Scholz, "The Earned Income Tax Credit: Participation, Compliance, and Antipoverty Effectiveness," *National Tax Journal* 7, no. 1 (1994): 3.

38. Scholz, "Tax Policy and the Working Poor," 2.

39. Greenstein, *Earned Income Tax Credit,* 10.

40. Anne Alstott, "The Earned Income Tax Credit and the Limitations of Tax-Based Welfare Reform," *Harvard Law Review* 108 (1995): 533; Barbara Kirchheimer, "The EITC: Where Policy and Practicality Collide," *Tax Notes* (Oct. 3, 1994): 15–18.

41. In 1983, for example, a family with earnings of up to $7,750 and a child under 18 would receive a credit equal to 18.5 percent of earned income. The maximum benefit would be $1,434. The maximum would apply up to $12,200. Then, the "phase-out" range applied— the credit was reduced by 13.2 cents for every additional dollar earned until the break-even point—$22,370—when the supplement would be zero. There are some additional benefits. For example, taxpayers with two or more children are entitled to a slightly higher credit, and taxpayers paying health insurance for a child are eligible for a supplemental credit. Blank, "Employment Strategy," 192; Scholz "Tax Policy and the Working Poor," 2.

42. See Alstott, "Earned Income Tax Credit," 553; Edgar Browning, "The Effects of the Earned Income Tax Credit on Income and Welfare," *National Tax Journal* 48, no. 1 (1995): 23–43; Richard Burkhauser, Kenneth Crouch, and Andrew Glenn, *Public Policies for the Working Poor: The Earned Income Tax Credit versus Minimum Wage Legislation* (Madison, Wis.: Institute for Research on Poverty, DP 1074–95, 1995), 12–15.

43. Stacy Dickert, Scott Houser, and John Scholz, "Taxes and the Poor: A Microsimulation Study of Implicit and Explicit Taxes: Tax Policy and the Social Agenda," *National Tax Journal* 7, no. 3 (1994): 21.

44. Alstott, "Earned Income Tax Credit," 554.

45. Quoted in Greenstein, *Earned Income Tax Credit,* 20–21.

46. Blank, "Employment Strategy," 193. The two most important studies of the effects of the EITC on labor supply are based on the Seattle-Denver income-maintenance experiment. However, that study was done twenty years ago and may be no longer relevant today. In addition, practically all of the EITC is a year-end lump-sum payment; therefore, the disincentive effects on the phase-out may be less evident. Finally, the most positive effects of the EITC are for households either not working or not earning much. The most serious negative effects are on households already working a significant amount. See also Alstott, "Earned Income Tax Credit," 546; Scholz, "Tax Policy and the Working Poor," 8–9.

47. General Accounting Office, *Earned Income Tax Credit: Design and Administration Could be Improved* (Washington, D.C.: Government Printing Office, September 1993), cited in Greenstein, *Earned Income Tax Credit,* 20.

48. Alstott, "Earned Income Tax Credit," 555.

49. Scholz, "Tax Policy and the Working Poor," 2.

50. Ibid., 3–4. For an example of outreach efforts, see Federation of Protestant Welfare Agencies, "A Model for Low-Income Communities: The New York City Earned Income Tax Credit Outreach Campaign," January 1994.

51. Scholz, "Tax Policy and the Working Poor," 5.

52. Ibid.

53. Kirchheimer, "The EITC."

54. More than half of the disqualified claims involved the child exemption; 30 percent were for misreporting earnings or adjusted gross income. One of the biggest parts of the noncompliance problem was addressed in the 1990 changes, which eliminated the support test for children in favor of a residency test (the child must be in residence more than 6 months). There are also changes in the form which are controversial. Alstott, "Earned Income Tax Credit," 570; Scholz, "Tax Policy and the Working Poor," 6.

55. For example, "A poor nonworker with two children . . . might receive a $3370 EITC simply by increasing the earned income she reports to $8425." Alstott, "Earned Income Tax Credit," 586. For other kinds of refund fraud, see George Guttman, "Improper Refunds Sapping Billions: IRS, Treasury, Hill Seek Answers," *Tax Notes*, Oct. 3, 1994: 19–28.

56. At present, it is unclear as to how much overreporting is going on, but one would guess that it will increase over time. As Scholz notes, the real danger may be the publicized "horror stories"—for example, households reporting fictitious incomes (and thereby qualifying for a refund) claimed to be earned by watching each other's children—that would undermine public support for the EITC. Scholz, "Tax Policy and the Working Poor," 8.

57. Lynn Olson, "The Earned Income Tax Credit: Policy Implications of Street Level Experience", paper presented at Annual Research Conference of the Association for Public Policy Analysis and Management, Chicago, October 1994.

58. Olson cites a 1988 Gallup survey of New Jersey families in which two-thirds of EITC filers paid a preparer.

59. There are inherent conflicts and trade-offs between a progressive income tax, equal taxation of married couple with equal incomes, and marriage-neutrality; in a word, marriage-neutrality cannot be achieved as long as policy opts for the first two propositions. Ann Alstott gives these examples. "Consider two individuals, each with two children and earnings of $10,000. In 1996, each individual would be entitled to the maximum EITC of $3,560, for a combined EITC of $7,120. If these individuals marry, . . . they would be entitled to a joint EITC of only $1,795, which represents a marriage penalty of $5,325." On the other hand, "if a childless worker earning $10,000 per year marries a nonworker with two children, the couple's total EITC, net of federal income tax, actually rises from $0 to $3,560. If two workers, each with one child and earning $5,000 per year marry, their total EITC rises from $3,400 to $3,560." Ann Alstott, "Alleviating Marriage Penalties in the Income Tax and the Earned Income Tax Credit," *Tax Notes*, Feb. 27, 1995: 1343–48. On the other hand, the EITC can provide a marriage incentive. If a nonworking AFDC mother marries a man with low earnings, she loses AFDC benefits and probably Medicaid. However, if she has one child, the couple gains an EITC benefit of up to $2,157, or up to $3,564 if they have two or more children. Greenstein, *Earned Income Tax Credit*, 22–23.

60. Alstott, "Earned Income Tax Credit," 559–64; Scholz, "Tax Policy and the Working Poor," 9–10.

61. For example, Alstott recommends a tax deduction for two-earner couples, similar to the deduction that was allowed under prior law, and she would structure the deduction to extend relief to EITC recipients. Alstott, "Earned Income Tax Credit."

62. Ibid., 581.

63. Olson, "Earned Income Tax Credit," 11.

64. Ibid., 21.

65. To encourage working, Michigan has applied for a waiver to experiment with EITC advance payments for AFDC and food stamp recipients. Scholz, "Tax Policy and the Working Poor," 7–8

66. Guttman, "Improper Refunds Sapping Billions."

67. Scholz recommends that various nontaxable benefits should be excluded (e.g., military benefits, housing allowances), changing the support-based definition of a dependent

(the GAO estimates that 9 million dependent exemptions were erroneously claimed) to rely on residency, and the age requirements for qualifying children, conducting outreach for the advance payment option, providing integration with AFDC and food stamps as proposed by the Michigan experiment, and possibly restricting the EITC to wage and salary income. Scholz, "Tax Policy and the Working Poor," 10. See George Yin, John Scholz, Jonathan Forman, and Mark Mazur, "Improving Delivery of Benefits to the Working Poor: Proposals to Reform the Earned Income Credit Tax Program," *Tax Notes Today*, Oct. 29, 1993: 224–41. Some reforms have been enacted and others are proposed. In 1990, changes were made in many of the EITC eligibility rules, a new form was introduced, and IRS verification procedures (e.g., matching Social Security numbers, verifying numbers of children in EITC families) were instituted. Requiring additional documentation in selected cases has been introduced. The GAO is of the opinion that these changes would remove principal sources of errors. Preliminary studies by the IRS indicate a significant reduction in the number of filers and in the error rates. Greenstein, *Earned Income Tax Credit*, 13–16. More recent legislation is designed to further tighten the EITC. Nonresident aliens are excluded; Social Security numbers are to be provided for children under age one; households with more than $2,350 in income from investments are ineligible. Additional tightening measures are proposed by the Treasury Department, the Senate, and the GAO. Ibid., 29–31.

68. Other proposals include repealing the small EITC for workers without children (designed to offset the increase in payroll and excise taxes), and canceling the final phase of the EITC expansion for families with two or more children. Ibid., 29–31.

69. Another proposal would reduce the investment income threshold to $1,000, thus preventing many working poor households from building up modest amounts of savings. Other proposals would count Social Security, tax-exempt interest, nontaxable pension distributions, and child support payments as part of adjusted gross income. Although there are arguments for and against proposals to count Social Security income, counting child support payments raises serious administrative (the IRS has no information as to the amount of the payments) and equity problems. The child support income would be taxed twice and reduce the income of the custodial parent, which is almost always the mother. Ibid., 33–9.

70. Haveman and Scholz, "Transfers, Taxes, and Welfare Reform."

71. For a review of wages subsidy demonstration programs for welfare recipients in seven states, with somewhat favorable results, see Stephen Bell and Larry Orr, "Is Subsidized Employment Cost Effective for Welfare Recipients," *Journal of Human Resources* 29, no. 1 (Winter 1994): 42.

72. For example, if the target wage were set at $10 per hour, a worker taking a job at $6 would receive an additional $2. They estimate that the cost of providing public service jobs would be $17,000 per worker per year. The authors also propose capital accounts for young people and poor families. For a less sanguine view of the effectiveness of wage subsidies, see Laurie Bassi, "Stimulating Employment and Increasing Opportunity for the Current Work Force," in Demetra Smith Nightingale and Robert H. Haveman, *The Work Alternative: Welfare Reform and the Realities of the Job Market* (Washington, D.C.: Urban Institute, 1995).

73. Edmund Phelps, "Raising the Employment and Pay of the Working Poor: Low-Wage Employment Subsidies versus the Welfare State," AEA *Papers and Proceedings* 84, no. 2 (1994): 54–8; Browning, "Effects of the Earned Income Tax Credit." Some countries allow the long-term unemployed to use part of their unemployment benefits as vouchers to firms that hire them. An innovative approach to encourage welfare recipients to "make work pay" through wage supplementation has been tried in Canada's Income Assistance program (the equivalent to AFDC). Under the Self-Sufficiency Program (SSP), recipients who work 30 hours per week or more receive substantial financial incentives to work, while being subject to a relatively low marginal tax rate on earnings. The SSP supplement is equal to half the

difference between the participant's gross earnings and a "target" earnings level. In British Columbia, the target was set at $37,000 (Canadian dollars). A recipient who worked for 30 hours per week at $7.00 per hour would earn $10,500 per year and receive a $13,250 SSP supplement. By comparison, the Income Assistance grant for a single parent with one child in British Columbia is $12,478. Eligibility for SSP is limited to recipients who have been on aid for at least a year, and the SSP supplement payments are limited to three years. The impact analysis of the first 18 months shows that there was a 13.1 percent increase in the employment rate (or a 50 percent increase relative to the average employment rate in the control group). The increase in average monthly earnings was $137 (or a 60 percent increase relative to the control group), even though the program group members were taking fairly low-wage jobs. There was also a 14 percent reduction in the proportion of the program participants receiving Income Assistance, yet the total income (earnings plus Income Assistance) increased by a monthly average of $235 (or 23 percent more relative to the control group). These findings are quite encouraging, showing how a combination of earnings and wage supplementation (in the form of income assistance) can lift recipients out of poverty. Yet, they also point to the fact that the participants were working in low-wage jobs, and unless their wages continue to improve after the three year limit, they may have to return to welfare. David Card and Philip Robins, *Do Financial Incentives Encourage Welfare Recipients to Work?* (Vancouver, B.C.: Social Research and Demonstration Corporation, February 1996).

George Yin and his colleagues suggest exempting low-income workers from paying the employee's share of the Social Security taxes. The example they give is a childless two-person household with a single worker at a minimum wage job. Under present law, the family pays no income tax and receives no EITC. With a Social Security exemption, the family would be within $590 of the 1993 poverty line. However, if the exemption were targeted only to low-income workers, there would be the usual disadvantages of requiring self-identification, possible stigmatization, and reduced participation. They think the better solution would be to apply the exemption to all workers, but make it applicable only to a certain wage level. The benefits would be recaptured through higher Social Security taxes on wages in excess of the exemption level. Yin, Scholz, Forman, and Mazur, "Improving Delivery of Benefits to the Working Poor."

74. Irwin Garfinkel and Sara McLanahan, "Single-Mother Families, Economic Insecurity, and Government Policy," in Sheldon Danziger, Gary Sandefur, and Daniel Weinberg, *Confronting Poverty: Prescriptions for Change* (Cambridge: Harvard University Press, 1994), 205–25.

75. The commission stated the arguments for the refundable tax credit: "Because it would assist all families with children, the refundable child tax credit would not be a relief payment, nor would it categorize children according to their 'welfare' or 'nonwelfare' status. In addition, because it would not be lost when parents enter the work force, as welfare benefits are, the refundable child tax credit could provide a bridge for families striving to enter the economic mainstream. It would substantially benefit hard-pressed single and married parents raising children. It could also help middle-income, employed parents struggling to afford high-quality child care. Moreover, because it is neutral toward family structure and mothers' employment, it would not discourage the formation of two-parent families or of single-earner families in which one parent chooses to stay at home and care for the children" (National Commission on Children, *Beyond Rhetoric: A New American Agenda for Children and Families* [Washington, D.C.: U.S. Government Printing Office, 1991], xxi, xxxv, 94–95). The commission recommended that the credit be available to all families. Some commissioners, however, felt that it should be limited to families with incomes under $150,000, thus reducing its costs by an estimated $1.1 billion. Ibid., 109–10.

76. Workers with low annual wage incomes (those with high capital income, affluent

teenagers, college students working summers, low-wage workers with high-earning spouses) would qualify for the Social Security tax exemption. The authors suggest that some of this problem could be handled by using weekly or other periodic bases rather than the annual one. There could also be age limits—the new EITC, for example, for childless, low-income workers eliminates teenagers, most college students, and seniors by restricting the age to between 25 and 65 years.

77. Rebecca Kim, Irwin Garfinkel, and Daniel Meyer, *Interaction Effects of a Child Tax Credit, National Health Insurance, and Assured Child Support* (Madison, Wis.: Institute for Research on Poverty, DP 1047–94, 1994).

78. Greenstein, *Earned Income Tax Credit,* 9.

79. *The Bottom Line,* U.S.DOL, available from http://www.dol.gov/esa/public/minwage/bottom.htm.

80. Bradley Schiller, "Below–Minimum Wage Workers: Implications for Minimum-Wage Models," *Quarterly Review of Economics and Finance* 34 (1994): 131–43.

81. David Card and Alan Krueger, *Myth and Measurement: The New Economics of the Minimum Wage* (Princeton, N.J.: Princeton University Press, 1995), 392: "Depending on how the question is phrased, and when it is asked, opinion polls consistently show that 65 to 90 percent of the general public favor an increase in the minimum wage. Support . . . is surprisingly broad and tends to be even higher among younger people, nonwhites, and those with lower family incomes."

82. Burkhauser, Crouch and Glenn, *Public Policies for the Working Poor.*

83. Schiller, "Below–Minimum Wage Workers."

84. Ronald Ehrenberg, "New Minimum Wage Research: Symposium Introduction," *Industrial and Labor Relations Review* 46 (1992): 3–5; Smith Ralph and Bruce Vavrichek, "The Wage Mobility of Minimum Wage Workers," *Industrial and Labor Relations Review* 46 (1992): 82–88.

85. Burkhauser, Crouch, and Glenn, *Public Policies for the Working Poor;* Card and Krueger, *Myth and Measurement,* 4. Since most minimum wage workers are teenagers, the research applies mostly to that group. According to Ronald Ehrenberg, prior research has shown—*ceteris paribus*—that a 10 percent increase in the minimum wage would result in a 1–3 percent decrease in teen employment. Ehrenberg, "New Minimum Wage Research."

86. One study was of the fast-food industry in Texas. Very few firms took advantage of the teen subminimum. Employers were aware of the option but thought that it was unfair or that they would be unable to attract workers. On the other hand, they were more likely to use the subminimum wage for Hispanic and black teens. In general, employers raised wages that were both below and above the new minimum. The researchers found that employment growth was positively related to the size of the wage increase; moreover, full-time employment increased and part-time employment per establishment decreased. Lawrence Katz and Alan Krueger, "The Effect of the Minimum Wage on the Fast-Food Industry," *Industrial and Labor Relations Review* 46 (1992): 6–21.

Similar results were found by David Card, who looked at the employment effects in California when, in 1988, the state increased the minimum wage from $3.35 to $4.25. About 11 percent of all workers and 50 percent of teenagers earned between $3.35 and $4.25. It was estimated that that teen employment would fall by 3–8 percent. About half of the "affected workers"—that is, those earning either below $3.35 or between $3.36 and $4.24—were in retail; and about 15 percent were in agriculture or low-wage manufacturing. Affected workers were more likely to be younger, female, Hispanic, and in school. Further, although a significant number of minimum wage workers are in high-income families (that is, they are teenagers), in California 44 percent of the affected workers lived in families with annual incomes of less than $15,000. Thus, the antipoverty aspects of raising the minimum wage were greater than is commonly assumed.

Card found that the wages of the low-wage workers *increased* and that, contrary to the received wisdom, there was no decline in employment—even in the retail trades. For teens, there was no drop in school enrollments; hourly and weekly earnings rose by 10 percent and employment by 4 percent. David Card, "Do Minimum Wages Reduce Employment? A Case Study of California, 1987–89," *Industrial and Labor Relations Review* 46 (1992): 38–54.

87. Card and Krueger, *Myth and Measurement,* 390–95.

88. Donald Deere, Kevin Murphy, and Finis Welch, "Reexamining Methods of Estimating Minimum-Wage Effects: Employment and the 1990–1991 Minimum-Wage Hike," *American Economic Association Papers and Proceedings* 85, no. 2 (1995): 232–37; David Neumark and William Wascher, "Minimum-Wage Effects on School and Work Transitions of Teenagers," ibid., 244–49. But see David Card and Alan Krueger, "Time-Series Minimum-Wage Studies: A Meta-analysis," ibid., 238–43.

89. Ehrenberg, in his introduction to "New Minimum Wage Research," says: "None of the studies suggests that at current relative values of the minimum wage, large disemployment effects would result from modest future increases in the minimum wage—increases up to, say, 10 percent."

90. According to the Department of Labor, quoting a recent analysis by the Economic Policy Institute and preliminary work by the U.S. Department of Health and Human Servies, 300,000 people, including 100,000 children, will be lifted out of poverty when the new law is in full effect. A family of four, with one worker employed full-time year round at $5.15 per hour, earns $10,300, plus a maximum EITC credit of $3,560, food stamps worth $2,876, less $788 payroll tax, for a total income of $15,600, which is above the poverty line. Futhermore, more female workers receive the minimum wage than men; most of these women (52 percent) are 25 years or older; therefore, raising the minimum wage will provide a modest pay raise to the poorest working women, many of whom are raising a family. *Bottom Line,* U.S.DOL.

91. Isaac Shapiro and Robert Greenstein, *Making Work Pay: The Unfinished Agenda* (Washington, D.C.: Center on Budget and Policy Priorities, 1993), 54.

92. LaDonna Pavetti and Amy-Ellen Duke, *Increasing Participation in Work and Work-Related Activities: Lessons from Five State Welfare Reform Demonstration Projects,* final report, vol. 1 (Washington, D.C.: Urban Institute, 1995), 13.

93. The description and evaluation of CAP is based on the report prepared by William Hamilton and Associates, *Child Assistance Program: Five-Year Impacts, Costs, and Benefits* (Cambridge, Mass.: Abt Associates, Nov. 6, 1996).

94. The treatment effects would have been considerably higher if the results were limited to the actual participants. However, restricting the analysis to this group would have violated the experimental design.

95. CAP probably produced much better results than GAIN, which measured its impact only on those recipients who came to orientation.

96. Food stamps is a federal program under the jurisdiction of the U.S. Department of Agriculture. The program has grown steadily over the years. In 1995, the total federal expenditures were more than $23 billion. *1996 Green Book,* 861. Benefits are available to nearly all "households" that meet federal eligibility financial (income and assets) requirements. AFDC recipients are automatically eligible, but the program is available to two-parent families and individuals as well, whether working or not, as long as they qualify financially. In other words, food stamps is basically a noncategorical income-maintenance program. There are work registration and employment and training requirements. State welfare agencies do the actual day-to-day administration of food stamps, but they operate under federal rules as to eligibility, benefits, and administrative requirements. On the other hand, the states have a significant role in administering the employment and training programs, as well as some administrative aspects—for example, verification.

97. The description of the food stamp program relies largely on *1996 Green Book*, sec. 16, 856–79.

98. Additional restrictions include a cap on the deduction for housing costs at 50 percent of income in calculating financial eligibility; childless able-bodied individuals will be limited to receiving benefits for three months within every three-year period, unless they are working or in training for 20 or more hours per week; and legal immigrants, with some exceptions (e.g., political refugees, veterans, and those with a ten-year work history), will not be eligible.

99. Participation rates vary. It is estimated that 74 percent of eligible persons participate. Most (86 percent) eligible children participate. Only 33 percent of the eligible elderly participate (most of those not participating live alone). Virtually all single-parent households are enrolled. Participation rates decline as household income rises. *1996 Green Book,* 873.

100. There are exceptions, which are probably not relevant for our purposes. For example, *unrelated* coresidents can be treated as separate households if they purchase food and prepare meals separately. However, coresident spouses or children under 18 may not be treated separately. *1994 Green Book,* 762.

101. E.g., unanticipated, irregular income up to $30 per month; income earned by schoolchildren, etc.

102. E.g., 20 percent of earned income; day care expenses up to $160 per month.

103. Income and benefit levels are for the 48 contiguous states and the District of Columbia. There are separate rates for Alaska, Hawaii, Guam, and the Virgin Islands.

104. Except for AFDC, SSI, and general assistance, the limit on "liquid" assets is $2,000, or $3,000 if there is an elderly member. In addition to the usual definition of liquid assets (e.g., cash, checking and savings accounts, lump sum settlements), other assets are also counted, including the fair market value of a car in excess of $4,500. Counted assets do not include the residence, business assets, personal property, EITC payments, cash value of life insurance, and other resources. Shapiro and Greenstein, *Making Work Pay,* 47–49.

105. Ibid., 47.

106. Ibid., 48–49.

107. If the household head fails to fulfill the work requirements, the entire household is disqualified, usually for two months; in some cases, only the noncomplying member is disqualified. *1996 Green Book,* 865.

CHAPTER 6

1. William Gormley, Jr., *Everybody's Children: Child Care as a Public Problem* (Washington, D.C.: Brookings Institution, 1995), 2.

2. Judith Musick, "The High-Stakes Challenge of Programs for Adolescent Mothers," in Peter Edelman and Joyce Ladner, eds., *Adolescence and Poverty: Challenge for the 1990s* (Washington, D.C.: Center for National Policy Press, 1991).

3. Ibid., 119 (emphasis added).

4. Ibid., 12.

5. Ibid., 125.

6. Gormley, *Everybody's Children,* 34.

7. Ibid., 4 (footnotes omitted). See also National Commission on Children, *Beyond Rhetoric: A New American Agenda for Children and Families* (Washington, D.C.: U.S. Government Printing Office, 1991), 29.

8. National Commission on Children, *Beyond Rhetoric,* 260.

9. U.S. Government, *Child Care: Child Care Subsidies Increase Likelihood That Low-Income Mothers Will Work* (U.S. General Accounting Office, GAO/HEHS-95–20, 1994), 2.

10. *1994 Green Book,* 543; Gormley, *Everybody's Children,* 19.

11. Gormley, *Everybody's Children,* 2–3.

12. National Commission on Children, *Beyond Rhetoric,* 27.

13. *1994 Green Book,* 532; Gormley, *Everybody's Children,* 17.

14. Sandra Hofferth, "Caring for Children at the Poverty Line," *Children and Youth Services Review* 17 (1995): 61–90.

15. Gormley, *Everybody's Children,* 16.

16. Proposed legislation in Wisconsin would require AFDC mothers to participate in work requirements 12 weeks after birth.

17. National Commission on Children, *Beyond Rhetoric,* 46, 260.

18. Hofferth, "Caring for Children," 61–90. D'Jamilia Salem, "Parents Flock to Organized Child Care: Report Shows Professional Facilities Steadily Gaining Ground Over Relatives, Other Baby-Sitting Options," *Los Angeles Times,* April 24, 1996: A5.

19. *1994 Green Book,* 542.

20. Peter Brandon, *An Economic Analysis of Kin-Provided Child Care* (Madison, Wis.: Institute for Research on Poverty, DP 1076–95, 1995); Gormley, *Everybody's Children,* 23.

21. Gormley, *Everybody's Children,* 24.

22. Barbara Bergmann, "Curing Child Poverty in the United States," *American Economic Review* 84 (May 1994): 79.

23. Gormley, *Everybody's Children,* 24.

24. Sandra Clark and Sharon Long, *Child Care Prices: A Profile of Six Communities* (Washington, D.C.: Urban Institute, 1995), 1–2.

25. Brandon, *An Economic Analysis.*

26. Gormley, *Everybody's Children,* 25.

27. *1994 Green Book,* 539–40.

28. Hofferth reports that only about half of centers accept very young children. Hofferth, "Caring for Children," 71–75.

29. In sum, "working-poor parents are more likely to work odd hours and to have changeable schedules. In contrast, most formal programs operated standard business hours. . . [Thus] locating a part-time slot might be difficult since it may mean denying someone else a full-time slot." Hofferth, "Caring for Children," 74–75. The six-city study reported similar findings, namely, an inadequate supply of child care slots for infants, school-age children, part-time care, and nontraditional hours. Clark and Long, *Child Care Prices,* 2.

30. Hofferth, "Caring for Children," 75–76.

31. For low-income families, there are four federal direct subsidy programs: AFDC Child Care and Transitional Child Care, At-Risk Child Care, and Child Care and Development Block Grant (CCDBG). The first two programs are for AFDC families who are currently working or in job training programs, and for families who left AFDC via employment—for up to a year. The At-Risk program is for families at risk of going on welfare because of the lack of child care assistance. And CCDBG serves the low-income population.

32. Other Federal assistance include the Social Services Block Grant, Title XX of the SSA, the Child Care Food program (subsidized meals for children in child care), and Head Start, as well as numerous other programs that provide services, training, and related activities. Sandra Clark and Sharon Long, "Child Care Block Grants and Welfare Reform," in Isabel Sawhill, ed., *Welfare Reform: An Analysis of the Issues* (Washington, D.C.: Urban Institute), 25–28.

33. *1994 Green Book,* 550.

34. Hofferth, "Caring for Children," 76–79.

35. Clark and Long, "Child Care Block Grants," 26.

36. Clark and Long, *Child Care Prices,* 3.

37. Hofferth, "Caring for Children," 80–82.

38. Some states use earnings disregards, which are limited to $200 a month for a child under 2 and $175 for all others; lesser amounts are permitted if the parent is working part-time.

39. Gormley, *Everybody's Children*, 80.

40. Ibid., 81–2.

41. Hofferth, "Caring for Children," 83–84.

42. Gormley, *Everybody's Children*, 67.

43. Ibid., 69–70. The National Commission on Children: "Research clearly documents that when caregivers are trained in child development, as well as basic health and safety practices, they are more likely to provide care and attention that fosters trusting, affectionate relationships. They are more likely to structure learning activities in ways that appropriately support social and intellectual development. . . . Specialized training is especially important for persons who care for infants, children with disabilities, and children from diverse cultural backgrounds. Yet, according to a recent study, approximately four-fifths of child care teaching staff do not have a college degree, and almost one-third of teachers and over half of assistant teachers have only three years or less of child care experience." The commission points out that despite the harmful effects of turnover, "high rates of staff turnover—as much as 40 percent annually—are often a direct result of low wages and poor benefits" (p. 269). See also Ellen Galinsky, Carollee Howes, Susan Kantos, and Marybeth Shinn, *The Study of Children in Family Child Care and Relative Care: Highlights of Findings* (New York: Families and Work Institute, 1994), 205.

44. "Cost, Quality, and Child Outcomes in Child Care Centers: Executive Summary," study conducted by the University of Colorado, UCLA, the University of North Carolina, and Yale University (1995).

45. Ibid.

46. Ibid.

47. Gormley, *Everybody's Children*, 166–67.

48. Barbara Bergmann, "The Economic Support of Child-Raising: Curing Child Poverty in the United States," *American Economic Review* 84, no. 2 (May 1994): 76–80.

49. Gormley, *Everybody's Children*, 179–80.

50. Clark and Long, "Child Care Block Grants," 27.

51. Karen Folk, *Welfare Reform Under Construction: W-2 Wisconsin Works* (Madison: University of Wisconsin, UWEX Extension, 1996).

52. LaDonna Pavetti and Amy-Ellen Duke, *Increasing Participation in Work and Work-Related Activities: Lessons from Five State Welfare Reform Demonstration Projects,* final report, vol. 1 (Washington, D.C.: Urban Institute, 1995), 57.

53. Ibid., 60.

54. Ibid., 61–62.

55. Gormley, *Everybody's Children*, 179–80.

56. Gormley thinks that "a serious effort to get good information into the hands of parents could revolutionize the child care system by empowering parents to protect their children through making judicious choices." He cites examples where information is provided. IBM, in order to give personalized assistance to employees looking for child care, subsidized a resource and referral agency that worked through a network of 250 community-based resource and referral agencies and consultants. Since 1984, more than 60,000 IBM families have used this service. Gormley reports that other companies are following this example. He argues for parent involvement and empowerment. Parents would help to design programs and policies, and participate in the selection of staff. They would serve as volunteers and help in special projects. He cites as an example Harrisburg, Pa., where several state-sponsored day care centers are governed primarily by parents. At each center, a con-

tract is issued to a private firm for a fixed time period. When the contract expires, competitive bids are invited; parents collectively choose the winning bidder, and contracts have been changed. Ibid., 87, 151.

57. Sheila Kamerman argues for parental leave with income replacement for the first year of each child's life; she claims that would benefit all children by moderating concerns about the expense and quality of programs and providing the children with a good start. The *Family and Medical Leave Act of 1993* is a step in this direction. Sheila Kamerman, "Starting Right: What We Owe to Children Under Three," *American Prospect* (1995): 63–73. The National Commission on Children also recommends family leave. National Commission on Children, *Beyond Rhetoric*, 261.

58. In Sweden, mothers may remain at home until their children reach the age of 18 months. They receive 80 percent of regular pay (for one year), followed by a minimum sickness benefit (3 months), followed by unpaid leave (3 months). For older children, day care is available at a nominal fee, with parents paying approximately 12 percent of the total cost. All parents may take as many as 60 days per year to take care of a seriously ill child. Germany provides 6 weeks off at full pay before childbirth, 8 weeks at full pay thereafter. All mothers are entitled to job-protected leave for 3 years, and approximately 80 percent are eligible for cash assistance for child raising for 2 years. Thereafter, a range of affordable arrangements are substantially subsidized. France has a generous family allowance and pays 20 percent of the costs of child care, with employers paying 5 percent. Gormley, *Everybody's Children*, 20, 169–77.

59. Ibid., 180.

60. Ibid., 183–85.

61. Irwin Garfinkel, Marygold Melli, John Robertson, "Child Support Orders: A Perspective on Reform," *Future of Children* 4 (1994): 84–100.

62. Judith Seltzer and Daniel Meyer, "Child Support and Children's Well-Being," *Focus* 17, no. 3 (1996): 33.

63. Elaine Sorenson, "The Benefits of Increased Child Support Enforcement," in Isabel Sawhill, ed., *Welfare Reform: An Analysis of the Issues* (Washington, D.C.: Urban Institute, 1995), 55–58.

64. Ibid., 55.

65. Ibid., 56–57.

66. *1994 Green Book*, section 11. Child Support Enforcement Program, 455.

67. Kathryn Edin, "Single Mothers and Child Support: The Possibilities and Limits of Child Support Policy," *Children and Youth Services Review* 17, nos. 1–3 (1995): 203–30; Irwin Garfinkel, Marygold Melli and John Robertson, "Child Support Orders: A Perspective on Reform," *Future of Children* 4 (1994): 84–100.

68. *1994 Green Book*, 455.

69. Garfinkel, Melli, and Robertson, "Child Support Orders," 86–88.

70. Judi Bartfeld and Irwin Garfinkel, *The Impact of Percentage-Expressed Child Support Orders on Payments* (Madison, Wis.: Institute for Research on Poverty, IRP Special Report 59, 1995).

71. Garfinkel, Melli, and Robertson, "Child Support Orders," 93.

72. Rich Bragg, "Child-Support Crackdown Shows Success and Limits," *New York Times*, April 14, 1995: 1.

73. Edin, "Single Mothers and Child Support." The father data is reported in Frank Furstenberg, Jr., K. E. Sherwood, and M. Sullivan, *Caring and Paying: What Father and Mothers Say About Child Support* (New York: Manpower Demonstration Research Corporation, 1992).

74. Edin, "Single Mothers and Child Support," 206.

75. Ibid., 212–14.

76. Ibid., 218–20.

77. Ibid., 220–25.

78. Seltzer and Meyers, *Child Support,* 33.

79. Edin recommends the following: (1) Rather than the current system of set amounts, with no adjustments for fluctuations in income (thus resulting in increasing arrearages), child support awards should be automatically adjusted, like Social Security taxes. Arrearages would only apply to voluntary quits. (2) Child support awards have to be more "progressive"; the amounts imposed on low earners are unrealistic and counterproductive. The one exception is the "Wisconsin standard" percentage of income, which is only used in a small number of states. (3) Because fathers of welfare children are not likely to have sufficient earnings to pay significant amounts, there should be guaranteed child support for families where the father is cooperating. (4) There has to be an improvement in the wages of unskilled and semiskilled men and women. Edin, "Single Mothers and Child Support," 226–27.

80. This section relies extensively on Barbara Wolfe, "Reform of Health Care for the Nonelderly Poor," in Sheldon Danziger et al., eds., *Confronting Poverty: Prescriptions for Change* (Cambridge: Harvard University Press, 1994), 253–88.

81. Ibid., 254.

82. Ibid., 254–55.

83. Ibid., 255.

84. Ibid., 254–5.

85. Barbara Wolfe and Steven Hill, "The Effect of Health on the Work Effort of Single Mothers," *Journal of Human Resources* 30, no. 1 (1995): 42–62.

86. Wolfe, "Reform of Health Care," 258.

87. Ibid., 262–64.

88. Ibid., 266.

89. Ibid., 266–67.

90. Ibid., 268.

91. Examples include: (1) expanding employer coverage through mandates, minimum packages, and subsidies, with an expanded public program as a back-up; (2) expanding Medicare and Medicaid; (3) modifying the current tax incentives (e.g., refundable tax credits for low-income families); (4) national health insurance (e.g., "single-payer"); and (5) competition (e.g., managed care).

92. CBO Analysis of Administration's Health Care Reform Plan, Hearing before the Committee on Finance, U.S. Senate, 103d Cong., 2d Sess., Feb. 9, 1994, 103.

93. Wolfe, "Reform of Health Care," 271–75.

94. Ibid., 275–77.

95. Ibid., 278.

96. Henry Aaron, "Small Steps: Health Care Reform Is Still Possible," *Brookings Review,* 1995: 34–35.

97. Martin Malin, "Unemployment Compensation in a Time of Increasing Work-Family Conflicts," *Michigan Journal of Law Reform* 29 (1995–96): 131–76.

98. Christopher Jencks, *Rethinking Social Policy: Race, Poverty, and the Underclass* (Cambridge: Harvard University Press, 1992), 222.

99. Rebecca Blank and David Card, "Recent Trends in Insured and Uninsured Unemployment: Is There an Explanation?" *Quarterly Journal of Economics* (November 1991): 1157–89.

100. Ibid.

101. Ibid.; Malin, "Unemployment Compensation."

102. Deborah Maranville, "Changing Economy, Changing Lives: Unemployment Insurance and the Contingent Workforce," *Public Interest Law Journal* 4 (1995): 291, 294; Malin, "Unemployment Compensation."

103. Lucy White, "No Exit: Rethinking 'Welfare Dependency' from a Different Ground," *Georgetown Law Journal* 81 (1993): 1961.

104. Richard McHugh and Ingrid Kock, "Unemployment Insurance: Responding to the Expanding Role of Women in the Work Force," *Clearinghouse Review* (April 1984): 1422–36.

105. This section relies on Maranville, "Changing Economy."

106. McHugh and Kock, "Unemployment Insurance."

107. Maranville, "Changing Economy."

108. Roberta Spalter-Roth, Heidi Hartmann, and Beverly Burr, *Income Insecurity: The Failure of Unemployment Insurance to Reach Working* AFDC *Mothers* (Institute for Women's Policy Research, Second Annual Employment Task Force Conference, March 20–22, 1994).

109. Ibid.

110. In addition to the above-cited authors, Lucy Williams, memo, Jan. 2, 1994.

111. Michele Adler, "Disability Among Women on AFDC: An Issue Revisited," report prepared for the Office of the Assistant Secretary for Planning and Evaluation, U.S. Department of Health and Human Services, 1993.

112. For a review, see Wolfe and Hill, "Effect of Health." In a recent survey of 1,347 single-parent AFDC recipients in four counties in California, 24.5 percent were classified as disabled, 6.8 percent of the households had a disabled parent and one or more disabled children, and 13.1 percent of the households had a nondisabled parent but one or more disabled children. The parent was defined as disabled if she answered yes to the question of having a physical, emotional, or mental health condition that limited the amount or kind of work she could do. A child was defined as disabled if the mother reported the child as having a chronic health problem—physical, emotional, or mental—that limited the kind of things he or she could do, or if the child was on SSI. Marcia K. Meyers, Anna Lukemeyer, and Timothy M. Sneeding, *Work, Welfare, and the Burden of Disability: Caring for Special Needs of Children in Poor Families* (Syracuse, N.Y.: Center for Policy Research, Maxwell School of Citizenship and Public Affairs, Syracuse University, April 1996).

113. Gregory Acs and Pamela Loprest, *The Effects of Disabilities on Exits from* AFDC (Washington, D.C.: Urban Institute, 1995), 8–9.

114. Ibid., 10–11.

115. Ibid., 5, 14–16.

116. Ibid., 18–19.

117. Wolfe and Hill, "Effect of Health"; Acs and Loprest, *Effects of Disabilities.*

118. AFDC *Based on Incapacity: Still Forgotten After All These Years* (Washington, D.C.: Center on Social Welfare Policy and Law, Publication 314, 1994). This section relies mostly on this report.

119. Little systematic research has been done on AFDC-I. According to surveys conducted by the Center on Social Welfare Policy and Law, several states had definitions of "incapacity" that did not conform to federal regulations—for example, failure to include limited employment opportunities for the handicapped, or requiring treatment, or disqualifying if the parent is able to work but at a more limited level or, even though unable to work in the paid labor force, can still perform usual caretaking functions. Advocates also think that in several states practices are unduly restrictive—for example, in addition to delays in the application process, doctors applying the more stringent Social Security and SSI disability standards, disallowing or discounting evidence of incapacity from social workers, nurse practitioners, and other nondoctor personnel despite explicit statutory authorization of qualified "other professionals," inadequate systems for obtaining medical information or paying for medical exams, and excessive verification practices. Finally, the respondents to the center's surveys thought that outreach was a serious problem.

120. *1994 Green Book.*

121. "SSI Modernization Project Final Report of the Experts," *Social Security Bulletin* 55 (Winter 1992): 22–35.

122. Joel Handler and Yeheskel Hasenfeld, *The Moral Construction of Poverty* (Newbury Park, Calif.: Sage, 1991).

123. *1994 Green Book,* 208.

124. Ibid., 235.

125. See Deborah Stone, *The Disabled State* (Philadelphia: Temple University Press, 1984).

126. *Sullivan v. Zebley,* 110 S.Ct.885 (1990).

127. Charles G. Scott, "Disabled ssi Recipients Who Work," *Social Security Bulletin* 55 (1992): 26–36.

128. This section relies on Frank Ravitch, "Balancing Fundamental Disability Policies: The Relationship Between the Americans with Disabilities Act and Social Security Disability," *Georgetown Journal on Fighting Poverty* 1 (1994): 240–57.

129. Ibid., 247–50.

130. As Ravitch points out, "The ADA was passed because of myths and stereotypes that create barriers to equal employment opportunity for disabled individuals. Those beliefs did not magically disappear with the passage of the ADA, and many employers may not comply, either intentionally, due to ignorance . . . or as a result of sincere but erroneous attempts to interpret the law. Thus . . . job applicants may often have to resort to litigation." Ibid., 247.

131. Ibid., 250–51.

132. Another issue is the treatment of earnings. Initially, the ssi treatment of earnings created major disincentives to work. This was changed in 1986. In calculating benefits for a recipient with earnings, in addition to an initial $20 a month exclusion, $65 of the earned income in any month is excluded, and thereafter ssi payments are reduced by $1 for every $2 earned until the ssi income disregard "break-even point." These earnings exclusions are considerably more generous than the $30 and the exclusion of expenses up to one-third of gross income in AFDC, although they do not include child care and regular work expenses. In addition, disabled recipients who are no longer eligible for ssi because of earnings can usually retain their Medicaid under certain conditions, such as continuing to be impaired, inability to remain employed without the Medicaid services, and insufficient earnings to provide for reasonable equivalent of ssi payments and Medicaid. Still, the experts who participated in the ssi Modernization Project recommended other incentives in addition to the change in the definition of disability, such as increasing the monthly earned income exclusion to $200 plus two-thirds of the earnings over $200, eliminating continuing disability review triggered by a return to work, and deferring scheduled medical reviews for workers for three years after work begins.

133. Pamela Loprest, "Reforming the Supplemental Security Income Program for Children" in Sawhill, *Welfare Reform,* 65–68.

134. Mark Kelman and Gillian Lester, *Jumping the Queue: An Empirical and Ethical Inquiry into the Legal Treatment of Students with Learning Disabilities* (Cambridge: Harvard University Press, 1996). In addition, the concept of cash benefits for disabled children is also being questioned. For adults, theoretically, ssi benefits replace earnings. For children, do ssi benefits replace additional costs or replace the earnings of parents who have to stay home and care for the children? A relatively small number of disabled children have significantly high medical costs, but it is not clear how many additional costs are incurred by the bulk of disabled children. At least half of the ssi children are in single-parent families; still, it is hard to be precise as to appropriate criteria for determining replacement assistance. In addition, despite ssi rules that payments for children be spent on the needs of the child—food, clothing, shelter, medical care, and personal comfort items—there is no requirement that ssi payments be used only for disability-related needs. Loprest, "Reforming the Supplemental Security Income Program," 66–67.

135. F. R. Rusch and C. Hughes, "An Overview of Supported Employment," *Journal of Applied Behavior Analysis* 22 (Winter 1989): 351–63.

136. Children's Defense Fund, "Summary of Legislation Affecting Children in 1996" (Nov. 22, 1996), 16.

137. Excepting veterans, refugees, asylum cases, and legal immigrants with a ten-year work history. P.L. 104–121.

138. Urban Institute, "Potential Effects of Congressional Welfare Reform Legislation on Family Incomes" (Aug. 8, 1996), table 2, p. 10.

139. Robert Greenstein, "Universal and Targeted Approaches to Relieving Poverty: An Alternative View," in Christopher Jencks and Paul Peterson, eds., *The Urban Underclass* (Washington, D.C.: Brookings Institution, 1991), 437–59.

140. Theda Skocpol, "Targeting within Universalism: Politically Viable Policies to Combat Poverty in the United States," in Jencks and Peterson, *Urban Underclass*, 411.

CHAPTER 7

1. Mark Rank, *Living on the Edge: The Realities of Welfare in America* (New York: Columbia University Press, 1994).

2. U.S. General Accounting Office, *Multiple Employment Training Programs: Overlap among Programs Raises Questions about Efficiency* (Washington, D.C.: Government Printing Office, 1994).

3. U.S. General Accounting Office, *Multiple Employment Training Programs: Information Crosswalk on 163 Employment Training Programs* (Washington, D.C.: Government Printing Office, 1995).

4. U.S. General Accounting Office, *Multiple Employment Training Programs* (1994).

5. Alfred J. Kahn, "Service Delivery at the Neighborhood Level: Experience, Theory, and Fads," *Social Service Review* 50 (1976): 23–56.

6. Lawrence Summers, *Understanding Unemployment* (Cambridge: MIT Press, 1990), 5.

7. Daniel Friedlander and Gary Burtless, *Five Years After: The Long-Term Effects of Welfare-to-Work Programs* (New York: Russell Sage Foundation, 1995), 197.

8. E.g., Jan L. Hagen and Liane V. Davis, *Implementing JOBS: The Participants' Perspective* (Albany: Nelson A. Rockefeller Institute of Government, State University of New York, 1994).

9. Thomas Bailey, Ross Koppel, and Roger Waldinger, *Education for All Aspects of the Industry: Overcoming Barriers to Broad-Based Training* (Berkeley: National Center for Research in Vocational Education, Graduate School of Education, University of California at Berkeley, 1994); Joleen Kirschenmann and Katherine Neckerman, " 'We'd Love to Hire Them But': The Meaning of Race for Employers," in Christopher Jencks and Paul Peterson, eds., *The Urban Underclass* (Washington, D.C.: Brookings Institution, 1991), 203–32.

10. Harry Holzer, *What Employers Want: Job Prospects for Less-Educated Workers* (New York: Russell Sage Foundation, 1996); Roger Waldinger, "Black/Immigrant Competition Reassessed: New Evidence from Los Angeles," *Sociological Perspectives* 40 (1997).

11. Kirschenmann and Neckerman, " 'We'd Love to Hire them But.' "

12. Demetra Smith Nightingale et al., *Evaluation of the Massachusetts Employment and Training (ET) Program* (Washington, D.C.: Urban Institute Press, 1991).

13. Ibid., 23.

14. James Riccio, Daniel Friedlander, Stephen Freedman, and Veronica Fellerath, *GAIN: Program Strategies, Participation Patterns, and First-Year Impacts in Six Counties* (New York: Manpower Demonstration Research Corporation, 1992).

15. County of Riverside Department of Public Social Services GAIN Program, *JOBS Program: Transferability Package for High Output Job Placement Results* (Riverside, Calif.: DHSS, March 1994).

16. Riccio et al., *GAIN*, 53.

17. Several experiments are currently underway to measure the impact of such services.

18. The sites are in Chicago, Portland, Riverside, and San Antonio.

19. Yeheskel Hasenfeld and Dale Weaver, "Enforcement, Compliance, and Disputes in Welfare-to-Work Programs," *Social Service Review* 70 (1996): 235–56.

20. Janet Quint, *Interim Findings from the Maryland Employment Initiatives Programs* (New York: Manpower Demonstration Research Corporation, 1984).

21. Daniel Friedlander et al., *Maryland: Final Report on the Employment Initiatives Evaluation* (New York: Manpower Demonstration Research Corporation, 1985).

22. Quint, *Interim Findings*, 75–85.

23. Participation in work experience required 40 hours per week up to 13 weeks. On average, participants spent 10 weeks in on-the-job training, and although education and training activities varied in length, they averaged almost 19 weeks. See Friedlander et al., *Maryland*, 67–68.

24. Friedlander and Burtless, *Five Years After*.

25. Ibid., 16–18. In all four programs, AFDC payments impact also converged toward zero by year five, but this is to be expected, given the dynamics of welfare.

26. Friedlander and Burtless indicate that Options had a greater impact on welfare applicants than on recipients, suggesting that the applicants might have used the program as an opportunity to improve their employability.

27. Stephen V. Cameron and James J. Heckman, "The Nonequivalence of High School Equivalents," *Journal of Labor Economics* 11 (1993): 43.

28. Lisa A. Lynch, "Entry-level Jobs: First Rung on the Employment Ladder or Economic Dead End?" *Journal of Labor Research* 14 (1993): 249–63.

29. Ann Gordon and John Burghardt, *The Minority Female Single Parent Demonstration: Short-Term Economic Impacts* (New York: Rockefeller Foundation, 1990), 92.

30. Alan Hershey, *The Minority Female Single Parent Demonstration* (New York: Rockefeller Foundation, 1988), x–xi.

31. Ibid., 41–42.

32. Gordon and Burghart, *Minority Female Single Parent Demonstration*, 98.

33. Hershey, *Minority Female Single Parent Demonstration*, 70–72.

34. Ibid., 71.

35. Ibid., 125.

36. Sharon Handwerger and Craig Thornton, *The Minority Female Parent Demonstration: Program Costs* (New York: Rockefeller Foundation, 1988). By comparison, the average costs for the educational and training component of Massachusetts ET ranged from $1,660 to $1,988, and about $3,000 in the Maryland Employment Initiative Program. In the GAIN program, the average cost per experimental ranged from a high of $6,622 (1993 dollars) in Alameda, which emphasized education and training, to a low of $2,963 in Riverside, which emphasized job placement. See Nightingale et al., *Evaluation of the Massachusetts Employment and Training (ET) Program* and Friedlander et al., *Maryland*.

37. Linda Gordon, "Social Insurance and Public Assistance: The Influence of Gender in Welfare Thought in the United States, 1890–1935," *American Historical Review* 97 (February 1992): 19–54.

38. Manpower Demonstration Research Corporation, *The Final Report: Summary and Findings of the National Supported Work Demonstration* (New York: MDRC, 1980).

39. Other target groups included in NWS were ex-addicts, ex-offenders, and young people.

40. Robinson G. Hollister and Rebecca A. Maynard, "The Impact of Supported Work on AFDC Recipients," in P. Kempter, R. Hollister, and R. Maynard, eds., *The National Supported Work Demonstration* (Madison: University of Wisconsin Press, 1984), 18–19.

41. Overall, about 11 percent terminated because of poor performance, while 45 percent terminated for such reasons as health, child care, transportation, and dislike of the experience. See Hollister and Maynard, *National Supported Work Demonstration*.

42. On the basis of a follow-up of 8 years after the experiment, on average, the experimental group earned from $375 to $525 per year more than the control group in 1978 dollars during the years 1982–86. Two years after enrollment, on average, 42 percent of the experimentals were employed as compared to 35 percent of the controls; experimentals worked 16 hours more and earned $80 more per month than the controls. The differences were large enough to make the program cost-effective. See Kenneth A. Couch, "New Evidence on the Long-Term Effects of Employment Training Programs," *Journal of Labor Economics* 10 (October 1992): 381–88.

43. Richard P. Nathan, *Turning Promises into Performance: The Management Challenge of Implementing Workfare* (New York: Columbia University Press, 1993), 1.

44. Robert D. Behn, *Leadership Counts: Lessons for Public Managers from the Massachusetts Welfare, Training, and Employment Program* (Cambridge: Harvard University Press, 1991), 9.

45. Hasenfeld and Weaver, "Enforcement, Compliance, and Disputes," 235–56.

46. Jan L. Hagen and Irene V. Lurie, *Implementing Jobs: Progress and Promise* (Albany: Nelson A. Rockefeller Institute of Government, State University of New York, 1994).

47. E.g., Catherine Alter and Jerald Hage, *Organizations Working Together* (Newbury Park, Calif.: Sage, 1991).

48. Behn, *Leadership Counts*, 95–103.

49. Mary Jo Bane and David T. Ellwood, *Welfare Realities: From Rhetoric to Reform* (Cambridge: Harvard University Press, 1994).

50. Michael B. Katz, *In the Shadow of the Poorhouse: A Social History of Welfare in America* (New York: Basic Books, 1986).

CHAPTER 8

1. P.L. 104–193, 110 Stat. 2105, *Personal Responsibility and Work Opportunity Reconciliation Act of 1996*, Title I—Block Grants for Temporary Assistance for Needy Families, Sec. 101, Findings.

2. The limit applies to the family in which the teenage parent lives, or to a minor child who is the head of the household or married to the head of the household.

3. Jodie Levin-Epstein, *Teenage Parent Provisions in the Personal Responsibility and Work Opportunity Reconciliation Act of 1996* (Washington, D.C.: Center for Law and Social Policy, November 1996).

4. Ann Phoenix, "The Social Construction of Teenage Motherhood: A Black and White Issue?" in Annette Lawson and Deborah L. Rhode, eds., *The Politics of Pregnancy: Adolescent Sexuality and Public Policy* (New Haven: Yale University Press, 1993), 86.

5. According to the U.S. General Accounting Office, from 1976 to 1991 the proportion of women receiving AFDC who gave birth as teenagers was about 42 percent. Of the mothers between ages 15 and 19, 27 percent received AFDC within 12 months of the birth of their child, and these mothers were likely to have longer welfare spells. See U.S. General Accounting Office, *Families on Welfare: Teenage Mothers Least Likely to Become Self-Sufficient* (Washington, D.C.: Government Printing Office, 1994). See also Mary Jo Bane and David Ellwood, *The Dynamics of Dependence and the Routes to Self Sufficiency* (Cambridge, Mass.: Urban Systems Research and Engineering, 1983); U.S. House of Representatives, Committee on Ways and Means, *1994 Green Book: Background Material and Data on Programs within the Jurisdiction of the Committee on Ways and Means* (Washington, D.C.: Government Printing Office, 1994), 453–54.

6. Frank Furstenberg, "Teenage Childbearing Reconsidered," unpublished paper, 1995.

7. Stephanie J. Ventura, Sally C. Clarke, and T. J. Mathews, "Recent Declines in Teenage Birth Rates in the United States: Variations by State, 1990–1994," *Monthly Vital Statistics Reports* 45, Supplement (Dec. 19, 1996).

8. Stanley Henshaw, *U.S. Teenage Pregnancy Statistics* (New York: Alan Guttmacher Institute, 1995).

9. Kristin Moore, Brent Miller, Dana Glei, and Donna Ruane Morrison, *Adolescent Sex, Contraception, and Childbearing: A Review of Recent Research* (Washington, D.C.: Child Trends, 1995).

10. Ibid.

11. In 1972, 76 percent of pregnancies ended in birth. The figure declined to 55 percent in 1980, but increased to 60 percent in 1990. For teenagers between ages 15 and 19 who had ever had intercourse, the abortion rate declined by 24 percent between 1980 and 1990 (from 95 to 72 per 1,000). See Henshaw, *U.S. Teenage Pregnancy Statistics.*

12. Moore, Miller, Glei, and Morrison, *Adolescent Sex, Contraception, and Childbearing,* xvii.

13. Brent Miller, "Risk Factors for Adolescent Nonmarital Childbearing," in *Report to Congress on Out-of-Wedlock Childbearing* (Washington, D.C.: U.S. Department of Health and Human Services, 1995), 220.

14. Judith S. Musick, *Young, Poor and Pregnant* (New Haven: Yale University Press, 1993).

15. Ibid., 36.

16. Charles Murray, "Does Welfare Bring More Babies?" *Public Interest* 115 (1994): 17–31.

17. Robert Moffitt, "Incentive Effects of the U.S. Welfare System: A Review," *Journal of Economic Literature* 30 (1992): 1–61.

18. Robert Moffitt, "The Effects of the Welfare System on Nonmarital Childbearing," in *Report to Congress on Out-of-Wedlock Childbearing,* 167–76.

19. Greg J. Duncan and Saul D. Hoffman, "Welfare Benefits, Economic Opportunity, and Out-of-Wedlock Births Among Black Teenage Girls," *Demography* 27 (1990): 530.

20. K. A. Moore et al., *State Variations in Rates of Adolescent Pregnancies and Childbearing* (Washington, D.C.: Child Trends, 1994).

21. Shelly Lundberg and Robert D. Plotnick, "Effects of State Welfare, Abortion and Family Planning Policies on Premarital Childbearing among White Adolescents," *Family Planning Perspectives* 22 (1990): 246–51; M. Hill and June O'Neill, *Underclass Behaviors in the United States: Measurement and Analysis of Determinants* (New York: Baruch College, Center for the Study of Business and Government, 1993). Hill and O'Neill calculated that a reduction of $100 in the monthly welfare grant would lower the nonmarital birth rate among young white women by 4 percent.

22. Robert Haveman and Barbara Wolfe, *Succeeding Generations* (New York: Russell Sage Foundation, 1994).

23. Ibid., 199.

24. Dennis Hogan and Evelyn Kitagawa, "The Impact of Social Status, Family Structure, and Neighborhood on the Fertility of Black Adolescents," *American Journal of Sociology* 90 (1985): 825–55; Mark D. Hayward, William R. Grady, and John O. G. Billy, "The Influence of Socioeconomic Status on Adolescent Pregnancy," *Social Science Quarterly* 73 (1992): 750–53.

25. Haveman and Wolfe, *Succeeding Generations.*

26. However, the relationship between race and nonmarital births is tenuous.

27. The researchers found that one standard deviation increase in high SES neighbors drops the rate of teenage nonmarital births from 8 percent to 5 percent, and that the effect is stronger for whites than blacks. See Jeanne Brooks-Gunn, Greg Duncan, Pamela Klebanov, and Naomi Sealand, "Do Neighborhoods Affect Child and Adolescent Development?" *American Journal of Sociology* 99 (1993): 353–95.

28. Jonathan Crane, "The Epidemic Theory of Ghettos and Neighborhood Effects on Dropping Out and Teenage Childbearing," *American Journal of Sociology* 96 (March 1991): 1126–59.

29. R. Olsen and G. Farkas, "The Effects of Economic Opportunity and Family Background on Adolescent Cohabitation and Childbearing Among Low-Income Blacks," *Journal of Labor Economics* 8 (1990): 341–62.

30. R. Haveman, B. Wolfe, and E. Peterson, "The Intergenerational Effects of Early Childbearing," cited in Moore, Miller, Glei, and Morrison, *Adolescent Sex, Contraception, and Childbearing.*

31. Ibid.

32. Dawn Upchurch and James McCarthy, "The Timing of a First Birth and High School Completion," *American Sociological Review* 55 (1990): 224–34.

33. Panel on High-Risk Youth, Commission on Behavioral and Social Sciences and Education, National Research Council, *Losing Generations: Adolescents in High-Risk Settings* (Washington, D.C.: National Academy Press, 1993).

34. Musick, *Young, Poor, and Pregnant,* 57–58.

35. Upchurch and McCarthy, "Timing of a First Birth and High School Completion"; David Ribar, "Teenage Fertility and High School Completion," *Review of Economics and Statistics* 76 (August 1994): 413–24.

36. Gina Adams, Karen Pittman, and Raymond O'Brien, "Adolescent and Young Adult Fathers: Problems and Solutions," in Annette Lawson and Deborah L. Rhode, eds., *The Politics of Pregnancy: Adolescent Sexuality and Public Policy* (New Haven: Yale University Press, 1993), 216–37.

37. David Landry and Jacqueline Darroch Forrest, "How Old Are U.S. Fathers?" *Family Planning Perspectives* 27 (1995): 159–65.

38. Musick, *Young, Poor, and Pregnant.*

39. Robert Lerman, "A National Profile of Young Unwed Fathers," in Robert Lerman and Theodora Ooms, eds., *Young Unwed Fathers* (Philadelphia: Temple University Press, 1993), 27–51.

40. William Julius Wilson, *The Truly Disadvantaged: The Inner City, the Underclass, and Public Policy* (Chicago: University of Chicago Press, 1987).

41. Ibid., 83.

42. Mark Fossett and K. Jill Kiecolt, "Mate Availability and Family Structure among African Americans in U.S. Metropolitan Areas," *Journal of Marriage and Family* 55 (1993): 288–302. They also found that average AFDC payments have a significant negative effect on family formation, but their study is not based on longitudinal data.

43. Greg Duncan, "How Nonmarital Childbearing Is Affected by Neighborhoods, Marital Opportunities and Labor-Market Conditions," in *Report to Congress on Out-of-Wedlock Childbearing,* 177–87.

44. Frank Furstenberg, Jeanne Brooks-Gunn, and S. Philip Morgan, *Adolescent Mothers in Later Life* (Cambridge: Cambridge University Press, 1987).

45. Mercer Sullivan, "Young Fathers and Parenting in Two Inner-City Neighborhoods," in Lerman and Ooms, *Young Unwed Fathers,* 52–73.

46. Elijah Anderson, "Sex Codes and Family among Poor Inner-City Youths," in ibid., 74–98.

47. Ibid., 81.

48. Frank Furstenberg, "Fathering in the Inner City," in William Marsiglio, ed., *Fatherhood: Contemporary Theory, Research, and Social Policy* (Thousand Oaks, Calif.: Sage, 1995), 119–47.

49. Ibid., 144.

50. Frank Furstenberg and Kathleen Mullen Harris, "When and Why Fathers Matter: Impact of Father Involvement on the Children of Adolescent Mothers," in ibid., 117–40.

51. Rebecca Maynard, Walter Nicholson, and Anu Rangarajan, *Breaking the Cycle of Poverty: The Effectiveness of Mandatory Services for Welfare-Dependent Teenage Parents* (Princeton, N.J.: Mathematica Policy Research, December 1993).

52. Sara McLanahan and George Sandefur, *Growing Up with a Single Parent* (Cambridge: Harvard University Press, 1994).

53. Haveman and Wolfe, *Succeeding Generations*, 208.

54. Douglas Massey and Nancy Denton, *American Apartheid: Segregation and the Making of the Underclass* (Cambridge: Harvard University Press, 1993).

55. Arline Geronimus, "On Teenage Childbearing and Neonatal Morality in the United States," *Population and Development Review* 13 (1987): 245–79; Arline Geronimus and Sanders Korenman, "The Socioeconomic Costs of Teenage Childbearing: Evidence and Interpretation," *Demography* 30 (1993): 281–90.

56. Kristin Moore, C. Nord, and J. Peterson, "Nonvoluntary Sexual Activity among Adolescents," *Family Planning Perspectives* 21 (1989): 110–14.

57. Anderson, "Sex Codes and Family among Poor Inner-City Youths."

58. Furstenberg, "Teenage Childbearing Reconsidered."

59. Musick, *Young, Poor, and Pregnant*, 61.

60. Panel on High-Risk Youth, *Losing Generations*, 2–21.

61. Elise F. Jones, ed., *Teenage Pregnancy in Industrialized Countries* (New Haven: Yale University Press, 1986).

62. Sara Brown and Leon Eisenberg, *The Best Intentions: Unintended Pregnancy and the Well-Being of Children and Families* (Washington, D.C.: National Academy Press, Institute of Medicine, 1995).

63. Moore, Miller, Glei, and Morrison, *Adolescent Sex, Contraception, and Childbearing*, 90.

64. Brown and Eisenberg, *Best Intentions*, 137.

65. Ibid., 142.

66. Frances Althaus and Stanley Henshaw, "The Effects of Mandatory Delay Laws on Abortion Patients and Providers," *Family Planning Perspectives* 26 (1994): 228–33.

67. Furstenberg, Brooks-Gunn, and Morgan, *Adolescent Mothers in Later Life*.

68. Frank Furstenberg, Jeanne Brooks-Gunn, and S. Philip Morgan, "Adolescent Mothers and Their Children in Later Life," *Family Planning Perspectives* 19 (1987): 142.

69. Kathleen Harris, "Teenage Mothers and Welfare Dependency," *Journal of Family Issues* 12 (1991): 492–518.

70. Arline Geronimus and Sanders Korenman, "The Socioeconomic Costs of Teenage Childbearing: Evidence and Interpretation," *Demography* 30 (1993): 281–90. The data sets they used were the National Longitudinal Survey Young Women's Sample, the Panel Study of Income Dynamics, and the National Longitudinal Survey Youth Sample. They were the first to point out that statistical analyses that rely on a cross-sectional rather than a fixed-effect model tend to overestimate the negative effects of teenage parenthood.

71. Saul Hoffman, Michael Foster, and Frank Furstenberg, "Reevaluating the Costs of Teenage Childbearing," *Demography* 30 (1993): 1–13.

72. Fifty-four percent of the teenage mothers graduated from high school. Had they delayed giving birth until they were 20, 71.6 percent would have graduated. The differences between the teenage mothers and their sisters in terms of being currently married were 48.7 percent and 61.5 percent, in terms of number of children 2.05 and 1.61, and in terms of poverty 28.4 percent and 15.6 percent, respectively.

73. Joseph Hotz, Susan McElroy, and Seth Sanders, "The Costs and Consequences of Teenage Childbearing for Mothers," in R. Maynard, ed., *Kids Having Kids: The Consequences and Costs of Teenage Childbearing in the United States* (Washington, D.C.: Urban Institute, 1996).

74. The researchers speculated that the difference might be due to the higher benefit level in California, where a large fraction of the Hispanic women resided.

75. Of course, even this sophisticated study may still overstate the consequences of early childbearing. Although a miscarriage is a random event, the women who miscarry may experience more health and other known problems than the teenagers who give births.

76. Furstenberg, Brooks-Gunn, and Morgan, *Adolescent Mothers in Later Life*.

77. Kristin Moore, Donna Ruane Morrison, and Angela Dungee Green, *Children Born to Teenage Mothers: Analyses of the National Longitudinal Survey of Youth-Child Supplement and the National Survey of Children* (Washington, D.C.: Child Trends, January 1995).

78. Sara McLanahan, "The Consequences of Nonmarital Childbearing for Women, Children, and Society," in *Report to Congress on Out-of-Wedlock Childrearing*, 229–37.

79. Furstenberg, Brooks-Gunn, and Morgan, *Adolescent Mothers in Later Life*.

80. For an extensive review of such programs, see Kristin Moore, Brent Miller, Dana Glei, and Donna Ruane Morrison, *Adolescent Pregnancy Prevention Programs: Interventions and Evaluations* (Washington, D.C.: Child Trends, 1995).

81. Andrew Hahn, *Evaluation of the Quantum Opportunities Program* (Waltham, Mass.: Brandeis University, Heller Graduate School Center for Human Resources, 1994).

82. Edward Pauly, Hilary Kopp, and Joshua Haimson, *Home-Grown Lessons: Innovative Programs Linking School and Work* (San Francisco: Jossey-Bass, 1995).

83. Although 64.1 percent of the young women in this project were 16 or younger, 59.1 percent of Redirection's participants were not in school at enrollment. On average, they had been out of school for more than a year (13.4 months). Whether they were in school or not, the skills of these teenagers were very poor; most were behind grade level and they had very low scores on a standard vocabulary test (i.e., in the tenth percentile). Although becoming pregnant is often a reason for leaving school, half of those who had dropped out reported leaving school before they became pregnant. At enrollment, 60.7 percent of the participants were pregnant (56.3 percent for the first time). Although 54 percent of the participants reported using contraceptives, only 60 percent did so regularly. See Denise F. Polit, Janet C. Quint, and James A. Riccio, *The Challenge of Serving Teenage Mothers: Lessons from Project Redirection* (New York: Manpower Demonstration Research Corporation, 1988).

84. Ibid., 8.

85. Janet C. Quint and Judith S. Musick, *Lives of Promise, Lives of Pain: Young Mothers after New Chance* (New York: Manpower Demonstration Research Corporation, January 1994); Janet C. Quint, Denise F. Polit, Hans Bos, and George Cave, *New Chance: Interim Findings on a Comprehensive Program for Disadvantaged Young Mothers and Their Children, Executive Summary* (New York: Manpower Demonstration Research Corporation, September 1994).

86. Quint, Polit, Bos, and Cave, *New Chance*, 20–23.

87. Ibid., 4.

88. David Long, Robert G. Wood, and Hilary Kopp, *The Educational Effects of* LEAP and Enhanced Services in Cleveland: Ohio's Learning, Earning, and Parenting Program for Teenage Parents on Welfare (New York: Manpower Demonstration Research Corporation, October 1994); Dan Bloom, Veronica Fellerath, David Long, and Robert G. Wood, "Ohio Boosts Attendance among Teenage Parents: LEAP Aims to Increase the Graduation Rate," *Public Welfare* 52 (1994): 18–31.

89. For a young mother living on her own with one child, a $62 sanction meant reducing her monthly AFDC grant from $274 to $212.

90. Implementation of LEAP as a large-scale program generally went smoothly. The most serious difficulty was to identify eligible teenagers, due to the limitations of the welfare computer system and the processing of the grant adjustments. A key to successful implementation of the program was access to alternative schools in which the teenagers could enroll.

91. The evaluation uses a random assignment design where participants were assigned either to LEAP or to the control group. If assigned to the control group, they could receive child care assistance and case management services through the regular JOBS program for adults. See Bloom, Fellerath, Long, and Wood, "Ohio Boosts Attendance among Teenage Parents."

92. For teenagers who were already in school, 29.2 percent completed school as compared with 20.4 percent of the controls, a difference of 8.8 percent. However, among teenagers who were *not in school* when LEAP was implemented, the difference between participants (11.1 percent) and controls (8.6 percent) was only 2.6 percent. These results are based on the Cleveland sample only. Ibid.

93. These enhanced services were provided in two ways. For teenagers attending high school, the services were located in the school and included intensive case management, child care, and instruction in parenting and life skills. For teenagers who did not "attend school regularly," the program, which included outreach, special GED preparation classes, and parenting and life skills instruction, was provided by community organizations.

94. Long, Wood, and Kopp, *Educational Effects of LEAP*, 66. Although not statistically significant, the enhancements appear to have increased the high school graduation rate very slightly—from 12.7 percent among those in the regular program to 15.1 percent in the enhanced version. It did not affect GED completion. As with the regular program, the enhanced services appear to have been most effective with teenagers *already in school*. The completion impact (as reflected in the numbers who either graduated from high school or completed a GED) was 3.1 percent higher for students in the enhanced program who were in school at random assignment than their counterparts in the regular program (30.6 percent versus 27.5 percent). In comparison to the control group, the combined impact of LEAP and the enhancements was 8.5 percent on school completion—6.5 percent LEAP impact plus 2 percent enhancement impact.

95. Rebecca Maynard, ed., *Executive Summary: Building Self-Sufficiency among Welfare Dependent Teenage Parents, Lessons from the Teenage Parent Demonstration* (Princeton, N.J.: Mathematica Policy Research, June 1993); Denise Polit, *Barriers to Self-Sufficiency and Avenues to Success among Teenage Mothers* (Princeton, N.J.: Mathematica Policy Research, November 1992).

96. All teenage mothers who, for the first time, began to receive AFDC for themselves and their families were required to attend a project intake session. Approximately 50 percent of enrollees were randomly assigned to the demonstration, while the others formed the control group. The controls were given regular AFDC services. See Maynard, *Executive Summary*, 2.

97. Ibid., 90.

98. David Olds, Charles Henderson, Robert Tatelbaum, and Robert Chamberlin, "Improving the Life-Course Development of Socially Disadvantaged Mothers: A Randomized Trial of Nurse Home Visitation," *Journal of Public Health* 78 (1988): 1436–45.

99. David Olds and Harriet Kitzman, "Review of Research on Home Visiting for Pregnant Women and Parents of Young Children," *Future of Children* 3 (1993): 53–91.

100. Olds, Henderson, Tatelbaum, and Chamberlin, "Improving the Life-Course Development of Socially Disadvantaged Mothers."

101. David Olds, Charles Henderson, Charles Phelps, Harriet Kitzman, and Carole Hanks, "Effects of Prenatal and Infancy Nurse Home Visitation on Government Spending," *Medical Care* 31 (1993): 155–74.

102. Deborah Rhode, "Adolescent Pregnancy and Public Policy," in Lawson and Rhode, *Politics of Pregnancy*, 312.

103. The main federal program for family planning is Title X. Other programs did not fare so well. The Adolescent Health, Services, and Pregnancy Prevention Care Act of 1978

was authorized at $60 million in 1979. Its funding was gutted by half during the Reagan administration when it was replaced with the 1981 Adolescent Family Life Act (AFL). The purpose of AFL was not to provide services but to undertake demonstration projects to discourage teen sexual activity and promote adoption. See Jennifer Mittlestadt, "Educating 'Our Girls' and 'Welfare Mothers': Discussions of Educational Policy for Pregnant and Parenting Adolescents in Federal Hearings, 1975–1995," *Journal of Family History* 1997 (forthcoming).

104. Moore, Morrison, and Green, *Children Born to Teenage Mothers;* Martha Burt, "Access to and Utilization of Preventative Services: Implications for Nonmarital Childbearing," in *Report to Congress on Out-of-Wedlock Childrearing,* 191.

105. Hotz, McElroy, and Sanders, "Costs and Consequences of Teenage Childbearing for Mothers."

106. Musick, *Young, Poor, and Pregnant.*

CHAPTER 9

1. Michael Katz, *In the Shadow of the Poorhouse: A Social History of Welfare in America* (New York: Basic Books, 1986).

2. See Lee Rainwater, "Poverty and the Income Package of Working Parents: The United States in Comparative Perspective," *Children and Youth Services Review* 17 (1995): 11–41. There are growing strains on the Western European social welfare system, especially with conflicts between national deficits and the impending requirements of the uniform currency, and there have been some attempts to scale back benefits. These relate primarily to the unemployed rather than the family (e.g., child allowances, etc.). In any event, despite the strains and reductions, the European system remains far more comprehensive and generous than the U.S. system.

3. The state allocations would generally be based on fiscal year 1994 federal spending for programs contained in the block grant. States are permitted to elect between fiscal year 1994 and fiscal years 1992–94 average. It should be noted that AFDC caseloads have been declining; the national caseload was 6.4 percent below the fiscal year 1994 average. Handsnet, "Welfare Reform Watch, AFDC Caseload Declines: Implications for Block Grants" (Sept. 19, 1996).

4. It is clear that this limit applies to the use of federal funds. The federal government claims that the limit also applies to any state funds used for these purposes—that is, states are to be prohibited from extending the time limit (for non-20 percent exemptions) even if they want to use only state funds.

5. Seventy-five percent must be participating by 1997; this increases to 90 percent by 1999.

6. For the relationship between TANF and state child support policies, see Paula Roberts, *A Guide to Implementing the Child Support Cooperation Policies* (Washington, D.C.: Center for Law and Social Policy, Dec. 12, 1996).

7. On the lack of effect of benefit levels on "family values," see Hillary Hoynes, *Work, Welfare, and Family Structure: A Review of the Evidence* (Madison, Wis.: Institute for Research on Poverty, DP 1103–96, August 1996).

8. Children's Defense Fund, "Summary of Legislation Affecting Children in 1996" (Nov. 22, 1996), 16.

9. Legal immigrants are also barred from receiving in-home support services.

10. The most dramatic requirement is to limit cash assistance for one year; then the recipient must wait a year before reapplying. There is still the five-year cumulative total.

11. Counties can reduce the grant levels substantially (up to 40 percent of the 1991 federal poverty level); can limit aid to those recipients deemed "employable" to three nonconsecu-

tive months per year as long as job training or placement is offered; can terminate recipients with substance abuse problems who refuse county-offered treatment; and can replace the cash grant with in-kind transfers, vouchers, or third-party checks.

12. Judith Havemann and Barbara Vobejda, "After Getting Responsibility for Welfare, States May Pass It Down," *Washington Post*, Jan. 28, 1997: A1.

13. There would also be problems of state comparability. These are difficult data sets, with expensive personnel and computational costs. John Marcotte, *Can Administrative Data Kept by States Be Used to Study the Duration of Program Participation?* (Washington, D.C.: Urban Institute, December 1994). See Robert Pear, "A Computer Gap Is Likely to Slow Welfare Changes," *New York Times*, Sept. 2, 1996: 1.

14. See Chap. 2 for the discussion of quality control.

15. Discussed in Chap. 2. See Robert Pear, "Burden of Welfare Changes Falls to State Case Workers," *New York Times*, Oct. 22, 1996: 1.

16. Major corporations are bidding for the Texas welfare system. Nina Bernstein, "Giant Companies Entering Race to Run State Welfare Programs," *New York Times*, Sept. 15, 1996: 1. For the problems in intergovernmental relations with contracting, See Joel Handler, *Down from Bureaucracy: The Ambiguity of Privatization and Empowerment* (Princeton, N.J.: Princeton University Press, 1996), Chap. 4.

17. Steve Savner, *Creating a Work-Based Welfare System under TANF* (Washington, D.C.: Center for Law and Social Policy, November 1996), 5.

18. Carla Rivera, "Welfare Law's Job Goal May Be Impossible," *Los Angeles Times*, Nov. 4, 1996: 1.

19. Jon Nordheimer, "High Profile Welfare-to-Work Effort Is Off to Slow Start," *New York Times*, Feb. 13, 1997: A11.

20. Melissa Healy, "Welfare-to-Work's Goal Is Ambitious, but Pace Glacial," *Los Angeles Times*, Feb. 16, 1997: A1.

21. Harry Holzer, *Employer Demand, AFDC Recipients, and Labor Market Policy* (Madison, Wis.: Institute for Research on Poverty, DP 1115–96, November 1996), 23.

22. That is, if the state caseload falls by, say, 10 percent since fiscal year 1995, then the state's work participation rate is reduced from 25 percent to 15 percent in fiscal year 1997.

23. Savner, *Creating a Work-Based Welfare System under TANF*, 6. The statute tries to mitigate this incentive by providing that a credit will be not given for cases that are reduced as a "direct result" of changes in state eligibility criteria. But given the data and monitoring problems and the multiple state rules and administrative practices, it is doubtful that the federal government can enforce this provision.

24. Urban Institute, "Potential Effects of Congressional Welfare Reform Legislation on Family Incomes" (Aug. 8, 1996), 3. See also Hoynes, *Work, Welfare, and Family Structure*. In California, assuming no growth in TANF rolls, there are 1.6 million children, approximately 36 percent of whom are long-term recipients. In the year 2002, cash aid will be terminated for 575,000 children. If present growth continues, the number of children subject to termination is 994,000. And this does not count the two-year time limit; the SSI cut-offs; cases terminated for substance abuse and alcoholism; and denials of aid for failure to establish paternity, children born to mothers under 18, and additional children born to current recipients—which could easily exceed several hundred thousand additional children.

25. This section relies on Center for Law and Social Policy, "Teen Parent Provisions in the New Law" (Jan. 22, 1997).

26. "The evidence suggests that family structure decisions are not sensitive to financial incentives." Hoynes, *Work, Welfare, and Family Structure*, 47.

27. They must also outline the state's statutory-rape education program.

28. For example, so far ten states (out of thirty) have proposed elimination of the entire cash grant as a sanction for failure to participate in work; five more states have proposed it

for failure to cooperate with child support enforcement, as well as denying or reducing benefits for other reasons (school or preschool attendance, immunizations, failure to provide social security numbers). Children's Defense Fund, "Selected Features of State Welfare Plans" (Nov. 13, 1996).

29. Urban Institute, "Potential Effects of Congressional Welfare Reform Legislation on Family Incomes."

30. The institute makes a "pessimistic" labor-market assumption: that only 40 percent of those facing time limits will find jobs; and a more "optimistic" one: that two-thirds will find jobs, and half of these jobs will be full-time. Concerning state behavior, the institute assumes that states will *not* reduce their welfare spending and that they will exempt the full 20 percent of the caseload. Significantly, neither labor assumption substantially changes the result. Under the pessimistic assumption, the number of people in poverty would increase by 2.8 million, and the number of children by 1.3 million.

31. Robert Pear, "Rewards and Penalties Vary in States' Welfare Programs," *New York Times*, Febr. 23, 1997: A16.

32. Children's Defense Fund, "Selected Features of State Welfare Plans."

33. Robert Pear, "Rewards and Penalties."

34. For example, some states have opted out of the TANF requirement that recipients participate in community service after receiving two months of assistance. Children's Defense Fund, "Selected Features of State Welfare Plans."

35. Several states are already seeking waivers from the food stamp provisions. Children's Defense Fund, "Legislative Update" (Dec. 20, 1996).

36. Robert Pear, "Rewards and Penalties."

37. Nancy Ebb and Deborah Weinstein, "Implementing the New Welfare Law" (Children's Defense Fund, Sept. 20, 1996).

38. A typical quote: "It will be virtually impossible for New York City and State to move hundreds of thousands of New Yorkers from public assistance into full-time jobs over the next few years, as the new Federal law overhauling welfare intends, according to many economists and job-training experts." Alan Finder, "Welfare Clients Outnumber Jobs They Might Fill," *New York Times*, Aug. 25, 1996: 1.

39. In California, for example, if only 10 percent of the children who lose eligibility need foster care, the cost to an already overburdened Los Angeles County system will be $16 million *additional* funds per month; if 5 percent of these children are older and have to go to group homes, the cost will be $81 million *additional* funds per month.

40. On the relationship between labor markets and welfare spells, see Hilary Hoynes, *Local Labor Markets and Welfare Spells: Do Demand Conditions Matter?* (Madison, Wis.: Institute for Research on Poverty, DP 1104–96, September 1996).

41. There is evidence that single unemployed men use general relief in much the same way. Kathleen Kost, *"A Man Without a Job Is a Dead Man": The Meaning of Work and Welfare in the Lives of Young Men* (Madison, Wis.: Institute for Research on Poverty, DP 1112–96, October 1996).

42. See Jeremy Rifkin, "A New Social Contract," *THE ANNALS* 544 (1996): 16–26; Barbara Gutek, "Service Workers: Human Resources or Labor Costs?" ibid., 68–82.

43. Claus Offe, "A Non-Productivist Design for Social Policies," in Philippe van Parijs, ed., *Arguing for Basic Income: Ethical Foundations for Radical Reform* (New York: Verso, 1992); Philippe van Parijs, *Real Freedom for All: What (If Anything) Can Justify Capitalism?* (New York: Oxford University Press, 1995).

44. Fred Block and Jeff Manza, " 'Ending Welfare As We Know It': The Case for a Negative Income Tax" (paper presented at the American Sociological Association Meetings, Washington, D.C., August 1995). The Negative Income Tax (NIT) was the subject of experiments in the 1970s in New Jersey, Denver, and Seattle and was proposed by President Nixon in 1972, as well as by Democratic Presidential candidate George McGovern.

45. To avoid a high marginal tax rate when a family is no longer eligible for the NIT, the positive tax would be changed to increase the size of the tax exemption for individuals and dependents.

46. Guy Standing, "The Need for a New Social Consensus" in Phillips van Parijs, *Arguing for Basic Income:* 47–60; David Purdy, "Citizenship, Basic Income and the State," *New Left Review* 208 (1994): 30–49.

47. Nancy Fraser, "From Redistribution to Recognition? Dilemmas of Justice in a 'Post-Socialist' Age," *New Left Review* 212 (1995): 68–94.

48. Even Western Europeans are seriously questioning whether they can or should maintain their welfare states. Western Europeans are impressed by the growth in U.S. jobs. Increasingly, and ironically, there is the call in Western Europe to follow the U.S. example. Low wages and a "flexible" work force—that is, people choosing work rather than welfare— are the keys to economic growth. Whatever the ultimate merits of the European reevaluation of the welfare state, it seems clear that, at present, there is very little support for expanding welfare state benefits that are not tied to labor market activity. See Joel Handler, "Questions About Social Europe by an American Observer" (unpublished manuscript, 1997).

49. Theda Skocpol, *Social Policy in the United States: Future Possibilities in Historical Perspective* (Princeton, N.J.: Princeton University Press, 1995), chap. 8.

50. Lucie E. White, "No Exit: Rethinking Welfare Dependency from a Different Ground," *Georgetown Law Journal* 22 (1993): 1961–2002.

51. Annette Bernhardt, Martina Morris, and Mark Handcock, "Women's Gains or Men's Losses? A Closer Look at the Shrinking Gender Gap in Earnings," *American Journal of Sociology* 101 (1995): 302–28.

52. Among young couples, the role of wives is changing from "contributor" to "coprovider." Aimee Dechter and Pamela Smock, *The Fading Breadwinner Role and the Economic Implications for Young Couples* (Madison, Wis.: Institute for Research on Poverty, DP 1051–94, 1994).

53. Rebecca Blank, "Does a Larger Social Safety Net Mean Less Economic Flexibility?" in Richard B. Freeman, ed., *Working Under Different Rules* (New York: Russell Sage Foundation, 1994).

Index

Aaron, Henry, 136

ABE. *See* Adult basic education

Abortion rate, among teenagers, 182, 260*n*

Abuse, and poverty, 17, 55, 221

Activities of daily living (ADL), to measure disability, 139

ADA. *See* Americans with Disabilities Act of 1990

ADL. *See* Activities of daily living

Adolescent Family Life Act (AFL), 265*n*

Adolescent Health, Services, and Pregnancy Prevention Care Act of 1978, 264*n*–265*n*

Adult basic education (ABE), in GAIN, 69

AFDC. *See* Aid to Families with Dependent Children

AFDC Child Care, 207, 251*n*

AFDC-I. *See* Aid to Families with Dependent Children-Incapacitated

AFL. *See* Adolescent Family Life Act

African Americans: in AFDC population, 45; children, 54; and child support, 128; earnings for, 43; and employment discrimination, 233*n*; and GAIN, 239*n*; and generational welfare, 46; and health care, 133; and job availability, 101; in low-wage jobs, 40; mothers, 50–51, 56; in National Supported Work, 159; and social security, 30; stereotypes of, 201; and teenage mothers, 56, 173, 179–80, 182–83; and teenage parenthood, 174–75, 177–80; unemployment rates of, 43

Age, and health care, 133

AICP. *See* Association for Improving the Condition of the Poor

Aid to Dependent Children (ADC), 10; enactment of, 27–28; expansion of, 31; myth and ceremony in, 29; opposition to, 28; restrictions of, 28

Aid to Families with Dependent Children (AFDC), 5, 19–20; administrative changes in, 34–37; ages of mothers receiving, 45, 169–70; bureaucracy in, 20, 35–37; caseloads, 265*n*; and child support, 128–29; clients of, 59; clients' responsibilities in, 35–36; eligibility rules of, 34; and exemption from JOBS, 60; and exemption from WIN, 59; expenditures for, 8, 31; family enrollment in, 44; family size in, 45; grants of, 44, 92; increase in clients, 31, 45; and JOBS, 61; liberalization of, 32; limitations of, 115; local offices of, 36; and Medicaid, 131–32; participation requirements, 237*n*; for people with disabilities, 140–41; under PROWR, 206; recasting majority of recipients, 145; reductions in, 8; reform characteristics, 38; in 1950s and 1960s, 31–32; simplification of, 35; tax rates of, 113; for teenage mothers, 264*n*; and unemployment insurance, 138

Aid to Families with Dependent Children-Incapacitated (AFDC-I), 141; research on, 255*n*

Alameda County, Calif., GAIN in, 67–70, 86

Alstott, Ann, 107

America. *See* United States

Americans with Disabilities Act of 1990 (ADA), 142–43, 256*n*

American welfare state: categorization in, 26; characteristic feature of, 26; development of, 26–34

Anderson, Elijah, 177

Andrews, Linda, 49, 99

Asset limitations, 115–16

Association for Improving the Condition of the Poor (AICP), 229*n*

At-Risk Child Care, 207, 251*n*

At-risk youth, 17

Automobiles, and asset limitations, 115–16

Hill, Steven, 140
Hiring patterns, 151
Hoffman, Saul, 173, 183
Hogan, Dennis, 174
Holzer, Harry, 100–102, 151
Home care: reimbursement for, 216; societal recognition of, 217
Homelessness, 212
Hostage strategy of welfare, 203
Hotz, Joseph, 183, 185, 196–97
Household composition, and earning opportunities, 40
H.R. 3734. *See* Personal Responsibility and Work Opportunity Reconciliation Act of *1996*
Human capital: deficits in, 155, 157; investments in, 52, 102, 218–19; and teenage pregnancy, 194
Hunt, Jennifer, 41

IADL. *See* Instrumental activities of daily living
Illinois Fund to Parents Act, 27
Illinois welfare system, 46–48
Illinois, work programs in, 82
Immigrants: denial of aid to, 7; discrimination against, 27; and federal meal programs, 208; in labor market, 43; and Medicaid, 207; and poverty, 9–10; under PROWR, 212; social service limitations on, 265*n*; stereotypes of, 201; and welfare morality, 25
Impairment-related work expenses (IRWE), 144
Incentives, in Utah work program, 72
Income Assistance, 247*n*
Income guarantee alternative, 215–18
Income-maintenance programs, 214; integration of, 113–16
Income-maintenance workers, 81–82
Income taxes. *See also* Negative Income Tax; and EITC, 107–08; of married couples, 245*n*
Individualized employment services, 155–56
Industrial Advisory Board of Center for Employment Training, 159
Inequality, of wealth, 38–41, 204
Infants, child care for, 120–21, 251*n*
Inner city, job availability in, 100–101, 233*n*

Institute for Research on Poverty, 75
Institutional movement, in welfare, 26, 203
Instrumental activities of daily living (IADL), to measure disability, 139
Intensive employment services, 157–60
Intensive service programs, for teenage parents, 192–94
Interest groups, and employment services, 161–62
Intergenerational welfare, 46
Iowa, definition of participation in, 86
"Iowa Plan Tries to Cut off the Cash," 98
IRWE. *See* Impairment-related work expenses
Isomorphism, in welfare offices, 83

Jencks, Christopher, 46, 106
Job availability, 204; discrepancy with number on welfare, 99–100; and employment services, 165–66; extent of, 99; government position on, 91; in inner cities, 100–101; studies of, 100; and unemployment, 242*n*
Job club, 150, 152
Job creation, 97–106; in welfare reform, 213; for youth, 104–05
Job development, 150–55; effectiveness of, 152; and postplacement case management, 154–55, 219
JOB GAP Project, 100
Job Openings Survey, 100
Job placement, 150–55; and postplacement case management, 154–55, 219
Job readiness, 83
JOBS (Jobs Opportunities and Basic Skills Training Program), 6, 60–61; and AFDC, 60; average monthly participation rate in, 61; in Chicago, 82; demonstration programs under, 66, 70; earnings rate with, 238*n*; exemption from work programs by age of children, 91; expenditures of, 61; in Florida, 70; impact study of, 61; under PROWR, 206; scope of, 61
Job search, 150
Job seekers, numbers of, 99
Job substitution, 103
Job Training Partnership Act (JTPA), 65–66, 70, 148
Johnson, Clifford, 104
Jones, Elise F., 181

Massachusetts: change from mandatory to voluntary work program, 88; Employment and Training program in, 62–63; GAIN in, 86; welfare-to-work programs in, 76–77

Mather, Cotton, 22

Maynard, Rebecca, 178

McElroy, Susan, 183, 197

McLanahan, Sara, 46, 179, 185

MDRC. *See* Manpower Demonstration Research Corporation

Mead, Lawrence, 90

Means test, 30

Medicaid, 131–32; as access to contraceptives, 181–82; and AFDC, 131–32; bright-line eligibility, 134; costs, 44, 134; under PROWR, 113, 207; restrictions on, 133; transitional, 72

Medicare, 132; costs, 44; government spending on, 8

Men: exclusion from public relief programs, 28; income estimates based on education, 38; part-time employment of, 42; on welfare, 10, 14, 221. *See also* Fathers

Meyer, Daniel, 130

Michigan: definition of participation in, 86; JOBS in, 66

Middle class, economic condition of, 8–9

Miller, Brent, 171

Minimum wage: decline in, 43; economists' view of, 112; increase in, 248*n*–249*n;* percentage of workers at, 112; and poverty rate, 249*n*; raising of, 111–13, 213; and reduction of employment, 112

Mississippi, JOBS in, 66

Moffitt, Robert, 172–173

Monitored employment, 86

Moore, Kristin, 171, 173, 181, 185, 196

Morality: and caseworker-client relationship, 81, 146, 161, 164; and family values, 210–11; and teenage mothers, 168; and teenage pregnancy, 194, 198–99; of welfare population, 9–10, 201; and work ethic, 4–5, 33

Morgan, S. Philip, 182–83, 185

Morrison, Donna Ruane, 196

Mothers: ages of, in AFDC, 45, 169–70; ages of, on welfare, 169–70; and child care, 119–120; conservatives on, 33; cooperation with child support collectors, 129–30; and mandatory work requirements, 220; and reimbursement for home care, 216–17; stay-at-home, 9, 216; stereotypes of those on welfare, 4; in Wisconsin Works, 75. *See also* Single mothers; Teenage mothers; Working mothers

Mothers' pensions, 28–29, 229*n*–230*n*

Multiple-job holders, 40

Murray, Charles, 9, 172

Musick, Judith, 118, 172, 180, 198

Nathan, Richard, 160

National Association for the Education of Young Children, 123

National Commission on Children, 55, 110, 119–20

National Longitudinal Survey of Labor Market Behavior, 176

National Longitudinal Survey of Youth (NLSY), 41, 173, 183

National Longitudinal Survey Young Women's Sample (NLSYW), 183

National Supported Work (NSW), 159–60, 259*n*

National Welfare Rights Organization (NWRO), 32

Neckerman, Katherine, 151

Negative Income Tax (NIT), 216, 267*n*–268*n*

Neighborhood, effect on teenage parenthood, 174–76

Network recruitment, 151

New Chance, 188–89

New Jobs Tax Credit (NJTC), 110

Newman, Katherine, 101

NIT. *See* Negative Income Tax

Nixon, Richard, 60

NJTC. *See* New Jobs Tax Credit

NLSY. *See* National Longitudinal Survey of Youth

NLSYW. *See* National Longitudinal Survey Young Women's Sample

NSW. *See* National Supported Work

Nurse Home Visitation program, for teenage parents, 193

NWRO. *See* National Welfare Rights Organization

Old-age assistance (OAA), 29, 31

Old-age insurance (OAI), 30–31

Olds, David, 193

Subsidies: for child care, 122, 153, 251*n;* for wages, 110, 246*n*–247*n*

Substantial gainful activity (SGA), 141–42, 215

Sullivan, Mercer, 177

Summer Food Program, 207

Summers, Lawrence, 149

Supplemental Security Income (SSI), 97–98; children receiving, 143–44; for immigrants, 7; and job availability, 142; for people with disabilities, 141; under PROWR, 207; treatment of earnings, 256*n*

Support services: of Center for Employment Training, 159; effectiveness of, 154; for low-wage workers, 152

Survey of Income and Program Participation (SIPP), 233*n;* to measure disability, 139–40

Sweden, child care in, 253*n*

SWIM. *See* Saturation Work Initiatives Model

TALS. *See* Test of Applied Literary Skills

TANF. *See* Temporary Assistance for Needy Families

Targeted employment-related services, 222–24

Targeted programs: failure of, 219; versus universalism, 218–22

Tax preparers, and EITC, 108–09

Tax rates, 97

Technology, and unemployment, 215

Teenage fathers, 176–79; ages of, 176; involvement with children, 178; profile of, 176–77; tolerance of, 199

Teenage mothers: on AFDC, 45; African American, 56, 173, 179–80, 182–83; ages of, 197–98; and child care, 189; children of, 56, 185; comparison with peers, 183–84; differing life circumstances of, 197–98; earnings of, 184; and education, 50–52, 262*n;* impact of motherhood on, 182–84; intensive service programs for, 192–93; likelihood of completing high school, 184; marital status of, 168, 170, 184; as moral symbols, 168; number of children in lifetime, 184; in poverty, 56; pregnancy rates of, 45, 260*n;* programs to keep in school, 187–88; public assistance for, 184; remarriage of, 185; requirements for living arrangements, 7;

seeming benefits for, 180; societal views of, 198–99; symbolic nature of programs for, 195; work experiences of, 182–83; work patterns of, 184; younger versus older, 183–85. *See also* Teenage parenthood

Teenage Parent Demonstration Project, 191–92

Teenage parenthood: among African Americans, 174–75, 177–80; authors' suggested approach to, 194–96; causes of, 168–82; children of, 56, 185; and child support, 178; consequences of, 169, 182–85; data on, 262*n;* and education, 179, 186–87, 264*n;* effect of family on, 173–76; effect of neighborhood on, 174–76; and employment opportunities, 186–87; and environment, 179–81; and health care, 169; intensive service programs for, 192–94; mandatory educational programs for, 189–92; MDRC study of, 190; Nurse Home Visitation program for, 193; patterns of, 169–70; and poverty, 56, 171–72, 179–81; preventive programs for, 196; programs for, 186–94; under PROWR, 210–11; risk factors for, 171, 179; and sanctions, 190–91; and single-parent families, 179; social service programs for, 187–92; social services for, 187–92; and TANF, 167–68, 206; voluntary educational programs for, 187–89; and welfare, 167–74, 194–200; in Wisconsin Works, 75. *See also* Teenage fathers; Teenage mothers

Teenage pregnancy rates, 45, 260*n*

Teenage Progress, 191

Teenagers: abortion rate among, 182, 260*n;* employment opportunities for, 174–75

Temporary Assistance for Needy Families (TANF), 6–7; and Child Assistance Program, 114; and child care, 125; and child support, 131; and employment services, 79; exemption from work programs by age of children, 91; federal funding of, 206; and Medicaid, 207; model for, 62; under PROWR, 206; and teenage parents, 167–68, 206; and working mothers, 147; work requirements under, 58, 209–10

Test of Applied Literary Skills (TALS), 69, 239*n*

employment disadvantages of, 50, 80; and morality, 9–10, 201; profile of, 44; redefinition of, 15, 18, 218; reduction of, 221; societal views of, 8–9, 25–26, 33–34; stereotypes of, 4, 44, 80–81, 88–89; unemployment rate and, 204

Welfare reform, 5–8, 205–13; aims of, 10; assumptions behind, 8–11; authors' approach to, 213–24; claims about, 19; and denial of benefits to children, 266n; effects of, 227n; funding needed to be effective, 212; funding of, 18; themes of, 6

Welfare-to-work programs, 58–93; and child care, 127; contradictions of, 90; costs of, 209; effectiveness of, 67–70, 93; failure of, 91; implementation of, 82; improving effectiveness of, 93; instability of, 93; and job development, 153; limited resources of, 92; localism of, 92–93; mandatory nature of, 85–93; paperwork in, 87–88; participation in, 92; political economy of, 85–86; problems with, 58; results of, 92; state's role in, 74; symbolic functions of, 91. *See also* Work requirements

Welfare workers: effects of sanctions on behavior of, 88; relationships with clients, 81–83, 88–89, 146, 161, 163–64

Wilson, Pete, 208, 211

Wilson, William Julius, 177

win. *See* Work Incentive

win ii. *See* Work Incentive II

Wisconsin Works, 74–76; and child care, 125; child care in, 75

Wolfe, Barbara, 133, 135, 140, 173–75, 179

Women: as target of welfare reforms, 10; discrimination against, 27; employment rates of, 41; exits from welfare, 51–52, 235n; income estimates based on education, 38; in labor force, 20–21, 49–50; low-income employment rates of,

41; and marriage, 40; part-time employment of, 42. *See also* Mothers

Women's Business Ownership Assistance, 147

Work: discouragement of, 113; moral importance of, 216; to supplement welfare, 46–50

Workers' compensation, 230n

Work ethic: of long-term dependents, 50–51; violation of, 4

Workfare. *See* Work-for-relief

Work-for-relief, 63, 70–71

Work Incentive (win), 156; and afdc, 59; exemption from work programs by age of children, 91; failure of, 59; myth and ceremony of, 59–60

Work Incentive II (win ii), 60, 237n

Work incentive programs, 59–60

Working mothers, 15; and child care, 123, 147; earnings of, 105; effect of eitc on, 106–07; societal views of, 10; and unemployment insurance, 137–39; wages of, 49

Working poor, 38–39, 220–21; and health care, 132

Work programs. *See* Welfare-to-work programs

Work requirements: incentive strategy for, 59; for mothers, 32–33; under prowr, 209–10; regulatory strategy for, 59; risks of, 217; in welfare reform, 6–7, 203. *See also* Welfare-to-work programs

Works Progress Administration (wpa), 30

Work test, 84

wpa. *See* Works Progress Administration

wtp, voluntariness of, 88

yiepp. *See* Youth Incentive Entitlement Pilot Projects

Yin, George, 110

Youth Incentive Entitlement Pilot Projects (yiepp), 102, 104–05, 175, 186

We the Poor People: Work, Poverty, and Welfare

JOEL F. HANDLER and YEHESKEL HASENFELD

Current welfare reforms—including recently enacted federal legislation—are largely symbolic politics, argue two experts in this important new book. According to Joel F. Handler and Yeheskel Hasenfeld, the real problem we face is not the spread of welfare but the spread of poverty among the working poor, a group that includes most welfare recipients. The surest way to solve the problem is to create jobs and supplement low-wage work. The authors offer proposals that would make it possible for individuals to support themselves and their families through working and that would establish a safety net for those relatively few individuals who are unable to do so.

The authors discuss current policies, efforts, and programs designed to deal with the poor and analyze what works, what does not work, and why. Instead of income maintenance strategies, they promote policies that would facilitate leaving welfare for work— particularly in the case of single mothers. Their proposals range from creating jobs and supplementing income through the Earned Income Tax Credit (EITC) to raising the minimum wage to providing health insurance and child care support. These are not inexpensive solutions, but they must occur if we truly wish to live in a society that strives to provide opportunities for all.

JOEL F. HANDLER is Richard C. Maxwell Professor of Law at the School of Law, University of California, Los Angeles. YEHESKEL HASENFELD is professor of social welfare at the School of Public Policy and Social Research, University of California, Los Angeles. Both authors have written extensively on various aspects of social welfare policy.

A Twentieth Century Fund Book

A Yale Fastback